FOLK-LORE AN
STORIES OF WALES

BY MARIE TREVELYAN

Author of "Glimpses of Welsh Life and Character,"
"From Snowdon to the Sea," "The Land of Arthur,"
"Britain's Greatness Foretold," &c.

INTRODUCTION BY

E. SIDNEY HARTLAND, F.S.A.

LONDON: ELLIOT STOCK
62, PATERNOSTER ROW, E.C.
1909

PREFACE

BRITISH mythology preserved by the ancient Druids, poems of the early bards, oral and written tradition, and legends, form the foundation- and corner-stones of the folk-lore and folk-stories of Wales.

About two thousand, if not more, years before Christ the Druids of Britain taught the belief that the sun, moon, and stars had mysterious and mighty influences. Evidences of this are numerous in Wales, where Druidism, merging into Christianity, left many survivals. in the form of May and Midsummer fire festivals and other periodical celebrations.

Mingled with these was the primitive imagination that the elements, animals, birds, trees, flowers, plants, and herbs were semi-human, and capable of working out actions of pleasure and pain. The wind conveyed secrets, the waves had warning voices, trees whispered, animals and birds provided omens and tokens, while flowers, plants, and herbs had mystic attributes.

With thunder, lightning, and storms the sorcerer and sorceress of old were supposed to be capable of destroying the enemies' hosts. With incantation and spell the wizard was enabled to perform his mysteries of defence and revenge. In later times their descendant, the Dyn Hysbys, or wise man, had rare gifts and magnetic influence, and the witch was associated with magical and uncanny deeds.

Many centuries reveal superstitions without a break, and here and there remnants of the Roman, the Saxon, the Dane, and the Norman are traced in the folk-lore and folk-stories of the Principality. Arthurian romance, mediæval monkish influence, and puritanical severity can be clearly identified in the lore so late as the seventeenth, eighteenth, and first half of the nineteenth centuries. That additions are unconsciously being made is evident, for the umbrella, the German band, and the locomotive are among later contributions.

Much of the folk-lore and many of the folk-stories, which formed a valuable contribution to the early history and condition of the Welsh people, survived the itinerary of Wesley in Wales, and were preserved by the oldest inhabitants, who considered it reverential to prayerfully assist in the laying of ghosts, the confounding of malign spirits, and the exorcism of evil-doers. During the religious revival of the fifties of the nineteenth century the lore and stories were regarded as gross superstitions, and were held in abeyance, but not wholly suppressed. Here and there families might be found holding these fragments as connecting-links between the past and the people of the day, who cherished loving memories of

"... the touch of a vanished hand,
And the sound of a voice that is still."

Love for ancestral sayings and doings is strong in the Welsh temperament, and while the religious revival already mentioned doubtless purged and purified Wales of gruesome superstitions and coarse practices, the minds of men winnowed the bad from the good, and the fittest of the lore and stories survived. In later years it was not unusual to hear people who had taken prominent parts in the religious movement of that period relating, quite in a spirit of reverence, the stories told by their grandsires and granddames, always prefacing them with the intimation that, personally, they did " not believe in such things," adding, " but my old grandfather was a Christian and a truth-teller."

Folk-stories are gradually diminishing, and in the present day can only be obtained from the very oldest inhabitants, or from private manuscripts and notebook collections. My late father's memory for the old stories told in his boyhood was reliable, and his collection of notes, taken from relatives and others, was very large.

All instances where the lore and stories are not attributed to informants, manuscripts, or printed sources, have been personally collected from old inhabitants, some of whom have passed away, while others still survive.

It has not been my purpose to dissect the lore and trace it back to its original sources, or to embellish the stories, but just to present them in their simple form, as a contribution to a fascinating section of the literature of Wales.

It is to be distinctly understood that the fairy-lore, fairy, giant, and dwarf stories of Wales have not been included in this work. They have a separate identity, and, if the present book finds favour among the lovers of folk-lore and of Wales, the genuine fairy-lore —of which the author has a large collection—will form a subsequent volume.

In conclusion, as a native of and resident in the Principality, I gratefully acknowledge my sincere appreciation of the invaluable suggestions, advice, and assistance so readily proffered and rendered to me by Mr. E. Sidney Hartland, the well-known and eminent folk-lorist, during the arrangement, classification, and revision of this book. His practical and indefatigable efforts to guide me in making the volume useful to students, and at the same time interesting to general readers, has been of the greatest possible service, and for these I am deeply indebted to him. Mr. Hartland's knowledge and experience of these and kindred subjects are very far-reaching, and he placed both unreservedly at my disposal. The preparation of the work, which entailed laborious research, time, and patience, has proved exceedingly pleasant from a personal point of view, and I earnestly hope it will be equally agreeable to all those who value the quaint old lore and stories of Wales.

MARIE TREVELYAN.

INTRODUCTION

THE following pages are so full of interest to students of tradition, and to Welshmen, whether students or not, as well as to that omnivorous but capricious abstraction known as " the general reader," that the question may well be put why it should be necessary that anybody should stand sponsor for them. To that question no answer is possible but that it was the wish of the author. Accordingly, though my qualifications for the task are small, I have undertaken with pleasure to write a few words by way of introduction.

The folk-lore here brought together is primarily that of Glamorgan and the immediately surrounding districts, but it also includes much from other parts of Wales. Folk-lore already on record has, as a rule, been avoided, and only referred to incidentally and by way of illustration. The author has had special facilities for the work. Not merely is she herself a child of Wales, enthusiastically devoted to the memories and the lore of her people ; she has had the advantage of inheriting a manuscript collection made by her late father, to which have been added contributions from other members of her family on both sides. Living among the people, she has made it her business to seek out those who were best versed in tradition, and to take methodical notes of the information they put at her disposal. The result, I venture to think, is a work which fills many a gap of the previous record, and helps us materially to an insight into the mind of bygone generations.

The favourite music of the Welsh is commonly pitched in the minor key. In harmony with this, the most obvious note of the folk-lore embodied in the following collection, I think, be found to be one of sombre mysticism. It pervades it all more or less, but naturally it is most insistent in the chapters on the Cŵn Annwn, Corpse-Candles and Phantom Funerals, Death and Transformation. This note is essentially human. It is found in the traditional lore of most peoples—at any rate, of most peoples who have attained a relatively high degree of civilization.   But it may be thought to have been intensified in Wales by the religious revival of the eighteenth and nineteenth centuries.   A careful examination of the folk-lore of Scotland, and particularly of Brittany, will dispel any such suspicion.   The populations of all these countries are reckoned Celtic.   Whether the characteristic in question, which belongs to the folk-lore of all of them, is to be attributed to the Aryan-speaking invaders, who seem to have subjugated the original inhabitants of the West of Europe a thousand years before the dawn of history, and not rather to those aboriginal inhabitants themselves, is a question we need not here consider.   It suffices to observe that mysticism of this cast is the natural outcome of the union of deep and easily excited emotion, passionate religious conviction, and vivid popular imagination.   These are the elements of which it is composed, and they are the endowment in equal measure of the Celtic populations of Scotland, Wales, and Brittany.

The dominant note, then, is that of sombre mysticism, and many of the best tales repeat that note with a grim intensity it would be difficult to beat—as, for instance, the weird story of the Vampire Chair, an exact parallel for which I hardly know.   Others will be recognized as part of the common stock of Europe.   The legend of Roch Castle is that of Cook's Folly at Bristol, and a hundred other places ; it is the story of inevitable fate.   The Swansea maiden who married the farmer of Anglesea is the Greek Lamia, but the girdle gives a new turn to the tradition.   Evidently the spell hung upon the girdle.   What we should have expected is that the husband would have seized the girdle, when thrown off by the wife in order that she might undergo her magical change, and that, on his refusing to restore it, and throwing it into the fire, the wife would have glided away for ever imprisoned in her serpent-form.   This may have been the original catastrophe.   But a deeper shadow rests here upon the ancient superstition which is the basis of the tale.

Lamia stories are only a variety of the Swan-maiden cycle. The Swan-maidens of Gower and Barry Island have nothing to distinguish them from their sisters elsewhere, though it is interesting to find them in Wales.   A tale of more unusual form was obtained near Carmarthen by Mr. T. H. Thomas, of Cardiff.   It does not appear in this volume, but was printed with some other folk-lore in a small pamphlet a few years ago, and reproduced, by Mr. Thomas's kind permission, in *Folk-Lore*, vol. xvi., p. 337.   In it the lady was a salmon, caught by a fisher-lad in the River Towy, and the union fails of its tragic end, lasting instead to the natural term of life. All the children, however, had in their lips the mark of the hook wherewith their mother had been caught.

Nor are the accounts of rites, festivals, and minor superstitions of less interest than the tales. The fulness of detail with which many of these are described from the statements of those who had taken part in them renders the record specially valuable, although they may have been described before. It is needless to discuss them here. I only desire to refer to one small point, on which I may be pardoned if I indicate incomplete agreement with the author's opinion. She thinks that " Lammas Day was not much regarded in Wales." I have no reason to impugn this generalization as applied to recent times ; but at an earlier period it may have been otherwise. There is at least one place where Lammas-tide was observed down to our own days. The story of the famous Lady of the Van Pool belongs to the Swan-maiden cycle. The first Sunday in August used to be regarded as the anniversary of her return to the lake, and large numbers of people visited the Van Pool on that day in the expectation of witnessing her reappearance. There can be little doubt that the first Sunday in August is a conventional substitution for Lammas Day, due, Sir John Rhŷs suggests, to Protestant influence. Probably rites were once performed at that season in honour of the divinity of the lake. They have long ceased, and the annual pilgrimage, if it be still performed, is no more than a pleasant picnic. But even so it is a witness, degraded and hesitating, to the sacred festivity at one time observed.

Many of the ceremonies and superstitions, as well as of the tales, recorded in the following pages are common to other parts of the kingdom—nay, of Europe. It would be remarkable if they were not, for they are the product of ideas and of social relations which are not a peculiar possession of the Welsh, or of any people. Ethnological science is built upon such parallelisms, and it is a gain to have their geographical boundaries extended and their variations made known. To students of anthropology, what the late Lord Salisbury contemptuously called " the Celtic fringe " is the most interesting part of the population of these islands. Its comparative seclusion from modern influences has enabled it to preserve much that has elsewhere passed away for ever. This collection shows what remains, even in a part of Wales in which the English tongue, and with it English modes of thought, have been predominant for centuries. They have not succeeded in abolishing the native traditions, though they have inflicted many irreparable injuries on them. A more dangerous, because a more insidious and inevitable, foe is, however, to be feared. The modern spirit is neither English nor Welsh. It is proper to no nationality. It broods over the Welsh as over the English, and by its aid the Welsh have already attained the van of intellectual progress. But for this advancement a terrible price is rigorously exacted—nothing less than the abandonment of ancient customs, institutions, and beliefs, and the acceptance of a new cosmos wherein such old elements as are retained have lost their most precious and most characteristic features, have been transformed and fused with modern speculation and modern aspirations. Fortunately, the modern spirit is not hostile to the preservation and study of ancient traditions when they are no longer living organisms. Like the fragments of an earlier world in our museums, they may be brought together for examination and comparison with those of other nations. This, to be done effectually in Wales, must be done at once. There is no time to spare. When the present generation is laid to its final rest, many of them will be irrecoverable. To collections like those of Sir John Rhŷs and Elias Owen the collection in this volume is now added, and there is yet more to be garnered. May other workers be stimulated, ere it be too late, to put on record the ways of their neighbours and the sayings of the men of old! If well and faithfully performed, it will be a patriotic work. Nor is it an unworthy ambition for any descendant of the historic Cymry to inscribe his name on the roll of recorders of their traditions, a roll headed with the memorable names of Giraldus, Geoffrey of Monmouth, and Walter Map.

E. SIDNEY HARTLAND.

HIGHGARTH,
    GLOUCESTER.

CONTENTS

FOLK-LORE AND FOLK-STORIES OF WALES

CHAPTER I

THE SEA, LAKES, RIVERS, AND WELLS

IN Wales the sea, lakes, rivers, fountains, springs, wells, cascades, torrents, and pools have much folk-lore and many folk-stories attached to them.

The seventh and ninth waves of the sea were regarded as rescuing waters, and of greater force than any that preceded. It is an old saying in the Principality that if a drowning man can catch the seventh or ninth wave he will be saved. On the other hand, if a man swimming to shore is overtaken by one of those waves, the chances are against his ever reaching land. It was customary to bathe nine mornings in succession in the sea, and this was considered to be a healing course. Nine plunges in the sea in one morning—in succession, if possible —were good for nervous people. It is said that if anybody began in childhood by taking a dose of sea-water immediately upon getting out of bed every day, he would live to attain a great age. People born near the sea were supposed to be brave. A bunch of seaweed kept hanging in the back kitchen scared evil spirits. On many parts of the shore-line of Wales the sea-mistletoe is a barometer. This is placed in a bottle of sea-water, and sealed down. When the water becomes dull or muddy, a storm or heavy rain may be expected. So long as the water remains clear and untroubled, the weather will be fair.

The sea, rivers, fountains, and springs were objects of devotion to the Welsh, and that was possibly why in former times

very little fish was eaten in Wales.   It was commonly believed
that " fishes lived on the bodies of the drowned," and this is
another reason why in some parts fish as a food is avoided.
White waves were watched with awe, and the old people used
to say they were the spirits of the departed who had met their
death by drowning.   They believed that at Christmas, Easter,
and All-Hallows Eve all those who had been drowned in the
sea came up to ride over the waves on white horses, and held
remarkable revels.   The white waves around the dangerous
sands of Nash, South Glamorgan, used to be called the " merry
dancers."

Welsh sailors call the sea " Davy Jones's locker," an expression supposed to have originated in Wales.

Welsh sea-captains and pilots of the Bristol Channel still
believe that a ship or boat of any kind is not a derelict if a
living person or animal is found on it.   It was formerly an
unwritten law that the occupant of the derelict should be
thrown overboard.   If the person or animal could swim a fair
chance was given, and the seamen humanely aided in the
rescue.   The mariners said they had " Parliament at their
back " for their deeds, which were evidently supported by
some obsolete Act concerning " man, woman, child, dog, or
cat " found in a forsaken ship or vessel of any kind.

From Welsh captains and pilots the following lore has been
gleaned :

When a sailor turns a hatch cover the wrong way up, or lets
a pail fall overboard, he feels " uncomfortable."   It is unlucky
to stitch or mend sails on the quarter-deck.   If a man spits to
windward before he has passed Lundy Island, he will have
trouble.   It is fortunate for a loaded ship with a list to star-
board, but unlucky if it is to port.   When first stepping ashore,
or entering a ship or boat, advance with the left foot first for
luck.   Heave a penny over the ship's bow when coming out
of the docks if you would have prosperity and a successful
voyage.   Welsh sailors' wives formerly gave their husbands a
piece of bread that had been baked on Good Friday to protect
them against shipwreck.   The mewing of a cat on board foretokens a serious voyage.   If the cat stretches so that her paws
meet before she reaches Lundy Island from any port in the

Bristol Channel, storms will be encountered. When cats are frolicsome on board a ship, the Welsh sailors say " a gale of wind is in their tails, and there is rain in their faces." If the ship's cat wipes its face often with its paw, trouble is ahead. When the animal turns its back to the captain, to the galley fire, or the cabin stove, the ship is likely to strike a rock or be stranded. If it scratches the mast with its claws, or singes any part of its body, " nothing in the world can save the crew, for all hands are bound to go down." Never hand anything through the ship's ladder. If, when ships go down the Bristol Channel, the Great Gutter, or Nash Passage, roars louder than Breaksea Point, the voyage will be uncertain and unsatisfactory. The reverse indicates a storm between Lundy and the Scilly Islands. There was an old Milford captain early in the nineteenth century who was always engaged to take ships out for their trial trips, because, whatever vessel he boarded, it " would sure to be lucky." A family of the name of Howe, who were well-known captains, pilots, and skippers along the Bristol Channel, had the same reputation as the Milford captain. Members of this family still live at Cardiff, Newport, and Bristol.

Those electric illuminations or phosphorescent gleams that are sometimes seen playing around the masts and rigging of ships were called by old Welsh sailors " canwyll yr ysbryd " (" spirit-candles "), or " canwyll yr ysbryd glân " (" candles of the Holy Ghost "), or the " candles of St. David," and were sometimes known by the English name of " comasants," a corruption of " corposants." These weird lights are known to Italians as " St. Elmo's Stars." By the French and Spaniards they are called " St. Elmo's Fire." To the Russians they are familiar as " St. Nicholas' and St. Peter's Lights." When two illuminations appeared, they were regarded as tokens of fair weather and a prosperous voyage. One solitary illumination was an unpropitious omen. Many lights seen suddenly in a storm indicated an early calm, or that the worst of the storm had passed.

Old Welsh sailors in the early part of the nineteenth century were fond of telling the following yarn : The devil made a three-masted ship from wood cut in the underworld. It smelt so

I—2

strongly of sulphur that it was a pest to the coast of Wales. In this ship the devil placed the souls of people who died in a very sinful condition. Whenever a fresh cargo of souls was taken on board the devil was extravagantly delighted. St. David, according to some sailors, St. Donat as others alleged, became greatly enraged, and pierced the hull with a spear. At that moment the devil was counting the souls on board, and only barely escaped by swimming. The ship was wrecked, and a giant on the coast of Gower, South Wales, made a tooth-pick of the mast and a handkerchief of the mainsail.

Welsh sailors object to going on board ships named after things that sting, because they are generally " doomed to destruction." They say that if anything is lent to another boat luck goes with it unless some portion of the article is first slightly damaged, broken, or wilfully torn. If an article is stolen from a ship, the thief has taken the luck too, and, if possible, it must be brought back at any price. The old Welsh sea-captains would not allow spinning-wheels on board, for they brought disaster, but a child of either sex indicated suc-cessful voyages. Good breezes were obtained when sailors found the ship becalmed by scratching the mizen-mast with a nail. Whistling at sea near the coasts of Wales was regarded as very unlucky, for unfavourable winds and misfortune were likely to follow the ship.

It was said in the older folk-lore that spring-water drawn between eleven and twelve p.m. on Christmas or Easter night turned into wine. This water was also considered good for colic and all abdominal pains. Running water drawn at mid-night from any important spring on St. John's Eve would remain fresh and pure a whole year. Water drawn before sunrise down-stream and in silence on Easter Day was proof against witches and evil spirits. Water drawn before sunrise on any Sunday morning in one jug from three separate and flowing springs was magical in its use and influence. It was customary in many parts of Wales for young men and maidens to walk to the nearest important spring on Easter Monday, draw water into jugs, and throw flowers on the surrounding grass, stones, or bushes. This was prevalent in Glamorgan and Carmarthenshire in the early part of the nineteenth century. My informant, who gleaned particulars from his grand-father of flower-offerings at springs, saw in this a remnant of Celtic water-worship. The youths and maidens believed this water-drawing would bring them good luck for the year.

Welsh girls formerly told their own fortunes in spring-water on May Day morning. A spring in Cadoxton-juxta-Barry, Glamorgan, flowed abundantly in an unfruitful year ; but if the water was slow in coming, there would be plenty of crops, grain, and sheep. The same used to be said of a spring near the foot of Plinlimmon. When the people went to see it, if the water ran quickly, they said : " This year everything will be very dear."

People were warned not to spurt or scatter the water from their hands after washing the first thing in the morning, else they would scatter their good luck for the day. To spill water while carrying it from the spring or brook was an omen of sorrow. Two persons should not wash in the same water without first making the sign of the cross in it. Water and corpses are said to disagree. The body of a drowned man always floats face downward, but a woman's keeps face upwards. The drowning man's body remains at the bottom of the sea or a river until the gall bursts.

Rain-water baths will make babies talk early. Water that will not readily boil is bewitched : to make it boil you must use three different kinds of wood.

Money washed in clear rain-water cannot be stolen. In getting water from a brook it is lucky to draw it with a pitcher down-stream. Pigs bathed in water in which killed swine have been scalded will thrive better and grow well.

The water in which a babe is washed for the first three months of its life used to be thrown under a green tree to make the child thrive.

There was an old belief in Wales that if a man wrapped up in the skin of an animal just killed was laid down alone beside a waterfall, he would have the future revealed to him by the sound of the waters.

It was customary in the first half of the nineteenth century for farmers to throw three ears of wheat, drawn from the first waggon-load to leave the harvest-field, into the nearest running water. When this was not possible, three ears were placed in the carter's or farmer's hat, and when reaching the farm-yard they were burnt. This was done for luck.

If a person washed or sprinkled any kind of animal in one of the fountains of healing, the water lost its virtue.

If a person bitten by an adder, viper, or any kind of serpent could leap across the nearest water before the reptile vanished, he would lose the venom and not die. If it was only a small rainpool, it would suffice.

The pouring out of water in seasons of drought was supposed to bring rain, and in the days of old this was done with considerable ceremony. It is a common expression among the peasantry of Wales to say : " Don't spill the water about unless you wish for rain." When rainy weather prevails, the farm-maids are told : " If you keep spilling the water about we shall have more rain, and we have had quite enough already." The old people used to say : " You must not throw stones into the well, or you will raise a storm." The same was said about lakes and rivers. At one time nothing irritated aged persons more than to see boys and girls pelting the well or river with stones.

Very old people always spat thrice on the ground before crossing water after dark, to avert the evil influences of spirits and witches. If you part from a friend beside a bridge you will part for ever. To avert the possibility of this, it was customary to cross together, take farewell on the other side, and the one who remained at home had to return alone.

It was unlucky to take any pay for water. Those who did so would have to cry in torment for a few drops.

If the water of any river, stream, or brook swept occasionally around a space of meadow-land so as to form an island, people said the tenant of that farm would be exceptionally fortunate in the harvest seasons succeeding the occurrence.

Washing-day lore is curious. If a new garment is washed for the first time when the moon is new, it will not wear well. If the washer-woman pulls out any garment from the tub upside down or to the left, the wearer of the article will never be bewitched.

The woman who wets her apron very much, or splashes the

water much about, will have a drunken husband. Soap frequently falling means " fresh work."

It is very unlucky to wash garments on New Year's Day.
To wash any articles on Good Friday was considered very
unfortunate.

Garments washed with the " right side out " would soon lose
their good colour. When the water boiling ready for washing-
day makes great steam, strangers may be expected. If it boils
quickly it is for luck, and when it boils slowly there will be a
delay in business.

The River Dee was supposed to be very sacred. It rises from
two springs near a farm-house called Pant Gwin, near Dolgelly,
in Merionethshire, and it is asserted it passes through Bala Lake
without mixing its waters with those of the lake. Beyond
Chester it runs to the Irish Channel. This river is supposed to
derive its name, not from " du " (black), or " dwy " (two), but
from " duw " (divine).*

Spenser the poet, in the " Marriage of the Thames and
Medway," includes it among the bridal attendants :

> " And following Dee, which Britons long ygone
> Did call divine that did by Chester tend."

Milton, in " Lycidas," writes :

> " Nor yet where Deva spreads her wizard stream."

An interesting story is connected with the Roodeye, a
spacious meadow near the Dee at Chester. This ground was
ages ago flooded by the tides in the Dee, but a bank or eye of
land in the centre remained above high-water mark. On this
piece of ground a plain and substantial stone cross formerly
stood. It acquired the name of the Roodeye, or Island of the
Cross. Tradition asserts that at one time drought was intoler-
able in the neighbourhood. In the church of Hawarden, in
Flint, a cross and image of the Virgin Mary stood, and to this
shrine of the Holy Rood people of all classes went to pray for
much-needed rain. Lady Trawst, the wife of the Governor and
Lord of Hawarden, prayed so fervently and continuously that
the image fell upon her, and caused her death. So angry were

* Pennant's " Tours," vol. ii., p. 217.

the inhabitants with this answer to their prayers that they selected a jury to sit in judgment. The verdict was " wilful murder " against the image of the Virgin Mary. The jury determined to lay the offender on the beach at low water, whence the next tide carried it to a spot under the walls of Chester. It is asserted that the citizens of Chester held an inquest, and seeing that the object was the image, decided upon " burying her where she was found." A cross was erected " over her grave." Another version affirms that the image was carried to St. John's Church, and there set up, and the crucifix was placed upon the Roodeye. There was an old rhyme on this subject. It ran thus :

" The Jews their God did crucify ;
The Hardeners theirs did drown,
Because their wants she'd not supply,
And she lies 'neath this cold stone."*

Near the banks of the Dee at Chester are the Wishing-Steps. The folk-story attached to this is that whoever stands at the foot of these steps and wishes for anything, and runs up to the top and down to the bottom without taking breath, will have his desires fulfilled.†

In several of the folk-stories of Glamorgan the Severn is described as crying, wailing, moaning, or groaning like a woman in sorrow, grief, or physical agony. Up and down the Bristol Channel skippers in the last half of the eighteenth century said that the apparition of a woman was seen swimming. Sometimes she was seen trying vainly to reach land, or gracefully swimming down Channel, or battling up the Severn Sea against the tide. This story probably owes its origin to a tradition regarding King Locryn and his amour. Locryn, the eldest son of Brutus, married Gwendolen, daughter of the Duke of Cornwall, who conquered Gog and Magog. After overthrowing Humyr (Humber), King of the Huns, Locryn found in one of the enemy's ships Estrildis, " a daughter of the King of Germany." She was very beautiful, and for some time Locryn kept her in a subterranean dwelling near the Severn. This charming lady bore him a daughter, named Averne Sabre, Sabren, or Sabrina.

* Thomas Hughes, F.S.A., " Handbook to Chester," p. 40.
† *Ibid.*, pp. 48, 49.

During the Duke of Cornwall's lifetime Locryn made it known that he visited the secret habitation in order to worship his gods in private. When his father-in-law died, Locryn divorced Gwendolen, married Estrildis, and made her Queen. The divorced wife raised an army against Locryn, who was slain at the first encounter. Gwendolen captured Estrildis and her daughter, and caused both to be drowned in the Severn. An edict was issued that the river should bear the name Sabrina to perpetuate her memory and the infamy of Locryn.* Milton put the legend into flowing verse, which describes the " daughter of Locrine " undergoing

> " a quick immortal change,
> Made goddess of the river."

The whirlpool of the River Taff at Cardiff forms a small lake when the bed is almost dry. In the days of old this whirlpool was called one of the " seven wonders of Glamorgan." People said it was fathomless, and in its cavernous depths a monstrous serpent dwelt, and gorged on the unfortunate victims that were drowned in the river and sucked into the whirlpool. When any bodies were not recovered from this whirlpool people said they had been swallowed by the serpent, and agonies of torture possessed the minds of those whose relatives were so ill-fated. When a body came to the surface it was thought that the person was very good, because the serpent would not touch the corpse of the righteous.

An old woman who was fond of telling nursery stories related to her by her grandmother said that the Taff whirlpool was frequented by a lovely lady, who lured people whilst bathing. Youths were known to swim or row towards her, attracted by her beauty. They were then sucked into the vortex, and their bodies could never be found. She said the lady was the devil in disguise. " It is a dreadful winch,"† said the narrator, " and it

---

* " Geoffrey of Monmouth," book ii., chapter i.
† In Wales the word " winch " is always associated with water. The Welsh scare children from deep water by saying, " There is a winch in it." It is believed that if a person falls into a winch his body will never be recovered. The Nash Sands, off the coast of South Glamorgan, have a winch into which ships are drawn. The Nash Passage, locally known as the Great Gutter, contains a winch, which at high-tide is very dangerous, and swimmers are warned against it. Renfig Pool,

is fathomless. It reaches from the Taff to the mouth of perdition, where Satan waits for the souls who are beguiled by the lovely lady."

A similar story used to be told about the whirlpool of Pontypridd, on the same river. The Black Pool, at Cefn, Merthyr-Tydfil, Glamorgan, has an evil reputation as " luring people to suicide."

A curious story is attached to Llyn Gwyn. St. Patrick passed it on his way to visit St. David. He was accompanied by another saint, and when they reached this lake one of them suggested resting awhile. This was done, and during the halt the saints discussed religion. Coming to a controversial point, the men grew irritable, and St. Patrick was very angry. Several Welsh people overheard the religious quarrel, and expressed surprise and annoyance. St. Patrick in spite turned them into fishes. One of the party was a woman, who was transformed into a white lady. She was often seen accompanied by flashes of light. On account of this insult to St. Patrick, the sun never shines upon the lake but during one week of the year.*

Llangorse Lake is said to be the site of a sunken city, the inhabitants of which were reported to be very wicked. The King of that part of Wales sent his ambassador to ascertain whether the rumour was true or not, adding that if it was well founded, he would destroy the place as an example to his other subjects. When the ambassador paid his surprise visit it was evening, and all the inhabitants were enjoying festivities and excesses. Not one of them offered the stranger any hospitality. Seeing the door of a humble cottage open, he entered, and found the place deserted, with the exception of a wailing babe in a cradle. The ambassador remained beside the babe, and acci-

---

near Porthcawl, is supposed to contain a winch. All along the coast of Wales there are shore and sea pools, each of which is supposed to contain a winch. It must be understood that the winch is not associated with every well, pool, and lake, but certain localities are thus famed.

Sly and underhanded people are commonly described in Wales as being " as deep as a winch."

At one time I thought the word belonged exclusively to Glamorgan and the Flemings, but wider and later investigation revealed the use of it in many parts of Wales, both with reference to water and people.

* William Howell, " Cambrian Superstitions."

dentally dropped one of his gloves into the cradle. In the morning before dawn he took his departure, intending to convey his unpleasant confirmation of the rumours to the King. He had only just left the outskirts of the city when he heard repeated peals of terrible thunder, accompanied by groans and shrieks. Then there were sounds like the dashing of waves. It was cold towards sunrise, and he missed his glove, which was of great value, so he returned to look for it. When he reached the outskirts of the city he saw that the houses had vanished, and the whole site was covered with water. While gazing at the lamentable scene, he saw a speck in the centre of the water, and as it was wafted towards him, he recognized the cradle in which he had left his glove. He drew the cradle towards him, and brought it up to dry land, and then found the babe safe and alive. The ambassador took the baby to the King, who adopted it as the sole survivor of the lost city.*

Kenfig Pool, near Porthcawl, Glamorgan, has a tradition attached to it. A local chieftain wronged and wounded a Prince, and the latter, with his dying breath, pronounced a curse against the wrongdoer. The curse was forgotten until one night the descendants of the chieftain heard a fearful cry : " Dial a ddaw !   Dial a ddaw !" (Vengeance is coming !). At first it passed unnoticed, but when the cry was repeated night after night, the owner of Kenfig asked the domestic bard what it meant. The bard repeated the old story of revenge ; but his master, to prove the untrustworthiness of the warning, ordered a grand feast, with music and song.

In the midst of carousal the fearful warning cry was repeatedly heard, and suddenly the earth trembled and water rushed into the palace. Before anybody could escape, the town of Kenfig, with its palace, houses, and people, was swallowed up, and only a deep and dark lake or pool remains to mark the scene of disaster. In the early part of the nineteenth century traces of the masonry could be seen and felt with grappling-irons in the pool. The sands near by cover many old habitations.†

A similar story is told of Llyn-y-Maes, a beautiful lake near

* Davies, " Mythology and Rites of the British Druids," p. 146.
† Iolo Manuscripts, p. 607.

Treflyn, in Cardiganshire. Its name means the lake of the field, which, according to tradition, covers the ancient site of Tregaron. The people of this old place were very wicked, and went to excesses in all ways. Most of their time was spent in revelry, feasting, hideous orgies, and incessant forms of every kind of pleasure known in those days. Many times had the people been warned that the place would be destroyed by fire and flood if they did not cease their wickedness, instead of which they grew worse as the years passed. One night, when the revelry was at its height, lightning caused a fire to break out, and a flood followed, completely overwhelming the place. Not a person escaped, for those who were not burnt were drowned. [*A. B.*]

In Carnarvonshire there is a lake called Llyn-Nâd-y-Forwyn, or the Lake of the Maiden's Cry. A man and a maiden were betrothed, but he was a deceiver, and one evening, when the mists were rising from the water, he pushed the girl in, and she was drowned. Her spirit was said to haunt the lake. Sometimes she appeared like a ball of fire rolling along the banks of the Collwyn. Her groans and shrieks could be heard a long distance away. Sometimes she arose out of the water with hair in disorder, and wildly waving her arms. People said she could often be heard weeping and moaning and plaintively uttering the words, " Lost ! lost !" [*Family Collection.*]

Llyn Dulyn is in one of the rugged valleys among the mountains of Snowdon. It is encircled by high rocks. The water of this lake is very black, deep, and turbid, and the fish that live in it have very small, withered-looking bodies, much deformed, and large grotesque heads. Wild-fowl and other birds shun this lonely lake, which is dismal in the extreme. A causeway of stones leads into this lake, and at the end of it there is a stone called the Red Altar. If even on the hottest day of summer any person throws water so as to wet this altar, rain will fall before night.*

This black lake is supposed to be an extinct and fathomless volcano, and shepherds in the surrounding mountains used to say that the appearance of a dove near those black and fateful

* *The Great* : Welsh magazine published in London, 1805.

waters foretokened the descent of a beautiful but wicked woman's soul to torment in the underworld.

In the seventeenth century people believed that if anybody had the courage on one of the " three-spirit nights " to watch beside Llyn Dulyn he would see who were to die within the next twelve months. Fiends would arise from the lake and drag those who had led evil lives into the black waters. Those who had led good lives would be guided past the causeway leading to the lake, and vanish in spirit forms robed in white. A reputed witch disappeared from the district, and a shepherd said he saw her being dragged into the black waters. [A. B.]

The Pwll-Gwen-Marw, or Dead Lady's Pool, is in the River Afan, at the foot of Moel Mynyddau, under Tewgoed Colliery. It is said that the spirit of a lady moans and hovers all night over the dangerous waters to warn people from the neighbourhood and point out tracts of safety. [A. B.]

Near Lake Tegid, now known as Bala Lake, there was a walled-in spring with a lid which had to be put on every night and locked, so that witches, fairies, and the devil might not disturb the waters. In close proximity to the spring there was a large and important town. One night the keeper of this spring forgot to put the lid on ; others said the devil had opened it. The waters burst out and overflowed the town, destroying everything before them. The site of the submerged town became Lake Bala. In the story, Old Bala is under the lake, which is about three miles long and one mile wide. A prophecy still unfulfilled is to the effect that New Bala is to meet the same fate. [C. D.]

There used to be a belief in Wales that lakes object to having their depths ascertained. Bala Lake was one of these. Two men went in a boat to what was regarded the deepest part, and ran out plummet and line to an almost endless extent. Presently a terrible cry rent the air, and a voice from the waters cried aloud : " Line cannot fathom me. Go, or I will swallow you up !" Since then no one has dared to sound the lake.

It was said that Bala Lake was bottomless. Centuries ago an expert diver tried it, but was terribly frightened by his experience. He asserted that a dragon was coiled up at the bottom of the lake, and if he had not been very careful the creature would have swallowed him. [A. B.]

Llyn-y-Gader is a round lake in the south-west of Snowdon. A man of the eighteenth century swam across this lake, and his friends, watching him, noticed on his return that he was followed by a long, trailing object winding slowly after him. They were afraid to raise an alarm, but went forward to meet him as soon as he reached the shore where they stood. Just as he was approaching the trailing object raised its head, and before anybody could render aid the man was enveloped in the coils of this water-monster, which dragged him to a deep hole in the end of the lake from which the Llyfin flows. There he was drowned, and the spot where he sank revealed blood-red waters. [A. B.]

Gellionen Well is in Glamorgan, not far from Pontardawe. It was formerly frequented by people in seasons of drought for the purpose of getting some of the water, which, when thrown or scattered about, would bring rain. This was customary in the early part of the nineteenth century. An old man who in his childhood remembered this said people would dance on the nearest green spot to the well, and throw flowers and bunches of herbs at each other. Then they would sing old-fashioned Welsh ballads, and play kiss-in-the-ring. The leader of the company, going to the well, would cry " Bring us rain !" three times. The people, chiefly youths and maidens, would then fill bowls or pitchers with the water, and either throw it there or carry it home to scatter upon the garden. Rain always followed. [Family Collection.]

The well dedicated to St. David at Henfynuw, Cardiganshire, had a curious story attached to it. An old man went to this well alone on Midsummer Eve, and while there he heard a voice from the waters calling " Help ! help !" He looked around everywhere, but not a person was visible. The man sat down to rest because he was tired, and thought no more of the cry. But later on he heard the same cry twice repeated. " Who calls for help ?" he asked, going to the well. " It is I," said the voice ; " I am calling." " Who are you ?" asked the man. A hand was stretched from under the well, and the voice bade the man to clasp it, and " hold tight."

He did so, but the hand was slippery, and he loosened his hold, and as the mysterious fingers vanished the voice cried : " I am bound for another fifty years !" [*Family Collection and Manuscripts.*]

Between Abergele and Llandudno there is a spring called Ffynon Elian.   People maliciously inclined formerly used to come from all parts of Wales, under the pretence of drinking the healing waters.   In reality, they came to obtain the waters for bewitching their enemies.   A farmer in Breconshire, having heard of this, took two small barrels, and, placing them pannier-fashion on his horse, went all the way to Abergele for water from Ffynon Elian with which to punish his enemies.   He returned home, and placed the barrels in his outhouse.   The next morning he went to get some water to throw after one of his enemies, but the barrels burst, and the water fell over him, with the result that he was bewitched ever afterwards.

This well was closely connected with many terrible superstitions.   Some of the old people generations ago called it the " well of evil," and it was shunned by all respectable persons. A man living beside this well was called the clerk of it.   He was consulted by persons who bore malice to somebody, and wished to injure them bodily or mentally, or both.   The clerk undertook to gratify their needs if they paid him a good sum for his work and secrecy.   One of the things done was to enter the man's or woman's name in a book.   A pin was stuck in the name, and a stone, inscribed with the initials of the person to be persecuted, was thrown into the well.   So long as it remained in the well the curse would work.   When anybody desired to remove the curse the pebble was taken out of the water, and the name erased from the clerk's book.   Sometimes a rude figure made of marl, wax, or dough was thrown into the well, and kept in the water for any desired period. A tale about St. Eliem's Well was as follows : A woman believed her husband to be guilty of infidelity, and desired to punish him ; so she made a figure of marl and stuck it with pins in the place where the heart would be.   She then registered his name in the clerk's book, and lowered the marl figure into the water.   There it remained for a week, during which her husband suffered tortures of pain in his heart.   At the end of the week she had the marl figure drawn up from the well, and stuck the head of it closely with the pins removed from the heart, and accordingly the suffering was removed from that organ to the brain, and he became almost mad. After successive tortures of various kinds and in different parts of the body for several months, the man altered his behaviour, and, expressing penitence, was forgiven by his wife.

Another story is about a man whose uncle had been cruel and unjust to him. He made an image of wax, stuck it with pins, tied to it a lump of copper, and suspended it over the well by a piece of cord. The man then uttered " secret words of cursing," in which he desired that his uncle might continually suffer severe pain, and lose money, property, and possessions. The figure was lowered into the well, plunged three times in succession, and then allowed to remain in the bottom. The uncle remained under the ban until the nephew promised to release him on payment of a certain sum of money. This was done, and the curse was removed. The story goes that the uncle suffered severe pain, some of his property was burnt to the ground, and a stranger robbed him while under the curse. [A. B. and Family Collection.]

The Silver Well at Llanblethian, near Cowbridge, Glamorgan, was a great resort of youths and maidens, who went there to test the fidelity of their sweethearts and lovers. The points of the blackthorn were gathered by breaking and not cutting them from the bush. One of these was thrown into the well. If it floated the lover was faithful, and if it whirled round he was also of a cheerful disposition. If it remained like a log on the water he was stubborn and sulky, and if it sank out of sight he was unfaithful. If a number of thorn-points fell accidentally into the water, the lover was a very great flirt. The same was said of Ffynon Saethon, in Lleyn, North Wales. [Family Collection and Manuscripts.]

People used to visit Gwyned Well, at Abererch, to ascertain the result of anybody's illness. A garment of the sick person was thrown into the waters. If it sank to the right he would get well, but if it went to the left he would surely die.

In the well of St. Peris, at Llanberis, North Wales, there was a large eel, and this was protected carefully. If this eel coiled around the person, he would be healed.   An old tale describes a young girl bathing in the waters, and when the eel coiled around her she died of fright.

According to the folk-stories, Mary's Well at Llandwyn contained sacred fish, the like of which was never seen in any " other well in Wales."   Still the same story used to be told of Peter's Well near Llantwit Major, South Glamorgan. [*Family Collection.*]

Eglwys Fair Well, in Lleyn, opposite Bardsey Island, has a folk-story attached to it.   It is said that in the far past a beautiful woman had a very important wish which she desired to obtain.   One evening about sunset a strange lady came to her, and said that her wish would be gratified if she descended the steps to the well, filled her mouth with water, then ascended, and went around the church once without losing a drop of the water.   To this day young people do the same thing, hoping their wishes will be obtained.

The well at Llanbedrog, in Lleyn, had oracular powers, and was frequented by people wishing to find out the thief who had stolen their goods.   It was customary for the inquirer to kneel down beside the well and utter the names of a number of people, suspected or not, at the same time throwing a piece of bread into the water.   At the name of the thief the bread would sink.   If the bread floated until it gradually soaked to pieces the thief would not be discovered.   [*A. B.*]

The waters of St. Fegla's Well, Carnarvonshire, were efficacious in cases of falling sickness.   People washed their hands in the well, and then dropped a fourpenny-piece into it.   Then, repeating the Lord's Prayer, they walked around the well three times.   The male patient had to take a cock, and the female patient took a hen, in a basket, which was carried by them in all their movements.   After going round the well, the patient entered the churchyard, went into the church, and laid himself down beside the altar, with the Bible under his head.   He then covered himself with a blanket or a thick shawl, and remained thus until daybreak, when he got up, and left the fowl in the church.   Should the bird die, it would be clearly understood that the disease had been transmitted to the fowl.   There are several wells in Wales where the same process used to be gone

2

through. A folk-story connected with one is that a woman who possessed considerable means went to the well one day carrying a hen in a neat basket. She did all that was required of the patients, but was too mean to drop a fourpenny-piece into the well. That night, while sleeping in the church, she was awakened by somebody pinching her severely. She immediately got up, and in the darkness tried to find her assailant, but was only plunged into worse torments. Some unseen hands laid hold of her, shook and beat her, and prevented her getting out of the church. When the day dawned, she found herself alone in the church. The fowl had been released from the basket, and was nowhere to be seen. It had mysteriously vanished. Instead of recovering, the patient grew gradually worse and died. Another version ascribes this tale to a man who threw a piece of gold into the well, and suffered in much the same way as the woman, and with the same results. [A. B. C. D.]

It was customary for a newly married wife to drop a pin or pins into the house-well immediately after entering her new home. If she neglected to do so, the first year of her married life would be unlucky. To pass a pin well without dropping a contribution in the shape of a pin or needle was regarded as very unlucky. In some places contributions of rags were expected, as well as of pins. Several wells or springs at Llancarfan, in the Vale of Glamorgan, were renowned as pin and rag wells. Marcross Well, in the south-west of the same vale, had deposits of pins for wishing purposes, and thank-offerings in the form of rags were fastened to the trees, brambles, and bushes in the close vicinity. The waters of Marcross Well were of medicinal efficacy, and especially in cases of eye affections. It seems to have been visited for various complaints, and an old rhyme about it runs thus :

> " For the itch, the stitch, rheumatic, and the gout,
>   If the devil isn't in you, this well will take it out."

People believed that the waters of this spring promoted the growth of the hair.

Penylan Well, near Cardiff, was visited for wishing purposes, and beside Taff's Well, near the Garth Mountain, rags, crutches, and sticks were deposited as votive offerings.

Wells were known to change colour when people quarrelled beside them. A well near Wenvoe, in South Glamorgan, was polluted by children throwing mud and manure into it. The respective parents blamed each other for allowing the children to do this. Both made disclaimers. When next people went to draw from the well, they found the waters partly brown and partly red. So long as the quarrelsome parents lived in the neighbourhood the waters remained discoloured. When the parties moved away to other villages, the waters resumed their normal condition.

Springs and wells in some districts were supposed to be guarded by serpents and dragons, and the killing or removal of the guardian was attended by dire consequences, frequently by an epidemic which swept away whole families. To offend a well or spring was regarded as dangerous.

An old woman living in the hamlet of Ogmore, to the south of Bridgend, Glamorgan, remembered a curious story which was told to children in the early part of the nineteenth century. Three springs hidden in a hill not far from the Ogmore Mills on the Ewenny River, to the south of Bridgend, Glamorgan, were regarded as very mysterious. The three springs united at a spot which is known as the Shee Well. My informant said the people believed that girls were carried off by water-ogres, and kept imprisoned at the source of the springs. Some of these maidens never escaped, but one came away, and was ever afterwards dumb, so that she could not describe what had happened during her absence. The Shee Well once ran away. Wild, wicked men formerly lived on the banks of the Ewenny and Ogmore Rivers. They never mowed the meadows nor sowed the fields, but lived by robbery and murder, so that often human blood tainted the waters of the rivers. Because of this neglect the Shee Well mourned and lamented, and one day it suddenly receded into the hills. The low cavern of the well became quite dry, and not a trickle of water could be seen. The robbers heard the moanings and groanings of the well, and said : " What matter is it ? The ogre of the Shee Well cannot deprive us of the fish in the stream." But when they looked where the stream flowed to meet the rivers, nothing was found but snakes and toads. When the men went to the Ewenny and

2—2

Ogmore Rivers, they found that the ogre of the Shee Well had charmed away all the fish. Then the robbers were penitent, and went humbly to the cavern from which the Shee Well sent forth its stream, and begged the ogre to let the waters return. The ogre promised to do this if the men agreed to till the lands, cultivate the fields, and mow the meadows. Then the robbers made the cavern and basin of the well sweet and clean, and planted trees around, so that the place looked cool and inviting. The people danced and rejoiced in honour of the return of the Shee Well, and it was said that old men and women grew young again for joy.

Near Nantle there is a spring near a brook, and sometimes sorrowful cries and wailings are heard there. They are supposed to come from this deep unseen spring, where a water-woman lives in imprisonment for her sins. The cries are ominous of death in the parish. [A. B.].

Llandowror is a corruption from Llandyfrgwyr, meaning the " church of the water-men." These men were the seven sons of Mainawe Matheu, who were called " water-men." They were born on the water, escaped from the water, and on land were maintained by " the fishes of the water." Mystery attended their origin, and they devoted themselves to a religious life. In old age the seven brothers went out on the water in a boat, and as they never returned mystery enshrouded their death. [A. B. and Family Manuscripts.]

The celebrated Swallow Falls at Capel Curig, Carnarvonshire, are supposed to keep imprisoned the turbulent spirit of Sir John Wynne for his many sins and wickedness. They say he is bound hard and fast to the bottom of the fall, and in his frantic efforts to get free from his fetters he makes terrible noises and cries as the cascades rush over him.

In the bed of the river under Haverfordwest Bridge a wicked man's spirit is said to be bound for a thousand years. When the time has expired, the most important man in the town is to release him. But as nobody knows when the thousand years began, it is impossible to say when they will expire, so the spirit still remains in " durance vile."

In the days of old, when ghosts were "laid," spirits were driven to a pool of water, a lake, a well, or the sea. Occasionally they were allowed to return from their watery prison by the length of a grain of corn or barley a day. It took ages to accomplish this journey. In the Vale of Neath, Glamorgan, an old story was formerly told of a spirit doomed to one of the pools of the Hepste, and returning in the shape of a frog.

In some of the old nursery stories told in various parts of Wales a beautiful clear fountain was described, the waters of which arose at the sound of singing, and fell when silence succeeded the song.

CHAPTER II

FIRES AND FIRE FESTIVALS

FIRE, like water, is closely connected with Welsh lore. Both were regarded as purifying, healing, and, in the days of old, more or less sacred. Ceremonies and superstitions with reference to fire were numerous and interesting.

The Bâltan, or sacred fire of the Druids, was obtained direct from the sun, and by means of it all the hearth fires in Britain were rekindled. These fires were accompanied by feasts in honour of Bel, or Beli, the Celtic deity of light, and in Druidical days they were carried out with much pomp and ceremony.

In later times the Bâltan, known by its corrupted name of Bealtine, or Beltane, was associated with much superstition and revels. The most important of the Beltane fires was held on the first of May, but sometimes on the second or third of that month. Midsummer was another occasion. Among the places in South Glamorgan where the latest Beltane fires were kindled were the common land beside the Well of St. John, Newton Nottage, Porthcawl, in 1828-1830, in Cowbridge about 1833, near Nash Manor in 1835, and at Llantwit Major between 1837 and 1840. The following information with reference to the Beltane fires was given me in these words :

" The fire was done in this way : Nine men would turn their pockets inside out, and see that every piece of money and all metals were off their persons. Then the men went into the nearest woods, and collected sticks of nine different kinds of trees. These were carried to the spot where the fire had to be built. There a circle was cut in the sod, and the sticks were set crosswise. All around the circle the people stood and watched the proceedings. One of the men would then take two bits of

22

oak, and rub them together until a flame was kindled. This was applied to the sticks, and soon a large fire was made. Sometimes two fires were set up side by side. These fires, whether one or two, were called *coelcerth*, or bonfire. Round cakes of oatmeal and brown meal were split in four, and placed in a small flour-bag, and everybody present had to pick out a portion. The last bit in the bag fell to the lot of the bag-holder. Each person who chanced to pick up a piece of brown-meal cake was compelled to leap three times over the flames, or to run thrice between the two fires, by which means the people thought they were sure of a plentiful harvest. Shouts and screams of those who had to face the ordeal could be heard ever so far, and those who chanced to pick the oatmeal portions sang and danced and clapped their hands in approval, as the holders of the brown bits leaped three times over the flames, or ran three times between the two fires. As a rule, no danger attended these curious celebrations, but occasionally somebody's clothes caught fire, which was quickly put out. The greatest fire of the year was the eve of May, or May 1, 2, or 3. The Midsummer Eve fire was more for the harvest. Very often a fire was built on the eve of November. The high ground near the Castle Ditches at Llantwit Major, in the Vale of Glamorgan, was a familiar spot for the Beltane on May 3 and on Midsummer Eve. I have also heard my grandfather and father say that in times gone by the people would throw a calf in the fire when there was any disease among the herds. The same would be done with a sheep if there was anything the matter with a flock. I can remember myself seeing cattle being driven between two fires to ' stop the disease spreading.' When in later times it was not considered humane to drive the cattle between the fires, the herdsmen were accustomed to force the animals over the wood ashes to protect them against various ailments. Sometimes the Beltane fire was lighted by the flames produced by stone instead of wood friction. Charred logs and faggots used in the May Beltane were carefully preserved, and from them the next fire was lighted. May fires were always started with old faggots of the previous year, and midsummer from those of the last summer. It was unlucky to build a midsummer fire from May faggots. People carried the ashes left after these fires to their homes, and a charred brand was not only effectual against pestilence, but magical in its use. A few of the ashes placed in a person's shoes protected the wearer from any great sorrow or woe."

It was said that Gwythyr, the son of Greidawl, fought with Gwyn ab Nudd for the fair Cordelia, daughter of Lear, every first of May, and they were to continue doing so until the day of doom. The ultimate conqueror was to be the winner of the maiden.* May Day contests were probably held in commemoration of this old belief.

May Day festivals in later times were survivals of the old Beltane fire celebrations.

On the morning of May Day—that is, at the first glimmer of dawn—the youths and maidens in nearly every parish in Wales set out to the nearest woodlands. The gay procession consisted of men with horns and other instruments, which were played, while vocalists sang the songs of May-time. When the merry party reached the woodlands each member broke a bough off a tree, and decorated the branch with flowers, unless they were already laden with May blossoms. A tall birch-tree was cut down, and borne on a farm waggon drawn by oxen into the village. At sunrise the young people placed the branches of May beside the doors or in the windows of their houses. This was followed by the ceremony of setting up the May-pole on the village green. The pole was decorated with nosegays and garlands of flowers, interspersed with bright-coloured ribbon bows, rosettes, and streamers. Then the master of the ceremonies, or the leader of the May dancers, would advance to the pole, and tie a gay-coloured ribbon around it. He was followed by all the dancers, each one approaching the pole and tying a ribbon around it until a certain number had been tied. The dance then began, each dancer taking his or her place according to the order in which the ribbons had been arranged around the pole.

The dance was continued without intermission until the party was tired, and then other dancers took their places.

The games or May dances were called " Cadi'r Fedwin " in South Wales, but in North Wales they were known as " Y

* "Mabinogion," pp. 251, 263.

Fedwin, neu y Ganghen Hâf." These dances and May feasts were very popular in all parts of Wales.

At these festivities a May beverage was distributed among the visitors. Sometimes this drink consisted of metheglin or mead alone, but frequently it was made of herbs, including woodruff. Elderberry and rhubarb wines were popular on these occasions, while among the men beers of various kinds were used.

On May Day morning a curious custom was prevalent in Wales until about forty years ago. The young men of the parish decked a large bunch of rosemary with white ribbons, and placed it at the bedroom windows of the maidens they admired. In some places people who wished to insult or annoy any enemy took a horse's head, and fastened it to the latch of the door. Sometimes a man did this to " spite " a girl, and *vice versâ*. On this day effigies were carried about the villages. These would be named after any man or woman who had made himself or herself notorious, ridiculous, or scandalous. The effigy was greeted with laughter, shouts of derision, and pelted with various missiles. This was done so late as the sixties.

In Wales, as in England, the May Day festivities were not complete without the customary fight between Summer and Winter.

An aged Welshman described the battle as conducted in South Wales in the following way : " When I was a boy, two companies of men and youths were formed. One had for its captain a man dressed in a long coat much trimmed with fur, and on his head a rough fur cap. He carried a stout stick of blackthorn and a kind of shield, on which were studded tufts of wool to represent snow. His companions wore caps and waistcoats of fur decorated with balls of white wool. These men were very bold, and in songs and verse proclaimed the virtues of Winter, who was their captain. The other company had for its leader a captain representing Summer. This man was dressed in a kind of white smock decorated with garlands of flowers and gay ribbons. On his head he wore a broad-brimmed hat trimmed with flowers and ribbons. In his hand he carried a willow-wand wreathed with spring flowers and tied with ribbons. All these men marched in procession, with their captain on horseback heading them, to an appropriate place. This would be on some stretch of common or waste land. There a mock encounter took place, the Winter company flinging straw and dry underwood at their opponents, who used as their weapons birch branches, willow-wands, and young ferns. A good deal of horse-play went on, but finally Summer gained the mastery over Winter. Then the victorious captain representing Summer selected a May King and the people nominated a May Queen, who were crowned and conducted into the village. The remainder of the day was given up to feasting, dancing, games of all kinds, and, later still, drinking. Revelry continued through the night until the next morning."

On May Day servants change their places in Wales ; half-yearly rents are paid, farms are taken, and house agreements and leases are signed. Llantwit Major, in Glamorgan, was renowned for a celebration held from time immemorial on May 3. It was called Llantwit's Anwyl, or Darling or Pet Day. Tradition states that an Irish pirate named O'Neil had for many years committed great havoc along the coast. Both sides of the Bristol Channel suffered at his hands, and many schemes were arranged to punish the offender. By-and-by the women of Llantwit set their wits working, and with success. The best-looking matrons and maidens in the town dressed themselves up in fine raiment, and went down to the meadows near Colhugh Point. There they danced and sang and held festivity until O'Neil and his men appeared in the offing. It was well known that the Irish pirate was exceedingly susceptible to the charms of women. Therefore, when he landed at Colhugh, he and his men hastened to join the fair ladies. So well were the pirates received, and so kindly were they treated, that the afternoon passed quickly. While in the midst of the dance one of the girls escaped without being noticed. She roused the men of Llantwit, and before O'Neil and his companions were aware of it they were surrounded and captured. The story goes that O'Neil was tied to a stake and burnt, while his companions were slain.

In commemoration of the occasion an effigy of the pirate was set up annually in Colhugh meadows and burnt. At the same time a King and Queen were chosen, and the usual festivities were carried out. Mrs. Wrentmore, a local lady of wealth and lands, and Mrs. Jenny Deere, a native of the town, were among the last Queens of the revels until they ceased, about 1850-1855. The Independent Order of Oddfellows then celebrated " Llantwit's Anwyl Day " by church parade and a dinner, and this was continued until the year 1907, when, like many other relics of the past, it went into oblivion.

The ancient tradition of O'Neil and his men probably owed its origin to something more than repeated acts of piracy. In the ceremony it is possible that the effigy of O'Neil represented winter or death, and the expulsion of one or both at the approach of summer and immortality. When the effigy was burnt the people sang at first sad and melancholy dirges, which, when the May King and Queen appeared, were followed by gay ballads and songs of rejoicing.

Midsummer fires and festivals resembled those of May. They were held on St. John's Eve and Day. Three or nine different kinds of wood and the charred faggots carefully preserved from the previous midsummer were necessary to build this fire, which was generally done on rising ground. Into this fire various herbs were thrown, and girls with bunches of three or nine different kinds of flowers would take the offered hands of boys who wore flowers in their buttonholes and hats, and jump together over the midsummer fire. Wild merrymakings these were, and the young people threw the flowers from their posies, hats, hair, and buttonholes into the heart of the flame. Roses and wreaths of various flowers were hung over the doors and windows on St. John's Eve and Day.

Describing a midsummer fire, an old inhabitant, born in 1809, remembered being taken to different hills in the Vale of Glamorgan to see festivities in which people from all parts of the district participated. She was at that time about fourteen, and old enough to retain a vivid recollection of the circumstances. People conveyed trusses of straw to the top of the hill, where men and youths waited for the contributions. Women and girls were stationed at the bottom of the hill. Then a large cart-wheel was thickly swathed with straw, and not an inch of wood was left in sight. A pole was inserted through the centre of the wheel, so that long ends extended about a yard on each side. If any straw remained, it was made up into torches at the top of tall sticks. At a given signal the wheel was lighted, and sent rolling downhill. If this fire-wheel went out before it reached the bottom of the hill, a very poor harvest was promised. If it kept lighted all the way down, and continued blazing for a long time, the harvest would be exceptionally abundant. Loud cheers and shouts accompanied the progress of the wheel.

Christmas, like Midsummer, had its fire associations. In many parts of Wales it is still customary to keep part of the Yule-log until the following Christmas Eve " for luck." It is then put into the fireplace and burnt, but before it is consumed the new log is put on, and thus " the old fire and the new " burn together. In some families this is done from force of habit, and they cannot now tell why they do it ; but in the past the observance of this custom was to keep witches away, and doubtless was a survival of fire-worship.

In the days of old Christmastide festivities extended into several weeks. Preparations for burning the Christmas log and for the various feasts were extensive and often elaborate. Then the bards and musicians of the Principality were active, and many kinds of amusements and entertainments were arranged. Nearly all the old Christmas customs have become obsolete, but the singing and literary festivals still remain in the form of local eisteddfodau. The old-time revelry has vanished, and with it the bringing in of the Christmas log ; the quaint morris or merry dancers, with the Aderyn Pig Llwyd, or " Bird with the Grey Beak "; the Mari Llwyd, or " Holy Mary "; and the wassailing amusements and festivities in connection with the New Year and Twelfth Night, or Old Christmas Day. In Wales burning torches were greatly in evidence with the Christmas log.

The morning watch to celebrate the birth of Christ was known as the Plygain. This early service was held in all the parish churches in Wales at four o'clock in the morning of December 25. It was continued until about the years 1850-1856, and in some localities a few years later. The churches were brilliantly illuminated and beautifully decorated ; a short service was held, and carols were afterwards sung. It is singular to note that when the Established Church discontinued the Plygain, it was held in Nonconformist chapels, and the services were conducted with great fervour every year. The Wesleyan Methodists were among the last to celebrate the Plygain, which, translated, means the early morn or dawn.

A curious custom was included in the Christmas festivities in many parts of Wales. On Christmas Eve a bowl of hot beer, sweetened with sugar and flavoured with spices, was prepared by the master of the household, while the mistress brought forward a basket containing a cake. The bowl and the basket were decorated with evergreens, holly, and ivy-wreaths. A procession was then formed, and the bowl and basket were carried in state to the stall of the finest ox belonging to the family. There the men of the household stood on one side, and the women were arranged opposite them. The mistress then placed the cake on the horns of the ox, and the master stirred the beer, drank a mouthful, and passed the bowl on after the fashion of the loving-cup. Meanwhile, a Welsh toast was heartily sung. While all this was going on, one or two persons in the assembly carefully noted the behaviour of the ox. If the animal remained quiet and peaceful, it was a token of good luck during the ensuing year. If, on the contrary, the animal became restless and angry, bad luck was supposed to follow. As it might be expected, the cake would not remain very long upon the horns of the ox. If it fell upon the side where the women stood, it was regarded as a token of feminine triumph during the ensuing year.

It may be mentioned that the bowls used on these occasions generally held about a gallon of beer. Some of these bowls had eighteen handles attached to them, and it was customary for the company to hold the handles while a Christmas carol was sung.

Carol-singing was, and is still, popular in many parts of Wales during the Christmas holidays. Formerly these carols were sung to the accompaniment of the harp, and sometimes the violin. Frequently they were sung without any instrumental accompaniment.

In the early part of the nineteenth century people firmly believed that between eleven and twelve on Christmas Eve and the first hour of Christmas Day the cattle knelt down in reverence. But the person who saw them would die within a year.

When the Christmas log is burning you should notice the people's shadows on the wall. Those shadows that appear without heads belong to the persons who are to die within a year.

If you tie wet straw-bands or hay-bands around your fruit-trees on Christmas Eve, they will yield plentifully during the next year.

If a hoop falls off a cask on Christmas Eve, somebody in the household will die within a year.

A bright and sunny Christmas foretokens full granaries and barns. A dull and cloudy Christmas promises empty granaries and barns.

If a spinster on Christmas Eve pours melted lead into cold water, it will turn into the shape of the tools her future husband will use. A doctor will be represented by a lancet, a writer by a quill, a surveyor by a chain, a mason by a mallet, and so on.

Put a small heap of salt on the table on Christmas Eve. If it melts during the night you will die within a year. If it remains dry and undiminished, you will live to reach a very old age.

It is considered unlucky to hang up the mistletoe in houses, or to decorate rooms with holly before Christmas Eve.

The morning after Twelfth Night all the Christmas holly and mistletoe is burnt. It is unlucky to keep it up longer, or to destroy it in any other way. Everybody tastes as many Christmas puddings as possible during the holidays " for luck."

The morris dancers formed a merry throng in the Christmas festivities. The party consisted of three, seven, or nine men, dressed as gaily and grotesquely as possible. Caps of any kind of animal's skin and short jackets were worn, all decorated with gay knots of ribbon. Sometimes the head and brush of a fox were prominent. Bells and any jingling ornaments were worn around the wrists and ankles, and frequently one or two of the party appeared as Megan, a hag of the night, in female dress. This party, accompanied by a harpist or fiddler and torch-bearers, went from house to house where money was to be

obtained, and danced a reel peculiar to Wales. The feet kept
time with the music, and occasionally two of the dancers would
hold each other's hands, and spin round and round in bewildering fashion. A Welsh jig and an old-style hornpipe were
included in the amusements, and these were often cleverly
performed by experts. A dance resembling the modern cake-
walk was also given.

The Aderyn Pig Llwyd, or the " Bird with the Grey Beak,"
sometimes accompanied the morris dancers, but frequently
went the round of the district on its own account. This
exhibition consisted of the skeleton frame of a horse's head
with artificial eyes and ears. The head was decorated with
ribbons, coloured paper, and almost any kind of finery. This
was carried upon the head and shoulders of a man wearing a
long fantastic robe adorned with tinsel. It was the duty of this
man to imitate the actions of a horse, and much amusement was
caused when the creature kicked, or reared, or curvetted. The
horse was attended by a groom, who held the reins and kept the
animal within bounds. This was often difficult, but productive
of much fun and merriment. After going through a performance, the groom placed a hat in the horse's mouth for any contribution that might be bestowed. The procession was accompanied by men holding burning brands.

The Mari Llwyd, or " Holy Mary," was an exhibition made up
of mummers dressed in all kinds of garments. The most prominent figure was a man covered with a white sheet. On his head
and shoulders he bore a horse's head, fantastically adorned with
coloured ribbons, papers, and brilliant streamers. Youths
bearing burning brands, and small boys dressed up as bears,
foxes, squirrels, and rabbits, helped to swell the throng. In
some parts of Wales, in the far past, it was customary for a
woman to impersonate the Virgin, while Joseph and the infant
Christ were prominent. But in later times these three characters were omitted, and a kind of Punch and Judy exhibition
was substituted. The Mari Llwyd was always accompanied by a
large party of men, several of whom were specially selected on
account of their quick wit and ready rhymes. The mode of
proceeding was always the same. All doors in the parish were
safely shut and barred when it was known that the Mari Llwyd

commenced her itinerary. When the party reached the doors of a house an earnest appeal was made for permission to sing. When this was granted, the company began recounting in song the hard fate of mankind and the poor in the dark and cold days of winter. Then the leading singer would beg those inside to be generous with their cakes and beer and other good things. It was customary for the householder to lament and plead that, alas ! times had been bad with him, and he had little to spare. Then began a kind of conflict in verse, sung or recited, or both. Riddles and questions were asked in verse inside and outside the house. Sarcasm, wit, and merry banter followed, and if the Mari Llwyd party defeated the householder by reason of superior wit, the latter had to open the door and admit the conquerors. Then the great bowl of hot spiced beer was produced, and an ample supply of cakes and other good things. The feast began and continued for a short time, and when the Mari Llwyd moved away the leader found contributions of money in his collecting bag.

Many specimens of the introductory rhymes, the challenge from without, the reply from within, together with the verses sung when the Mari Llwyd entered the house, and afterwards departed, are still preserved and well remembered.

When the Mari Llwyd was badly treated, the revenge of the party was boisterous. In some places the men forced an entrance, raked the fire out of the kitchen grate, looted the larder, and committed other depredations.

Some people think that the bony horse's head used in what is called the " Mari Llwyd " celebration was an emblem of death, or a symbol of the dead, and not a remnant of pre-Reformation days and the Virgin Mary.

I have been told that in the seventeenth and early eighteenth centuries this celebration was called in many parts of Wales the " Marw Llwyd," meaning the " Grey Death," a symbol of the dying or dead year.

The skeleton head and shoulders and the skull of the horse, accompanied by a procession of sight-seers and dancers, point to the Mari Llwyd celebrations as a lingering vestige of ancient horse worship common to the Celts, Teutons, and Slavs.

In the far past the Mari Llwyd was looked forward to with

pleasure, but in later times it was surrounded by a riotous throng, and became so degenerate in some places that it was regarded with terror.

The city of Llandaff annually provides the performers for a Mari Llwyd kind of Christmas waits, and to this several old Welsh customs are attached. Trecynon, Aberdare, had its Mari Llwyd as late as, if not later than, 1900. Llantwit Major has its Mari Llwyd, which visits several places in the Vale of Glamorgan ; but here the custom is becoming spasmodic, and is not carried out every winter. There are, doubtless, other places in the Principality in which the old custom still survives.

But the genuine wits, the ready rhymesters, and the clever leaders and mummers of the Mari Llwyd, are no longer to be found.

In connection with fire superstitions there are many curious survivals. People in out-of-the-way places, when troubled in mind, touch the stone over the chimney-piece, and afterwards throw a handful of dry earth into the fire. As it burns, they whisper the cause of their trouble to the flames, and this is supposed to avert any impending evil ; or they kneel down beside a low-placed oven or stand by the high, old-fashioned ones, and whisper any secret or trouble to the bottom of the oven.

Here may be mentioned a curious habit of the old women who bake their own bread in ancient ovens which are heated with wood. When cleaning them out, they take very good care to leave some of the wood ashes, together with a small charred stump, inside. When the next fire is to be lighted, the old stump is first ignited, and the new faggots are thrown on, so that all burn together. This has been done for generations, and in one instance personally known to me, the aged great-grandmother sees that the custom is duly observed at the present day when baking-fires are lighted.

The people say, while a fire burns on the hearth lightning will not strike the house. Never leave a frying-pan on the fire without something in it, or else the wife of the house will have puckers in her face. If the town clock strikes while the church bells are ringing there will soon be a fire in the parish.

3

When the fire under the oven hisses, there will be quarrels in the house. If sparks of fire fly from the candle when lighted, the person they go towards will get money that day. A crackling fire betokens strife ; a dull fire betokens sorrow. When there is a hollow in the fire, people say a grave will soon be dug for a member of the family. When the fire is slow in lighting, they say " the devil is sitting on top of the chimney," or " is in the chimney."

CHAPTER III

THE HEAVENS AND EARTH

SIGNS and symbols of earthly beings are mingled in the folk-lore of Wales with the stars, and the names of many distinguished heroes, heroines, and giants are to be found connected with the silent and pathless heavens.

The Via Lactea, or Milky Way, is known to the Welsh as Caer Gwydion or Gwydion's Circle, and the other constellations as follows : the Northern Crown is the Circle of Arianrod ; the Lyre is Arthur's Harp ; the Great Bear is Arthur's Plough-tail ; Orion is Arthur's Yard ; the Pleiades is the Group of Theodosius ; Cassiopeia's Chair is the Circle of Don ; the Ecliptic is the circle of Sidi ; the Twins is the Large Horned Oxen. The rest are named thus : the Smaller Plough-handle, the Great Ship, the Bald Ship, the Triangle, the Grove of Blodenwedd, the Chair of Teyrnon, the Chair of Eiddionydd, the Conjunction of a Hundred Circles, the Camp of Elmur, the Soldier's Bow, the Hill of Dinan, the Eagle's Nest, Bleiddyd's Lever, the Wind's Wing, the Trefoil, the Cauldron of Ceridwen, the Bend of Teivi, the Great Limb, the Small Limb, the Great Plain, the White Fork, the Woodland Boar, the Muscle, the Hawk, the Horse of Llyr, Elffyn's Chair, and Olwen's Hall.

The Pleiades were known as the Twr Tewdws and the Group of Theodosius. They were described as the " agitated, thickly collected, cheering, and solacing stars."

The Milky Way was supposed to be peopled by the souls of heroes,* kings, princes, and all just and honourable persons, who thronged the Circle of Gwydion. The brighter the stars

* Davies, " Mythology," p. 262.

in this part of the heavens, the more exalted the character whose soul had entered the charmed circle.

Gwydion of the Milky Way has been identified with Hermes, and yet he appears similar in many respects to Wodan of Norse fame. Gwydion, the son of Don, invented writing, practised magical arts as a renowned magician or wizard, and was the builder of the rainbow. His Caer, or fort, was by his magical power transported from earth to heaven, and the great pathway leading to and from it is known to the English as the Milky Way.

Gwydion, the most intellectual of the Welsh heroes, is described as being able by means of his magic wand or rod to be always surrounded by a glorious host, whose deeds of chivalry and daring entitle them to places in the great Caer of the heavens.

With reference to Arthur's Plough-tail, a farmer living in the Vale of Glamorgan said his grandfather always declared that when the tail of the plough was low down bread would be cheap, but when the tail was high bread would be dear. The same farmer pointed out the stars forming Orion's belt as the " Mowers." This, perhaps, was because the constellation rises about the hay-harvest.

In the mythology of Wales Hu Gadarn, or Hu the Mighty, the primitive leader, hero, and law-giver of the ancient Britons, was deified when earthly honours were exhausted. He is described as inhabiting the sun. His symbols were a wren with outspread wings, which conveyed a similar meaning as the dove in Syria and other parts of the East, and an ox. His spouse, elevated to the rank of a goddess, appears under the name of Ceridwen, or Cariadwen,* and her symbols were a boat and a cow. Hu received the homage due to the sun, and Ceridwen received that due to the moon. The subordinate deities were the three Bull Demons of Britain. Their names were the Ellyll Gwidawl, or the Demon of the Whirling Stream ; the Llyr Merini, or the Demon of the Flowing Sea ; and the Ellyll Gurthmwl Wledig, or the Demon of the Earth.

The sun was personified under various names. He was

* This spelling was used in the fourteenth century (Iolo Manuscripts, p. 79).

Arthur, the controller; Taliesun, the light-giver; Merddyn, the hero of the sea; Morgan, when risen from the sea-barge of Ceridwen;* and Dofydd, as the conqueror of Black Wings, or Satan, known to the Ancient Britons as Avagddu. The barge of Cariadwen is known as the Llong Foel, and the crescent moon was regarded as its emblem in the sky. In Welsh the crescent moon is called Llun, and Monday, Moonday, is known as Dydd Llun. Cariadwen, the Queen of the Heavens, is supposed to protect the sacred barge or boat from the fury of Black Wings. The Druids asserted that the personified sun was mortally wounded at noon on the shortest day of the year. All through the afternoon the sun struggled to live, but at sunset he perished and fell into the water beyond the horizon. Then the divine soul of the sun escaped into the barge of Cariadwen, while Black Wings usurped the authority over the heavens and the earth. After that the sun was born again, and arose in all his glory in the morning.

The garden of the life-giver contained his three daughters and three golden apples. These three daughters correspond with the three personifications of the sun on March 25, June 25, and December 25. The golden apples growing on a tree in the sun-garden transmitted their juice to the Cauldron of Cariadwen, and thus became three drops of divine essence which fertilized vegetation and entered the human system.

In the folk-lore of Wales the sun was supposed to hide his face before any great sorrow or national disaster. Eclipses were, therefore, regarded as ominous of wild warfare and danger of defeat. An ancient myth describes Hu Gadarn as determined to punish Black Wings for his misdeeds; but he is not to be found, having hidden himself under the earth. Cariadwen, the Moon-Mother, reveals his whereabouts, and Black Wings is punished. In revenge, Black Wings pursues the sun and the moon, and whenever a hand-to-hand encounter ensues an eclipse occurs.

A Carmarthenshire veteran said that when he was a boy all the people in his home district firmly believed that if a person went up early enough into the mountains at any time in the summer, he would positively see the sun dancing.

* " Welsh Archæology," vol. ii., p. 278.

The British Druids* decreed that every official act was to be discharged " in the eye of the light and the face of the sun."† Thus, their great convocations were held at the solstices and equinoxes, while the minor congresses were held at the new and full moon.   All Druidic services and rites were celebrated between sunrise and sunset.

At the spring festival of the Druids the Bâltan, or sacred fire, was brought down from the sun.   No hearth in Britain was held sacred until the fire on it had been rekindled from the Bâltan.   This festival became the Easter season of Christianity.   The midwinter convocation of the Druids—who then cut the mistletoe with a golden crescent or sickle from the sacred oak—represented our Christmas.   The three berries of the mistletoe represented the Deity in His triple dignity.   The growth of the mistletoe on the oak was the symbol of the incarnation of the Deity in man.

In Welsh folk-stories all magical herbs are represented as gathered before sunrise.   All healing waters should be drawn and quaffed before sunrise.

A superstition of very old standing was to say of the sun : " He is going to rest, and he is awaking."   In his morning splendour on great festivals the sun was always described as " dancing."   This evidently gave rise to the expression prevalent in many parts of rural Wales, " I can see the sun dancing before my eyes," meaning that it glittered.

" Toriad-y-dydd " (the " break of day") and " Y seren ddyd " (the " day-star ") waited upon the sun, and heralded its rising.

In some superstitions the sun is described as laughing and being joyful.

People born at sunrise were regarded as likely to be very clever.   Those born in the afternoon or about sunset are described as lazy.

During an eclipse of the sun people in Wales covered their wells, fearing the water would turn impure.

May-flowers gathered just before sunrise keep freckles away.

Dragons and flying serpents were supposed to count their gold at sunrise.

The new moon is considered propitious for all fresh under-

---

* Davies, " Mythology," p. 270.
† " Welsh Sketches," 1853, p. 19.

takings. Thus, in Welsh lore it is mentioned that if you move into a new house or change from one residence to another at the time of new moon, you will have " plenty bread and to spare." Again, if you count your money at the time of new moon, you will never have an empty purse.

Wedded happiness and household stores will thrive, and money will increase, if you gaze at the moon on the first new-moon night. Never look at the new moon through glass or trees, for it is unfortunate.

It is lucky to cut the hair and the nails on new-moon nights.

If one member of a family dies at the time of new moon, three deaths are likely to follow.

Healing herbs and dew should be gathered at new moon.

Trenches made at new moon time will fall together.

To turn your back to the new moon when wishing for any-thing is unlucky.

Wood cut at new moon is hard to split; at the full, it is easily cut.

The full moon, as opposed to the new, was propitious to all operations needing severance.

Grass should be mown at the full of the moon. In this way the hay dries quickly.

If a bed is filled with feathers when the moon has passed the full, the newly plucked feathers will lie at rest.

Trenches made at full moon will grow wider and deeper.

Winter crops must not be sown in the moon's idle or third quarter.

The spots on the moon are accounted for in the following way in Wales : A man went out gathering faggots of wood on Sunday, and God punished him by transporting him to the moon. There he is doomed to walk for ever with a large bundle of sticks on his back. In some parts they say his dog went with him, and may be seen at his heels.

The colour of the new and full moons had certain indications.

William Cynwal, a Welsh bard of the sixteenth century, composed a rhyme, which, translated into English, runs thus :

> " Observe, ye swain, where'er ye stand,
> The pale-blue moon will drench the land ;
> Cynthia red portends much wind ;
> When fair, the weather fair you'll find."

The pale new moon is indicative of rain, especially when surrounded by a cloud film.

A red full moon means a coming storm of wind.

A single " ring," or halo, around the moon was indicative of a storm ; a double ring meant " very rough " weather ; a triple ring indicated a spell of unusual weather.   If, when three days old, the moon appears very bright and clear, fine weather is promised.   A clear moon denotes frost, but a dull moon indicates rain.   If the new moon looks high, cold weather may be expected ; when it seems to be low down, warm weather is promised.   When the moon is clearly seen in the daytime, cool days may be expected.   If the new moon appears with points upwards, the month will be dry ; if her horns point downward, the month will be more or less rainy.   The Welsh say, when the moon looks like a golden boat—is on her back— the month will be wet.   The boat-like appearance of the moon is possibly a remnant of the Cariadwen myth.

It is considered very dangerous to sleep in the moonlight, and especially for moon-rays to fall on a sleeping child's face. Moonlight falling on the eyes of any sleeping person causes blindness, and this is difficult to cure.   People say it will cause the person to become moonstruck, or a lunatic.   If the moon is allowed to shine in through the pantry window, much crockery will be broken.   If you hold a sixpence up to the new moon, you will never be short of money.   If lovers crossed the moon-line together they would never be married.   Fisher- men avoided the moon-line when setting out to sea.   Never cross the moon-line without wishing for something.   Plants, herbs, and flowers should not be planted at the time of the waning moon.   Calves weaned at the time of the waning moon grow very lean.   It is unlucky to kill a pig when the moon is waning.   The curing will be unsatisfactory, and the meat will shrink in boiling, roasting, or toasting.   This applies to fresh pork, as well as to cured bacon and ham.   If in the summer the new moon is seen with the old moon in her arms, the weather will be fine for the next quarter.   Fleecy clouds across the face of the moon are indicative of rain.   A misty moon means wet weather.   A very red moon rising is a " sign of great heat." There was an old belief in Wales that all lunatics had been moonstruck in infancy, and incessant talkers were " moon led."

Cader Ceridwen, the chair or seat of Ceridwen, is a name for the rainbow in Wales. In the days of old the Welsh believed that the souls of heroes, Kings, Princes, and just people entered heaven by means of the rainbow, which was built by Gwydion, the son of Don. By some it was formerly called God's Chair. in which He sat watching those who entered heaven. In the early part of the nineteenth century people considered it very unlucky to pass under the rainbow. It was an omen of impending death. In some places there was an old story that if you passed under the rainbow, or it fell between you and other people, your sex would be changed. Where the rainbow sprang out of the ground, a pot of gold or some kind of treasure was to be found. The Welsh say that the rainbow will cease appearing before the end of the world.

Comets were supposed to appear before the birth or death of a King, a Prince, or a very exalted person. The birth of Owain Glyndwr was said to be heralded by a comet and curious meteors, with falling stars.

There was formerly a belief in Wales, even so late as the middle of the nineteenth century, that if the tail of a comet swept the earth the world would be burnt, and afterwards be effaced by a flood. The end of the world would be accomplished by means of fire and water. Donati's comet struck terror among the rural population of Wales.

Meteors falling like balls of fire to the earth indicated calamity to the nation or to some distinguished person. Dread followed the event. These meteors were supposed to form the fiery chariots in which the souls of the Druids were conveyed to heaven.

A substance which fell from meteors, or was found where the latter had fallen, was formerly known as " Tripa'r Ser," or " star-jelly." It was considered very fortunate to find it.

A meteoric stone found by anybody was carefully kept for luck, and the finder would have prosperity so long as he preserved it. If he gave the stone away he must expect misfortune, and if he sold it some calamity would befall him and his family.

Shooting or falling stars are regarded as ominous. In some parts of Wales they say you should express a wish while the star falls, or you will be unlucky during the whole year. In other localities they say you should utter a few words of the Lord's Prayer " for luck."

When shooting stars fell over a house it foretokened the death of one of the inmates. If they fell to the west of a town or village there would be sorrow therein ; if to the east, some pleasure or festivity may be expected. To the north they indicated a hard winter, and to the south an unusually warm summer. If they fell to the east, it would be " bad for man and beast."

Thunder and lightning, above all other natural phenomena, were supposed, by the older inhabitants of Wales, to indicate the anger and punishment of God. During a thunderstorm old people used to say, " God is angry."

The name Taranis is handed down as one of the Celtic deities, from whose name the word *taran*, or thunder, was derived. and is still used in the Welsh language.

A very old man remembered his grandfather saying that his great-grandfather, living in the end of the seventeenth century, used to tell a story of an ox being led up and down the fields when thunder brooded, and the herdsmen would implore God to drive the thunder away, or to send protecting rain with it. The same authority said there was an old belief that the thunderbolt dived into the earth—it was in the shape of a black wedge—and remained in the earth for seven or nine years, when it returned to the surface again. Every time it thundered the bolt ascended nearer the surface. If a thunderbolt or wedge was preserved indoors, the house would be proof against damage by lightning. The thunder-stone was supposed to possess healing and restorative powers, especially in nervous affections and fits, for which it was carried in the pocket.

The Welsh still dread a thunderstorm without rain, for it is regarded as extremely dangerous. During the storm it was formerly, and still is, customary to fasten all doors and windows. Sometimes two sheathed knives were crossed outside a window to prevent the house being struck. In former years, when a person heard thunder for the first time in the season, he took a stone and tapped his forehead with it three times, to prevent headaches during the next twelve months.

In the older folk-lore thunder was supposed to be caused by God pursuing the devil and dashing him to the underworld. Fearing the devil would take refuge in the house, all entrances were instantly closed.

It was considered dangerous to take refuge under an oak during a thunderstorm, for the lightning penetrated fifty times deeper into it than into any other tree. Animals struck by lightning were considered unfit for human food, being poisonous. Places struck by lightning were cursed. People struck by lightning must have been very sinful. At one time church bells were rung to drive the thunder and lightning away. This practice was kept up in Wales until early in the nineteenth century. Shooting into the sky was supposed to be efficacious for the same purpose. The redbreast and the beetle attracted lightning. Glass, steel, and all glittering articles had the same power. For this reason looking-glasses, pewter-vessels, and bright brasses were covered at the approach of thunder and lightning. Stonecrop was formerly planted on the roofs of old thatched houses to keep the thunder and lightning away. On many habitations in Wales the stonecrop is still to be seen, and also on old barns and granaries. People at one time gravely asserted that if a thunderbolt or lightning struck a building in any hamlet, village, or town, there was an evil inhabitant in it. When a person was struck by thunder or lightning, the old inhabitants said it was " God's judgment " for some secret sin or wickedness. When thunder was heard and lightning was seen between the first day of November and the last day of January, the people said the most important person in the parish would die within the year of the occurrence. The year in which thunderstorms were unusually prevalent was called " bad and wicked," and it was generally believed that very serious crimes were committed in it.

Folk-lore concerning earth is not abundant, but it has its curiosities. It was formerly customary with farmers, upon changing farms, to take some earth from the place they were leaving to the new home. This earth was strewn here and there among the gardens, orchards, and lands " for luck." Sometimes the housewife carried with her the charred stump and wood ashes from the last baking, to kindle the first fire in the oven of the new home. [*Family Collection.*]

At one time it was customary to throw a handful of earth over the next of kin or heir to the deceased after the funeral.

Among the peasantry in the eighteenth century, a person taking a voluntary oath in the course of his daily work frequently swore placing a bit of turf or earth on his head. This was customary in Glamorgan later than in many parts of Wales.

To get a good crop of wheat, barley, oats, or any cereal, farmers used to fetch some mould from three adjoining fields inherited by one person. This they mixed with their seeds before sowing a field.

If anybody wished to overcome an enemy or discover a thief, he had to cut a piece of sod trodden by the suspected person, wrap it in a rag, then place it under his pillow. In his dreams the guilty person would appear. This was to be done three nights in succession.

" If I wass to sink into the earth this minute," says the Welsh peasant-girl, in proof of the truth of her assertion, and " as sure as I am standing on the earth," to prove the certainty of a circumstance. Again, the farm-boy says, " If the earth wass to swallow me up," he could not be more astonished.

" Black " earth was, and still is, in great request for putting on graves without tombstones, and those with flower-beds.

It was formerly the custom of Welsh farmers and peasants to obtain earth from certain important places, for the purpose of sprinkling it through their stables, pig-sties, gardens, and even their house, to avert evil. Portions of this earth were also strewn over the coffins and graves of their relatives and friends. In the eighteenth century earth from Llancarfan and Llantwit Major, both in the Vale of Glamorgan, was in much request. It was obtained in the former place from the Garden of St. Cadoc, and in the latter from beside the Cross of St. Iltutus, and from the Côr Tewdrig, formerly the Côr Eurgain, to the north of the parish church.

Earth from the fissure of the Skyrrid Fawr, in the parish of Llantheweg Skyrrid, Monmouthshire, was used for similar purposes. The Skyrrid is popularly known as St. Michael's Mount and the Holy Mountain. On its summit there was formerly a small chapel dedicated to St. Michael, and on the eve of that saint's day, it was the scene of many quaint and weird practices customary at that season. The legendary story of the fissure on the Skyrrid is that the mountain was rent asunder by the earthquake which happened at the time of the crucifixion of Christ. From this the Skyrrid derived the name of the Holy Mountain.

St. Gowan's Chapel, in Pembrokeshire, had what was formerly called " sprinkling earth " in fissures close beside it. Bardsey Island, Priestholme, and Holyhead in the North, and St. David's, Caldy Island, and Barry Island, in the South, had earth which was locally in request for sprinkling purposes.

Churchyard mould, passed through a sieve and added to mortar, caused the stonework to knit more strongly than if ordinary sifted ashes were used.

It was at one time customary for persons suffering from rheumatism to be buried in earth in the churchyard. The patient was stripped naked, but his face was covered. He was then buried in a standing position for two hours, with only his head above the ground. If then relieved of pain, the process was to be repeated for the same time every day nine times in succession. If not quite rid of pain, the patient omitted the treatment for three days, resumed it on the fourth, and again repeated it nine times in succession.

An expression formerly much in use in Llantwit Major and the Vale of Glamorgan was : " It is panwaen days with him," or, " He has fallen on panwaen days." Of a horse unable to render further services, they would say : " He has come to pan-waen days at last," or, " Panwaen days have come for him "— that is, his fortunes have reversed, and he has fallen from good ground into bad ground. Y panwaen was peat-moss or bog, and useless or poor ground. There were patches of this ground in various parts of the Vale, particularly at Llancarfan, Llancadle, Boverton, supposed to be the Bovium of the Romans, and Llantwit Major, where, according to tradition, St. Patrick was captured and taken by pirates to Ireland.

In former times it was customary for the farmers in springtime, when they turned up the first furrow with the plough, to take a handful of the earth and sprinkle it in the four corners of the kitchen for luck " with peace and plenty."

Earth placed in the lining of a hat, or a small piece of turf fastened in the hatband, was supposed to guard a man from magic and witchcraft.

It was a token of extreme scorn if anybody spat on the earth before another person. Formerly such an action would end in a " free fight " among villagers and others.

A handful of earth flung after anybody was equivalent to the challenge of the thrown gauntlet.

Late in the eighteenth century those called " witches and evil people," who wished to " destroy " an enemy, used to cut out a piece of turf, to which a thickness of earth was attached, that had been trodden by the offending person. This was suspended by a cord on a hook in the chimney. As it dried up the enemy would waste to death !

An old remnant of magic remained prevalent in the early part of the nineteenth century. This was told by an aged person who had seen it done. When anybody wished a relative or lover to come home from a distance or from abroad, it was customary to boil a clod of earth or turf, or the person's old stockings or old shoes, in a crock, and keep the water boiling for twelve hours, replenishing as it wastes. The person wanted would at once start for home.

Gaps in the earth in any person's garden or field were said to foretoken death to the owner or tenant.

When the earth sinks mysteriously in a field, or anywhere near the premises of anybody, it is a token of misfortune.

A landslip was formerly avoided by children in their play, for they were told that such a thing never happened without sucking in evil men and naughty children. Deep hollows in fields were said to have been caused by the curses of witches or the bans of enemies. [*Family Collection.*]

CHAPTER IV

HOUNDS OF THE UNDERWORLD, AND OTHERS

THE Cŵn Annwn are celebrated as spirit-hounds passing through the air in pursuit of objects of their malice, and their howling was regarded as an omen of death. These dogs have been variously described. Sometimes they appear as very small dogs, white as the drifted snow, with tiny ears quite rose-coloured inside, and eyes that glittered like brilliant moon-beams. In some parts of Wales they are described as being black and very ugly, with huge red spots, or red in body, with large black patches like splashes of ink. The most terrible of these spirit-hounds were said to be of a blood-red colour, and when seen were dripping with gore, while their eyes resembled balls of liquid fire. In some places they were known as small liver-coloured dogs, all " spots and spangles " of red and white, or " flame-coloured."*

They were heard in the " dead of night " by travellers in lonely districts, or by people who lived in remote places far away from towns. Sometimes they howled in the air with a wild kind of lamentation, or bayed and yelled in appalling chorus, to the terror of those who heard them.

The eves of St. John, St. Martin, St. Michael, All Saints, Christmas, the New Year, St. Agnes, St. David, and Good Friday, were important occasions for the Cŵn Annwn. Then these dogs went in procession through the lonely lanes and by-ways of Wales. Sometimes they travelled in weird packs alone, but frequently they were guided by their master. He is de-scribed as a dark, almost black, gigantic figure, with a horn slung around his swarthy neck, and a long hunting-pole at his back.

* " Jones of Tranch," p. 33.

In Carmarthenshire he is represented as a fleet-footed pedestrian, with two black hounds in a leash, and a creature, half wolf, half dog, behind him.   There, too, the Brenin Llwyd, or Grey King, favours him, and receives his hounds with those of the Cŵn Wybyr, or Dogs of the Sky, in his Court of the Mist.

In Glamorgan, Brecon, and Radnor Arawn, the master of these hounds rides a grey horse, and is robed in grey.   In North Wales he walks or rides, and is always dark and gigantic.

In North and South Wales alike he is sometimes accompanied by Mallt y Nos, or Matilda of the Night, a hag who, with evil force, drives the dogs onward.

If any person by accident, design, or curiosity joins these hounds, on one of the processional nights, " blood falls in showers like rain, human bodies are torn to pieces, and death soon follows the victim of the nocturnal expedition"*

Their favourite meeting-places were cross-roads, and whenever their feet touched the mandrake the latter " screamed aloud."   Sometimes they frequented the graves of those who before their death had in spirit form visited their last resting-place.   On cross-roads and around graves these hounds left their uncanny traces in the shape of human bones, torn-up turf, and lumps of earth, which, when trodden upon, emitted a flame, with a " strong smell of sulphur."†

Sometimes they were known to go in pursuit of people who were doomed to die within twelve months from one of the processional nights.   Then they went quietly, stealthily, without so much as a faint cry to announce their approach.   They were seen, but not heard, as they ran quickly from room to room in the ancient mansion or humble cottage in pursuit of their victim.   It was stated that on certain occasions the spirits of those pursued people were seen running out into the night followed by the hideous hounds.

An old Mid-Wales story describes the death of a very vain lady, who desired to be buried in her ball-dress.   Her wish was gratified, but ever afterwards her soul was hunted by Arawn and his hounds.

It was said in the past that those souls which were not good enough to enter heaven, nor yet bad enough to merit hell, were

* " Jones of Tranch," pp. 20-30.   † " Vale of Glamorgan," p. 300.

doomed to ride about following the Cŵn Annwn to the end of all time.   The cavalcade of doomed souls included " drunkards, scoffers, tricksters, attorneys, parsons' wives, and witches !" [A. B.]

The horses used in these processions are described as " coal-black, with fiery eyes that glow like furnaces, and the hunting-crops are of red-hot iron, while the bridles and reins are of steel."*

Arawn, with his Cŵn Annwn and fiery steeds, can be heard for miles, and Mallt-y-Nos, or Matilda of the Night, cries aloud during the chase.   The story of Mallt-y-Nos, as it used to be told in the early part of the nineteenth century, is curious.

There was once a beautiful but wicked Norman lady, who came in with Fitzhamon from Gloucester to South Wales. She so passionately loved riding after the hounds that once she exclaimed : " If I cannot hunt in heaven I would rather not go there."   At her death her soul was doomed to join Arawn and his Cŵn Annwn, and sometimes with them, or with the fiery steeds, or with the Cŵn Wybyr, poor Mallt-y-Nos is to be seen as she wished, hunting through all the centuries until the end of time.   The folk-story asserts that Matilda has long repented her impious wish, and for this reason her cries are often sad and pitiful as she runs low down beside the spirit-hounds, or takes an aerial flight with the Cŵn Wybyr, or mounts a fiery steed, and rides through lonely villages on Christmas or New Year's Eve. [Family Collection.]

Another form taken by this story runs thus : A maiden very fond of hunting was betrothed to a man who made her promise to give up her favourite sport as soon as she married him.   For a year or more after her marriage she gave up all thoughts of hunting, but one day her husband went from home, intending to remain away a little time.   During his absence his wife could not resist the temptation of the chase, so, mounting a splendid horse, she gaily rode away to the meet.   Feeling sure that none of her friends would divulge her secret, she followed the hounds for a whole day.   Coming home in the twilight, her horse threw her.   When her husband returned soon afterwards, he found his wife had broken her leg.   One version of the story describes the

* " Jones of Tranch," pp. 28, 29.

4

husband throwing her out into the courtyard, where she was seized by a whirlwind, carried away, and doomed to ride on the storm for all eternity.   Another version describes her husband seeking the advice of a local Dyn Hysbys, " a man well informed in matters that are dark to others," who by incantations " threw her to the winds," among which she is doomed to " whirl for ever and ever !"   [J. R.]

So late as 1850 old people mentioned her name with bated breath, and referred to her as the wicked Norman lady who would " rather hunt than go to heaven."

Mallt-y-Nos was supposed to search St. Donat's Castle, Glamorgan, once a year for the soul of Colyn Dolphyn, the notorious pirate.   This wandering and unhappy spirit was sometimes seen dressed in dull green, with a hooded cloak.   In the Vale of Glamorgan she was seen in dark red or in dark blue.

Cross-roads appear to have been her bane, and if ever she chanced to reach one between Christmas Eve and Twelfth Night, she could be heard crying for help.   Then the Cŵn Wybyr or the Cŵn Annwn would come to her assistance, and set her on the direct route to her haunts.

In several instances and districts the Cŵn Annwn, or Dogs of the Underworld, whose haunts were solitary woodlands, ravines, and lonely valleys, had rivals in the Cŵn Wybyr, or Dogs of the Sky, whose clamorous noises in various keys were startling indications of disaster.   The latter frequented marshy places and lonely moorlands far away from the busy haunts of mankind.   The cries of both dogs resembled those of hounds and huntsmen in full chase.

The nearer these dogs were to mankind, the fainter were their voices ; the farther away, the louder they sounded.*   Their voices were like those of great hounds, or of bloodhounds, sounding in the night very deep and hollow.

In Welsh mythology† these dogs belong to Arawn, the King of the Underworld, who is described as a great huntsman, clothed in grey, and always riding a grey horse, while the dogs from the royal kennel were grey, with scarlet spots.   This huntsman-king and his dogs were accused of sometimes doing

* " Jones of Tranch," pp. 28, 29.
† Davies, " Mythology," p. 420.

harm to mortals, and they were supposed to inflict perpetual torment on disembodied spirits who were doomed to everlasting wanderings on earth or in the air.

In Welsh folk-lore these dogs when heard in packs prophesied disaster and doom to ancient families, and to the peasantry misfortune, calamity, or death. Heard singly, the dog always denoted sickness and death. Excepting on processional nights, they were seldom seen in whole packs; but parties of them—three, seven, or nine—were frequently encountered. Sometimes a stray dog wandered from the pack and prowled the countryside, howling near comfortable homesteads, or in the grounds of castles and ancient manor-houses.

Out of innumerable stories about the Cŵn Annwn and the Cŵn Wybyr which are to be found in every county of the Principality, the following have been selected:

From Aberffraw, in Anglesey, comes the story of an evil fisherman, who was supposed to " brew storms," being chased by the Cŵn Annwn into the sea, and was never afterwards seen.

Merionethshire has a story of a girl who, having lost her way among the Berwyn Mountains, fell in with a pack of these hounds, and was only saved from death by repeating the Lord's Prayer over and over again until the creatures ran away.

In the beautiful Vale of Clwyd an Englishman was " nearly killed by the Cŵn Annwn," and gladly made his escape from Wales, saying its demons were " the curse of the country !"

Aberdaron, in Lleyn, Carnarvonshire, had a pack that pursued a clergyman who from the pulpit one Sunday denounced all smugglers as " children of Beelzebub." From the neighbouring villages homeward on several occasions the Cŵn Annwn chased the unfortunate clergyman, and harried him so much that he gladly promised not to preach against smugglers any more.

A pack of the Cŵn Annwn, accompanied by Arawn, the master, frequented Montgomeryshire, and were said to have their kennels in the recesses of Plinlimmon.

The Radnor Forest Mountains had a terrible pack of these hounds. They frequented a deep ravine on the road to Llanfihangel-nant-Melan, and many stories were formerly told about the depredations they accomplished in the neighbourhood of Old and New Radnor. [*A. B. and Family Collection.*]

All the dreary valleys of South Wales were supposed to be haunted by these hounds.   The Vale of Taff, above Cardiff, the Rhondda Valley, and the Vale of Neath, were celebrated for these mysterious visitants, attended by the master and Mallt-y-Nos.

Near Wilton Crossways, in the Vale of Glamorgan, one of these spirit-hounds was frequently to be seen even so late as a " few years ago." This creature is described as having features and upper part of the body of semihuman form.   The other part and lower limbs were those of a " light-spotted dog." The eyes were large and " like moons," and sometimes " smoke came out of its mouth."   This animal made unearthly howlings, and " glared fiercely," rendering people senseless with his glances."*

Another roadway in the same locality is haunted by a terrible coal-black dog, with eyes like balls of fire.   This creature is said to follow people like a footpad, and to snarl and howl if any person halts or looks backward.

Near Lisworney, in the vicinity of this creature's haunts, people so late as forty years ago spoke with bated breath of Entwisle and his pack of phantom hounds tearing along the road between Marlborough Grange and Nash Manor.

It was gravely stated in the locality that if any unlucky persons coming late home from market chanced to fall in the way of these hounds, their clothes were torn to pieces, they were left almost for dead, and the next morning it was only just possible for them to crawl home.

Doubtless these spirit-hounds had to bear the blame for many a drunken brawl or midnight orgy of the long ago !

In many parts of Wales one of the Cŵn Annwn is supposed to be seen before a death.   The mysterious animal is generally found sitting perfectly still on the doorstep or close to the threshold of the house in which a person is sick, and its appearance there is a certain indication of death.

An old manor-house in Glamorgan is haunted by a large black dog of the Cŵn Annwn pack before a death in the family. It is described as large, quiet, and almost lazy in its movements. Sometimes it is seen in the grounds, from which gardeners and

* " Vale of Glamorgan," p. 40.

gamekeepers fail to scare it. Occasionally it is found in the hall-way, or crouching low at the foot of the grand staircase. It remains on or near the premises during the illness of any member of the family who will ultimately die.

A Breconshire farm-house is frequented by a white Cŵn Annwn that mysteriously comes and goes before a death in the family.

In Cardiganshire a brown creature of the pack, with white ears, is the bringer of evil omens, while in Carmarthenshire a grey hound appears to be the favourite.

In a story formerly attached to Pwyllywrach, Glamorgan, it is asserted that one of the huntsmen was approaching the kennels one evening, when he heard the wild barking of dogs in the air immediately above his head. It was twilight, and no animals were at hand. The hounds in the kennels were silent. Presently the unseen dogs barked again, and somebody called out " Tally-ho-ho !" It was more like a wail than a cry. When the sound was repeated the huntsman responded with a wailing " Tally-ho-ho-ho !" The next moment all the pack of hounds in the kennels broke loose, surrounded the huntsman, and tore him to pieces, so that nothing but bones remained. People said it was the revenge of the Cŵn Wybyr, whose cry the un-fortunate man had imitated. In after-years the peasantry declared that often in the night-time the cries of the huntsman and the baying of hounds could be heard distinctly. It was stated that the huntsman had forgotten to feed the hounds, and they fell upon him and killed him. The kennels were pulled down because of this calamity. The spot is still called " the old kennels." [J. R.]

Long years ago people said they heard Arawn cheering his Cŵn Annwn on the Aberdare Mountains, and in their wild hunting flight they trampled pedestrians to death unless the people got out of the way. The old story of that district described a bad man who would hunt even on Sunday, and for this desecration of the Sabbath he was banished into the air, where he was doomed to hunt for ever without rest.

In some parts of Wales it was stated that Arawn and his Cŵn Annwn hunted only from Christmas to Twelfth Night, and was always accompanied by a howling wind.

Arawn left one of his hounds behind him in an old barn not far from Llancarfan, Glamorgan.   There the hateful creature, who had assumed material shape, remained for three months, defying all attempts to dislodge him.   Because the strange dog would not go away, people said it was one of the spirit-hounds. The barn was left to the dog, and everybody avoided the place. One night when the tempest was high, Arawn and his hounds were heard shouting and baying above the howling of the wind. Two men passing the barn saw the strange dog springing out and jumping with joy.   It ran yelping and barking along the roadway, then with one wild bound vanished, and was never seen again. [C. D.].

The entrance-gate to the drive of an ancient mansion in Glamorgan was formerly the scene of tragedy.   For three or four generations the head of the family had met his death by accident while riding to or from the hunt.   The last of the family in the male line broke his neck near the entrance-gate on his return from hunting.   He was a wild young man, and always laughed when warned of reckless riding.   He was not coming to an " end like the others."

After his death people said his spectre was doomed to hunt every night with the Cŵn Annwn, and never had any rest. They heard him coming through the gate shouting to his hounds and cracking his whip, and his roaring laughter was a thing to remember.   Loudly he went out, and was heard madly crossing the country.   On his return he was seen silently riding a grey horse, whose flanks were foaming, and from whose nostrils flames of fire issued.   Reaching the gate, he immediately vanished.   At one time people dreaded passing the mansion in the evening or late at night, and when wild noises were heard, people said, " It's the Squire a-huntin'."   [Family Collection.]

Vampires were said to be dead men doomed to join Arawn and his Cŵn Annwn.   They visited the earth to suck blood from people and corpses.   An old dower-house, long since turned into a farmstead in Glamorgan, had a vampire story attached to it.   The house was evidently enlarged in Tudor times, and had some additions made in the reign of Queen Anne. In the reign of George I. it ceased to be a dower-house, and became a farmstead. Part of the premises were shut off at first, but when the next tenant came all the rooms were in occupation. Some of the old furniture that was bought by the ingoing tenant when the place ceased to be a dower-house remained. This furniture was distributed in various rooms, but one apartment, used as a guest-chamber, was wholly filled with it. A very pious Dissenting minister visited the farm in the eighteenth century, and as an honoured guest he was given the best bed-room. He was to stay there three or four days on his way to Breconshire. In those times people travelled on horseback everywhere, and the minister arrived on a Friday night, riding a grey mare. A service was to be held in the house on Saturday evening, and two were to be held on Sunday. On Friday night the minister went early to bed, and on Saturday was up " with the lark." Not wishing to intrude upon the early domestic arrangements, he sat in an old armchair of quaint design beside one of the windows which commanded a fine view of the surrounding country. There he remained for some time, reading the Bible and musing over his sermons for Sunday. When he got up from the chair to go downstairs, he observed that the back of his hand was bleeding freely. He immediately dipped it in his washing-basin, but it was quite a few minutes before he could stanch the blood, and the scar resembled teeth-marks more than anything else. The marks were on his left hand. This he bound with his handkerchief, and when he reached the break-fast-room the hostess kindly asked how he had slept. " Very excellently, I thank you," was the minister's reply. " The room is handsomely furnished, and the furniture is valuable, but I fear me there is a nail in the old armchair by the window ;" and he held forth his hand. " I quite forgot to have it overhauled," said the hostess, " for more than one visitor has complained of having scratches in that chair." She examined the hand, and then exclaimed : " But this is in the back, and not on the palm. The other persons had scratches on the palm." Nothing more was thought of the affair until Monday morning, when the minister was disturbed in his sleep long before dawn by a gnawing sensation in his left side. He described it " as though a dog was gnawing my flesh." There was much pain in his side, and he had some difficulty in striking a light. When he got up and examined his side, all across his ribs he discovered marks

similar to those upon his hand, and they had been bleeding
freely.   It took some time to stanch the blood, and then the
minister dressed himself, and, reading the Bible, awaited the
dawn.   After breakfast he went to see his grey mare, and when
he stroked its fine head he was surprised to find marks on the
left side of the neck similar to those on his own hand and side.
These he quickly bathed, and went indoors.   Before leaving
the house he mentioned these occurrences to his hostess, adding:
" Madam, you may not know it, but I believe a vampire
frequents this house.   The dead man who owned the furniture
comes to suck the blood from intruders, even to the grey mare in
your stable.   And probably he is not pleasantly disposed
toward ministers of the Gospel."   " It has happened to two
ministers before," said the goodman of the house, " but not to
the ministers' nags."

The descendant of this minister who related the story said
that long after her great-grandfather died, other ministers who
slept in the same room had suffered alike.   " It was supposed
that a Christian minister had effectually laid the vampire,"
said the narrator, " but in the year 1850 a dignitary of the
Church of England had the same unpleasant experience so far
as his left hand and left leg were concerned.   Science failed to
account for these occurrences, and it was not until a year later
the old vampire story was remembered.   The house is still
occupied by a farmer, but the outgoing tenant had a sale of all
the antique furniture and effects, and nothing more was
heard about the vampire. [*A Glamorgan lady who desires
anonymity.*]

A handsome Elizabethan chair of genuine sixteenth-century
workmanship was bought in a sale in South Wales, in the year
1840.   The purchaser wanted to complete a set of similar
chairs.   After it had been in use for some time one of the chairs
was set in a corner apart from the others, because people complained they were always scratching their hands until they
bled whenever they sat in it.   This could not be accounted
for, because the chair was absolutely free from nails.   In the
course of time the set of chairs was sold for a high price to a
rich merchant.   His family, in turn, complained about scratches
received when sitting in one of the chairs.   At his death the

offending chair was separated from the others, and given to a lover of antique furniture, who valued the old Elizabethan article because he considered it to be a " vampire chair." [C. D.]

A Cardiff family possessed an old four-posted bedstead of the reign of James I. It was bought at a bankruptcy sale, and has been described as a " handsome but heavy piece. of furniture." The man who bought it for the proverbial " song " set it in his best bedroom, and was proud to exhibit it to his friends. After it had been in his possession for some months, it was found necessary to take up a portion of the flooring of the room usually occupied by the man and wife, and the latter, as her husband was away, decided to sleep in the best bedroom. The young people had one child, an infant of four months old. The first night when the mother and child slept in the best bedroom the infant was restless. The second night the child cried out violently, and the mother could not pacify it for some time. In the morning she sent for the doctor, and he prescribed for the infant. That night the babe was more restful, but still uneasy. The fourth night the child screamed, and the mother immediately got up and took the infant in her arms. A few moments later it was dead. The mother saw at the throat of her babe a large mark with a red spot in the centre, through which blood was oozing. When the doctor came he examined the affected part carefully, but could not account for the extraordinary mark. He said : " It is just as though something had caught at the child's throat and sucked the blood, as one would suck an egg." Time passed, and the mother gave birth to another child. On this occasion the husband occupied the best bedroom. The first night he was awakened by feeling something clutching at his throat, and he believed himself to be a victim of nightmare. The second night he had the same experience, and was troubled in mind about it, but said nothing. The third night he was almost suffocated. He sprang out of bed, and went to the looking-glass. There he saw reflected a large space of skin as if it had been sucked, and from the centre blood was oozing. He mentioned these occurrences to a friend, who asked to sleep in that bed. He did so, and his experiences were exactly like those of the babe and its father.

A person who was acquainted with folk-lore told him it was a
" vampire bed." The bedstead still stands, but is never used,
and is regarded as an " uncanny piece of furniture."

In many parts of Wales people believed that vampires came
to suck corpses. An old story attached to a Carmarthenshire
yeoman was very curious. The family had lived for generations in the same house, situated in a lonely spot. The old
yeoman in question was very grasping, and in his generation
they said he would " suck blood out of a stone." He died,
leaving his money and possessions to his eldest son. When
that man died, he was duly laid out, and the death-chamber
was shut for the night. In the morning they found marks on
the body, which everybody said had been made by a vampire.
The family came to the conclusion that the old yeoman had
been sucking the corpse to see if he " could get something out
of it." In later generations, if any marks were found upon the
body of a dead member of the family, they said the " Old wretch
had been at work again." [C. D.]

A reputed witch died in the Vale of Neath. After her death
the few friends she had shut up the room and sat by the fire
all night. During their vigil they repeatedly heard a scratching
noise in the death-chamber, but were afraid to enter it. In
the morning they found the witch's body covered with innumerable marks as if formed by suction. Then the women said
vampires had been at work all night, and the funeral was
hastened, " for fear the body would be entirely devoured."
[A. B.]

CHAPTER V

WEIRD and grotesque are the stories connected with the spectral lore of Wales.

Far back in the past the list of spectres included those of the waterfall, the forest, the mountain, and the valley. Taliesin, the bard of the fifth century, mentions the magic wand of Mathonwy, which, if found in the woodlands, would cause the fruit and flowers to appear more beautiful on the mysterious banks of the spectral waters.

Spectral stags and vast herds of spectral oxen were supposed to frequent the dense forests of Britain, and spectral horses lured huntsmen to leave the chase and go in pursuit of them.

The Ceffyl-dwr, or water-horse of Wales, was described as a beautiful but small creature, who, after tempting the unwary traveller to mount him, soared over river and mountain, then suddenly melted into thin air or mist, and threw his rider to destruction.

About fifty years ago people living in the rural districts firmly believed in the water-horse.

Near Glyn-Neath, a beautiful locality which is much frequented on account of the cascades caused by the rivers Perddyn, Little Neath, Mellte, and Hepste, a man, tired out after a long journey, lingered to rest in a shady nook.

A water-horse slowly came up from under the foaming cascade, shook the spray from its snow-white mane, and ascended the slope upon which the tired man rested. By-and-by the animal neighed, then snorted, and tossed its head proudly in the sunlight. The weary man was tempted to mount the fine creature, and this he found was remarkably easy of

accomplishment.   Soon he was safely astride the noble horse.
Saddle and bridle he had not, but the grateful man felt the
white mane of the animal to be an excellent substitute.   He
had not long mounted before he observed that the horse was
going at an unusual speed.   Moreover, he noticed that the
horse's hoofs did not appear to touch the ground.   For a time
the astonished rider enjoyed the rapid rate at which the horse
conveyed him, but after a while he became slightly alarmed.
Wonder took the place of enjoyment, and soon terror sup-
planted both, as, up hill and down dale, the horse went with the
speed of lightning.   It was moonrise when he found himself
thrown on the slope of a hill.

The shock of the fall was very great, and for a few moments
he was completely dazed.   Upon recovering his composure,
he looked around for the horse which had carried him so swiftly
and so far.   To his surprise, the animal's graceful form became
gradually indistinct.   Then by slow degrees it appeared to
merge in a vapoury cloud that hung low over the hill.   By-
and-by it vanished altogether.   In the early night the man
descended the slope, and after walking a mile or more he found
himself in the ancient village of Llanddewi Brefi, Cardiganshire.

It was sunset when he left Glyn-Neath, and the long distance
extending between that place and the remote village in Cardiganshire had been traversed in the short space of about an
hour.   [C. D.]

Another story of the kind comes from the banks of the
Honddû.

Near the town of Brecon the remains of a Roman camp are
still to be seen.   It is supposed to have been formed by Ostorius
Scapula, on the site of the British camp " Caer Bannau," from
which the local Roman station was called " Bannium."   This
camp stands on the north bank of the River Honddû.

About a century ago a weary man was lured by a small
grey water-horse from the camp to the edge of the river.   Opportunity was too inviting to be lost, so the man mounted the horse,
and in a very short space of time was set down on the banks
of the Towy, not far from Carmarthen.   Three days later the
man was again lured by the small grey horse, and carried back
to the Honddû—but, as the narrator said, " in a worse state

than when he left, for the Ceffyl-dwr had dragged him through mire and water, through brambles and briars, until he was scarcely knowable." [*A. B.*]

The water-horse of the Honddû had a " tormenting " reputation.

Flemingston, locally called Flimston, in the Vale of Glamorgan, was regarded as a favourite haunt of evil spirits in the form of water-horses. These creatures always appeared when people were benighted or lost on the desolate moorlands stretching for miles on each side of the River Thaw.

Sometimes the water-horse was luminous, and then more peculiar and bewildering.

In the early part of the nineteenth century an old man wended his way down these moors to Old Mill, near Aberthaw. It was a dark and cold night, late in December, and the traveller quickened his pace, for the clouds promised snow. When he had reached half-way to his destination, he was surprised to see, going slowly along before him, a solitary and small horse, ridden by a somewhat long-legged man.

The shape of the horse, from the ears to the tail, was distinctly outlined by a steady glow. The rider's boots, spurs, hunting-crop, and arms appeared tipped with light. The man was astonished to find that, although he used every effort to overtake the horse, he failed to do so.

Within an arm's length from the door of the Old Mill the horse and its rider vanished mysteriously in the darkness that could almost be felt. When the old man entered the house he related his experiences. The people said he had seen the water-horse—the Ceffyl-dwr.

Before midnight the whole valley was flooded by an unusually high full-moon tide, and the traveller ever afterwards attributed his escape to the guidance of the water-horse, who lured him rapidly onward through the darkness to a place of safety.

It was said that clergymen and ministers of all denominations could ride the water-horse without falling until the desired destination was reached.

Two stories regarding the Ceffyl-dwr come from the Vale of Glamorgan.

The parson and parish clerk of Bouvilston, in the Vale, were walking homeward from Cardiff one dark night in the eighteenth century.   Seeing a fine horse near the old bridge that spanned the River Ely, the parson said : " Here is a stray : let us mount the animal, and get quicker home."

" Well and good, sir," said his companion; and they mounted, the parson in front and the clerk behind.

In silence, but swiftly, the horse reached the foot of the Tumble Hill, and they were ascending agreeably, when the clerk said : " He is a good one to go, sir."

With that the horse began to snort, and threatened to throw its riders.   Again the clerk praised the horse, and then the animal pranced and reared dangerously.

" Hold your tongue, will you !" said the parson authoritatively, and the clerk remained silent.

The horse rapidly ascended the Tumble Hill, and soon went rushing through St. Nicholas.   As they approached Cottrell the clerk said : " Darker and darker 'tis getting, sir.   I do wish we were safe home !"

A moment later the clerk found himself in a ditch on the side of the road, while the horse whisked the parson in safety to his own door.   When asked about this adventure, the clerk persisted the stray was the " Ceffyl-dwr, and no other, for he carried the parson safe, but threw the clerk."

The other " old story " comes from Lydmoor, below Duffryn. An itinerant minister, wending his way past Lydmoor Mill, paused to rest beside the stream.   He was then joined by one of the deacons of Trehill Calvinistic Methodist Chapel.   Not far from the mill-pond at Duffryn the men saw a horse.   Tired after a long walk, the minister suggested that he and his companion should mount, and so reach the chapel quicker.

" You can ride the horse home again to-night," said the minister, " and restore him to his owner, whoever he may be."

" Ay, ay !" responded the deacon.   " It is the miller's horse, an' he'd be willing enough for you to ride him."

So the men mounted, and the horse bore them rapidly up and down hill until they reached Tinkin's Wood, near which are several cromlechs.

Then the horse went on at a jog trot, to the discomfort of the riders.

" He is getting lazy and stubborn," said the deacon ; where-upon the horse reared fearfully.   " I can never hold on !" ex-claimed the deacon ; and he urged the minister to dismount, or allow him to do so.

Even as he spoke the horse again reared, and threw the deacon into the hedge.

The minister tried to alight and assist his friend, but the horse galloped away " like lightning," and the deacon had to walk to Trehill.

There the people assembled for service said : " Serve thee right ! He that talks on the back of the Ceffyl-dwr is sure to be thrown."

The banks of the Towy, which flows through Carmarthen, were frequented by the Ceffyl-dwr.

A story was formerly told of a man who went down the Towy in an ancient coracle, but was seen returning home on a Ceffyl-dwr, which had eyes like balls of fire, and a snort like a blast. [C. D.]

In Carnarvonshire and several parts of North Wales the water-horse was supposed to fraternize with mountain ponies, and there is a tradition to the effect that the merlyns, or small horses known by that name, are the direct descendants of the Ceffyl-dwr.

It is singular to note that in Carnarvonshire, Montgomery, Merioneth, and Cardigan, the Ceffyl-dwr had the reputation of being able to transform itself into other shapes, and thus become a terror of the night.   Sometimes it took the form of a goat, and rushed towards its victims with such force as to cause serious injury.   In the Vale of Clwyd a Ceffyl-dwr delighted in leaping in the shape of a frog upon the backs of the people, clasping them with a fiendish embrace.

A Cardiganshire butter dealer of the old school declared that a Ceffyl-dwr followed him from the market town, and, in the form of a creature between a man and a goat, crushed him so severely with its superhuman weight that " great black bruises " were to be seen " for weeks " upon his shoulders and arms. [O. S.]

Near the town of Montgomery a Ceffyl-dwr, taking a hideous, indescribable shape, was accustomed to leap upon pedestrians and horsemen, almost crushing them to death with its weight. A man living in the wilds of the Rhondda, in Glamorgan, was riding down to Pontypridd early in the nineteenth century, when a Ceffyl-dwr, in the form of a squirrel, leaped between his shoulders. The creature clasped his neck so closely as to make the man gasp for breath. Then he was shaken and beaten so badly that the next day a mysterious illness assailed him, from which he never recovered, but lingered on in misery for nearly two years. [J. R.]

The stories of South Wales represent the Ceffyl-dwr generally as a small horse which allowed people to ride him. This animal was a temptation to weary pedestrians and benighted travellers. But in the stories of North Wales the Ceffyl-dwr was capable of varied transformations. In the North the horse was generally dark, with fiery eyes and a forbidding appearance. In the South he was often luminous, fascinating, and sometimes a winged steed.

The Ceffyl-dwr was frequently seen on the seashore, where he appeared with a dapple-grey coat, or was very like the sand in colour. The old people said he could be identified by his hoofs being turned the wrong way. If anybody mounted him, he plunged with his rider into the foam. A man once caught a Ceffyl-dwr on the shores of Carmarthen Bay, and afterwards tried to break the creature in. By means of an artfully contrived bridle he led the animal home, and used it as a cart-horse. But one day the bridle became unfastened, and the Ceffyl-dwr darted with the cart and driver into the sea, and was never afterwards seen. [C. D.]

In some parts of Wales a Ceffyl-dwr, in the shape of a hulking or clumsy chestnut or piebald horse, trotted up and down the shore. The animal was seen in St. Bride's Bay just after a storm. A farmer caught it, and put it to the plough. All went well for some weeks; then the Ceffyl-dwr, seized with an impulse, dragged both the plough and ploughman through the field at a furious pace, and, reaching the shore, rushed into the sea, and was lost in the waves. [O. S.]

The Ceffyl-dwr, in the form of a huge and clumsy horse, was seen plunging up and down in the sea when thunderstorms were brewing, or before great gales. Sometimes its colour was grey or dappled white and brown, while in very stormy seasons it would be snowy white, like the foam, or leaden-hued, harmonizing with the dark clouds and steel-coloured under-waves.

The Gwrach-y-rhibyn resembled the Irish banshee. Welshmen say this night-hag never troubles new families, only those whose ancestors have for long generations lived in the same place ; in other words, the " old stock."* This spectral form is described as having long black hair, black eyes, and a swarthy countenance. Sometimes one of her eyes is grey and the other black. Both are deeply sunken and piercing. Her back was crooked, her figure was very thin and spare, and her pigeon-breasted bust was concealed by a sombre scarf. Her trailing robes were black. She was sometimes seen with long flapping wings that fell heavily at her sides, and occasionally she went flying low down along watercourses, or around hoary mansions. Frequently the flapping of her leathern bat-like wings could be heard against the window-panes.

St. Donat's Castle, on the seashore of Glamorgan, has always been inhabited since the coming of the Normans into Wales, even though occasionally it was not in the owner's occupation. The Stradlings were holders of it from Norman times until the middle of the eighteenth century, when it was the subject of a romantic law-suit, which lasted over fifty years. The heir of the Stradling family went on a tour with his friend Tyrwhitt, and before starting it was agreed by the two young men that if during their travels anything should befall the other, the survivor was to inherit the deceased's estates. Both were rich, and their estates valuable. In the meantime the father of Thomas Stradling died, and the absent heir came into possession of the St. Donat's estate. In 1738 Thomas Stradling was killed in a duel at Montpellier, in France, and Tyrwhitt, of Wiltshire, according to agreement, became the owner of St. Donat's. The Stradling family believed the rightful heir had been the victim of foul play, and laid claim to the possessions. During the long years of litigation the Tyrwhitts let the castle in succession to highly respectable people, from the descendants of whom many stories of the place have been obtained.

* " Vale of Glamorgan," p. 331.

In the lore connected with the castle the Gwrach-y-rhibyn appears. One night early in the nineteenth century a stranger who was visiting the family resident in the castle, distinctly heard a moaning and wailing sound close under his window. It was like " the pitiful sound of a woman in the greatest possible agony." The visitor ventured to look out, but was alarmed by the flapping of wings against the lattice, and a rattling noise like that of talons. In the morning he told his host and hostess of his experiences, and they said it was the Gwrach-y-rhibyn, who always frequented the castle, and lamented the death of the last of the Stradlings in the direct line. They said that sometimes this mysterious figure wandered through the empty and silent rooms of the disused part of the castle, and the sounds of her lamentation were " enough to turn one's blood to ice." Once the Gwrach-y-rhibyn traversed the village from end to end, and in the dim uncertain twilight of a November evening her flowing robes and outstretched arms were " against the wind," and caused a " roaring noise." She was once seen beating the boundaries of the whole estate, and was accompanied by black hounds with red eyes and horrible fangs.

Near a small creek that runs into the land from Oxwich Bay stand the ruins of Pennard Castle, which was built on the site of a stronghold of Danish rovers. The castle was the property of a Norman lord, and the old story goes that it was built in a single night by a Welsh sorcerer, who in this way saved his life from threatened imprisonment and assassination by the Normans. Around this castle the Gwrach-y-rhibyn often wandered, and was seen and heard by people so late as the first half of the nineteenth century. People along the country-side used formerly to say that if anybody slept for the night among the ruins of Pennard Castle he would be bewitched. It was solemnly stated that centuries ago a man once slept in the ruins after being told not to do so. During the night, the Gwrach-y-rhibyn attacked him violently, and almost " left him for dead." He was found in the morning quite unconscious, with bruises on his body, scratches upon his face, and other evidences of maltreatment. When he " came to himself " he described the terrible appearance of the hag who attacked him, and said she " clawed " him just as an eagle might have done. Then she " pecked " at his body and beat him. The man went home to Carmarthen, and ever afterwards was bewitched, as the people near Pennard Castle said he would be " for all time." [*A. B. and O. S.*]

Beaupré Castle, on the banks of the River Thaw, near Cowbridge, Glamorgan, became uninhabitable in the eighteenth century, when a residence known as New Beaupré was erected. It originally belonged to the Welsh Seisyllt family, from whom the present Lord Salisbury is said to be descended, the family name Cecil being a corruption of Seisyllt. Beaupré was restored by the Normans, and descended by heirship to the Bassett family, who came into possession about the year 1200. Later on it was sold to the Edmunds family, and subsequently to the Treharnes of St. Hilary, from whom it was bought by a solicitor. During the Edmunds ownership, and while the Treharnes possessed the castle, the Gwrach-y-rhibyn frequented the place.   There was an old story prevalent that the hag had been seen rising up out of the River Thaw, and wringing her hands and flapping her bat-like wings in the twilight. She also seemed to have a grievance against New Beaupré, for late in the eighteenth century she was seen and heard in the grounds. Early in the nineteenth century workmen staying in the neighbourhood declared they had seen the Gwrach-y-rhibyn among the ruins of the old castle, and the wailing and sobbing were painful to hear. Soon all the neighbourhood rang with the story, and as time passed the hag became more persistent. When the solicitor bought the estate he heard the story of the Gwrach-y-rhibyn, and was much interested in it. A year or two before this owner's death the following story was told by an old man in the Vale of Glamorgan : Above the entrance doorway of the castle a panel bears the Bassett arms and motto, *Gwell angau na chwilydd* (" Rather death than shame "). The old man was doing some work near this door, and it was twilight. While busily engaged, he heard a low, sad wailing sound wandering around the courtyard, and immediately opposite, in the grand porch of the castle, he saw a shadowy figure standing wringing its hands and flitting in and out like somebody in distress. The spectator crossed the courtyard and approached the porch, and as he did so the figure vanished.

Curiosity prompted him to venture farther in, and as he went a voice seemed to whisper in his ears, " Lost ! lost ! lost !" He looked around, but could not see anybody.   Quietly he re-entered the porch, and the wailing, moaning, and sobbing began again.   Then the figure with the waving hands reappeared, and the old man distinctly heard a sweet but sad voice, in wailing accents, crying : " Restore ! restore ! restore !"   The old man went home, and the next day told the solicitor who owned the castle the story of the Gwrach-y-rhibyn.   " I know all about it," said the gentleman, who was one of the kindest-hearted in Glamorgan.   " Strange voices often come from the past, and act as monitors for the future.   I know all about it."   The old man understood that the owner also had seen and heard the Gwrach-y-rhibyn in her wanderings and wailings and whisperings around picturesque old Beaupré.   Whether this story was true or not, it is certain that the then owner, Mr. Daniel Jones, left the Beaupré estate by will to Captain Bassett, a direct descendant of the original owners, in whose family it still remains.   The grand old porch (designed by Inigo Jones, and built by Gwylim Twrch) of Beaupré is one of the " show places " of the Vale of Glamorgan.   It is said that at the castle of Beaupré arrangements and terms were made to compel King John to sign the Magna Charta.   Sir Philip Bassett of that period was afterwards Lord Chief Justice of England. [*Family Collection.*]

The Caerphilly swamp, through which the stream Nant-y-Gledyr flows, was frequented by the Gwrach-y-rhibyn.   This swamp, when the river was dammed up, formed a lake, and was used for the defence of the fortress-castle of Caerphilly, where the powerful De Clares dwelt.   In the last half of the eighteenth century the hag was seen by many living in the district.   An old man, who remembered his father's version of the story, said that in rainy seasons the stream overflowed the marshy ground, and from the midst of the lake formed thereby, the Gwrach-y-rhibyn arose, and dipped herself up and down in the water.   From her bat-like wings, her long black hair, and talon-like fingers the water dropped sparkling in the moonlight. Each time she arose from the water she would wring her hands and moan, or utter a long-drawn wail, or a groan which was terrible to hear.   Then, suddenly flapping her wings, she would fly to the castle and take refuge within its walls.   Boys and men were known to watch the hag, and used every endeavour to catch her, but without success.   The old man said his father had seen her several times, and was afraid of the rainy weather and the gloomy swamp.   Sometimes the hag wandered up and down beside the stream in dry weather.   His father had seen her. It was " as true as the Bible—iss, indeed !" he said.   [C. D.]

Stories about the Brenin Llwyd, the Grey King, or Monarch of the Mist, were told in most of the mountainous districts. In the North he was described as being very mighty and powerful.   He was represented as sitting among the mountains, robed in grey clouds and mist, and woe to anybody who was caught in his clutches !   Snowdon and the ranges of it, Cader Idris, Plinlimmon, and other lofty places, were his favourite haunts.   In the South he was regarded as " hungering " for victims, and children were warned not to venture too high up the mountains, lest the Brenin Llwyd should seize them.   So late as the first half of the nineteenth century, whenever an adult or a child was lost on Gellionen, near Alltwen, or on the Garth Maelog, Glamorgan, people said the Brenin Llwyd had seized its prey.   An old woman said that when she was a child, and visited relatives at Llantrisant, Glamorgan, the children believed the Brenin Llwyd lived among the local mountains.   She said that many a time she shuddered when they ascended to the mineral wells on the Smaelog, and was glad to come down, because the people and children warned everybody not to linger late, for the Brenin Llwyd would be after them.   She was further told that there was no trusting him, for sometimes on the brightest summer evening he would come suddenly and draw them into his clutches.   [U. S.]

A resident in the North said that formerly the old guides among the Snowdon ranges were fond of telling stories about the Brenin Llwyd, who came stealthily and silently up through the ravines, or sat waiting among lonely peaks to imprison the unwary.   In the childhood of those old men few cared to make long ascents, and even the guides were nervous occasionally, when the old people talked in the fireside corners about the ever-silent and gloomy but treacherous Brenin Llwyd, whose movements were never heard when he came to take his prisoners.

CHAPTER VI

ANIMALS, BIRDS OF PREY, AND INSECTS

ANIMALS and birds have prominent places in Welsh lore. Many of the Kings, Princes, and chieftains of Wales have names derived from those animals which were considered brave.

Arth—the Welsh for bear—with *ur* added to it, was the name of Arthur, the King, hero, and warrior. Llewellyn is derived from Llew, the lion, and Bleddyn from the wolf. Cadno, the name of a Welsh Prince, is derived from the fox.

In the ancient mythology of Wales, Hu Gadarn, known as Hu the Mighty,* is described as drawing the Afanc, or beaver, out of the lake with the aid of his wonderful Ychain Banawg, or oxen.

In the British triads it is stated that when the Lake of Llion overflowed and submerged the whole of Britain, the people were all drowned excepting Dwyfan and Dwyfach, who escaped in a naked or sailless boat. These two personages afterwards repeopled the island. The boat or ship was called the Nefydd, nâf neifion, and had on board a male and female of every creature. The deluge has never broken out since, because Hu Gadarn undertook the difficult task of dragging the Afanc, or beaver, out of the Lake of Llion with the aid of his oxen, known as Ychain Banawg. It is said that one of them, in drawing forth the Afanc, overstrained himself, and his eyes fell out of their sockets. He dropped down dead the moment his task was over. The other, in grief of mind at the loss of its companion, refused food, and wandered about until it died of a broken heart at Llanddewi Brefi, or St. David's

* Davies, " Mythology," p. 267.

the Lowing, in Cardiganshire, which derived its name from the miserable moaning of the sacred ox. In former times the villagers of that parish exhibited as a relic a large horn, which they said belonged to one of the oxen of Hu the Mighty.*

In Druidical times—and, it is stated, many centuries afterwards—the Welsh were accustomed to have a festival in commemoration of the Deluge. It took place on the morning after the Eve of May. Sacred oxen, and in later ages the best oxen to be found in the country, were stationed near the lake, in the midst of which was a holy island, where a shrine or ark was kept. These oxen, by means of a chain attached to the shrine, drew it through the shallow water to dry ground. Meanwhile, the finest singers in the district sung a chant known as " Cainc yr Ychain Banawg." The melody closely resembled the lowing of kine and the rattling of chains. The first person in the great procession was the Arch-Druid, or the chief bard, bearing his magical wand. Then came about two hundred Druids and bards, with various kinds of harps, and after them came the ark or shrine of Ceridwen, or Cariadwen, which had been removed from the chains of the oxen to the shoulders of minor priests. Before the ark went the hierophant, who represented the Supreme Creator, a torch-bearer who represented the sun, and the herald-bard, who was regarded as the special official of the goddess and symbol of the moon. Then the general public made way for a large body of singers and dancers, who, with wreaths of ivy on their heads, or cornute caps, surrounded the Afanc, or car of the diluvian god. Some of these kept blowing horns; others carried double pateras, and many clashed their shields with crooked swords. Ultimately the procession entered the Druidical temple in the centre of the grove of oaks. The rampart of earth surrounding the temple was crowded by the heads of tribes, with their standard-bearers, and people of importance, while the general population of the district stood beyond. In these ceremonies two or more black beavers were exhibited.†

Welsh mythology describes the Afanc, or beaver, as a creature of monstrous size, which, when taken and fastened with

* Davies, "Mythology," p. 140.
† Meyrick. "Costumes," p. 34.

huge iron chains, was so heavy that he could only be dragged
out of the great lake by twin oxen of great strength.

In support of the tradition about the beaver, the local name
Nant yr Afancon, or the Valley of the Beavers, in Carnarvonshire, still exists.

Some Welsh authorities discard the beaver theory for that
of the alligator, or a huge kind of otter.

Under the name of Llostlydan, or " broad tail," the beaver
is particularly specified in the laws of Hywel the Good.   The
skin of the beaver was then valued at one hundred and twenty
pence ; while that of the Dyfrgi, or water-dog, known to us as
the otter, was considered only worth eightpence.

The beaver is described as being generally about three to five
feet in length, with hind-parts like the seal.   The skin was thick,
and the hair, which was very plentiful, was exceedingly black
and glossy.   Beneath the hair was a soft down.   The legs were
short and thick, and the toes, joined with a web, were covered
with hair.

In the time of Giraldus Cambrensis the River Teivi was
inhabited by beavers.   These animals are now unknown in
Wales.

The sacred animals of the Druids were milk-white oxen,
and the spotted cow procured blessings.   In many of the old
festivals of Wales milk-white oxen were led in the processions,
and those with pink ears were much valued.   They were decked
with garlands and flowers.   If these oxen had curly hair on
any part of the body, they brought luck to their owners.
Cattle and cows of pure white were formerly much sought
after by Welsh farmers, because they brought luck to the
herds.

Black cattle and cows, especially those of the Castlemartin
breed, were much valued ; and although they have a certain
ferocity, the people in South Wales still regard them as luck-
bringers.

Oxen were credited with the power to dig up wild winds,
or hurricanes ; and even now, when these animals gambol or
are frisky, people say, " A storm is coming."   A bull-calf, it
is said, was specially reared to fight any dragon that might
enter the district.   The black cow was regarded as an omen

of care and sorrow when met in the morning. The hoof-prints of the same animal seen near any dwelling were unlucky to the inmates.

An old Cardiganshire butter-dealer said that the birth of twin calves on a farm foretokened prosperity, and if the animals were parti-coloured, all the better.

When cattle and cows lie down quietly in the meadows, people say a very warm summer may be expected. If the animals are very restless and uneasy in May, the weather during the ensuing summer will be variable. If they are wild and frisky, windy weather and rain will prevail for the next three months. The deep lowing of kine indicates a prosperous harvest.

Sheep and lambs are slightly connected with Welsh folk-lore, but they are more generally associated with charms and divination, or disease.

When sheep congregate in corners of the fields storms may be expected. If they keep close to the cattle rain is coming. When they are scattered abroad or wander about people say great heat may be anticipated. If the sheep go quickly to the shearing-place a very warm summer is indicated. A single black sheep in a flock is regarded as an unlucky omen, while three of them mean " plenty."

If the first lamb of the season faces the farmer, he will have good luck for the remainder of the year. If the farmer turns money in his pocket when he sees the first lamb of the season, he will have much prosperity.

The boar is prominent in Welsh lore, and, according to a very ancient tradition, men learnt from him the way to plough.

In the Mabinogi of Kilhwch* and Olwen, Arthur the King is described as chasing the " Boar Trwyth " with his " seven young pigs " from Ireland through South Wales, and on into Cornwall, where the animal was " driven straight into the deep sea. And henceforth it was never known where he went."

Arthur told his warriors that the Boar Trwyth was " once a King," but " God had transformed him into a swine for his sins."

The same Mabinogi also contains details of the " son of

* " The Mabinogion," p. 253.

Dadweir." Its name was Henwen. At Maes Gwenith (Wheat-
field in Gwent) the sow left three grains of wheat and three bees,
since when the best wheat and honey have been found in
Gwent.   In Dyfed she left a grain of barley and a little pig, and
at Lleyn, in Arfon, she left a grain of rye.   In another part of
Wales Henwen left a wolf-cub and an eagle.   At Maen Du, in
Arfon, she left a kitten, which was thrown by Coll ab Collfrewi
into the Menai Straits.   The sons of Palug in Anglesea found
and reared this kitten, which came to be known as the Palug
Cat, one of the " three plagues of the Isle of Mona."

Some of the coins mentioned by Camden had the figure of a
sow carrying on her back a basket of fruit and flowers.   The
bards and mythological triads represent Ceridwen or Cariadwen, the British Ceres, assuming the character of a sow.   In
her pontifical capacity she is described as a " twrch," or boar.
Her priesthood was called " meichiaid," or swine-herds.   Her
disciples were known as " moch," or swine, and her novitiates
were described as " perchyll," or young pigs.

In an old nursery tale rescued from the past a black pig was
born to a sorceress, and in punishment for her wickedness the
animal grew so big that his bristles stood up above the trees
in the forests of North Wales.   The creature rooted up
the earth so deep that the sea ran in and made lakes all
through the land. He went on through the north and
south of the country, and ate up naughty little children
who told fibs. He destroyed many villages that were noted
for their sins and wickedness, and finally rushed into the
sea.   This probably owed its origin to the suppression of the
Welsh by the English, and inroads made by the sea on the
northern coasts. [O. S.]

A black hog rooting near a house and frequenting the premises
foretold disaster to the inmates.   To meet a black pig upon first
going out in the morning was unlucky.   It was deemed unfortunate to be followed by a black pig.

The bear was regarded as the king of all animals.   Arthur is
described as the mighty bear, and as a god and hero.

Among the rural population about eighty years ago it was
customary to call the Great Bear Arthur's Plough.   People
said that in the dead of the night, if anybody cared to listen, the

plough and waggon of the Great and Lesser Bear could be heard turning. The little, almost invisible star just above the middle one in the tail of the plough was called the " ploughman," or " driver."

The morris dancers never went forth in former times without a man wrapped in a bear-skin.

With reference to the bear, there is a saying which runs thus : " Gwrnerth Ergydly a laddes yr arth mwyaf a welwyd erioed a saethwellten," or " The keen-eyed Gwrnerth killed the largest bear ever seen, with a wheat-straw."

Here it may be mentioned that wheat-straw was sacred to the goddess Ceridwen. It was used in making contracts and casting lots. Even in the present day the peasantry of Wales cast lots in the following way : If six persons are to be drawn in the lot, six pieces of a wheat-straw are cut into different lengths, and then put together, the tops being all even, and the ends concealed. Each person draws one of these pieces. He who happens to draw the shortest piece has to do or not to do the action thus to be determined by lot.

A wheat-straw was used for ratifying a bargain, contract, or engagement. Two pieces of equal length were held by each of the two contracting parties as proof of the contract. To cut one of the pieces of wheat-straw appears to have meant the breaking of the contract.

The ancient Welsh poet Sion Rhys Morus says to a love-messenger : " If she converse no more, break the straw with my fair one "—that is, " break my engagement with her."

Associated with the bear was the wolf. In the morris dances, the Mabsant, and all revels, the wolf was represented.

There was formerly a saying in Wales that the devil made the wolf and the goat.

If the name of a wolf was uttered between Christmas Eve and Twelfth Night, the farmers believed adversity would soon visit their homesteads.

In the eighteenth century very aged people in many parts of Wales would talk seriously about the wolf-men, or persons said to be descended from wolves, who dwelt in the forests and woodlands, and at night emerged to prowl about farm-yards and villages for the purpose of stealing poultry and pigs. These men were notorious robbers, and sometimes carried infants and young children away, in the hope of ransom. They went more like animals than men, in packs, and thought nothing of making raids on lonely farm-houses and hamlets in the outskirts of the forests and woodlands where they dwelt. In appearance it is said they closely resembled wolves, and during their raids they had a curious wolf-howl, which scared people, who would willingly assist the victims of these robbers. In a nursery rhyme, now believed to be obsolete, children were warned not to wander into the woods, because of the wolf-men, who would eat them.

The fox was regarded as the devil's spy, and any place much frequented by foxes, or neighbourhoods where these animals had their dens, were " in the power of Satan."

In the old folk-stories they were described as being capable of conversation at certain seasons of the year, especially late at night. Like a fragment of the past wafted to the present comes an old story once prevalent in Glamorgan. A drover going down to the Vale of Glamorgan for cattle was benighted in the woods of Porthkerry, and sought shelter and a resting-place in a comfortable nook. In the night he heard somebody talking, and, sitting up, he saw beside him a fox, who looked old and grey in the bright moonlight. The animal appeared to be in trouble, and when the drover asked the cause, the fox said he was burdened with sorrow that had descended to him through many long generations. Thereupon the drover blamed him for taking to heart anything that happened to his forefathers. The fox said it was the sin of remorse for misdeeds done by one of his far-back ancestors. At this the drover laughed. Then the fox was angry, and the drover, to pacify the animal, asked what the sin and remorse meant. The fox answered that he was directly descended from Einion ap Collwyn, who betrayed the Welsh to Robert Fitzhamon, and thus helped the Normans to become possessed of Glamorgan. The animal told the drover that the soul of Einion had passed into the body of a fox, and from him he had directly descended. When the drover reached his destination he related his experiences, and the villagers said they were glad the traitor was punished, for Einion was a " sly old fox, who was paid for his treachery on the Golden Mile."
[A. B. and Family Collection.   Told in local Mabsants.]

A similar story is told with reference to Coroticus, with whom St. Patrick remonstrated between A.D. 480 and 490. This Coroticus is said to have been Ceredig, the son of Cunedda, who conquered and drove the Irish away from Wales early in the fifth century. For this deed St. Patrick cursed him. Soon after Coroticus was cursed he led a wandering life. Ultimately he was turned into a fox, and in this form he ran away into the forests, and was never seen again. This story appears in the legends connected with St. Patrick.

To see several foxes together was regarded as unlucky, but to see one alone in the morning was good. A grey or white fox seen anywhere or at any time in South Wales was an omen of a death in a family.

Early in the nineteenth century a farmer living near Brecon said that whenever a white fox was seen in the vicinity of a very large farm, a stroke of good luck might be expected. During the next year all undertakings would be successful, and the harvest would be unusually abundant.

The appearance of a white fox on the farms in Mid-Wales indicated a fortunate marriage. If seen just before a birth, the child would be fortunate in all its undertakings.

It was regarded as a very bad omen if a litter of any kind of foxes entered the courtyard. Disaster, death, or trouble always followed their appearance.

When foxes barked and howled or made uncanny noises in or near the village of St. Donat's, Glamorgan, people said that the head of the family living in the castle would die.

Black or very dark foxes seen in Gower indicated death, misfortune, or disaster to farmers on whose lands they appeared.

The hare took a prominent place in connection with Druidical mysteries. It was used by the Druids in their auguries, and generally to indicate the fate of war or the veracity of a person. From the various movements of the animal success or misfortune was predicted.

In later times the hare entered largely into folk-lore, and its comings and goings were watched with considerable curiosity, and sometimes anxiety. The peasantry, as well as the lords of the soil, in Wales regarded the hare as a herald of death. A white hare and a white weasel crossing any person's path foretold death, disaster, or misfortune. If these creatures ran before a man, he would be able to conquer his enemies and avert calamity. When they ran to the right from a man, he might expect danger, and perhaps an accident. When they ran to the left from a man, he had enemies in his household. If they went in a zigzag way before a man, he would have much success; but if they turned and ran backwards along the path it was an omen of sudden death.

In the neighbourhood of Carreg Cennin, Carmarthenshire, a white hare was regarded as a bringer of good luck to the farms. After its appearance the harvest was exceptionally plentiful.

The white hare, white weasel, and white mole were formerly regarded in Glamorgan and Cardiganshire as heralds of misfortune or disgrace to the families near whose premises they were to be seen.

In the old mythology and stories of Wales the horse held a worthy place.

Milk-white steeds were ridden by Kings, Princes, and chieftains.

It was considered very fortunate to meet a white horse, especially in the morning. To meet a white horse without spitting before it was unlucky.

If anybody, hearing horses neighing, listens attentively, he will know they announce good luck.

If a person in the first stages of consumption walked up and down the stables early in the morning, while the horses yet slept, he would be cured. The process was to be continued for not less than six months.

When the Bâltan fires were lighted a horse's head was thrown therein to keep witches away, and to prevent any disease spreading among the flocks and herds. In some parts of Wales, so late as the first quarter of the nineteenth century, the old belief was current that every churchyard which had been laid out in the far past contained the bones of a horse. People said the horse was buried alive.

During the eighteenth century horses' heads were nailed above barn-doors to keep witches away. The uncanny musicians of the witches' revels played unholy tunes on horses' heads, and drank to the health of each other in goblets made of horses' hoofs. [*Family Collection.*]

Horses were supposed to see ghosts' apparitions of all kinds quicker than men could. In all the old stories of phantom funerals, and apparitions connected with riders and drivers, the horse sees first, and halts before the obstacle, which then appears to the person holding the reins.

A country doctor of the old school, and one of the fourth generation of surgeons in the same family, who lived on the borders of Monmouthshire, said that so long as a white horse was kept in the stables good luck predominated. If a white horse died, sorrow, misfortune, or death always happened in the family.

The dog was an animal of importance in the mythology and folk-lore of Wales. Ceridwen, the moon goddess, had for one of her symbols a "milast," or greyhound bitch. When initiating Gwion the Little into her mysteries, Ceridwen transformed herself into a "milast."

The canine symbol of Ceridwen was well known in Wales, and is perpetuated in many places to this day. Gwâl y Filast, "the lair of the greyhound bitch," in the parish of Llanbendy, Carmarthenshire, consists of a large stone supported by four pillars. There is another Gwâl y Filast in Glamorgan, and in Cardiganshire a similar stone is called Llech yr Ast, "the flat stone of the bitch." In the parish of Llanhamlwch, Breconshire, there is a place called Maen yr Ast, "the bitch stone," abbreviated into Mannest. On the south side of the Roman road between Bassalleg and St. Mellon's, Monmouthshire, there is a farm-house called Gwael-y-filast, which has some reference to a greyhound bitch. A maenhir, or tall stone, stands near this farm. A sketch of this stone by Viscount Tredegar appears in the Rev. W. Bagnall-Oakeley's "Rude Stone Monuments." In Merionethshire there is Ffynon Maen Milgi, "the greyhound's stone well."

Camu ar Camulus, the name under which Mars was known to the ancient British, had the dog, the greyhound bitch, and the horse dedicated to him. These animals were offered on his altar. The dog-grass, a weed, was also sacred to him.

The figure of a woman on or with a mare represents the latter as another symbol of Ceridwen.

In the folk-lore of Wales the dog, like the horse, is credited with being able to see spirits before they are apparent to a man. A dog will bark or howl in the night at spirits that may be passing. It always knows a haunted castle, house, or locality, and makes known the fact by its incessant howling or barking, and reluctance to pass the place. A dog with spots over its eyes is supposed to be able to see the devil ! People said that dogs would go mad if they were given a bone of lamb at Eastertide.

A family living near St. Nicholas, in the Vale of Glamorgan, would not be without a black-and-white sheep-dog "for worlds." When asked the reason why, they said that whenever the farm was without one, trouble and misfortune attended the tenant, whoever he might be.

A greyhound with a white spot on its forehead was supposed to be a luck-bringer to people in Gower.

If a black dog strayed into a farmstead people were glad, because it betokened good luck.

Cats were supposed to be endowed with magical powers, and therefore granted many privileges and indulgences. It was not considered lucky for the inmates of a house to be without a cat.

Girls are told to feed their cats well, so that the sun may shine on their wedding-day. Black cats keep care and trouble away from the house. It is lucky for a black and strange cat to stray into anybody's house. If a black cat is lost, trouble and sorrow will fall upon the house. It is very fortunate to have a purely white and a thoroughly black cat on the premises. When the cat has a cold, the sickness will seize all in the house. Cat's blood cures the shingles !

When cats trim their whiskers, guests may be expected. If cats suck the breath of babes, the latter will die. When cats are frisky, wind and rain may be expected. If the cat sits with its back to the fire, snow is coming. When a cat stretches its paws towards the fire, strangers are approaching the house.

The goat has long been associated with Wales, but it is not

clear why, for the reason that nearly all references to it appear to have been dated since the Norman Conquest.

In an old nursery rhyme a story is told of a goat tethered with a wooden collar at the foot of Snowdon. Two others were sent to Bardsey Island. The latter fought with each other so furiously that the vibration of their conflict caused the church tower of Abermaw to fall, and it was never rebuilt.

The devil had the credit of creating the goat.

Witches were supposed to take their nocturnal rides on a he-goat, a wolf, or a cat.

In some parts of Wales black goats were regarded as keepers of treasure. Their presence among solitary bridle-paths indicated hidden money or some kind of goods.

Many of the old Welsh stories describe the devil's goat-feet appearing, and with claws like a wild goat.

An old Welsh saying is that " Goats are on good terms with the fairies."

Stags appear occasionally in Welsh lore.

The stag that took refuge with Illtyd, the knight and saint, when the hounds of King Merchion hunted it, is mentioned in the " Vita Sancte Iltuti."

There is a tradition connected with the ancient town of Llantwit Major, where Illtyd founded his fifth-century college or University, that a golden stag with its head buried to the west is concealed in the immediate neighbourhood. When found, the former importance of the town will be restored, and prosperity will quickly follow

The eagle is described in Welsh lore as the king of birds.

Sacred eagles screamed and prophesied down from their crag-built nests on the summits of all the great mountains in Wales. In poetical language Snowdon was called Caer Eryri, the stronghold of the eagle.

Many superstitions were attached to the eagle, but they are remote and almost lost to oral tradition. A few have survived, and among the most curious of these is the old story that the descendants of a person who had eaten eagles' flesh to the ninth generation possessed the gift of second sight. They had the power to charm various complaints away, and especially shingles. [A. B. C. D.]

6

To destroy an eagle's brood was a token of revenge to follow the slayer. An eagle's egg, boiled and eaten by two persons, would keep witches away.

The eagles of Snowdon were regarded as oracles. When they soared aloft and circled, triumph was near ; when they descended nearer the earth, disaster was at hand. If they stood sentinel-like on the grim crags, enemies were in the near distance. When they brooded, or nestled together, or congregated in numbers in various places, or appeared indifferent, peace would come for a season.

The man who was daring enough to rob an eagle's nest of its eggs could expect to be bereft of repose ever afterwards. The eagles of Snowdon and Cader Idris could never be caught. Their cries meant calamity, and when they hovered over the plains, it was a sign that disease and death would soon stalk abroad.

Eagles are prominent in all the legends connected with King Arthur, and several caverns in Wales are pointed out where chained eagles once were supposed to guard the resting-place of the monarch, who, in the golden age, would return and rule triumphantly over Britain and all the isles of the sea.

In the North they used to say the " whirling " wind, or whirlwind, was caused by the great eagles of Snowdon when they prepared for flight.* A folk-story describes a great meeting of eagles on the summit of Snowdon. To this assembly the eagles, vultures, and other birds of prey were bidden, from Plinlimmon, Cader Idris, and other mountains of the North. When busy in debate, they all shouted, and at the conclusion the birds sprang upwards and flapped their wings mightily, so that a great whirlwind passed over Wales, destroying all as it went. In some parts of the Principality they formerly said, when exceptionally high winds prevailed : " The eagles are breeding whirlwinds on Snowdon !"

The owl is prominent in the mythology and folk-lore of Wales.

Dafydd ap Gwylim† gives an excellent rendering in verse

* " Welsh Sketches," 1850, p. 20.
† Dafydd ap Gwylim was the celebrated idyllic poet of Wales in the fourteenth century, and contemporary with Chaucer. He has been likened to Petrarch, and was the writer of many beautiful verses, a

of the ancient tradition with reference to the owl.   The translation runs thus :

THE OWL'S PEDIGREE.*

POET.

" Bird of wondrous sorrows, thou
    With thy countenance of age,
Wilt thou to the bard avow
    What thy name and lineage ?"

OWL.

" By the men of noble race
I am called ' Unrivalled Face.'
At the banquetings of yore,
I the name ' Flower Aspect ' bore.
I was daughter of a chief,
Proudly through the land of Mon
As the son of Merchion known.
Rich in golden stores——"

POET.

        " O Grief !
Maiden who art called ' The Morn,'
Who, then, wrought this fearful change ?"

OWL.

" Gwydion, son of Don, in scorn,
With his wand of magic sway,
Changed my beauty's proud array
For the aspect you behold !
In revenge, because of old
Gronwy, Pevyr, Garanhir,
Of tall form and noble cheer,
Penllyn's lord to me was dear !"

From time immemorial the owl has been regarded in Wales
with ill-favour. Innumerable stories are told against this
bird. Woe, sorrow, death, and tribulation attend its flight,
and its hootings are listened to with dread in many parts
of the country.

In several villages in North and South Wales, when an owl
hoots in the midst of houses, a maiden inhabitant will lose her
chastity.

---

collection of which was published in 1789 by Dr. Owen Pughe, and in
1834 by Mr. Arthur J. Johnes.   The latest articles on Dafydd ap Gwylim
are to be found in " Y Cymmrodor " and the Transactions of the
Honourable Society of London Cymmrodorion.
  * Translated by Mr. Arthur J. Johnes. 1854.

" When an owl was heard hooting early in the night from one of the yews in the churchyard, it was looked upon as a sign that some unmarried girl of the village of Llangynwyd had forsaken the path of chastity.   There are even now persons who maintain the trustworthiness of this sign."*   Llangynwyd is a village near Maesteg, near Bridgend, Glamorgan.

In South Glamorgan, if an owl hoots in the early part of the winter close to any small town or village it is regarded as a sign of snow.

The flight of an owl across a person's path was considered very baleful.

The raven in Welsh lore is closely connected with King Arthur, whose soul was supposed to hover in the form of that bird over his favourite haunts.   For this reason in Wales, as well as in Cornwall, it is considered unlucky to kill a raven. If this birds alights and halts on any part of a homestead, it is regarded as a token of prosperity and pleasure.

Old Welsh superstition states that if blind people are kind to ravens, they will soon learn how to regain their lost sight.

In Wales it is considered fortunate to see two crows before setting out on a journey.   Old rhymes on the crow run thus :

" Two crows I see ;
Good luck to me"; and

" One for sorrow, two for mirth,
Three for a wedding, four for a birth."

A single crow is regarded as an omen of evil if it crosses a person's path.   In former times people said if a crow hovered or circled above a person's head, it was a sign of decapitation.

If a carrion crow makes three circles around a field, croaking all the time, the owner or tenant of the land may expect heavy losses in flocks and herds.

Magpies were regarded with disfavour by the Welsh.   If they crossed any person's path, disaster would follow.   If a magpie hovered over a man's head, it was formerly believed that he would be decapitated.

There is an old Welsh couplet running thus :

" One magpie means misfortune,
Two magpies mean good luck."

* T. C. Evans, " History of Llangynwyd," p. 150.

And another runs :

> " Three magpies mean a burying,
> Four magpies bring a wedding."

Among insects, various kinds of beetles were associated with the old folk-stories.

The dung-beetle was called the devil's coach-horse.

The small gold-beetle was placed to creep upon unmarried girls' hands, and then allowed to fly away. The direction in which it flew indicated the quarter where the future bridegroom lived.

If on the gold-beetle's wings more than seven black spots are found, the corn harvest will be scanty ; if less than seven, the harvest will be unusually abundant.

As in England, so in Wales, the rhyme of the ladybird is popular and well-known :

> " Ladybird, ladybird, fly away home !
> Your house is on fire, your children will burn !"

Bees, in the traditional lore of Wales, draw their origin from Paradise,* which they had to leave owing to man's transgression. But God gave them His blessing, and bade them descend from heaven to earth, where they suck out of every blossom Divine nectar ; therefore Mass could not be sung without wax.

The clear, sweet honey was a chief ingredient of the Divine drink sacred to the Druids.

If the queen bee flew to any child in his sleep, people said he would be unusually fortunate in life.

In Wales they say if you do not confide all your joys and sorrows to the bees, all your hives will waste away within the ensuing year.

In the superstitions regarding bees, the Welsh say a hive given to or bestowed upon any person will bring good luck to the homestead ; but a hive of bees bought will not thrive so well.

Sunday is considered a lucky day for swarming bees.

A strange swarm of bees settling on a house or entering a garden is a token of prosperity or good luck.

It is very unfortunate for a swarm of bees to leave a house.

* Davies, " Mythology," p. 260.

At the same time, if a swarm of strange bees enters a house, misfortune and death will soon follow them.

It was formerly customary in Wales for the head of the household to tell the bees whenever a death took place in the family. The news should be whispered cautiously.

A widow, at her husband's death, knocked several times at the beehive, saying, " He's gone ! he's gone !"   The bees hummed in reply, and by this the woman understood they decided to remain where they were.   If they had not responded, she would have known they intended quitting the place. [*J. R.*]

Beehives were always turned completely round before a funeral.

In some parts of Wales they say a swarm of bees settling on a house foretokens a fire.

It is said bees and crickets bring blessings to the house, and it is unlucky to kill them or spiders.

CHAPTER VII

PLANTS, HERBS, AND FLOWERS

ALL growths that did not owe their origin to seed or root were regarded as miraculous and endowed with magical power. For this reason the mistletoe was held in awe, and gall-nuts were suspended from the kitchen beams and rafters, to protect the house against the mischief of Satan and witchcraft.

The mistletoe* was regarded as particularly sacred, and in Druidical days the cutting of it was attended by great ceremony. The blossoms of the mistletoe generally appear just before the summer solstice, and the berries within a few days of the winter solstice. Thus they indicated the return of two of the usual seasons for holding bardic conventions. When the sacred rites were finished, the berries were gathered and preserved for medicinal purposes.

In ancient times it appears to have grown only on the oak, but in later centuries it grew on the ash, birch, hazel, apple, and pear trees.

It still grows in profusion in the border counties of Wales.

This plant† is called by the Welsh Pren Awyr, or merry tree; Pren Uchelvar, or tree of the high summit; and Pren Puraur, or tree of pure knowledge.

So late as the early part of the nineteenth century, people in Wales believed that for the mistletoe to have any power, it must be shot or struck down with stones off the tree where it grew.

There was formerly a superstition in Mid-Wales that if the mistletoe was found growing on an ash or hazel, a snake or a viper, with a jewel on its head, would be discovered under the

* Davies, " Mythology," pp. 278, 279. † *Ibid.*, pp. 280, 281.

tree, or some kind of treasure was concealed beneath the roots.

In some parts of Wales people believed that a sprig of mistletoe which had been used in the Christmas decoration of a church would bring good luck for the ensuing year to its possessor. If an unmarried woman placed a sprig of mistletoe taken from the parish church under her pillow, she would dream of her future husband.

In some parts of Wales it was considered an act of desecration to include mistletoe in church decorations, and whoever did so would be unlucky for the next twelve months.

In rural places where mistletoe was abundant there was always a profusion of it in the farmhouses. Welsh farmers used to say, when mistletoe was scarce : " No mistletoe, no luck." They also said that mistletoe brought good luck to the dairy. To insure this, a branch of mistletoe was given to, or placed beside, the first cow that gave birth to a calf after the first hour of the New Year. In the agricultural districts where mistletoe grows the farmers believe that when it is unusually abundant an exceptionally prosperous year may be expected.

It was considered fatal to allow the mistletoe or any Christmas decoration to remain in the house after Twelfth Night, and it was lucky to make a bonfire of the evergreens.

In Wales, like all other places, the mistletoe is an emblem of love, and a kiss given to any matron or maiden under it was regarded as a compliment, and not an insult.

A sprig of mistletoe gathered on St. John's Eve, or any time before the berries appeared, and placed under the pillow, would induce dreams of omen, both good and bad. It would also reveal events likely to take place during the year. It was considered particularly unlucky for anybody to bring mistletoe into the house before Christmas.

Holly was regarded with superstition. If brought into the house before Christmas Eve strife, family quarrels, and disputes would ensue. Here it may be mentioned that the old people said, if you pluck a sprig of holly in flower, there will be a death in your family. If you bring holly-flowers into the house you live in, or into a friend's dwelling, there will be a death on the premises within a year and a day. The person who severs the holly-flowers from the bush will meet with misfortune, accident, or death.

Selago,* or hedge-hyssop, is said to be the herb formerly known to the Welsh as Grâs Duw. It was a Druidical herb, and the orthodox way of gathering it was with the right hand well covered. The herb was then to be drawn with the left hand under a cloth. The person who gathered it had to be robed in white, and his bare feet were to be previously washed. He must also be bare-headed. Iron was not to touch or be used to cut the herb. Among the Druids a sacrifice of bread and wine was made before the plant was gathered, and it was carried in a clean napkin to a place near the altar. This plant was in the days of old regarded as a charm against all misfortune. It was seldom found, and then generally by a holy person. This herb shines like gold, and it was customary to pluck it in the meadows before sunrise.

He who accidentally trod upon selago fell asleep, and afterwards awoke to be able to understand the language of birds and animals.

Some think the selago to be the lycopodium.

Valerian had healing and magical powers of high repute. Girls used to conceal it in their girdles and inside their bodices, in order to secure the admiration of the opposite sex. In the Middle Ages it was considered efficacious against the plague. It is still used for various purposes in Wales.

Basil-roots were chopped up finely and mixed with pig's wash, to keep them free from disease.

In Mid-Wales the fern had curious properties. The people used to say that the man who could gather fern-seed would be able to daunt the devil ! It was formerly customary for waggoners to place a bunch of fern over their horse's ears or on the horse-collar, to " keep the devil away " and to " baffle witches." [*Family Collection.*]

Fern-seed was supposed to render people invisible.

A very amusing story about fern-seed came from the neighbourhood of the Garth Mountain, Glamorgan. An aged Welshman said that when he was a small boy he heard his grandfather gravely relating the experience of a neighbour

* Davies, " Mythology," p. 280.

who chanced to be coming homeward through the mountain
fern on Midsummer Night between twelve and one o'clock. At
that hour fern-seed is supposed to ripen, to fall off directly,
and be lost.   Some of the fern-seed fell upon his coat and into
his shoes.   He thought nothing of this, but went home ; and
as the family had gone to bed, he, being tired, flung himself
into the fireside corner of the old-fashioned oaken settle.   In
the morning he was much surprised that his mother and sisters
took no notice of him.   Thinking they were offended, he said :
" Well, come, now ; I won't be so late coming home again—
no, indeed."

His mother and sisters looked frightened, for they heard the
man's voice, but could not see him.

" Come, now ; what's on me ?" he asked.   " You look as if
you'd seen a ghost."

His mother and sisters screamed with fright.

" Come on, now ; no joking," said the man.   " 'Tis me myself, and nobody else."

Again the women screamed.

Then he chanced to stroke his coat, and, feeling something in
one of his shoes, he took it off, and removed what he thought
to be grit in it.   Instantly he stood revealed to everybody.

The fern-seed had rendered him invisible !

The man who told this story said that when he was a boy
not a person would wear a fern of any kind—first, because it
caused men to lose their paths ; and secondly, because adders
were likely to follow you so long as it was worn.   [C. D.]

Rosemary was regarded as an excellent remedy against
chronic drunken habits.   For this reason an infusion of it was
often put in the cask or measure of beer.   It also kept beer
from turning sour.

The smoke of its burning bark would release a person from
prison.   The leaves pressed and applied as a poultice kept
wounds from running.   Placed on the doorpost, it prevented
adders and snakes from entering the house.   Spoons made
from the wood of it rendered all food placed therein highly
nutritious.

A bush of rue was always kept in old-fashioned gardens,
and an infusion of it was administered to people suffering from

convulsions or fits of any kind. Rosemary and rue kept witches away.

Mugwort was connected with several superstitions. It was asserted that if a man wore a bit of mugwort in his coat he would never get weary. A bit of it kept in the house " would scare the devil away," and protect the property from fiends and witches. The juice of this plant was regarded as a cure for consumption.

An old rhyme, well known in some parts of South Wales, runs thus :

> " Drink nettle tea in March,
> And mugwort tea in May,
> And cowslip wine in June,
> To send decline away."

Nettles boiled and eaten were supposed to quicken the senses and clear the brain. If you would cultivate a good memory, use nettles as a vegetable in the spring. A bunch of nettles in broth was supposed to induce appetite and promote sleep. Marigolds were used for the same purpose.

Vervain was one of the sacred plants of the Druids. With it were associated the trefoil and the hyssop.

The Druids* used it in casting lots and foretelling future events. It was also in great request as a love-philtre. Vervain was to be gathered at the rising of the Dog-star, " without having been looked upon by the sun or moon." The earth around it was prepared by a libation of honey. The left hand was to be used in digging it up, and the moment that process was over the plant had to be waved above the head of the person who dug it. All the leaves, stalk, and root were to be divided and dried separately in the shade. The floors of banqueting halls, the tables for feasts, and the cushions of regal apartments were always sprinkled with the water in which vervain had for a long time been infused.

The sow-thistle had magical properties, and people said he that carried it in his belt or put a leaf of it in his hat would be able to run and never get tired. At the same time, it would take the strength out of his companion, and if by accident a man gave some of the leaves of it to his wife, one of the persons would waste away and die. It was generally applied to a cut or

* Davies, " Mythology," p. 276.

gash made by the hoof or teeth of a hog. Sometimes it was thrown in or near the swine-trough, that the pigs might fatten quickly ; and formerly some of it was tied to the tails of horses before a ploughing match. Neither the devil nor any witch or hag of the night could harm the person who wore a leaf of the sow-thistle.

Betony is known in Welsh as " St. Bride's comb." It was lucky for the girl whose sweetheart was the earliest to find the first betony. Worn in the hat, it was supposed to confound witches and keep evil spirits away. In some parts of Wales it is called the " Bishop's flower." The Bâltan fire was incomplete without betony.

Henbane was regarded as a plant of evil repute, and people told the children that if they ate ever so little a bit of it, they would " go raving mad." A decoction of it given to persons suffering from tendencies to insanity, or any kind of mental trouble, would quickly work a cure. There was a belief that if any young child fell asleep near the henbane, he would " sleep for ever."

The periwinkle is called " the plant of the dead." It used to be grown chiefly on graves. It is unlucky to uproot the periwinkle from a grave, as to pluck a flower of it, for the dead will appear to the person who takes either, and his dreams for the next twelve months will be very wretched and miserable.

In many parts of Wales the black bryony, with its dark green and glossy leaves and brilliant red berries, which clings to trees and shrubs, and has no tendrils, was known as the mysterious and uncanny mandrake. The leaves and fruit were called " charnel food," and formerly it was supposed only to grow beside the gallows-tree or near cross-roads. Witches gathered the leaves and flowers, and uprooted the plant for magical purposes. When uprooted it shrieked and groaned like a sensible human being, and its agony was dreadful to hear. From its stalk a sweat like blood oozed, and with each drop a faint scream was heard. There was an old saying that people who uprooted the mandrake would die within a year. They would die groaning as the mandrake died, or approach their death raving, or uttering penitent prayers for having uprooted the unholy plant.

Witches kept the mandrake, and were said to sell portions of it to people who wanted to find out secrets, to wives who desired offspring, and to people who wished for wisdom.

In some of the old stories the origin of the mandrake was curious and mysterious. If an innocent man suffered on the gallows-tree, and his tears fell to the earth, there would grow on the spot the broad-leaved, yellow-flowered mandrake. It was also supposed to grow mysteriously near the cross-roads where suicides were buried. A process for uprooting the mandrake was described as follows : " The person who wished to do so had to put cotton or wax in his ears, and go before sunrise on a Friday. With him he had to take a black dog that had not a white hair on him. After making the sign of the cross thrice over the mandrake, the man or witch, as the case might be, had to dig around the plant till the root held by thin fibres only. Then he had to tie the roots with a string to the dog's tail, hold a piece of bread before him, and move away. The dog would rush after the bread, and thus wrench up the root of the mandrake. Then, pierced by the agonizing groans of the mandrake, the dog would fall dead at the man's feet.

Leeks are associated with victory by the Welsh. It is one of the national emblems of Wales, and, in common with the Scandinavian races, was probably used by the early Britons when victorious on the battlefield. It was at one time supposed that a person who had leeks or garlic on his body at the time of a fight would be victorious without a wound. Men notorious as fighters in Wales wore the leek in their caps, and were accustomed to rub their bodies with leeks, wild onions, or garlic before encounters with opponents. In the days of old a leek was thrown into the loving cup. At Courts Leet in Glamorgan so late as 1850 this was done. [C. D. *Family Collection.*]

With the leek people made divinations, and when worn, it scared evil spirits and enemies away. It is considered lucky to have a bed of leeks growing in the garden.

With reference to the leek as one of the national emblems of Wales, there are many theories. Whether the common or garden leek or the daffodil was used in battle is a disputed point. In the traditions of Wales the matter is not very clear. The daffodil is called in some places the leek of St. Peter, sometimes the leek of the Goslings, and the leek of the spring. It is also called " Croeso 'r Gwanwyn," the " welcome of spring," and " Gwanwyn 'r brenin," the " king of the spring." St. Non the Blessed, the mother of St. David, was associated with the daffodil, which grew in profusion in the Vale of Aeron, where the patron saint of Wales was born on March 1. At that season of the year the daffodil would be the most prominent flower. [C. D.]

Whatever may be said in favour of the daffodil, the claim of the common, wild, or cultivated leek is strongly supported by the assertion that in primitive times victorious warriors wore it, and so late as the last half of the eighteenth, and first part of the nineteenth, century champions and fighters patronized it.

Poor Robin's Almanack for 1757 contains the following verse for the month of March

> " The first of this month some do keep
> For honest Taff to wear his leek,
> Whose patron was, they say, of Wales.
> And since that time—cup-plutter-a-nails !—
> Along the street this day doth strut,
> With hur green leek stuck in hur hat,
> And if she meet a shentleman,
> Salutes in Welsh ; and if hur can
> Discourse in Welsh, then hur shall be
> Amongst the green-horned Taffys free."

The *Diverting Post*, 1705, refers to the pungent odour of the leek :

> " Why on St. David's Day do Welshmen seek
> To beautify their hats with verdant leek,
> Of nauseous smell ?   ' For honour 'tis,' hur say,
> *Dulce et decorum est pro patria.*
> Right, sir, to die or fight it is, I think,
> But how is't *dulce* when for it you—stink ?"

The house-leek, so often seen upon the garden-walls and housetops, or somewhere on the premises, was considered to be a protection from thunderbolts, lightning, and fire.

The lungwort is called the " herb of Mary," and was a proof against witches. Many flowers and herbs are associated with the Madonna and St. Bridget, and all of them were worn or used as a protection against witches and evil spirits.

Springwort was supposed to indicate where hidden treasures might be found, and particularly minerals. Enclosed in a man's stick, it would lead the owner to places where iron-ore could be found, and also protect him against robbers.

Saxifrage, or sassafras, was regarded as a rock-breaking plant. People said it would split the hardest stone growing near it. When worn near the heart it had the power of rendering the wearer victorious over his enemies, and removing all obstacles from his way.

The devil's bit, or *Scabiosa succisa*, was regarded with awe. Old people said it was once very beautiful and powerful in the healing art, but the devil bit it away, because he envied mankind its virtues.

Elecampane was considered a lucky plant to wear in the hat or cap, because it had the power to frighten robbers, thieves, and all sly people. If placed in the cap of a deceptive person, the latter would immediately get very red in the face. Welsh children have a rhyme running thus :

> " Elecampane, what is my name ?
> If you ask me again, I will tell you the same."

The common teasel was a protection against witches. Water or dew standing in the hollow of its leaves was a remedy for freckles.

Stonecrop is seen on many of the thatched and other cottages and farmsteads in Wales. It was originally placed there as a protection against thunderbolts, lightning, and witches.

Ground-ivy, with its small blue flowers, was a sanitary herb or weed, and a safeguard against sorcery. In the past, milkmaids wore it when first milking the cows in the pastures.

An infusion of ground-ivy grown near eye-wells was considered good for bathing weak eyes. A poultice made of ground-ivy leaves applied to sore eyes invariably cured them. The clover or shamrock, sometimes called the trefoil, was connected with the name of Olwen, the beautiful daughter* of the " hawthorn-headed " giant. Wherever Olwen trod a four-leaved shamrock sprang up. It was considered lucky, and a token of marriage, to find the four-leaved variety. Worn upon the person, or placed under the pillow, it induced cheerful-

---

*„" The Mabinogion," p. 219.

ness of mind, and made people light-hearted. It is given and accepted as an emblem of good luck.

Parsley was regarded as a root the leaves of which " cleared the brain." It was considered very unlucky to accept a root of parsley, but you could take the leaves for luck. If the parsley withers, there will be a death in the house. If it grows and flourishes, peace and plenty are promised. If you give away a root of parsley, you will give away your luck.

Lemon-thyme, thyme, marjoram, and savory were grown in old-fashioned gardens for luck, and these herbs were shunned by witches and fairies. They scared spirits away, and it was customary to scatter them upon the dead, to throw bunches of them on the coffin when in the grave ; and some of the old women say that when they were girls, they would wear sprigs of those herbs, with mint and lavender, to bring them sweet-hearts. Mint and peppermint leaves were worn for luck in business transactions.

Meadow-sweet is regarded as a fatal flower in Wales. There is an old story to the effect that if a person falls asleep in a room where many of these flowers are placed, death is inevitable. It is called a death-flower and a poisonous plant, for the effects of which there is no antidote. It is considered quite dangerous for anybody to fall asleep in a field where it is to be found in abundance.

Primroses, apple, and all wild-fruit blossoms were among the sacred offerings of the Druids, with whom the selago and crocus were popular.

Triple leaves, plucked at hazard from the common ash, were in the days of old worn by those who desired prophetic dreams concerning a dilatory lover. Leaves of the yellow trefoil answered the same purpose.

Lilac blossoms were supposed to indicate changes of the weather. If they kept closed longer than usual, fine warm weather might be expected. If they opened rapidly, rain would fall soon. If the lilacs quickly droop and fade, a warm summer will follow. Late-flowering lilacs indicate a rainy season.

May blossoms, buds, and flowers from certain old thorns were never gathered or brought into the house, for fear " death would follow." Branches of whitethorn were suspended outside houses on May Day to keep witches away. For outdoor use and decoration may blossoms and whitethorn sprays were lucky.

Cowslips are still used as a pretty test by children in Wales, who make the blossoms into flower-balls. These they toss up, and catch with the right hand only, while repeating :

"Pistey, postey, four-and-forty,
How many years shall I live ?
One, two, three, four,"

and so on, until the ball falls at the fateful number.

Cowslip-tea and cowslip-wine were said to " strengthen the senses."

In Wales the daisy is generally selected by the doubting maiden who is wishful to test the fidelity of her lover. Gathering a daisy, she commences plucking the petals off, saying with each one, " Does he love me ?—much—a little—devotedly—not at all !" And the last petal decides the question. An old Welsh belief indicated that the daisy was first planted on a baby's grave by infant angels. Another belief was that the first daisy owed its origin to the death of a beautiful and royal infant, who was transformed into a new and lovely flower in the land. [O. S.]

Marjoram, St. John's wort, and white heather were capable of scaring the devil. Wild marjoram and thyme, thrown into a fairy ring, would bewilder and confuse the fairies.

St. John's wort blossomed on St. John's Day, and in honour of that festival people formerly decorated their houses with it, adding thereto birch, larch, fennel, and the flower of St. John. In Wales St. John's wort is frequently called the " school or ladder of Christ."

The scarlet pimpernel, known as the " poor man's clock," which opens at 7 a.m. and closes about 2 p.m., was regarded as a barometer. On the approach of rain the flowers will not open, or, if open, close at once. Gloomy and melancholy people, and those who were very much depressed in spirits, were accustomed to drink an infusion of pimpernel. Worn in the hat, cap, coat, or bodice, it was supposed to keep sad thoughts from

7

the wearer. Placed under the pillow at night, it brought pleasant and soothing dreams.

In some parts of Wales daffodils are known as " babies' bells." People say that only infants and very young children can hear them ringing. It is considered very lucky to find the first daffodil, for you will have more gold than silver that year.

Forget-me-nots were associated in Wales with hidden treasure, and their talismanic power was considerable. This flower promoted prosperity and fidelity. At the same time, it was regarded as unlucky for lovers to give each other a forget-me-not, because it indicated estrangement, a severance, or improbability of marriage between the pair.

Lavender blossoms brought luck to the wearer. Sprigs of lavender worn about the person were capable of bewildering witches and confusing evil spirits. They also quickened the wits or senses of dull-minded people, and cleared the brains of poets and preachers. Lavender-water purified the face.

Golden broom is called by the Welsh the " goldfinch of the meadows,"* and was among the wedding blossoms. It was used as a charm, and if waved over a restless person, it induced sleep.

In the parish of Llanganten, Breconshire, it is asserted that the broom has never grown again on the spot where Llewelyn, the last native Prince of Wales, was slain. The dingle was formerly overgrown by broom.

The old-fashioned bridal flowers of Wales were pansies of all colours, roses of every description, excepting any shade of yellow, prick-madam, gentle heart, lady's fingers, lady's smock, prickles, blossoming gorse or furze, red clover bloom, scarlet fuchsia, golden rod, ivy, shamrock, a few straws, and heather, which is considered very lucky. May blossoms are unlucky for weddings.

Yarrow, sprigs of yew and box, are funeral tokens in Wales. The yarrow, sometimes named " boy's love," is called the " death flower " in Wales, where it is considered a token of death if brought into the house.

On the wild-rose brambles and the whitethorn there is often a moss-like excrescence. In Wales they say if this is placed under the pillow of a person who cannot sleep, it will perfectly

* Davies, " Mythology," p. 283.

restore him. But it was necessary to remove it at a given time, or, according to the old story, he would never awake.

The thorn-apple was considered in some mysterious way to be closely connected with, and used by, wizards and witches. It assisted their incantations, and helped them to develop the cult of second sight. In Puritanical times those who grew it in their gardens were in danger of being persecuted, or burnt for wizards or witches.

It is regarded as very unlucky to a household when flowers that only flourish in the summer bloom in the winter. Quite recently an old Welsh woman said : " I thought death was coming, because all my geraniums have been in flower from November to February." Three of her very near relatives died within those months.

On the small islands of the Steep and Flat Holms, Sully and Barry, in the Bristol Channel, the blossoming of the burnet rose out of its proper season was regarded as an omen of shipwreck and disaster.

The blossoming of Christmas roses late in the spring indicates unexpected events in West Wales. A primrose blooming in June, and a summer rose unfolding in November or December, are regarded as signs of trouble and bad luck by people living in Mid-Wales.

If ivy growing on an old house begins to fall away from the walls or becomes shrivelled, people predict financial disaster or misfortune to the owner of the property, or the property will soon pass out of the present owner's possession.

With reference to the blossoming of fruit-trees out of season many stories are told. Their untimely appearance indicates trouble, calamity, sickness, or death. In Wales, when blossoms appear in the orchards and hedgerows through a whole district out of their proper season, people predict epidemic sickness, many deaths, and a " hard winter." Individual instances of untimely blossoms in orchards and gardens indicate misfortune, trouble, or death to the occupant of the house. When plum-trees blossom in December it is a " sure sign of death." In a remote village, when a certain crab-apple-tree overhanging a well blossoms out of season, there are said to be more births and marriages than deaths during the ensuing year. Whenever a very old plum-tree blossoms in a certain Glamorgan farm, a wedding takes place in the family.

With reference to fruit, the following particulars are interesting : An old house-book in South Glamorgan contained this note : " The old greengage-tree has produced two plums only this year (1830). By this we know something unusual will happen, but good or evil I cannot tell. It mostly goes by reverses. Nine years ago it bore one plum, and my mother died. Seven years ago two plums came, and my sister Gwen was married. Five years ago one plum came, and my brother John died. And now I wait to see what will happen." [C. D.]

The same book, bearing date 1837, has the following record : " In my uncle's garden the old apple-tree next the churchyard-wall has borne three apples, after being fruitless for the past nine years, and then there were three weddings in the family within one month." [C. D.]

" Untimely fruit, untimely news," is an old Welsh saying.

CHAPTER VIII

TREES, BIRDS, AND WATER-FOWL

AMONG all the trees of the forests and plains the oak stands pre-eminent. It was the sacred tree of the Druids, and the people held it in great reverence.

Remnants of old-time superstitions with regard to the oak were to be found in Wales so late as sixty years ago, when it was customary in many districts for the young men and maidens to dance and sing around the oldest oak in the village. This was called a " round dance." It took place as a rule at Easter, but Whitsuntide and Midsummer festivities were held under its branches.

The oak and the ash, or the walnut, cannot grow close together without perishing. The blackthorn and the white-thorn " cannot agree," for the white one always gets the " upper hand " and " kills the black one." It is further said that a piece of oak rubbed upon the left hand in silence on Midsummer Day will heal all open sores.

The oak was prophetic. The curling of its leaves foretokened heat. A fly in a gall-nut or " oak-apple " gathered by anybody was a " sure sign of a quarrel." A worm in it was a token of poverty ; a spider in it was a sign of illness.

An aged Welshwoman told me that when she was a girl it was customary for young unmarried women to take two acorn cups, and name one for their sweetheart and one for self. These acorn cups were then set to float in a pan or bowl of water. If the acorn cups sailed together, marriage would follow ; if they drifted apart, there would be a separation.

There was a belief prevalent in some parts of Wales that at certain seasons of the year, particularly in the summer or early in the autumn, the oak-leaves whispered secrets of the ancient Druids, and any person gifted with prescience, if so minded, could understand what was said.

It was considered dangerous to enter a grove of oaks at midnight, for the spirits of the past assembled there for Druidical service. This is probably the reason why there are so many " haunted oaks " in Wales. Each of the counties of Wales has its venerable " haunted oak," from which mysterious sounds are sometimes heard. Children and superstitious people do not care to wander where oaks are abundant.

Groves of oak were sacred to the Druids, and the most beautiful tree of all was fixed upon as an emblem for their ceremonies. The Druids cut off all the side branches, and then joined two of them to the higher side of the trunk, so as to fashion it into a figure of a cross. Above and below the insertion of these branches the word " Thau " (God) was cut into the bark. Under this the most sacred rites of the Druids were performed.*

Next in importance to the oak was the ash.

It is still considered unlucky to break a branch off an ash-tree.

A garter made of the green bark of the mountain-ash was a talisman against witches, conjurers, sorcerers, and the devil.

When cock-fighting was popular, it was customary to place a few crossed twigs or a ring of mountain-ash bark in the cock-pit. This was done to prevent any evil power impairing the courage of the combative birds.

It was a charmed wood, and the bards of Wales invariably carved their Coelbren, or record stick, on wood of this tree.

The ash was regarded as one of the spirit-haunted trees, and people avoided remaining long near it. At the same time they had a curious regard for the ash, which was supposed to find out the secrets of lovers, and to whisper them to the wind. The ash-grove is much mentioned in the poetry and songs of Wales, and the name is very frequently given to houses and even modern villas. Triple leaves of the ash worn at the breast caused prophetic dreams.

Pollard-ashes had an important place in the old-time remedies

* Meyrick, " Costumes," p. 25.

of Wales. People used to catch a mouse, and shut it up in the ash, thereby " shutting up " their " bad luck." The bark of the ash or pollard-ash kept in the pocket, or rubbed in the hands, would scare away snakes, vipers, and other reptiles.

The ash, the pollard-ash, and the mountain-ash, known as the rowan-tree, had many peculiar and magical attributes. The man who carried a stick made of mountain-ash could readily find out the hiding-places of snakes, trace the route taken by witches, and defy the temptations of the devil.

It was considered lucky to have a mountain-ash growing near your premises. The berries brought into the house were followed by prosperity and success. A bunch of the berries worn in girdle or bodice kept women from being bewitched.

The birch was held in high estimation among the Welsh. In former times, when a girl accepted an offer of marriage, she presented her lover with a wreath of birch-leaves. If she rejected the offer, she sent him a rod, or twig, or wreath of hazel. Many of the Welsh bards in the Middle Ages mention groves and summer-houses of birch, and the birch crowns or hats which their sweethearts sent them in proof of their affection.

The Welsh maypole was always made of the birch-tree, and the birchen rod dealt its rebukes upon the neglectful schoolboy.

The elder was regarded with considerable awe. In South. Wales it was deemed very dangerous to build any premises on or near the spot where an elder-tree stood.

In the past an elder planted before the door of a cow-shed or stable protected the cows and horses from witchcraft and sorcery.

Charms were made of elder-twigs that grew on willows. Nine sticks were tied with red ribbon or red rag, and worn by children to protect them against pain.

In Wales people formerly would not burn elder-wood for fear of ill-luck. It was considered dangerous to build houses or any other premises where elders had stood, for the tenants would be continually changing.

Elders were frequently found near stables and out-buildings, and it is said they would " bleed " if cut. An old Carmarthenshire man said that in his grandfather's days people declared that the elder-tree wept or bled when cut. When hewn they were generally allowed to decay, because if burnt the witches would be roused. It was asserted that the elder-mother lived between the bark and the tree, and it was unlucky to burn her ; therefore she must be allowed to die.

Infusions of elder flowers were used for whitening the skin. If the flowers were worn by a girl she might expect to see her lover in her dreams. The berries are used for wine-making, and at one time they were eaten to induce sleep and peace of mind.

From the hazel, the rods of divination and wishing were made. The way in which these were formed in Carmarthenshire, Breconshire, and Glamorgan is thus described :

The wood must be cut when the moon is new, and in a perfect crescent. It should have nine ends or twigs, and be taken from " an old hedge." The rod was held in the hand so that two tips were firmly grasped. The stem would then point to hidden things. Some said that if the point of the forked hazel was held up firmly in each hand, one of the twigs would bend irresistibly to the ground, and then you may be sure ore was not far away. By means of the hazel, or wishing-rod, men were able to discover springs of water, hidden treasure, veins of ore, and new fields of coal.

The wishing-cap or hat of Wales was generally composed of hazel leaves and twigs, but sometimes it was made of juniper sprigs and berries. Old people told the children that if one of these caps was worn on the head, it would be possible to obtain any wish ; but the twigs and leaves must be gathered at midnight, and at new or full moon, and they should be made up as quickly as possible. These caps would also enable the wearer to go to any part of the world " in the twinkling of an eye." If a skipper wore one under his usual headgear, his ship would ride safely through every storm. The wishing-cap could render people invisible if they so desired. It was sometimes called the " thinking-cap," by means of which the wearer could readily remember or invent nursery and other stories. A common expression at present in Wales when somebody desires to obtain anything is to say : " I must put on my wishing-cap." If anybody wishes to invoke memory, he says : " I must put on my thinking-cap."

A quaint nursery story describes old " Molly Holly " sitting in the fireside corner of the settle, and grumbling and crooning because her husband was so peevish, her children were noisy and troublesome, and her neighbours were unkind.   Then she put on her wishing-cap, and desired to be away from them all. " In the twinkling of an eye " she was gone, not to return until her husband, children, and neighbours put on hazel or juniper caps and sincerely wished her home.   The origin of this story is obscure, and has some connection with the holly-tree.   It was a popular story in Glamorgan years ago.   [O. S. and Family Collection.]

People said that he who cut down a juniper would die within the year.   For this reason, in many parts of Wales aged junipers are carefully preserved, and it is customary to " let it die of its own will," or a natural death.

Twenty years ago an old farmer living in Glamorgan asserted that three deaths in his family followed by disaster happened when " the old juniper was cut down."

A resident in Carnarvonshire attributed losses in the family to the destruction of some aged junipers.

Willow caps were presented to all people who were disappointed in love.   It is customary in the present day for villagers in Wales to ask a rejected suitor on the morning of his sweetheart's marriage to another man, " Where is your willow cap ? " or " We must make you a willow cap."   The same applies to a spinster whose lover discards her for another girl.

The yew was regarded as the gentle guardian of the dead, and was formerly revered so much in Wales that to cut it down was considered an act of desecration, while to burn any part of it was looked upon as sacrilege.

Box-trees, plain or variegated, were much in request in gardens and for bordering flower-beds.   Sprigs of box were used at weddings and funerals, because they bewildered witches and scared the devil.   To cut down a box-tree was considered a rash act, invariably punished by disaster.   It was asserted that if a young or newly-married man uprooted or cut down a box-tree, his first child would be stillborn.

Myrtle is much esteemed in Wales, where they say that if it grows on each side of the door the blessings of love and peace will never depart from the house.   To destroy a myrtle is to " kill " both love and peace. Sprigs of myrtle, with its blossoms, were not only used by brides, but in some parts of Wales they were worn in the girdle or bodice of young girls when going to their first Holy Communion. Sprigs were also placed in cradles to make babies happy.

At Aberglasney, Carmarthenshire, many years ago, there was a hawthorn which flowered every Christmas Eve, but by the next morning the blossoms were faded. The thorn was cut down, and since then the grass has grown green around it every Christmas Eve, and withered in the morning. [*A. B.*]

A lonely house in Canton, near Cardiff, had a hawthorn that always bloomed for three nights only, and then withered. Occasionally it blossomed for a week, and whenever it did so there was a death in the family. The house has long since been demolished, and the garden covered by small habitations, but members of the family are still living. [*Family Collection.*]

In many of the rural districts of Wales where tumuli abound people said that whenever a hawthorn-tree stood in the centre of a single barrow, it denoted the resting-place of a renowned warrior. The children still call mounds and barrows with hawthorns in their midst " the warriors' graves." This is particularly noticeable in Glamorgan.

The hawthorn was regarded as a safeguard against lightning, and the same virtue was attributed to the laurel and the vine.

The dove appears to be more closely connected with woe than with joy in the Principality.

Whenever a dove is seen hovering around the mouth of a colliery, the Welsh colliers of the present day regard its appearance as an omen of disaster.

In July, 1902, there was a panic in Glyncorrwg, because a dove had been seen hovering over the colliery level, and other omens of trouble had been experienced.

Glyncorrwg, near the head of the Cwmavon Valley, is one of the most dreary and desolate places in Glamorgan.

The *South Wales Echo* of July 15, 1902, contained the following particulars, under the heading " A Batch of Evil Omens," which caused three hundred colliers to refuse to work in the pit :

" The men have been whispering their fears to each other for some time past, but the drastic action of Monday was probably the outcome of so-called evil omens which are said to have been heard in the mine. About two months ago the night-men began to tell ' creepy ' tales of the strange and supernatural happenings which took place in the colliery every night. . . . Now and then a piercing cry for help would startle the men . . . and during the night-shift horrid shrieks rang through the black darkness of the headings, and frightened the men nearly out of their wits. . . . There is, of course, the usual tale of the dove hovering over the mouth of the level."

The dove was seen before the Llanbradach Colliery explosion, and also at the Senghenydd and at Morfa Collieries before similar disasters.

Shepherds among the mountains surrounding the extinct volcano known as Llyn Dulyn, or the Black Lake, believed that the appearance of a dove near those dark and fateful waters foretokened the descent of a beautiful but wicked woman's soul to torment in the underworld.

Swallows are regarded in Wales as messengers of peace.

When swallows build new nests in the eaves of a house, there will be a death in that habitation within a year.

In some parts of Wales people say if swallows forsake their old haunts under the eaves, it is a token of misfortune to the inmates of the house.

It is also said that swallows are the first to pluck borrowed plumes from the jackdaw. The young of the swallow are commonly believed to be born blind, but eventually gain their sight. If one of the offspring is blind, or anything happens to its sight, the mother bird knows where to find a powerful herb of healing, which she places on the eyes. Sight is thereby restored.

Sometimes the bird has been watched by people who desire to find out the remedy ; but she always goes stealthily and in secret, and thus evades discovery.

An old story describes the swallow to have been a seamstress who, for stealing a ball of white yarn, was changed into a bird. The white spot on the swallow indicates the stolen ball. [O. S.]

The woodpecker is associated with Welsh lore. In the days of old this bird was regarded as being especially acquainted with the magical virtues of various herbs.

Two stories about the woodpecker were formerly told in Wales.

In the North of the Principality the people said that when Christ was on earth, He, after walking a long and weary distance, felt hungry. Seeing a woman making cakes, He begged one. He also asked for a draught of water. The woman refused both, whereupon Christ said: "Thou didst refuse Me both food and drink, and for this thou shalt be turned into a bird. Every day thou shalt feed of the stuff to be found between the wood and the bark of trees, and thou shalt only drink when it rains." The woman was instantly turned into a bird, and in this form she taps or pecks at hollow trees for food, and pipes loudly before rain. [O. S., *Family Collection, and C. D.*]

This story was also told in Carmarthenshire and Pembrokeshire about fifty years ago.

In South Glamorgan, between fifty and sixty years ago, and in Gower still later, the following story about the woodpecker was popular: A woodman neglected his wife and children and left them to starve. After their death he became a wanderer, but nobody knew where he went. But in after-years his spirit haunted the woods, and he could be heard here and there through the country-side felling oaks. In summer twilight and winter moonlight he could be heard alike. From morning until sunset he rests, but from twilight to dawn he may be heard tapping or felling the oaks. But his task is never done. This, they say, is the origin of the woodpecker, who is constantly tapping the "hollow beech-tree." [*A. B., C. D., and Family Collection.*]

Bats, whether grey, white, or black, are regarded in some parts of Wales as heralds of good luck. If an unmarried person chances to see one flapping its wings, he or she may be expected to be married within the year.

In certain parts of the country it is regarded as very unlucky if a bat circles or flutters over a person's head.

In all parts of Wales the cuckoo is generally regarded as a bird of good luck.

It is a common saying among the farmers and peasantry that if the cuckoo is seen before the leaves appear on the blackthorn, the year will be dry and unproductive.

A child born on the day that the cuckoo is first heard will be lucky and truthful.

It is fortunate for lovers when together they hear the cuckoo first on a Sunday morning.

The women say that if you remove the shoe from your foot when you first hear the cuckoo, you will find on your stocking a hair resembling in colour that of your future partner in life.

It is fortunate if you have a piece of silver in your pocket when you first hear the cuckoo.

In Wales, as in England, the following rhyme is popular :

> " The cuckoo's a fine bird :
> She sings as she flies ;
> She brings us good tidings,
> And tells us no lies.
> She sucks little birds' eggs
> To make her voice clear,
> And when she sings ' Cuckoo !'
> The summer is near."

The cuckoo has a herald or " handmaiden," who comes quite fourteen days in advance of the harbinger of summer. This bird is the wryneck, known in Welsh as Gwas-y-gôg.

In many parts the cuckoo is regarded as a prophet.

The children cry out :

> " Cuckoo, cuckoo, true answer give :
> How many years have I to live ?"

As many times as the bird says " cuckoo " after the question is asked will be the number of years left to live.

Girls ask :

> " Cuckoo, cuckoo, on the tree,
> How long before I wedded be ?"

If in answer the cuckoo calls more than three or six times, the girls say the bird is bewitched.

An old woman in Mid-Wales told me that the cuckoo was once a beautiful lady who wept over her brother's death until she was changed into a bird.

In West Wales and in some parts of the North it is said that if, when you hear the cuckoo for the first time in the season, you are standing on grass or green moss, you will live to hear the bird next year. If you are standing on the earth or any red soil, you will die before the cuckoo comes again.

In North and Mid-Wales the people say if the cuckoo cries more than six times, it is sitting on a bewitched bough, and bodes no good.

In some parts of Wales the boys would roll their lazy companions in the grass when the cuckoo was first heard. This was to cure them of idleness.

At one period the peasantry of Mid-Wales, when they heard the cuckoo for the first time in the season, rolled themselves three times in the grass, to insure freedom from back-ache, lumbago, and sciatica.

If the cuckoo cries three times in succession immediately above a person's head, it means good luck. To see a cuckoo before the bird cries is a token that you will be able to find out hidden secrets in the season. To catch a cuckoo without killing it and let it go again means remarkable prosperity.

The cuckoo is considered a miser, for it is said when the leaves come out in spring, she will not eat as much food as she desires, for fear it should run short before she takes flight.

This bird is supposed to eat up the eggs of the hedge-sparrow, and put her own into that bird's nest.

It is stated that when the cuckoo grows up the bird devours its foster-parents, and in winter it is transformed into a bird of prey.

This bird is regarded as the embodiment of ingratitude, selfishness, and carelessness.

It is a common phrase in Wales to call a young foolish woman a cuckoo, or to say, " What a cuckoo you are !"

An old foolish woman is described as " An old cuckoo !"

The robin redbreast and the wren are prominent in Welsh lore.

With reference to the robin, the following story is told in Wales : " Far, far away, in the land of woe, darkness, spirits of evil, and fire, day by day does the little bird bear in its bill a drop of water to quench the flame. So near to the burning stream does he fly that his little feathers are scorched, and hence his name Bron Rhuddyn, or breast-scorched. To serve little children the robin dares approach the infernal pit. No good child will hurt the benefactor of man. The robin returns from the land of fire, and therefore he feels the cold of winter far more than his brother-birds. He shivers in the wintry blast. Hungry he chirps before your door. Oh, my child, then, in your gratitude, throw a few crumbs to the poor little robin redbreast !"*

The poem by the American poet Whittier charmingly illustrates the old Welsh nursery story.

" My old Welsh neighbour o'er the way
    Crept slowly out in the sun in spring,
Pushed from her ears the locks of grey,
    And listened to hear the robin sing.

" Her grandson, playing at marbles, stopped
    And, cruel sport, as boys will be,
Tossed a stone at the bird, who hopped
    From bough to bough in the apple-tree.

" ' Nay,' said the grandmother, ' have you not heard,
    My poor bad boy, of the fiery pit,
And how, drop by drop, this merciful bird
    ·Carries the water that quenches it ?

" ' He brings cool dew in his little bill,
    And lets it fall on the souls of sin ;
You can see the marks on his red breast still
    Of fires that scorch as he drops it in.

" ' My poor Bron Rhuddyn, my breast-burned bird,
    Singing so sweetly from limb to limb ;
Very dear to the heart of our Lord
    Is he who pities the lost, like Him.'

" ' Amen,' said I to the beautiful myth ;
    ' Sing, bird of God, in my heart as well ;
Each good thought is a drop wherewith
    To cool and lessen the fire of hell.'

" Prayers of love like raindrops fall,
    Tears of pity are cooling dew ;
And dear to the heart of our Lord are all
    Who suffer like Him in the good they do."

In the colliery districts of Wales the robin redbreast is regarded as a harbinger of calamity. The accompanying illustration of this superstition appeared in a leaderette in the *South Wales Weekly News* on September 14, 1901 :

" There is a pathetic and melancholy interest in the mention

* Well-known nursery story.

of a 'bird of ill-omen' in connection with the Llanbradach explosion. It is reported that several days before the explosion a robin redbreast was seen in the pump-house underground, where it had made its home. It was declared by some of the more superstitious of the miners that this was an ill-omen of coming disaster, for a similar bird had been noticed in the Senghenydd Mine just before the explosion there. A further paragraph announces that the bird was caught and brought to bank after the explosion, and when liberated, 'it flew away over the hilltops, apparently delighted to find itself once more in its native air.' Belief in omens and auguries may not be general amongst the miners, for the School Board and the railways have been too long in South Wales, but it is neverthe-less a fact that a section hold very strong beliefs in signs and portents of coming disasters. The black crow, or two black crows, flying east and west, are held to be a certain sign of coming accidents. Of course, the two black crows flying in opposite directions over Llanbradach were noticed, and simi-larly at Senghenydd, and some other collieries on the eve of disasters. The miners who are supposed to notice these signs and portents speak of them with the greatest mystery, and shake their heads gravely. But it was at Morfa where the greatest excitement was created over portents and auguries. The Morfa Colliery is situated near the sea, in a wild region. Shortly before the explosion at that colliery the men were dis-turbed by strange noises and tappings in one of the stalls.   A bird had been seen, and the crows had flown over the colliery. Two of the miners had even noticed the spirits of two men pass on the road before them as they left the colliery for their homes. The workmen were in a state of consternation for some time, and a meeting was held secretly at dead of night to discuss the subject and decide what should be done. Either from fear of being laughed at or in dread of offending the 'spirits,' which wanted to warn them of 'the wrath to come,' those who were present at the meeting kept silence and would not speak of it. That there was amongst the miners at Morfa a wholesome dread of spirits and a belief in their manifestations was placed beyond doubt, for rumours of spirits and knockings were rife throughout the colliery village, and the terrible disaster, no doubt, confirmed many of them in that belief. The Celtic imagination has peopled the West with stories of signs and portents, mysterious beings, corpse-candles, and death-hounds, and the Cornish miner is perhaps far more superstitious than the small section of Welsh colliers who repeat these reports of black crows and strange tappings and warnings of disaster."

A robin singing quite close to a window means vexation, sorrow, or annoyance. If this bird ventures over the threshold, it is a harbinger of illness or death.

If you destroy the nest of a redbreast, there will be a death in the family within a year, or there will be a fire in the house, or lightning will strike the premises.

If you kill a redbreast, a series of misfortunes or some unusual calamity will befall your family.

To steal the redbreast's eggs was very unfortunate. The theft made the person a victim of witches or the devil.

The wren's life was particularly sacred because of its Druidical associations. The robin and the wren must never be killed.

The following story about these birds is told in several localities :

The robin cannot fly through a hedge, say the people, but always goes over it. The wren cannot fly over a hedge, but always through it. For this reason it is said the birds were " under a curse."

If you kill a wren your house will be burned down.

The water-wagtail is called in Wales " little lady wash-dish." The old women used to tell the children that Merlin the enchanter set several animals and birds to dig a channel for the overflow of a brook ; but the wagtail sat on a branch of a tree and watched the others at work. Merlin said : " Thou canst do nothing but trim thyself up and be idle." The bird answered : " I do not like to soil my fine white feet." " Oh, thou fop !" said Merlin. " Henceforth thou shalt have black feet, and drink out of puddles and gutters, and sing only before rain and storms." From that moment the wagtail slaked her thirst in the rain-pools, and hopped about the rain-wet road, and flew low, skimming the ground, before heavy showers or in rainy seasons. [O. S., C. D., and Family Collection.]

8

Another story says the bird was so vain and fine that he was doomed by a wizard to be always looking for dish-water for clean and tidy housewives.   Hence she was called " little lady wash-dish."   [*O. S. and Family Collection.*]

Farmers and shepherds in Wales never kill a wagtail, because it is considered unlucky to do so.

The yellow-hammer was supposed to suck or taste blood from the veins of vampires, and it was formerly regarded as a herald of the approach of evil spirits.

The hen was an emblem of the goddess Ceridwen, or Ceres, and was sacred to the Britons.   Taliesin, the bard, says of Ceridwen : " The red-fanged hen with the parted crest received me, and I rested nine nights in her womb."   In another poem he says that when Ceridwen pursued him in a fury, she took the form of a black high-crested hen, and scratched him out of a heap of wheat, where he attempted to conceal himself, and then swallowed him in the shape of a grain of corn.

The swan appears in many of the legends and traditions of Wales, and in the fairy-lore the bird is very prominent.

An old Welsh story describes the eggs of the swan as being hatched by thunder and lightning, and, in common with other nationalities, the people believed that the bird sang its own dirge.

A swan's egg—because of its rarity, perhaps—was a lucky thing to be kept in the house.

A curiosity of this kind was carefully kept in the family of a Welsh farmer, who said the specimen was about two hundred years old.   If ever it was shattered, all the freehold property of the family would pass into other hands. This actually happened in 1850, and the prediction was fulfilled.

It was unlucky to see a wild swan alighting in any person's garden, for it meant disaster to a member of the family.   A wild swan flying hurriedly inland alone promised sad tidings from the sea.   If wild swans flew in flocks inland, wrecks of numerous and costly ships were to be expected.

Geese cackling and making much noise at midnight, or any unusual hour after going to roost, are said to portend theft and robbery on the premises.   When they turn back home after starting out, a stranger may be expected.

If a goose or a duck lay one soft and one hard egg, or two eggs in a day, misfortune in the family is foretokened. Farmers' wives will not allow eggs to be brought into or taken out of the house after dark, for it is unlucky. If sittings of the eggs of a goose, fowl, or duck are brought indoors between sunset and sunrise, the farm-wife says they will never be hatched.

A grey goose straying into a neighbour's yard is a token of slander. When flocks of geese or ducks or fowls desert their homes, death is coming among the inmates.

If geese, fowls, or ducks wander far, and seek new abodes among strangers, there is danger of a fire in their old haunts.

It is very lucky to find the feathers of geese, ducks, fowls, or any wild bird stuck in the ground as you are walking through fields or meadows. You will soon have unexpected money, and good news before the day is out.

It is unlucky to find a grey gander's feather in the same position.

When a goose is flying over a house the goodman's shroud is being woven. To meet three geese when starting on a journey is a token of success. If geese hiss at you, be sure enemies are working against your interests. Many grey geese in a flock portend many experiences. A black goose in a flock means that the devil is at work in the household. The shells of geese and ducks are always thrown on the fire, lest witches should find them and use them for coracles on their nocturnal trips to the opposite coast. It is considered unlucky to eat cooked goose unless before or after it you partake of giblet-soup or giblet-pie.

CHAPTER IX

WIND AND WEATHER

WINDS and storms take their place in Welsh lore. In the North the raising of the whirlwind was attributed to the eagles of Snowdon; in the South they said it was brought about by wicked and malicious elves and fays, and in Mid-Wales they said it was raised by the devil and his hosts when they had a meeting among the Black Mountains.

The wind blowing wildly on New Year's Night was regarded in some parts of Wales as an omen of pestilence. In other parts it foretokened death. In some places they used to say when a sudden wind sprang up, " A man has hanged himself," while a roaring wind foretokened a case of suicide in the parish. The howling wind breathes " misfortune," and the whistling wind means " mischief somewhere." The wind " blowing over the feet of the corpse," or over the " breast of the corpse," or the " breast of the grave," was sad to hear, for it was unlike any other sound, and promised " heavy grief " and " care and sorrow in plenty."

In the past the old people regarded the wind to be both hungry and thirsty, for it was customary to throw out a handful of flour, barley-meal, or oatmeal into the wind, and it was generally followed by a bowl of water or a cup of milk. These offerings were supposed to pacify the storm. They also breathed their wishes to the balmy west and south winds, and the soft breezes of summer foretokened pleasant news.

If Lundy Island can be seen clearly from a long distance, people on the shores of South Wales predict storms and rain. The same is said of Caldy Island and the Steep and Flat Holms.

When these islands are enveloped in summer mist or haze, great heat may be expected.

In the seventeenth century, people on the shores opposite Bardsey Island saw the shadowy forms of monks before wild winds and disaster at sea and sickness on land. The voice of an imprisoned monster was heard around Braich y Pwll before storm winds, and the spirits of the drowned wailed while the sea-horses galloped with them on the sands before a tempest around the Stack Rocks. Before a storm in some parts of Radnorshire they used to say, " The old men are quarrelling," or " The old men are beginning to quarrel." Radnorshire people had the reputation of being fond of quarrels and legal disputes. When a storm brooded and the waves made much noise around the Bishop's Rocks, Pembrokeshire, people said, " The Bishop and his clerks are praying." [C. D.]

Pentregethin, Pembrokeshire, had its cunning man, who preferred selling foul winds if he could, so that wreckers might have a good time and pay him well. Dafydd Lloyd ap Llewellyn* was a confederate of the man of Pentregethin and a conjurer. David Lewis, of Eithin-duon, in the parish of Trelech Cannar, sold winds fair and foul, raised storms, was a conjurer, and could pass through keyholes at will.

Jack o' Sheer-Gâr was an adept at these arts and practices, and plied his trade in Swansea in the days of old. Shoni Hoi frequented the Gower Coast, and many were the gifts he received from wreckers and smugglers in the eighteenth century.

Many parts of the Principality had men and women who sold winds and weather to sailors. Modryb Sina (Aunt Sina) was one of the cunning women who could procure " a fair wind or foul " for sailors and others who went to her haunts, Lavernock, Sully, and Cadoxton-juxta-Barry, in the eighteenth century. Ewythr Dewi (Uncle David) was prepared to do the same. He lived on Barry Island, and used to travel down to Swansea in the days before the great ports and trading places at Cardiff and Barry were known. Bill o' Breaksea accommodated people in the same way at the little harbour of Aberthaw, South Glamorgan. These kinds of people were to be met

* William Howell, " Cambrian Superstitions," p. 86.

all along the coastline of North and South Waies. Mari, of Lleyn, in the North, and Modryb Dinah, of Sker, in the South, were experts. [*A. B., C. D.*]

Whichever way these men or women turned their hats and wished, therefrom the desired wind would blow. On the Gower peninsula whole families were adepts in the art of storm-raising. They were accustomed to tie up the foul wind and weather in an eggshell, from which the white and yolk had been set free by a slight perforation, or sucked carefully out. The latter was then stopped up with shoemaker's wax. At the evil moment the cunning woman or man dashed the egg-shells on a stone; then the storm rushed out, and played havoc on land and sea. In some parts they used bags instead of eggs. Flogging the water with rods was customary with these storm-raisers, and it is said they beat until vapours arose which formed into a black cloud, producing deluges of rain and hail. In Carmarthenshire and Breconshire it was said that these cunning peasants used to eat, drink, and dance to the tune of the fiddle around three stones, by means of which they could produce wet weather or dry at will. If they set them upright, it would be dry; if they laid them down, it would be very wet. They also were accustomed to put their head-coverings askew and wish for rain, or set them straight for dry weather. [*C. D.*]

Light clouds, called "fleeces," "mares' tails," "horses' manes," and "streamers," indicated luck if they appeared directly above anybody's head. Gold-tinted or pink cloudlets floating or remaining stationary immediately over a person's head, house, or garden were, and are, regarded as omens of exceptional prosperity and good fortune, with unusual happiness during the following year.

Among the mountains they say when a thick mist is rising, "Old Nick or Andras is boiling his supper," or "washing his feet," or "brewing," or "making his fire," or "putting out his fire." Along the coasts the mists are variously called "sea-maidens," "merry women," and "hags of the night." The mist that rises from the River Cymmal is said to be the wraith of a beautiful woman who was unfaithful to her husband, and was turned into a mist for her sin.

The morning fog is said to go a-fishing or a-hunting. When it fishes or is lowering, it is a sign of bad weather; when it hunts, or rises from the ground, it is a sign of rain.

The Welsh say when fogs come from the sea, the bees make a fine harvest; when fogs come from the hills, the corn harvest will be good and plentiful. Fog in the spring, especially during May, indicates a very warm summer.

When snow falls people say, " The old woman is feathering her geese," or " Mother Goose is moulting," or " The goose-mother is feathering her nest." If snow falls before December 25, the people in some parts of the Principality say, "Mother Christmas is feathering her flock early." If the first fall of snow comes after that date, they say, " Mother Christmas is after the fair."

It was customary between 1823 and 1830 for aged people in Wales to foretell the weather by means of the shoulder-blade of a sheep or a pig, or by the breast-bone of a cooked goose, a duck, or the merry-thought of any bird. These bones were placed in the fire for a time, and then withdrawn. If the fire left many dark marks on the blades, the coming winter would be mild; if more white streaks than dark appeared, it was a token of snow and hard frost. If the breast-bone or merry-thought of a bird turned red, a long-continued frost might be expected; but if the bone remained white and transparent, the winter would be exceptionally mild. St. Martin's Day was generally selected for this purpose. [C. D. and Family Collection.]

Before storms on the coast of Gower, in South Wales, the Lord and Lady of Rhosilly, seated in a coach drawn by four fiery and headless horses, are driven wildly along the sands near the Worm's Head.

In North Wales the warning voice of Helig is heard before boisterous weather and shipwrecks.

In Glamorgan a phantom light is seen hovering along the Sker Rocks and the Tuskar Rocks before storms.

Smoke ascends from the devil's chimneys, three in number, in Kenfig Pool, the site of a submerged township and churches in Glamorgan, before wild gales and continued wet weather. This pool or lake ebbs and flows with the sea-tides, and at

Newton Nottage, in the same district, St. John's Well is influenced in a similar manner.

In South Glamorgan the following rhyme is well known :

" When Breaksea Point doth roar and cry,
    Gileston Lane is never dry."

When ducks and geese flit to and fro restlessly, or are unusually sportive, and frequently wash themselves in ponds and pools, rain may be expected.

When fowls congregate outside the hen-house instead of going to roost, wet weather is at hand.

When guinea-fowls clamour rain may be expected.

Peacocks crying in shrill notes prophesy high winds and rain.

A severe winter is indicated by the early appearance of woodcock.

Fair weather is at hand when many quails are heard in the evening.

When rooks fly high, storm winds are following. If these birds stay at home, or return to their nests in the middle of the day, rain is coming ; but if they go far abroad, it is a token of fine, warm weather.

When thrushes sing at sunset fair weather will follow.

When three or four magpies fly together and utter harsh cries very windy weather may be expected.

Pigeons always wash much before rain, and return home slowly.

Larks flying high and singing long predict fine, warm weather.

Swallows and water-wagtails skimming the roadways predict rain. When these birds keep high in the air warm weather may be expected.

In South Wales the children say :

" Every swallow slain
    Means a month of rain."

When seagulls remain on the shore fine weather is coming, but if they fly inland storms may be expected. This applies to all kinds of sea-birds.

If wild geese leave the marshes for the sea, it is a token of very fair weather.

If a strange parson comes into the parish rain will soon follow.

A modern piece of folk-lore asserts that the " German band brings rain."

Heavy white clouds are called " chancellor's wigs " in Wales, and they indicate high winds.

If the cows and cattle lie down in the pastures rain may be expected.

Pigs carrying straws in their mouths foretoken rain. If they walk with their heads against the wind a strong gale may be expected.

When the cat washes her ears it is a sign of rain. If she turns her back to the fire a snowstorm can be expected. If the cats are frisky rain and wind are coming. If they stretch so that their paws meet it is a sign of prolonged bad weather.

When sheep are restless and crows croak more than usual, wet weather is probable.

An old verse runs thus :

> " Bwa Drindod y boran, ami gawodau ;
> Bwa Drindod prydnawn, tegwch a gawn,"

which, translated, means :

> " A rainbow in the morning
> Is the shepherd's warning ;
> A rainbow in the night
> Is the shepherd's delight."

The following weather rhyme, translated by Edward Williams, better known as Iolo Morganwg, is :

> " When the hoarse waves of Severn
> Are screaming aloud,
> And Penllyne's lofty castle's
> Involved in a cloud,
> If true the old proverb,
> A shower of rain
> Is brooding above,
> And will soon drench the plain."

If you gather pansies on a fine day rain will soon follow. Lilac blossoms bend before rain ; red sunsets bring wind ; pale sunsets promise rain.

In some parts of Wales the coast people say they see white hares before winter storms, and the howling of dogs foretokens a south-westerly gale.

If the oak-leaves appear before those of the ash, the summer will be rainy. If the ash puts forth its leaves before the oak, the ensuing summer will be very dry and warm.

Owls hooting in or very near a village prophesy snow.

When cords snap rain follows.

When the floors and stones " give," the Welsh housewife says very warm weather is coming. To " give " means to look damp.

Crows croak before windy weather.

When distant mountains look nearer than usual rain may be expected.

An old man of Porthcawl, Glamorgan, said that when wild swans and geese congregated in large numbers among the sand-dunes along the shore, unusual storms could be expected. If the swans and geese went in flocks towards the north, a hard winter would come; but when these birds kept near the shore, the next summer and autumn would bring great heat.

If the pimpernel, or " ploughman's weather-glass," closes in the daytime, it is regarded as a sign of rain. It is said in Wales that the pimpernel can forecast rain twenty-four hours in advance of a downpour.

When aspen leaves " clatter " or make a great noise, rain may be soon expected, accompanied by wind, and sometimes by a thunderstorm.

If the leaves of the horse-chestnut spread like a fan, wide and broad, fine, warm weather is coming; but long before rain the leaves begin to droop and point downward towards the earth.

Before fine, warm weather the chickweed expands its leaves, but before rain each leaf is folded.

When the down of the dandelion is fluffy, fair weather will come; but if it becomes limp and contracted, rain may be expected.

Clover-leaves fold before rain, and expand some hours before great heat.

If the cowslip stalks are short, a dry, warm summer is coming; but when they are long, a wet season may be expected.

French grass or clover is very rough to the touch before storms.

The stalk of the trefoil swells before rain.

If marigolds do not open their petals before seven in the morning, the day will bring rain before many hours pass, or a thunderstorm may be expected. These flowers always close before storms.

Sweetbriar has a fresher fragrance before rain. This is observed several hours in advance of a downpour.

Lavender and roses emit their strongest perfumes before wet weather.

A weather rhyme, translated from the Welsh, runs thus :

> " Ladybird, ladybird, tell to me
> What the weather is going to be.
> If it is to be fair,
> Fly high in the air ;
> If it is to rain,
> Fall down again."

The children say the ladybird always falls down before rain, and flies away before wet weather.

The country people say, if the blackbird and thrush sing before February they will cry before May.

If birds flock early in the autumn, a very hard winter may be expected.

If they separate early in spring and congregate again, the peasantry say, " Winter will rest on the lap of May."

When the sea sounds heavy with ground swells, or the waves murmur, or a dull, deep roar is heard around distant rocks, storms and gales may be expected.

If it rains at the flow of the tide, the next morning will be fair for haymaking ; if it rains at the ebb-tide, the next days will be wet.

Rain comes soon when fish bite readily and appear near the surface of the water. Before thunderstorms they remain in-active. When the wind is in the east, the fish bite little or not at all. This applies to trout and all other fish.

Cockles have much sand sticking to their shells before storms.

Crabs burrow in the sand before strong gales.

If eels are exceptionally lively, rain may be expected.

When dolphins or porpoises swim to windward, foul weather will come within twenty-four hours. When dolphins or por-poises are seen tumbling up and down the Bristol Channel, exceptionally favourable weather may be expected.

An old Welsh fisherman of Porthcawl, Glamorgan, said that when he was a boy the men were accustomed to set three nets in the sea, and closely watched the middle one. If into that, crabs, lobsters, and shell-fish came, bad weather and a poor season for fish would follow. If scaly fish entered the middle net, they could expect fair weather and a plentiful year.

On the extreme west and north-west coast of Wales it was customary among fishermen at the beginning of the herring season to see if the first herring on board be a male or female. If it was a male, the next season would not be lucky; if a female, the results would be very fortunate.

CHAPTER X

STONES AND CAVERNS

THE whetstone of St. Tudno, near the ancient oratory on Great Orme's Head, was included among the thirteen curiosities of the Isle of Britain. It was said that if the sword of a brave man were sharpened on it, anybody wounded thereby would surely die; but if the sword of a coward were sharpened on it, the blade would hurt, and not kill.*

Another stone on Orme's Head is known as Cryd Tudno, or Tudno's Cradle. It is supposed to have been a rocking-stone, but has long since been dismounted. People said two centuries ago that if any mothers wanted their children to learn to walk quickly, they should put their babes to crawl three times in succession once a week around the cradle of Tudno. [O. S.]

On the summit and sides of Cefn Carn Cavall, a mountain near Builth, in Breconshire, there are several carns scattered here and there. Among them is a stone resembling the impression of a dog's foot. The story connected with this is that if anybody carried the stone away for a day and a night, the next morning it would be found on the carn in the same place as usual. It is said that King Arthur, when hunting the swine named Twrch Trwyth, Cavall, his favourite dog, impressed the stone with his footprint. The warrior king collected a heap of stones together, and on the top he placed the curiously marked one, and called the mount Carn Cavall. It is still to be seen in the spot where it has stood for a thousand years or more.†

At Llandyfrydog, in Anglesea, there is a curious stone, resembling a humpbacked man. It is said that a man who had

* "The Mabinogion," p. 286 notes.   † Ibid., p. 292 notes.

stolen several valuable articles from the parish church at last desired to obtain the Bible from a cupboard under the altar, where it was kept locked up when not in use. The sacred volume was contained in a special cover made of carved wood, inset with precious stones and gold. It took the man several hours in the night to secure the Bible, and, under cover of the darkness, he ran away with it on his back. For this shameful theft he was turned into stone.*

Moelfre Hill, Carnarvonshire, has three curious stones. The story goes that three women went to the top of the hill to winnow corn on Sunday, and a neighbour rebuked them for desecrating the Lord's Day. The women laughed, and were turned into stone, which assumed the colours of the gowns they were wearing at the time. One was a dark and dull red, one was white, and the third was slate colour.†

Duffryn, near St. Nicholas, in the Vale of Glamorgan, has Druidical stones scattered about in various places. Some of these have stories attached to them. Old people in the beginning of the nineteenth century said that once a year, on Midsummer Eve, the stones in Maes-y-felin Field whirled round three times, and made curtsies ; and if anybody went to them on Hallowe'en, and whispered a wish in good faith, it would be obtained. The field in which these stones stand was unprofitable, and people said the land was under a curse. The stones in Tinkin's Wood, some distance away, but belonging to the same Druidical series, were said to be women turned into stone for dancing on Sunday. The great cromlech in the Duffryn Woods was an unlucky place to sleep in on one of the " three spirit nights," for the person who did so would die, go raving mad, or become a poet. These stones were haunted by the ghosts of Druids, who were in the habit of punishing wicked people by beating them, and were particularly hard in their treatment of drunkards. A man fond of drink slept there one night, and his experiences were terrible. He declared the Druids beat him first, and then whirled him up to the sky, from which he looked down and saw the moon and stars thousands of miles below him. The Druids held him suspended by his hair in the mid-heaven, until the first peep of day, and then let him drop down

---

* Rev. Elias Owen, " Welsh Folk-lore," p. 260.   † Ibid., p. 230.

to the Duffryn woods, where he was found in a great oak by farm-labourers.

Standing stones supposed to be of Druidical or memorial origin are seen in Glamorgan near Cottrell, the seat of Mrs. Macintosh, wife of the Macintosh of Macintosh. The story about these stones is that some women had sworn falsely against an innocent man, who was put to death on the gallows on Bryn Owen Mountain, subsequently known as the Stallingdown. These women were turned into stones on their way home. [*A. B. and O. S.*]

The Sogranus Stone at St. Dogmell's, Pembrokeshire, was formerly used as a bridge. On the " three spirit nights " it was frequented by the devil, and at midnight in winter a white lady haunted it.*

On a certain day in the year the dancing-stones of Stackpool were said to meet and come down to Sais's Ford to dance. If anybody witnessed this performance, it meant exceptional good luck to him. The witches held their revels and the devil played the flute occasionally around the dancing-stones.*

Carreg y Lleidr, near Llandyfrydog, Anglesea, has the Robber's Stone. A man once stole the church bells, and was turned into stone for his theft.*

Three gigantic stones, called Tre Greienyn, are to be seen standing at the foot of Cader Idris. An old tradition says that these stones were three grains of sand which the gigantic astronomer Idris Gawr shook out of his shoes before he ascended to his stone chair or observatory on the top of the mountain. On the summit of Cader Idris there is an excavation in the solid rock which resembles a couch or seat. It is said that if anybody remained in the seat of Idris for a night, he would be found in the morning either dead, raving mad, or endowed with remarkable genius. Mysterious lights are, it is said, to be seen on Cader Idris on the first night of each New Year.†

About a mile from Cynwyl Gaio there is a boulder which has fallen from the mountain. On this stone St. Cynwal once stood in ecstasy of thanksgiving and prayer. The river flowing below has worn hollows in the rock, and these are popularly

* William Howell, " Cambrian Superstitions," pp. 127, 128, 129.
† " Welsh Sketches," p. 15 (*Cambro-Briton*, 1821).

supposed to have been made by the saint when he knelt by the stream.   Within the memory of old inhabitants the neighbourhood farmers used to lead their cattle there, lift the water from the hollows, and pour it over the animals to insure their good health and immunity from any epidemic during the ensuing twelve months. [O. S.]

The Goblin Stone of Cynwyl Gaio occupied a spot which few people cared to pass at night.   In the seventeenth century a young man who had gone far in search of work came in the twilight to a large stone surrounded with grass.   The place looked tempting for a night's resting-place.   After making a good but simple supper, the traveller placed his bundle containing clothes on the grass in shelter of the stone.   For a time he slept soundly, but about midnight he was awakened by somebody pinching his arms and ears and pricking his nose.   He got up, and, looking around in the starlight, saw a goblin sitting on the stone, with many others around him.   The man tried to run away, but the master goblin would not permit him, and at his command his minions interlaced their grotesque arms around him and prevented him moving.   They tweaked his ears and nose, pinched him, gave him pokes in his ribs, and tormented him all through the night in every conceivable manner.   He sat down to rest and wait for the dawn, and in the meantime the goblins screamed and laughed and shrieked in his ears until he was nearly mad.   When the first streak of morning light appeared, the goblins vanished.   The stranger got up in the dawn, and when he went onward he met some workmen, to whom he related his adventure.   They said he had slept under the Goblin Stone. [O. S. and C. D.]

At Trelyfan, in Pembrokeshire, is St. Brynach's Stone.   It is the shaft of a cross about ten feet high, with interlaced ornamentation.   Pembrokeshire people say that the cuckoo sounds its first note when perched there on April 7, the day of St. Brynach.   George Owen, in his " Description of Pembrokeshire," says : " The parish priest of this church would not begin Mass till this bird, called the ' citizens' Ambassador,' had first appeared, and began his note on a stone called St. Brynach's Stone, standing upright in the churchyard. . . .   One year, staying away very long, and the people expecting the cuckoo, the bird came at last, and, lighting on the said stone, its accustomed preaching-place, and being scarce able to once sound his note, presently fell dead."

A stone in Llowes Churchyard, in Radnorshire, has a story attached to it. Maud of Hay, the wife of William de Breos or Bruce, Lord of Brecknock and Abergavenny, was the daughter of Fitz-Walter, Earl of Hereford. The story goes that she built the castle of Hay in Breconshire in a single night, and without assistance. Owing to her occult powers, gigantic stature, and mysterious deeds, people thought she could accomplish any feat, however difficult. In the folk-tales and nursery stories of Wales she is known as Mol Walbee, a corruption of her father's surname, Waleri. While carrying stones in her apron for the purpose of building Hay Castle, a " pebble " of about nine feet long fell into her shoe. At first she did not heed the discomfort, but by-and-by, finding it troublesome, she indignantly threw it over the Wye into Llowes Churchyard, in Radnorshire, about three miles away. It remains there at present.*

Another time, when she was busy with incantations at midnight, she was interrupted by a monk, who besought her to cease her unholy work. Mol Walbee caught him up in her arms, and ran to the banks of the Wye, wherefrom she threw him into the middle of the river ; and as the man could not swim, he was borne away down the river and drowned. People used to say that at midnight a wailing was heard on the Wye, and a gurgling sound followed it. These were attributed to the struggles of Mol Walbee's victim. [O. S.]

The fate of Mol Walbee used to be recited in the nurseries and by the firesides of Wales. During the feuds between King John and her husband, Maud of Hay presented his Queen with four hundred kine and a bull, all milk-white with pink ears. When her husband failed to make good his payments for Munster and Limerick, John wanted her children as hostages. She promptly said she could not and would not trust her offspring to a man who had murdered his own nephew. John then forcibly gained possession of Maud and her children, but ultimately accepted a ransom. Several times she broke

* Hoare, " Giraldus," vol. i., p. 91.

her bargain with the King. In the meantime her husband had made good his escape into France. By-and-by John again captured Maud and her children, and they were imprisoned in Bristol, from whence they were taken to Windsor. There a few small rooms isolated from the other part of the castle were placed for their use. The sad story goes that hundreds of masons were employed to build around her apartments, and rapidly a tower was in formation. Maud's incantations and spells were unavailing against the masonry, and her gigantic powers were no good.

Higher and higher rose the tower, and when the pangs of hunger attacked the pitiful and spirited woman and her children, she cried and stormed, and besought the King for mercy. But he would not listen. Maud and her children were actually buried alive in the tower.*

Lechlaver, the " talking-stone " of St. David's, was a marble slab where the bridge over the brook now stands. Once, when a corpse was carried over it, the stone broke into speech, and cracked the coffin.

Not far from Aber, and about two miles and a half from Llanfairfechan, in one of the wildest and most lonely valleys in North Wales, is the celebrated Arrow Stone, upon which the chieftains of old sharpened their battle-axes and other implements of war. Labourers going home from field work and people living near the valley declared that if ever the sound of any instrument being sharpened upon the stone reached them, it was an omen of bad luck to the hearer, and foretokened an epidemic in the country, or some disaster in Wales.

Arthur's Stone, in Gower, is in a solitary spot, from which a fine view of land and sea can be obtained. It is said that when King Arthur was on his way to the Battle of Camlan, he felt a pebble in his shoe. As it lamed him, he took off his shoe and flung the pebble as far as he could, and it fell on Cefn-y-Bryn, exactly on the stone where it is still seen, and quite seven miles from the spot where King Arthur stood.†
At midnight and full moon maidens from Swansea and district used to deposit on the stone a cake made of barley-meal

* Rees, " South Wales," pp. 25-30.
† William Howell, " Cambrian Superstitions," p. 101.

and honey wetted with milk and well kneaded. Then, on
hands and knees, the girls had to crawl three times around the
stone. This was done to test the fidelity of their lovers. If
the young men were faithful to their sweethearts, they would
make their appearance. If they did not come, the girls regarded it as a token of their fickleness, or intention never to
marry them.

Beneath this stone is a spring which is said to flow with the
ebb and flow of the tide. It is called Ffynon Fair, or Our
Lady's Well. The water therefrom was lifted in the palm
of the hand while the person who drank it wished. This is
situated on Cefn-y-Bryn, near Reynoldstone, Gower.

Arthur's Quoit, at Lligwy, near Moelfre, in Anglesea, is one
of the stones of a cromlech once very important, and to it
curious stories were formerly attached. A fisherman going
down to the sea was overtaken by a storm, and halted to shelter
beside Arthur's Quoit. When the rain was over, he looked
towards the sea, and felt sure that somebody was struggling
in the water. He hastened to the shore, and then discovered
that a woman with very long dark hair was endeavouring to
swim to land ; but the ground swell was very strong, and each
attempt proved unavailing. The fisherman, fearless of the
sea, sprang in, and bore the swimmer to the shore, only just
to escape a dangerous roller. The man observed that the
woman was beautifully robed in white, and had jewelled
bracelets on her arms. After squeezing the water out of her
garments, she asked him to assist her to the " huge stone,"
meaning Arthur's Quoit. He did so, and while she sat to rest
against the stone, he noticed that she was very beautiful and
youthful. The man was about to ask her how she came to
be in such peril, but she anticipated his question with a harsh
voice, by no means in keeping with her beauty. " Ha, ha !"
she cried. " If I had been swimming in my usual raiment,
you would have allowed me to sink. I am a witch, and was
thrown off a ship in Lligwy Bay ; but I disguised myself,
and was rescued." The man shrank back in terror, fearing
the woman would bewitch him. " Don't be frightened," said
the witch ; " one good turn deserves another. Here, take
this." In the palm of her hand she held a small ball.

" It is for you," she said, " and as long as you keep it concealed in a secret place where nobody can find it, good luck will be yours.   Once a year you must take it out of hiding and dip it in the sea, then safely return it to its place of concealment. But remember, if it is lost, misfortune will follow."   The fisherman took the ball and thanked the witch, who gravely said : " That ball contains a snake-skin."   Then she vanished mysteriously.   But an hour later he saw her leaping from rock to rock in Lligwy Bay, where a boat was waiting for her, and in it she sailed away.   Returning to Arthur's Quoit, the fisherman thought he could do no better than conceal the ball in a deep hole which he dug close beside the great stone which was reputed to be haunted, and accordingly avoided.   He did this, and once a year he took it from concealment and dipped it in the sea.   The ball was carefully preserved, and the family had remarkable runs of luck.   But one evening when the fisherman went to look for the ball, it was nowhere to be found.   He searched for many days, but without avail, and at last gave up his search as hopeless.   Somebody evidently discovered his secret, and had stolen the precious ball.   Seven years passed, during which time misfortune pursued the fisherman.   At the end of that period a dying neighbour confessed to the theft of the ball, and restored it to its lawful owner. Good luck was at once restored to the family.   When the fisherman died, he bequeathed it to his eldest son, who carefully preserved it.   In the first half of the nineteenth century the fisherman's eldest son, accompanied by his only brother, started for Australia, where they eventually made large fortunes.   A descendant in the female line of the old fisherman considered the ball one of her most precious treasures, and carefully preserved it in her far-away home in India.   It was last heard of about forty years ago.   [A. B. and O. S.]

In the parish church of Llantwit Major, Glamorgan, there is a peculiar stone.   It was formerly part of a shrine of the Madonna, and has recently been replaced in its original position at the base of a very beautiful niche in the church, representing a finely carved Jesse-tree.   When this stone was embedded in the wall of the ruined Lady Chapel, a folk-story was attached to it.   People said the recumbent figure was that of a woman who had swallowed a cherry-stone, and after her death a tree grew out of her body, and formed branches. Children always pointed out this stone to their friends from a distance, saying it was the wonderful woman who once had a tree growing out of her body.

The Druids' Circle, which is about a mile distant from the Green Gorge on Penmaenmawr, contains two stones among other Druidical remains. The Deity Stone was formerly held in considerable awe. An old story told by a North Welshman was to the effect that if anybody used profane language near it, the stone would bend its head and smite the offending person. A man from South Wales played cards with some friends beside this stone on a Sunday, and when the men returned to the village with cuts about their heads, the people knew the Deity Stone had smitten them, though they would not admit having had punishment. A notorious blasphemer who came from Merionethshire laughed to scorn the story of this stone. One night he went to the Druids' Circle alone and at a very late hour, and shouted words of blasphemy so loud that his voice could be heard ringing down the Green Gorge. People shuddered as they heard him. The sounds ceased, and the listeners ran away in sheer fright. In the morning the blasphemer's corpse was found in a terribly battered condition at the base of the Deity Stone. [*A. B. and Family Collection.*]

Immediately opposite the last-named relic is the Stone of Sacrifice, on the top of which there is a cavity large enough to hold a full-grown child. There was an old belief that an infant placed in this cavity for a few minutes during the first month of its life would be lucky. Rain-water conveyed from the cavity was proof against witches if sprinkled on the threshold. Sometimes terrible cries were heard issuing from the Stone of Sacrifice, and frequently moanings, sobbings, and wailings sounded above the wind on stormy nights. It was stated that the witches once held a revel outside the Druidical circle, and when the orgies were at their height, stern maledictions were heard coming from this stone, and so frightened were the weird women that two of them died suddenly, and one went raving mad. [*A. B.*]

Marcross, in the Vale of Glamorgan, had a stone about which

the old people told more than one story.   In the eighteenth
century they said that once a year a stranger used to be seen
near the stone.   Nobody knew from whence he came nor
whither he went.   One night a villager who had long made
up his mind to accost the stranger did so.   " In the name of
God, what do you want ?" asked the villager.   Then, in low,
grave tones the stranger said : " Since you ask me in God's
name, I will tell you what I want.   I am looking for the bones
of my brother, and cannot rest until they are found.   But
I am a spirit, and I cannot dig.   Will you help me ?"   The
villager said he would.   Silently he went for a pick and shovel,
and was told to dig beside the stone.   This he did carefully
in the summer night, when everybody was in bed and asleep.
After some hard work the man came upon human remains,
which were closely examined by the stranger, who said :
" Thank God !   They are his !"   He then asked the villager
to go with him and bury them in the parish churchyard.   The
man did so, and when all was over the stranger said : " He was
a good man and brave, and fought valiantly for his Queen and
country against the Spanish Armada !"   Then he disappeared,
never to return.   In the morning the stone had fallen.   There
is a local tradition to the effect that portions of the woodwork
in Marcross Church are remains of one of the ships of the Great
Armada which was wrecked under Nash Point.   [C. D. and
Family Collection.]

In Donovan's " Descriptive Excursions in South Wales,"
1805, an account is given of a very curious stone.   On the eve
of Corpus Christi Donovan saw a man lying bare on Sir John
Colmer's gravestone at Christ Church, Caerleon.   This stone
was supposed to perform miraculous cures.   People witnessed
this scene.   The man passed the night of Wednesday and
Thursday after Trinity Sunday on the stone, and when he got
up he was cured.

Near Dolacauthi,the seat of Sir James and Lady Hills-Johnes,
in Carmarthenshire, there is a hill-top which is supposed to
have been scooped out by the Romans in search for gold.   Into
this cavernous place there are tunnels, which were evidently
" bored at a very remote period."   In one of these, five saints
are said to sleep.   They are known as the Five Sleepers.

These were the five sons born at one birth of Cynyr Fârfdrwch, and brother of Cai, who was sewer to King Arthur. Their great-uncle was Caswallon Lawhir, who drove the Irish out of Mona. In a storm of thunder and lightning the five brothers took refuge in this spot. They laid their heads on a stone pillar and fell asleep. It is said that they will not awake from their sleep until King Arthur reappears, or a genuine and faithful apostolic bishop occupies the throne of St. David. Old inhabitants of the neighbourhood used to assert that the five brothers have worn the stone into hollows with the pressure of their heads, and they have turned it three times, so that each side is marked by depressions. The first pillow they used was cast away, and it was set up near a great tumulus at the entrance to the mines, which is close to the grounds of Dolacauthi. Then the sleepers took up a new stone pillow. The hollows in the stone are mortars in which the quartz was ground by the Romans to obtain the particles of gold. Gwen of Dolacauthi, led by the devil, paid a visit to the five sleepers. But, like the uninvited guest, she was not welcomed. The sleepers punished her by keeping her imprisoned for ever in the cave. But they still allow her out when storm winds and rain are abroad; then her vaporous form may be seen sailing around the old gold-mine. Her sobs and moans are heard far and near, , and when the storm passes she has to return to the Five Sleepers. [O. S.]

The story of Craig-y-Dinas, in the Vale of Neath, is well known. A version of it appears in " Glimpses of Welsh Life and Character," published by Mr. John Hogg, London. A Welsh drover accustomed to attend Barnet Fair stood to rest on London Bridge. He leaned on his strong hazel-stick, similar to those used by drovers in the present day. He was very tired after the long march from Wales, and presently left the bridge for an eating-house on the other side of the Thames. There he was joined by a queer-looking stranger, who asked where he got his stick. The drover replied that it grew near his home. The stranger then said the stick must have grown on a spot where treasures of metal, gold, and silver could be found. He offered to make the drover the master of much treasure if he would take him to the spot where the stick grew. To this the Welshman agreed, and the next morning they started for Wales. In the morning after their arrival at the drover's home the stranger accompanied his host to the grassy hollow where the hazel grew from which the long stick had been cut. The stranger then said that in a dream he had seen the hollow before, and directed the drover to get a spade and pick, and dig as he directed. The Welshman at once began to dig up the roots of the hazel, and after digging for some time the men discovered a very broad and flat stone. Underneath the stone there was a flight of broken steps, where the men descended, and soon reached a long corridor, from the roof of which a huge bell was suspended. The stranger warned the drover never to touch the bell, for the consequences would be dreadful. Then they went on until a vast cavern was reached. It was filled with warriors in shining armour, with shields beside them and swords unsheathed. In the midst of these warriors a circle of twelve knights surrounded a King, and all the men were asleep. The stranger told the drover that these warriors were King Arthur and his knights and squires. They were waiting there until the Black Eagle and the Golden Eagle should go to war. The clamour of the eagle warfare would make the earth tremble, and cause the bell to ring so loudly that the warriors would awaken, and go forth with King Arthur to destroy all the enemies of the Cymry, and establish the King's rule again in Britain. But terrible would be the results if a false alarm ever rang. In the midst of the space where the King slept were several heaps of gold, silver, and precious stones. The stranger told the drover that he was at liberty to take as much as he could carry from one heap at a time, but the precious metals and stones were not to be mixed.

The drover did as he was bidden, and when the stranger ascended, he said : " Beware you never touch the bell. But if by·chance you do, one of the sleepers will lift his head, and ask, ' Is it day ?' and in peril of your life you must answer, ' It is not day ; sleep thou on.' "

The stranger went away, and the drover never saw him again.

Many times in the next few years the drover visited the cavern and brought away treasure, so that he became ex-

ceedingly rich.   Twice he chanced to touch the magic bell, and
one of the warriors on each occasion asked " Is it day ?" and
the drover answered, " It is not day ; sleep thou on."   One day
he eagerly endeàvoured to carry away a larger quantity of
treasure than usual, and accidentally touched the bell.   One of
the warriors cried out, " Is it day ?"   Too excited in his greed
for gain, the drover forgot to reply, whereupon, quick and
angrily, the warriors took the treasure away from the man.
Then they dragged and beat him, and finally threw him out
of the cavern, triumphantly drawing the stone over the
entrance.   The drover never recovered from the effects of the
beating, and although he often went to Craig-y-Dinas to search
for the spot where the stone covered the entrance to the cavern,
he never found it.

In a cavern near Carrig Cennin Castle, Carmarthenshire, Sir
John Goch, known also as Owen the Red Hand, is doomed to
sleep for a thousand years.   He has fifty-one comrades with
him, and when he awakens there will be peace all over the
world.*

A similar story is told of Owen of Cymru (Owen de Galles).
This hero is not dead, but sleeps in a cavern far from his native
land, on the banks of the Gironde.   There he will remain with
his captains and soldiers around him, waiting until a great bell
shall ring to summon him to fight again for the honour of
Wales.†

Owen Glyndwr is supposed to be sleeping in a great cavern,
with all his men in armour, their spears resting against their
shoulders, and their swords close at hand.   There they wait
until the bell rings that shall call them out to march forth and
fight for the needs of their native land.

Merlin's Cave is in Merlin's Hill, above the secluded village
of Abergwilli, near Carmarthen.   Old stories state that Merlin
is held there in bonds of enchantment by Nimue-Vivien, and
it was firmly believed in the eighteenth century that the celebrated magician could be heard at certain seasons of the year
bewailing his folly in allowing a woman to learn his secret spell.

In Carmarthen, where the magician was born, Merlin's Tree

* William Howell, " Cambrian Superstitions," pp. 104, 105.
† Froissart.

stood. It was struck by lightning many years ago, and very soon withered. An old Welsh folk-rhyme runs as follows :

> " When Merlin's Tree shall tumble down,
> Woe shall betide Carmarthen town !"

Among the mountains called The Rivals in North Wales is the beetling and furrowed Craig Ddu, with its almost black rocky surface and inaccessible sides rising sheer against the sky. In the eighteenth century people said that the apparition of an old man with long white hair and flowing beard used formerly to be seen wandering down the valley, and pausing to mutter unknown words beside the Craig Ddu. Sounds of strange music were heard, and magic signs were made by the old man. If anybody fell asleep in the shadow of Craig Ddu he would sleep for ever, and be carried away by unseen hands, so that his resting-place could not be known. [A. B.]

Tresillian Cave is a short distance to the east of St. Donat's, Glamorgan, and was once the scene of a romantic wedding.

Cecil Powel, heiress of Llandow, was a high-spirited girl with many admirers. Among them was Thomas Picton, of Poyston, Pembrokeshire, who was determined, if possible, to win the wilful damsel. At last she consented to be married in the cave. She cleverly arranged a bogus ceremony to defeat the bridegroom, and dissolve the marriage as soon as the fun was over. A masked man did duty as a clergyman, and although the wedding party numbered many friends of the bridegroom, the wilful bride gaily pronounced the ceremony to be invalid. Whereupon the bridegroom produced the special licence, and the officiating clergyman removed his mask, revealing the features of the Rev. Edward Powel, Rector of Llandow, and father of the bride, who had bribed the hired man to let him take his place. This bride and bridegroom's wedded life proved, contrary to expectations, to be exceedingly happy. Thomas Picton and his beautiful wife Cecil became the father and mother of General Sir Thomas Picton, one of the most renowned of the British officers in the Peninsular War. He fought and fell at Quatre-Bras.

At the mouth of this cavern it is said that one Peter the Pirate, who had been a terror to the country-side, was buried in the long ago. The people bound him hands and feet, and buried him alive in a deep grave of sand, on which they piled rocks and stones. It was formerly asserted that if you listened on New Year's Eve you could hear Peter the Pirate raving for freedom, and sometimes when high tides filled the cave he might be heard moaning and groaning. This used to be told by the old people who cherished the folk-stories of the neighbourhood.

This cavern bears the name of the early British Christian who was slain by the pagans : Tre—the home of Sillian ; hence Tresillian. In former times there was an ancient chapelry near this spot.

There is a cave or underground passage leading from Morda to Chirk Castle, North Wales. If anybody went near the entrance of this cavern, he would be mysteriously drawn in and never seen again. People were afraid of it, and in the course of time the entrance became overgrown with briars and brambles and tall rank grasses. A fox once tried to hide there, but became so greatly alarmed by what he saw that his hair stood on end, and he ran wildly into the middle of the pack of hounds, not one of which would touch him because he smelt so strongly of brimstone !

Iolo ap Hugh, a merry wandering minstrel, was determined to solve the mystery of the cave. On Hallowe'en, one of the " three spirit nights," Iolo provided himself with a basket of provisions, including a good supply of bread and cheese, seven pounds of candles, and his beloved fiddle. People advised him not to go, but away he went. Like the fox, poor Iolo was drawn into the cave by mysterious hands, and never was seen again. For many weeks people smelt " brimstone," and some said that " the devil was having a fine feast over poor Iolo ap Hugh !"

Long years afterwards, on Hallowe'en, a shepherd, hurrying . past the mouth of the cave, suddenly heard a burst of wild music. He looked towards the cave, and who should he see but Iolo ap Hugh, in body as young as ever, fiddling and capering in fantastic fashion to the tune of his own fiddle. But his head was quite loose, as if it would fall off, and his face wore an expression of indescribable agony. A lighted lantern suspended by a rope hung between his shoulders, and the head and horns of a goat were fastened upon his breast, and all the time he danced right merrily. The shepherd gazed for some time, fascinated by the music, until at length the fiddler was drawn back by some mysterious power into the cave. Two years later the shepherd went to church early on Christmas morning when the clerk was lighting the candles. He heard strange sounds of music passing through the church. It seemed as if the melody ascended from under the flooring or from a crypt, and passed on and out into the snowy air, then soaring sweetly upward. The shepherd recognized the melody as that played by Iolo ap Hugh when he revisited the earth after his absence in the under-world. He was able to whistle the tune to the vicar, who transposed it into music. Iolo never returned, but his melody lives in the well-known Welsh air entitled " Ffarwel Ned Pugh."*

Another version of the story contains the additional information that the fiddle of Ned Pugh became a bugle, and the musician undertook the duties of chief huntsman to Gwyn ap Nudd. In this tale he is described as wandering every Hallowe'en and other spirit nights in many places. Sometimes he is below Plinlimmon, occasionally among the Black Mountains, and there was a story about him among the wild places around Aberdare. There he is heard cheering the Cwn Annwn, blowing his bugle, and shouting as he goes. [C. D. and Family Collection.]

Similar stories are told of other caverns. The Black Cave of Cricceth is supposed to conceal musicians who entered and lost their way back. They played on certain nights, and the people heard them. At Braich-y-Bidi and Braich-y-Cornor the mysterious pipers and horn-blowers send forth wild music into the night. The tunes they play are known as " Ffarwel Dic-y-Pibyd " (Dick the Piper's Farewell) and " Ffarwel Dwm Bach " (Little Tom's Farewell).*

* Cambrian Quarterly, 1829, vol. i. ; Rhŷs, " Celtic Folk-lore," pp. 210, 211.

CHAPTER XI

SECRET HOARDS AND TREASURE

CASTELL COCH, or the Red Castle, has many stories attached to it. In the twelfth century it was the stronghold of Ivor the Little, Lord of Morlais, who boasted that his twelve hundred men were capable of defeating any twelve thousand in the then known world.

Robert of Gloucester, keeping a keen eye upon Robert of Normandy, at that time occupied Cardiff Castle. The descent of Ivor the Little upon Cardiff, and the capture of the Earl of Gloucester, are matters of history.

In the traditionary lore connected with the castle is the story of the great eagles placed there, it is said, by Ivor the Little, to protect a huge iron chest filled with treasure, including precious stones.

The old story goes that down in a deep subterranean vault at the head of a passage leading to Cardiff Castle, several miles away, there is a vast cavern, containing the iron chest of Ivor the Little. To this chest three huge eagles are chained, but with sufficient length of links to permit the gigantic birds to seek relaxation by returning as far as the vault outside the cave. These fierce birds are described as having dark grey plumage. Their eyes are large and brilliantly red, with a light that flashes like fiendish lightning through the gloom of the cavern. In certain seasons of the year, chiefly between October and March, these birds make fearful commotion in their retreat. They scream and shriek, causing terror to the dwellers in the country-side around the castle. In ages gone by men sought to destroy the eagles, but failed. During the seventeenth century a search-party, armed from head to feet, explored the vault and cavern, but were beaten by the birds, and gladly made their escape. Another party took the precaution to have their weapons blessed by a priest, while a more devout company sought the aid of a holy friar who had never tasted wine or strong drink; but they were treated in the same ferocious manner as former explorers.

In the eighteenth century a party of brave and fearless men, who had seen active service abroad, started on an expedition to the cavern. They were armed with pistols and cutlasses; but although they fired and slashed away for hours, the eagles with the great red eyes beat the men unmercifully, so that they were glad to retreat. And as the men left the gloomy vault, the eagles screamed in exultation, while the flapping of their wings sounded like distant thunder.

It was said that those who cared to seek might find the chained eagles of Ivor the Little guarding the huge iron chest in the cavern of the Red Castle, but to this day human power has been unable to dislodge them. A century ago aged people declared that their forefathers believed the three gigantic eagles intended guarding their chieftain's treasure until Ivor the Little could come back to his own again, with his brave twelve hundred men of Glamorgan.

These gigantic eagles appear in another story connected with Castell Coch.

Early in the eighteenth century an aged gamekeeper and his wife occupied a few rooms in the castle. At first they found the place very quiet and peaceful, but afterwards they were disturbed by strange noises and unearthly sounds, which they attributed to rats and night birds. Last of all they heard whisperings and mutterings in the night. The woman was disturbed in her sleep by a curious tapping. She quickly looked around, and saw, not far from her bedside, a venerable gentleman in a full dress suit of Charles I.'s reign. His face was deadly pale, and his countenance looked worn with sorrow. He retreated to the door and appeared to be lost in shadows. When the woman went to the door she found it locked. She did not tell her husband, but later on, when relating their experiences, the latter said he had frequently seen the apparition of the old gentleman in the turret garden and elsewhere.

There is a tradition of a Royalist who secreted plate, jewels, and money in an iron chest somewhere in Castell Coch. He was killed in the Civil Wars, but his spirit form wandered to the spot where the treasure was deposited. People searched for the Royalist's precious hoard, but were beaten back by the three gigantic eagles of Castell Coch. [*O. S. and C. D.*]

The River Ogmore appears to have been a favourite depository of all kinds of treasure. In the folk-stories of the Vale of Glamorgan it is recorded that hoarders of money, or people who secreted any precious stones or metals, even if only a piece of old iron, never rest if they die while the treasure remains hidden. In order to give the spirit rest, the treasure must be taken by a " living human hand " and thrown into the River Ogmore " with the stream." If thrown against it, the unfortunate person would be terribly tormented ever after.

It is strange, but true, that the other rivers and streams of the Vale were never to be recipients of treasure, which must be thrown into the Ogmore, and that only. The following stories out of several of the kind indicate the popularity of the Ogmore.

Barbara,* the wife of Edward, the tailor of Llantwit Major, was a hale and hearty woman, until a secret pressed sorely upon her mind. For a long time after her husband's mother's death she kept as a profound secret the fact that the old woman had entrusted her with a bag of money, which was to be divided equally between several members of the family. Barbara decided to keep this for her own use. But the spirit of Mollans, as the old woman was called, would not give her peace. By-and-by Barbara became very miserable and emaciated, and seemed to be gradually pining away. For the spirit teased and pinched her in the night, and would not allow her to sleep because she persistently refused to take the hoard and honestly divide it, or throw it into the Ogmore. Barbara selfishly consented to the latter course. The spirit then led her out of the house, and wafted her so high in the air that she saw the church loft and all the houses far below her. In her flurry she threw the bag of money up the stream, instead of down with it, whereupon the spirit, in a great rage, and with a savage

* " The Vale of Glamorgan," p. 300.

look, tossed her into a whirlwind. One evening the bellringers found her in a sad plight and in a fainting condition near the church lane. She was wet and bedraggled, and her hair was filled with sand. The whirlwind bewildered her so much that she could not remember how or when she came home. From the moment after her return Barbara never had peace. Her husband, a very good and truthful man, declared that supernatural noises and knockings were always heard in the house, and the garden was haunted because of Barbara's folly. People are living to-day who said Barbara's children were " ghost-walked," or ghost-ridden. [*Family Collection.*]

An aged woman still living says that Barbara invariably refused to open the door when, as she said, the spirit of her mother-in-law knocked. But the spirit assumed the shape of a crow, and entered by means of an open window or down the chimney. When my informant was about ten years of age, she remembered being in Barbara's house when a crow chanced to fly in through the window. Barbara screamed with terror while the crow flapped its wings around her head and beat her unmercifully. Neighbours, hearing the commotion, entered from the back of the house and offered to kill the bird, but Barbara said : " Don't, don't ! if you kill the crow you'll kill my mother-in-law, and I shall go to perdition." When the front-door was opened the crow flew out.

The following story was given me by the grand-daughter, still living, of one who took part in the religious service held in the miser's house in St. Donat's, Glamorgan.

A middle-aged woman, who for many years had been housekeeper to a " money-hoarder," could not have peace or rest after the man's death. She appealed to the Wesleyan Methodists, asking them to hold a prayer-meeting in the house. In the midst of a fervent prayer the woman cried out : " There he is ! There he is !" The people stared, but saw nothing. They told the woman to ask in the Holy Name what the spirit wanted. She did so, but they could not hear any response. Then they heard the woman asking : " Where is it ?" She immediately went to the fireplace, stretched her arm up the chimney, and brought down from a secret nook what appeared to be a bag of money. The woman then turned quickly round, and cried : " Let me go ! Let me go !" She slipped out of the house " in a twinkling." Young men, following her, saw her leaping over the stile in the moonlight, and whisking rapidly away out of sight. Later on the woman returned, tired and bespattered with wet sand. She said the spirit carried her to the Ogmore River, and held her in mid-air over it, until she had thrown the bag of money with the stream. He then whisked her home again.

In a pasture-field near the ruins of a very ancient house at Brincethin, Glamorgan, there was a well of clear spring water. A girl going to this spot was suddenly surrounded by forked lightning, which made her run home terrified. Next evening the same thing happened. This time the girl looked across the well, and among the wild-rose bushes she saw a lady dressed in a curiously antique costume with high-heeled " peaked shoes " and immense silver buckles. The girl mustered up courage to address the spirit in the holy name, and ask what was desired. The lady then told her to remove a hoard of money and precious stones contained in a bag that was concealed under the hearthstone of a ruined house near at hand. The girl told her friends of this, and they helped her to find the treasure. The lady requested the girl to throw the bag into the River Ogmore. It was to be sent with the stream, and not against it. She did so, and never afterwards saw the lady.

An old inhabitant of Newton Nottage, near Porthcawl, said that when he was a boy he remembered people talking about a tall man dressed in a costume of a century or more previously. For some time this figure was seen pointing to one of the sand-hills that abound in this district. After several months had passed, one of the inhabitants of the village ventured to address the stranger in the Holy Name, and asked what he wanted. The man then desired the person who accosted him to dig into one of the mounds close by, where gold and jewels would be found. When the treasure was discovered, it was to be taken to the Ogmore River, and thrown with the stream. This was done, and the apparition never again appeared.

Where the Rivers Rhondda and Taff meet and mingle their waters at Pontypridd, there is a spot which in the days of old was much frequented by treasure-throwers from various parts of the district. These people were bidden by supernatural strangers to dig for, and carry, hoards from the Rhondda and Taff Valleys to the confluence of the rivers. When swollen by heavy rain the waters here form a strong current. A woman from Hafod and a man from Treforest, who had been borne through the air by some unseen power, hesitated when they reached the wild waters. For this they were badly beaten in the night, and in the morning when they tried to throw the treasure with the stream, the current carried it backward. For this they were thrown into the water and swept away. Nothing more was heard of them for two days, and then they were discovered in a bedraggled condition some miles lower down the River Taff. Their treasure had followed them, and they were fortunate enough to seize the bags, which they threw downstream in the orthodox manner. [*O. S.*]

There are many stories connected with secret hoards thrown with or against the stream, but, for some unaccountable reason, South Wales holds the majority.

The following story is told in connection with an old Glamorgan family, and the origin of their wealth : Centuries ago a young girl was engaged as a servant to the wife of a farmer. She had not been there very long before she begged to be released from her situation. When asked the reason, she said that if she went alone through a lane near at hand, she always met a strange man. If she changed her route the stranger did the same, and he always followed her when the night was dull or dark, never in the moonlight. This reached the master's ears, and he advised the girl that if she met him again to ask the stranger what he wanted. The girl summoned up courage to do so, and in response he beckoned her to a small field not far from the house. He requested her to come the next night, and bring a spade with her, but she was not to tell anybody a word about it. The girl obeyed, and the stranger pointed to a spot in a corner of the field. He told her to dig. She did so, and found a pot containing a large number of gold coins. The stranger told her that so long as she kept seven of the coins and handed them down to posterity, there would be good luck in her family.

Soon after her find, her former mistress died, and a year later the owner of the farm married her. When she had been married a few weeks, the stranger appeared to her for the last time. He directed her to be very careful in handing the seven coins down to the future generations, from father to son, or mother to daughter, as the case might be. If this was done the farm would always remain in possession of her descendants. If she or any of her descendants lost the coins, or any portion of them, the property would also be lost, or parts of it, in proportion to the number of the missing coins. This was done, and the owners of the farm became more wealthy as the generations passed. In the course of time the people bought a large estate near the farm, and became important land-owners. Eventually succeeding generations were careless, and lost some of the coins. Part of the lands were then sold to pay the debts of a spendthrift owner, who afterwards gambled away his fortune. His son kept two of the coins, and in manhood went to America, where he accumulated a large fortune. His descendants had great pleasure in visiting the old farm in Glamorgan, associated with the origin of their wealth. [*A. B. and Family Collection.*]

A similar story is told of a Pembrokeshire county family; but they kept their coins and retained the estates, and became more wealthy as the generations passed.

In a village near Cowbridge, in the Vale of Glamorgan, a middle-aged bachelor and his two sisters lived. The eldest sister one night heard a voice calling her from under the bedroom window, but she did not answer it. Twice in succession this happened, and she told her brother and sister about it. They advised her to answer the voice if it called again. The third night another call came. She went to the lattice, opened it and looked out, but not a person was visible. " What dost thou want ?" she asked ; and the voice answered : " Go down to the second arch of the gateway leading into St. Quintin's Castle, Llanblethian, and there dig. Thou wilt find buried in a deep hole close to the inner arch a crock full of gold pieces. It's of no use to me now. Take it, and may the gold be a blessing to thee." The brother and sisters dug, and with very little trouble found the treasure. People said it was a large sum of money. [*Family Collection.*]

10—2

Effy'r Gwecrydd, whose proper name was Elspeth John, was born about the year 1795, and when between ten and fourteen she entered the service of a farmer at Prisk, near Cowbridge, in the Vale of Glamorgan.   While there, and when well on in her teens, a shadowy figure of a man dressed in dark clothes repeatedly met her.   This blurred-looking personage at first merely gazed steadfastly at her, and she paid little heed to it, but later on she was vexed and tormented by it.   As time passed, and she could not get any rest from mysterious pinch-ings and other molestations, the girl became very sad, and her master and mistress, who were kindly and godly people, begged her to tell them if she had any trouble on her mind.   She then confessed what her experiences were.   Her employer urged her to address the apparition, but she could not muster up courage to do so.   Gradually the family came to know when, even in the midst of household duties, she was tormented by the look of terror in her countenance, and by her cries in bed.   Means were taken to " lay " the spirit, as they said in those days, but all were unavailing, and Elspeth declared she was being treated worse than ever.   Her master at length urged her to put her " trust in God," and question the spirit.   She did so, and the spirit told her he was glad she had spoken, for until she spoke he was under a spell, and had been " waiting for her before she was born."   He told her to trust herself entirely to him, and he would do her no harm.   Then he beckoned her to follow him upstairs and into a room, where he asked her to remove a board. She did it with ease, even though it was perfectly firm before. The spirit told her to take up what she could find underneath, replace the board, and follow him.   She did so, and he led her downstairs.   Then she passed rapidly through the living-room, where the family and neighbours tried to hold her.   Once out-side, she "went like the wind," and several saw her carried " up into the air " in the dim starlight.   Her flight with the spirit continued, she said on her return home, until she reached the fish-pond at Hensol Castle, or some part of the River Ely— probably the latter, for these hoards always were to be thrown into running water, and " with the stream."   There she was requested to throw the burden she carried, which fell from her hands with a splash into the water.   Then the flight home was resumed. There the spirit said : " Now I shall have peace, and you shall have peace," and he never troubled her again.   It was understood that Elspeth was under a bond of secrecy never to reveal what she had found under the boards in the old house at Prisk.   To the day of her death she did not care to talk of her experiences, but when anybody asked if the story was true, she would solemnly say, " It is as true as the Bible." [*Family Collection, and the David Jones Manuscripts.*]

It was generally supposed that when hawthorn-trees stood on mounds in fields, and quite apart from hedges, they marked the site of a warrior's grave.   Long years ago, in a corner of a field near Llantrissant, Glamorgan, there was a very old hawthorn.   A man living near at hand had heard his great-grandfather telling a story of buried treasure in places like that, and determined to try his luck.   He must first gather some springwort and forget-me-not flowers and leaves, and make them into a girdle, which had to be worn around the waist next to the skin.   A sprig each of the herb and flower were to be worn in the hat.   In this way the man went to seek the treasure. A condition to be fulfilled was that each time treasure was taken away the sprigs of the herb and flower worn in the hat were to be left as an acknowledgment of the transaction.   The man dug beside the hawthorn-tree, and soon found a way down past the warrior's grave to a large cavern, where there were many human bones, beyond which he saw high heaps of gold. The entrance from the grave to this cavern was hidden by a stone covered with strange inscriptions.   The man went for some months to the spot, and, unknown to anybody, secured as much treasure as he could carry.   A year passed, and the man grew very rich.   One night he brought a heavier load of gold than usual, and in his eagerness to be quickly home with it he forgot to leave the herb and flower in acknowledgment of the treasure.   When next he went for treasure, he could not remember in which field the old hawthorn grew, and was never able to find it again.   [*C. D.*]

CHAPTER XII

THE DEVIL AND HIS DOINGS IN WALES

IN the sixteenth, seventeenth, and eighteenth centuries it was generally asserted by the Saxons that His Satanic Majesty lived among the mountains in the heart of Mid-Wales, wherefrom he could keep one eye upon the North and one upon the South. To prevent the Prince of Darkness entering their houses, the Welsh whitewashed their doorsteps and sanded the floors—at least, so said the Saxons; but the house-mothers of the Principality declared they took these precautions to please the " little people," or fairies, and to keep witches away.

An old Glamorgan house-book, kept in the first half of the nineteenth century, contained the following scrap of auto-biography illustrative of the position held by Satan in Welsh folk-lore. It was written above the initials " W. T.," and runs thus :

" I was brought up to understand that the Devil was not an imaginary Terror, but a real Evil, which assumed a multi-tude of Shapes to entrap the unwary.

" My earliest dread of the Evil Being began as far back as I can well recollect, even to days when as a child I went with my father and mother on horseback to various places in Glamorgan. On the way I was shown ugly corners, where it was rumoured the Devil stood with arms akimbo, ready to pounce upon dilatory travellers. One of the places said to be frequented by the Evil Being was a nook near ' The Dusty Forge ' Inn on the coach-road to Cardiff. Whenever I passed that spot I closed my eyes, and buried my face in my hands, and kept my head well down until we had made our way over the great hill known as The Tumble-down-Dick, which was to me the place of the great Temptation.

" People in the long winter's evenings alluded to the Evil Being's aid in forming the Devil's Bridge on the Rheidol River ; to the Devil's Kitchen in the Vale of Nant Francon ; to the Devil's Blow-Hole in Gower ; and to other places connected with the Prince of Darkness.

" In play, I avoided the Devil's Messenger, or great dragon-fly, and I shuddered when told of the Devil's fish which came wallowing up the River Taff on full-moon tides ; or of the Devil's gold ring to be found near any spot where the gallows-trees stood.

" Whenever the Devil's name was mentioned in Church, the whole congregation began spitting, and continued to do so violently for a few seconds, in contempt.   Second only to the Devil in this respect was Judas Iscariot, at whose name the people smote their breasts in abhorrence." [*Family Collection.*]

In Welsh folk-lore the dragon-fly is the devil's messenger ; the caterpillar is the devil's cat ; the iris is the devil's posy ; the wild clematis is the devil's yarn, or thread ; the wild convolvulus is the devil's entrails ; the lycopodium is the devil's claw ; the euphorbia is the devil's milk ; the palmatum is the devil's hand ; the *Scabiosa succisa* is the devil's bite ; and the wild orchid is the devil's basket.

If it rains while the sun is shining, the Welsh say, " The devil is beating his wife."

If thunder is heard while the sun is shining, they say, " The devil is beating his mother."

A Welsh proverb runs : " Fear God and shame the devil." Another old saying is : " Idleness is the devil's pillow."

When a child or adult is full of mischief, half fun and half obstinacy, people in Wales say, " He is possessed," meaning in the power of the devil.

A quaint old preacher of the early part of the nineteenth century frequently referred to the " Evil One's blow-bellows."

In the days of old the devil was sometimes known in Wales by the curious names of Andras, or Andros, and Y Fall.

He was always described as black or very dark, appearing sometimes in the shape of a man with horns and cloven hoofs, or, taking animal form, he was known to resemble a he-goat. In witch lore he appeared as a very black male goat, with fearful and fiery eyes. In some of the old stories of Wales he took the shape of a raven, a black dog, a black cock, a horse, and a black pig. Sometimes he appears in the stories in the shape of a fish, or as a ball of fire, or as a huge stone rolling downhill, or as a mysterious presence without form, that caused terror.

In some of the older folk-lore the devil assumes the form of a blacksmith, who may be seen busy at the anvil or replenishing the forge-fire. He was described as a maker of horseshoes, bolts, bars, and ploughshares.

The black calf of Narberth was said to be the devil in disguise. On more than one occasion a black calf was seen near the brook, and, to the surprise of everybody, a calf it remained through the four seasons. People said there must be some mistake, and it could not be the same black calf all the time. Inquiries were made at all the farms in the neighbourhood, but each farmer declared that his black calves had not strayed. At intervals the black calf continued to appear. At last one of the farmers caught it, and locked it up in a shed with other cattle. In the morning, when the men went to turn the animals out, the black calf was nowhere to be seen. But it always haunted the brook, and deluded new-comers, as well as the old inhabitants.*

On Hallowe'en, or any one of the " three spirit nights," the devil, in the shape of a pig, a sow, a horse, or a dog, prevented people getting over stiles ; or, in the guise of an old woman spinning or carding wool, he frequented lonely spots and scared people away. On New Year's Eve he was seen in the form of a sleuth- or bloodhound in lonely ravines.

It was said in Wales that the devil could assume any shape but that of white sheep. On the other hand, he was supposed to be able to appear at any time as a black sheep or black lamb.

He was supposed to frequent moorlands and marshes, lonely mountain-sides, cross roads, the neighbourhood of forges, and frequently was seen with arms akimbo, blocking the entrances

* William Howell, " Cambrian Superstitions," p. 132.

to dark ravines and narrow passes. He could walk on water as well as on land, and when put to rout by any good man, he could cross a lake with ease, or fly up to the mountain-tops.

In the folk-stories the devil has a prominent place, with his bargain-driving, building, flights through the air, and encounters with people in lonely places.

Nightmare, bad dreams, and delirium, owing to fever or drink, were said to be the devil's means by which he sought to get possession of people's souls.

In past centuries people would not bury their dead in the north side of the churchyard, because in that part of the hemisphere were " the Old Gentleman's " dominions. He claimed all places that lay due north. It was commonly believed that at the Judgment Day all buildings would fall to the north, and then the devil could " take his share."

There were various lonely spots in Wales where the devil kept nine apprentices. Sometimes the number was named as three, five, or seven. The conditions were that when these apprentices had learnt their trade, the last to finish and go away had to be caught by the devil before he had a chance to escape. Once, when three apprentices prepared to leave, one was ordered to remain, and the latter, pointing to his shadow, said, " There is the last of all !" The devil had to be satisfied with the shadow. But the apprentice became a man " without a shadow " to the end of his life. [C. D. and told in Mabsants.]

From the shores of Cardigan Bay comes the following story : " A fisherman was told that he would be lucky and rich, and have the largest catch of fish in his life, if he had the courage to watch the tide flowing into the River Aeron when it was new moon on December 29 : for then the devil went to seek or ' lift ' treasure. Unfortunately, the man had to wait a few years before the new-moon night of December 29 came. Then he went on to the banks of the River Aeron, and was gratified, while sitting in a hollow place, by seeing a dusky figure lifting a large black object out of the water. In fright, the fisherman tried to get out of the hollow place, but found himself held tightly back. A moment later the devil stood before him. ' You caught a fish last week,' said the devil, ' and in it you found a ring. It was not a ring of gold, but a black one of stone.   Give me that black ring, and I will let you free.'   From midnight to dawn the fisherman remained in misery in the hollow.   Some comrades tried to set him free, but they could not.   So the fisherman sent for the black ring he found in the fish, and as soon as he placed it beside his enemy, the devil took the ring and flew up into the air with it.   Then the fisherman was free to go where he wished."

It was not stated whether he ever became lucky or rich, or had the largest catch of fish in his life.   Probably his release from the thrall of the devil was a sufficient reward.   [A. B.]

Another coast story of Wales describes the devil as a fish, inducing unwary people to throw nets into the sea, in the belief that a fine sturgeon was in the water.   In this way they were snared to destruction.

An old Glamorgan man gravely asserted that his grandfather, a " truth-teller." was once fishing off Penarth Head, near Cardiff, and, seeing a large fish, harpooned it.   Instead of red blood, the wound emitted a thick black fluid, and the odour thereof was like " fire and brimstone."

A Merionethshire blacksmith is said to have enticed the devil into his forge, and there hammered his right foot upon the anvil, after which the Evil One was lamed " for ever."

In Glamorgan, St. Quintin is said to have lamed the devil on the heights near Llanblethian, and put him in misery for three days.   The marks, called the Devil's Right Kneecap and Left Foot, are to be seen upon the hill-side to this day.

A man in Llanidloes was heard saying to another : " The devil would have had Ianto Bach long ago, but he is waiting to find his partner, because his grandmother wants a pair of cart-horses."

A similar story comes from the Vale of Taff, and is equivalent to the English story of " The Devil and his Dam."

The card-playing devil was known in many parts of the Principality.

A Cardigan story describes him as a good-looking stranger appearing in a village inn, where he offered to play a round with a merry party.   But when the name of Christ was mentioned, the devil vanished up the chimney like " a ball of fire."

In Carmarthen he played cards beside a pool, in which, as

the sun arose higher in the heavens, his horns were reflected. When these were noticed by one of the party, the visitor vanished " in a flash of fire."

In Glamorgan, near Llanmaes, a party of young men were playing cards on the Sabbath near a spot known as the Gallows Way. By-and-by a stranger came along, and offered to teach them a " new trick." Eagerly the merry party invited the stranger to do so, and for quite half an hour play went on rapidly. Suddenly one of the party glanced downward. " How well your boots are polished !" ventured one of the youths. Then the others glanced down. Instead of boots, they saw hoofs, and immediately the cards were scattered over the stile into the field. The next moment, in the midst of dire confusion, the stranger vanished, and the place where he sat " was as black as a coal " and smelt of brimstone.

In a field not far from this spot the devil might be seen tossing burning hay at midnight, while his great black dog, with " eyes like balls of fire," rattled his chains, to the terror of benighted wayfarers. [*Family Collection.*]

Bargains or compacts with the devil were mentioned in many parts of Wales ; but in all these stories the Welsh devil never commits himself to do anything in writing.

In a Carmarthen story the devil bargained that the man who made the compact with him should never sing the *Venite.* So the man always repeated it from beginning to end. Thus he cheated the devil.

A man in North Glamorgan desired to grow rich by any means. The Evil One promised a large sum of money from November " until the falling of the leaf " of a certain tree. In the following autumn the devil, presenting himself for payment, was shown the tree, which had been cut down so low in the late summer that not a leaf remained to fall.

A famous compact was made between John of Kentchurch and the devil. This extraordinary man was known as " Sion Kent," and he was a terror to everybody in South Wales. He made verbal contracts with the devil on many occasions, and always managed to outwit him. When a mere boy he was told to scare the crows from the field on a fair-day. In

order to go to Grosmont (Monmouthshire) Fair, he conjured the
crows into a barn without a roof, and, by the force of incantations, caused them to remain there during his absence.   It is
said that he built the bridge over the River Monnow at Monmouth, with the aid of the devil, in a single night.   People said
he kept a stud of horses at the service of Satan.   They were
such swift coursers as to outstrip the wind.   The stable where
they were kept is still shown.

Welsh folk-lore describes him as going hunting on Sundays,
and forcing the peasantry to turn out with him.   They came
home jaded and miserable after a terrible ride on the devil's
steeds to places they had never before seen.   On one occasion
Sion Kent left one of the fiery coursers in a wayside barn.
There the horse remained for three weeks, and all attempts to
dislodge him proved vain.   At the end of that time, when
Sion Kent passed with his notorious steeds, the horse
suddenly sprang from the barn, and, snorting and neighing,
joined the uncanny stud.

Sion Kent agreed with the devil that at his death he would
surrender his body and soul, whether he was buried in or out of
the church ; but, by ordering his body to be laid under the
church wall, he managed to slip out of the contract.   A stone
in the churchyard at Grosmont, near the chancel, is pointed
out as Sion Kent's grave.

This remarkable man, around whom many stories cling, was
very learned.   The Iolo and other manuscripts place him at the
close of the fourteenth century.   He was supposed to be a native
of Pembrokeshire, but either from Kentchurch, where he lived for
some years, or from Gwent, the Welsh name for Monmouthshire,
where he passed his later days, he derived his designation, Sion
Kent.   He was a Doctor of Divinity and a stern Lollard.   An old
tradition stated he was no other than Owen Glyndwr himself.
This was probably owing to the friendship existing between
him and the Scudamore family, with whom Glyndwr passed his
last years.   Dr. John Kent flourished in various forms—now
as a wizard, then as an author.   He was a bard, poet, and
essayist, and a clever linguist.   Verses composed by him on
his death-bed are to be found in the Iolo Manuscripts, and
a list of his poetical pieces is contained in the Welsh Charity

School Manuscripts, quoted in " The History of the Literature of Wales," by Charles Wilkins, Ph.D., F.S.A., pp. 50-59.

There are more stories of compacts or treaties with the devil in Wales. To the unfortunate, to those in adversity, misfortune, or debt, he frequently promised temporal blessings for a term of years. At the same time, he made unwritten bargains for their souls at the expiration of the treaty. In rare instances a written bond, signed with the man's blood, ratified the agreement.

An ancient family, living in Carmarthenshire, had a curious story attached to it. The head of the family in the early part of the eighteenth century was a Colonel in the British Army, a Justice of the Peace, at one time a Deputy-Lieutenant for the county, and regarded in every way as irreproachable and honourable. He was high-spirited, and had a very fiery temper, which led him at times to acts of cruelty. He had a strong-room or dungeon attached to his mansion, and there he was accustomed to lock up culprits waiting to be brought up before the magistrates. Beside the dungeon was the Colonel's study. Many people to whom the Colonel owed a grudge were, on the slightest pretext, incarcerated in the dungeon. A neighbouring farmer, who some years previously had much offended the Colonel, was brought to the mansion for having, as it was supposed, murdered the Deputy-Lieutenant's head-gamekeeper. He had long been suspected of poaching, and the Colonel now saw his opportunity for revenge. He treated the man cruelly, had him beaten and almost starved, and thus kept him for some time before he was brought to justice. The last night for the prisoner to remain in the dungeon the Colonel went down to see him. Hearing voices in the room, he paused to listen, but could hear little. A stranger came out, and said : " A person will bring you a large bag of gold if you will leave the key in the lock of that door." The Colonel was indignant at being offered a bribe, and refused to grant the request. " You'll need that bag of gold badly one day," said the stranger, who, while the Colonel went for a weapon, suddenly disappeared. When the Colonel went to the dungeon, the door was wide open and the room vacant. The Colonel was furiously enraged, and ordered the county to

be scoured for the culprit.   A year later a poacher confessed to
the murder, and proved the innocence of the farmer.   In the
course of a few years the Colonel found himself in the midst
of embarrassments, gambling debts, and other troubles.   He
was too proud to let his friends know the state of his affairs,
and suddenly wished he could find the stranger who once
offered him a bag of gold as a bribe.   The next night there was
a wild storm of wind and hail, with thunder and lightning.
The door of the Colonel's study blew open, and in strode a
stranger, who asked, " How many bags of gold do you need to
clear your debts ?"

The Colonel was amazed, and pointed to the pile of accounts
before him, and then told the stranger the amount necessary
to pay them.   The world would then be in ignorance of his
troubles.   Looking down to the floor, he saw that the stranger
had hoofs instead of feet.   It was the devil who now demanded
the Colonel's soul for the loan.   The bribe was too tempting
now, and the Colonel signed with his own blood a compact
with the devil.   No term of years was mentioned, only at
death his soul was to be claimed by the devil.   Many years
passed, and when the Colonel died, a large black dog with glaring
red eyes was found sitting by the corpse.   It was driven out
of the room, but the hideous animal lurked about the house
until the day of the funeral, and then joined the procession to
the church.   For an hour or more the dog howled over the
grave, and went away, never to be seen again.   People said
the devil had sent the Colonel's soul into the black dog, and it
vainly cried to be restored to its human body.

A later member of the same family inherited the fiery and
sneerful temper of the old Colonel.   He derided a tailor who
worked for him, and challenged the man to show him something " the like of which " he " had never seen."   The tailor
promised to do so.   He thereupon took him to a wood, and
introduced him to the devil.

The Colonel's descendant never would tell what he had seen.
Some said it was his ancestor in the shape of a black dog.*

Many places are pointed out in Wales as being associated
with the devil.

* William Howell, " Cambrian Superstitions," p. 129.

On the east side of St. Donat's, in Glamorgan, is a place called the Devil's Stairs. The Devil's Bridge is well known, and is classed among the folk-stories.

On the land belonging to Rhiwogo, on the side of Cader Idris, there is a crag known as the Rock of the Evil One. It is said that long years ago the parishioners of Llanfihangel, Pennant, and Ystrad-Gwyn used to frequent that spot on Sunday to play cards and throw dice. One Sunday the devil came to join the people in their games, and afterwards, to their dismay, he danced wildly around the rock. It is said that the marks of his feet are to be seen on the rock " to this day."*

In Pembrokeshire two stones are called the Devil's Nags. This spot people said was haunted by spirits, who tormented evil-doers when they passed that way.†

One of the caves in Little Orme's Head, Llandudno, is known as the Cave of Devils.

At the head of the Ogwen Valley, near Bethesda, North Wales, among grand scenery, is the Devil's Kitchen, which in seasons of storm is a pandemonium of weird noises and steaming, dripping fogs. The spot thus known is the west side of Llyn Idwal, Carnarvonshire.

The Devil's Punch-Bowl, also called the Devil's Blow-Hole, is to be seen at Bosheston Mere, on the coast of Gower, South Wales. It is a small aperture, which, like a winding funnel, spreads out into a cavern. The sea, driven in by the winds, is ejected through the upper hole, in jets of foam and spray from forty to fifty feet high, just like geyser spouts. The noise is fearful.

The Devil's Chimneys, three in number, were in Kenfig Pool, Glamorgan. The devil was a frequenter of that place.

The Devil's Bridge, near Aberystwyth, is in a beautiful spot over the falls and grand cascade of the Rheidol and Mynach rivers.

There are several versions of the story regarding the origin of the ancient bridge. One is to the effect that farmers and shepherds had for many years begged the monks of Strata Florida,

* Rev. Elias Owen, " Welsh Folk-lore," p. 190.
† William Howell, " Cambrian Superstitions," p. 50.

who had considerable property in the neighbourhood, to build a bridge over the ravine for their convenience. Finding the monks neglectful, the people expressed the wish that the devil would come and throw a bridge across. The fiend instantly appeared and offered to build a bridge, provided that the first creatures to cross it should be sacrificed to him. The devil was of opinion that numbers of people would eagerly hasten to cross the bridge, and thus insure a large harvest of souls for him. The bridge of one arch was built during the night, and at dawn the devil awaited his victims. Just before sunrise an old woman appeared, enveloped in a cloak. By her side was a sheep-dog. Going to the bridge, she paused, and then from the folds of her cloak she threw a roll of bread across the bridge. The hungry dog ran swiftly over, and the devil was outwitted. The people learned that the old woman was one of the monks of Strata Florida in disguise, who, knowing all about the devil's bargain, had come to rescue the souls of their tenants from everlasting destruction. In some versions credit is given to a wise old woman, and not to a monk, for thus outwitting the devil.

The Devil's Stone at Llanarth, near Aberaeron, in Cardiganshire, has a quaint story attached to it. The good people discovered the devil had been tampering with the bells in the old church-tower. This happened on more than one occasion. The parishioners requested the vicar to watch one stormy night, and, doing so, he saw the devil entering the belfry. Presently the vicar, with book and candle, went into the belfry, and saw the devil among the bells. The good man conjured him to go away, and in such eloquent tones that the devil, much frightened, mounted the ladder of the tower. Promptly the vicar followed, and so closely that the devil jumped from the battlements, and came down among the gravestones in the churchyard. In his fall the devil came down so heavily that his hands and knees made the four holes afterwards visible in the stone. [A. B.]

In Mid-Wales there was a story of the devil being shut up in a tower, with permission to get out at the top, but only by mounting one step a day. There were 365 steps, and the ascent took him a whole year. [C. D.]

A blacksmith down in Gower was working late one night, when the devil came into the forge, greeted him, and asked what he was doing. The man said he was forging a chain for a master mariner, who wished it to be strong enough to hold a ship, a giant, or the devil. Laughing boisterously, the devil asked if he could accomplish the work. The man said he could. " Well," said the devil, " I am a strong man, and should like to test the chain." The blacksmith agreed, and a week later, when the chain was finished, the devil came to test it. " I should like to know the name of the man who is come to test the chain," said the blacksmith. " Any name will do," said the devil ; " and as I came in the nick of time, you shall call me Nicholas." The blacksmith told him he must be bound with the chain around the waist, and pull with all his might. The devil agreed, and the blacksmith called his apprentices to hold the other end of the chain. The devil laughed. " Only yourself and three apprentices ? You'd better have a few more." " Nay," said the blacksmith. " Four strong men can do much." The tug-of-war began, and the devil gradually dragged the men out through the door. Beyond the forge there was a deep pool, in the middle of which was an old winch. Just as the devil gave one mighty tug the four men slackened their hold, with the result that the fiend fell into the winch, and the water hissed and steamed like a boiling caldron. " Old Nick " was never again seen in that part of Gower. [*C. D. and Family Collection.*]

Breconshire, South Glamorgan, and Cardiganshire supply stories much alike, in which a blacksmith throws over the devil's head a noose of iron which he is unable to break, and in that state he is dragged to the anvil, and his leg is hammered until he is lame.

More than one story describes the devil as a blacksmith, making bolts, bars, ploughshares, and harrows. A young farmer bought a harrow cheap of a new blacksmith near Radnor Forest. The maker told him that if he took the harrow into the forest on Good Friday, or one of the " three spirit nights," and stretched himself on his back under it, he would see all future events which were to happen for the next two years. The farmer did so, and for some time remained looking through the holes.   He presently saw a number of black imps with fiery tongues darting out of their mouths.   Frightened at the scene, the man tried to creep from under the harrow, but was held fast, and the devil stood beside him grinning and asking : " Have you got a coal-black dog ?   If so, give it to me, and I'll let you loose."   For a day and a night the farmer remained under the harrow, and then an old woman came along. Seeing his sad plight, she went to the village and begged a black pup of the publican.   When the devil received the pup, he seized it and flew high in the air over Radnor Forest. [C. D.]

The wife of a Glamorgan blacksmith, during her husband's absence for three days and nights, heard the forge fire roaring at midnight.   Going quietly to a place from whence she could see the forge, to her surprise she beheld at the anvil a gigantic blacksmith with horns on his head, a very long tail, and horse's hoofs instead of feet.   The devil was hammering a horseshoe for his own hoof, and presently he shod himself.   The good wife quietly crept to the fowl house, and disturbed the hens, and the next moment the cocks began to crow, whereupon the devil fled in anger, leaving one shoe unfinished on the anvil. [*Family Collection.*]

A similar story used to be told about an old forge from which the inn called " The Dusty Forge," on the main-road leading from Cardiff to St. Nicholas, took its name.

Crack Hill, on the high-road leading from Bridgend to Cowbridge, Glamorgan, is credited with peculiar and uncanny associations.   An aged Welshman related his personal experiences, and he was a native of the district.   The second narrative was proffered by an Englishman, a stranger to the neighbourhood, and he did not know anything about the story told by the Welshman.   The former told me he went to Bridgend for some goods which could not be obtained on that day, and he had to come home without them.   He assured me that he did not indulge in " pipe or pot," and was perfectly cheerful when leaving Bridgend in the late autumn twilight.   He walked briskly until he reached the foot of the Crack, and then began the ascent.   As he went upward he found walking unusually heavy work.   Yet the road was dry and hard, and particularly agreeable for walking.   He therefore thought that either he was more tired than usual or lazy; so he tried to adopt a better pace, but could not. To make matters worse, night was approaching. When half-way up the hill something, he knew not what, seemed to spring upon his back, and afterwards pressed heavily between his shoulders. In the starlight he looked over his right shoulder, and saw a shape clinging closely to him. Being a strong man, he promptly endeavoured to shake it off, but it pressed heavier than ever. He felt great difficulty in proceeding on his journey, and the effort brought a "heavy sweat" to his forehead and face. When just at the top of the hill he groaned with agony, and so great was his distress that he cried aloud: "O Lord, I pray Thee, deliver me of this burden!" While uttering these words he crossed his arms upon his breast. Instantly he was relieved of his load. Turning round to see if anybody had been playing a practical joke on him, he saw in the starlight a huge shape, which looked like a "great bundle," or a "fat, short man" enveloped in a dark wrap. The shape rolled rapidly down, and fell into a disused quarry at the foot of the hill. Immediately afterwards the sound of a loud explosion was heard, and from the depths of the quarry sparks of fire shot up and were scattered across the road. He hastened home, and when he related his experiences to an aged neighbour, the latter said he remembered his father telling a similar story of the "devil on the Crack." [C. D.]

The second version of this story was told by a civil engineer, who had never heard the above narrative. He said he had engaged a horse and trap at a Bridgend hotel to convey him to Cowbridge, when the Taff Vale Railway extension was being made to the last-named town. Unaccompanied, he started rather late in the evening, and it was quite dark when he reached the foot of the Crack Hill. The sky was obscured, but occasionally the moon shone through cloud-rifts. The carriage-lamps were lighted, and he was in a very cheerful state of mind. Soon after beginning the ascent the horse became very restless, and snorted vigorously from time to time. By-and-by somebody or something appeared to be thrown into the back of the trap. Thinking it to be an intrusive traveller, he called out, but there was no response. He whipped his horse, but the animal was hardly able to struggle upward, and toiled as if under a very heavy weight.   Nearing the top of the hill, the horse made a desperate effort, and then stood still.   The civil engineer descended from his seat, and, to his amazement, he found the horse quivering, as if panic-stricken.   Looking down the hill, he saw in the fitful moonlight a monstrous bundle rolling downhill, where it fell into the quarry.   It was followed by a loud explosion and sparks that were scattered across the road.   The civil engineer had never heard the old story, and was much interested when, in 1896, I related the Welshman's account of his experiences with the " devil on the Crack."

CHAPTER XIII

DRAGONS, SERPENTS, AND SNAKES

"Y DDRAIG COCH," the Red Dragon which forms the national emblem of Wales, heads the list of serpents and other reptiles prominent in the folk-lore of the Principality.

In "The Mabinogion"* is found the first account of the dragon of Wales. The story of Lludd and Llevelys contains the following particulars. Lludd, King of Britain, consulted his brother Llevelys, King of France, with reference to troubles in his kingdom, and the cause thereof. Thereupon Llevelys stated that one of his troubles was caused by a home dragon and "another of foreign race fighting with it." He then gave the following directions : "After thou hast returned home, cause the island to be measured in its length and breadth, and in the place where thou dost find the exact central point there cause a pit to be dug, and cause a caldron full of the best mead that can be made to be put in the pit, with a covering of satin over the face of the caldron. And then in thine own person do thou remain there watching, and thou wilt see the dragons fighting in the form of terrific animals. And at length they will take the form of dragons in the air. And last of all, after wearying themselves with fierce and furious fighting, they will take the form of two pigs upon the covering, and they will sink in, and the covering with them, and they will draw it down to the very bottom of the caldron. And they will drink up the whole of the meal ; and after that they will sleep. Therefore do thou immediately fold the covering around them, and bury them in a kistvaen, in the strongest place in thy dominions,

* "The Mabinogion," p. 459.

165

and hide them in the earth.   And as long as they abide in that strong place no plague shall come to the Island of Britain from elsewhere."

These dragons were imprisoned by Lludd in Dinas Emrys, in Snowdon.   Their combats five centuries later led to the acquaintanceship of Vortigern and Merlin.   Vortigern, after the treachery of the Saxons, fled to one of the most romantic parts of Wales, and ordered the building of a great tower of defence, the foundations of which were swallowed up as soon as they were filled in.   Merlin was sent for, and soon discovered under the foundations the red and white sleeping dragons that symbolize the Celtic and Saxon races.   The red was the British dragon, and the white the Saxon.   The remains of the castle said to be built under Merlin's direction are to be found in Nant Gwrtheryn, or Vortigern's Valley, near the mountains called, The Rivals.   There, too, is the cairn known as Vortigern's Grave, where the bones of a tall man were found.   One story describes Vortigern fleeing from his enemies, and leaping over the precipice into the sea.   This crag, haunted by sea-birds, is called " Carreg-y-Llam," or the Rock of the Leap.

From time immemorial the Red Dragon has been the national standard of Wales.   In later times this emblem was adopted by Henry VII. at Bosworth, and the heraldic office of Rouge Dragon, now held by Mr. Everard Green, was established in honour of that victory.

Welsh stories, like those of other lands, reveal formidable dragons, griffins, and winged serpents, many of which were connected with Arthurian romance and the ancient traditions of Wales.

In the Mabinogi of Peredur* a hideous serpent is described. It had upon its tail a ring of gold, or was seated on one.   Peredur fought with and killed the knights of the serpent, and afterwards destroyed the loathsome creature, from which he obtained the ring, and carried it away

Legends and traditions about dragons, griffins, and various kinds of winged serpents were popular among people in the far past, and traces of the belief that such creatures were lurking in the dim caverns and wilds of Wales survived the stress of

* " The Mabinogion," p. 81.

time, and existed in folk-stories of the seventeenth, eighteenth, and nineteenth centuries.

In North Wales a place called Llanrhaiadr-yn-Mochnant was associated with a dragon, or winged serpent, which went forth through a large district, and not only destroyed whole flocks and herds, but thought little of capturing men, women, and children. Many plans were devised for the destruction of this monster, but without avail. By-and-by one man, wiser than the inhabitants of the district, suggested a curious arrangement. A large stone pillar was built and studded with sharp spikes of iron. As the colour red allures a dragon or a serpent as well as a bull, the post or pillar was " cunningly " draped with scarlet cloth, so that the spikes were carefully concealed. When the dragon next came forth, he was allured by the red drapery, and at once rushed towards it. The colour caused the infuriated creature to beat itself against the pillar for many hours, with the result that it died from exhaustion and loss of blood. The spot where the man-eating dragon beat itself to death is called Post Coch, or Post-y-Wiber, or Maen Hir-y-Maes-Mochnant to this day.* The district frequented by this dragon, or winged serpent, is in the extreme south of Denbigh-shire, on the River Rhayadr, which forms the highest waterfall in Wales. The cataract of Rhayadr descends a rock over 210 feet in depth, and the river below marks the boundary between the counties of Denbigh and Montgomery.

The Vale of Neath, in South Wales, had a dragon, or winged serpent, which is said to have frequented the districts near the celebrated waterfalls of the Perddyn, Mellte, Hepste, and to have concealed itself in the lonely gorges around Pont-Neath-Vaughan. Winged serpents were to be seen flying beside the waterfalls of Erwood, Resolven, and Ystradgynplais. In the same district a crested serpent with brilliant colouring around its head frequented the fertile glades surrounding Ynys-y-Gerwn, near Aberdulais. [A. B.]

Trelech-ar-Bettws, in Carmarthen, had a winged serpent. This creature was generally to be seen on or near a tumulus or barrow known as " Crug-Ederyn." In this barrow was found a kistvaen or stone-lined grave covered with rough slabs.

* Rev. Elias Owen, " Welsh Folk-Lore," p. 350.

This is said to have been the burial-place of Ederyn, an early Prince or chieftain of Wales.

Lesser dragons and winged serpents frequented Lleyn and Penmaenmawr, in Carnarvonshire ; the ravines of the Berwyn Mountains, in Denbighshire ; the district around Cader Idris and Penllyne, in Merionethshire ; under Plinlimmon, in Montgomeryshire ; the wilds of Cardigan ; Radnor Forest ; the Brecon Beacons ; the marshes of Carmarthen ; and the lands around Worm's Head, in Gower. In South Glamorgan, Llancarfan had the reputation of being haunted by winged serpents and other reptiles, while into the parish of St. Donat's, in the same county, these loathsome crawling creatures could not make their way, for in the long ago, according to tradition, Irish earth was mingled with the soil.

Linked with all the dragon, griffin, and winged serpent stories was the belief that in lonely ravines, moorlands, and forests treasures of gold and hoarded gems were guarded by these creatures, who sometimes conveyed their goods through the air at midnight when the old hiding-places were discovered.

The griffin, like the dragon, had a prominent place in the lore of Wales.   At one time it was used as a tavern sign.   The Griffin and the Two or Three Griffins were names of inns in some of the towns of Wales and of wayside hostelries, and were very popular as late as the early part of the nineteenth century.

The woods around Penllyne Castle, Glamorgan, had the reputation of being frequented by winged serpents, and these were the terror of old and young alike.   An aged inhabitant of Penllyne, who died a few years ago, said that in his boyhood the winged serpents were described as very beautiful.   They were coiled when in repose, and "looked as though they were covered with jewels of all sorts.   Some of them had crests sparkling with all the colours of the rainbow."   When disturbed, they glided swiftly, "sparkling all over," to their hiding-places.   When angry, they "flew over people's heads, with outspread wings bright, and sometimes with eyes, too, like the feathers in a peacock's tail."   He said it was "no old story," invented to "frighten children," but a real fact.   His father and uncles had killed some of them, for they were " as bad as foxes for poultry." This old man attributed the extinction of winged serpents to the fact that they were " terrors in the farmyards and coverts." [*J. R.*]

An old woman, whose parents in her early childhood took her to visit Penmark Place, Glamorgan, said she often heard the people talking about the ravages of the winged serpents in that neighbourhood. She described them in the same way as the man of Penllyne. There was a " king and queen " of winged serpents, she said, in the woods around Penmark, and " more of them in the woods around Bewper " (Beaupré). The old people in her early days said that, wherever winged serpents were to be seen, there " was sure to be buried money or something of value " near at hand. Her grandfather told her of an encounter with a winged serpent in the woods of Porthkerry Park, not far from Penmark. He and his brother " made up their minds to catch one, and watched a whole day for the serpent to rise. Then they shot at it, and the creature fell wounded, only to rise and attack my uncle, beating him about her head with its wings." She said a fierce fight ensued between the men and the serpent, which was at last killed. She had seen the skin and feathers of the winged serpent, but after the grandfather's death they were thrown away. That serpent was notorious " as any fox " in the farmyards and coverts around Penmark. Buried money had been found not far from Penmark Place in her childhood, and she said it had been " hidden away by somebody before going to the great Battle of St. Fagan's, when the River Ely ran red with blood." This old dame was a direct descendant of an aged woman who, in the memory of Edward Williams (Iolo Morganwg), said she distinctly recollected the Battle of St. Fagan's, near Cardiff, during the Civil War. The family was renowned for its longevity, several members having passed the age of 105 and 107. The old dame who gave these accounts of the serpents died at the age of 99, and retained full use of her faculties to the last. [*O. S.*]

Similar stories about winged serpents were told in the neighbourhood of Radnor Forest and in several parts of North Wales. All are agreed that this kind of serpent was dreaded as much as foxes, and their extermination was due to their depredations in farmyards and coverts.

There was also a much-dreaded cockatrice that sucked the milk from cows, blood from fowls, and was fond of eggs. Children were told that if they were naughty the cockatrice would come and suck their blood. It had "eyes in the back of its head as well as in front," said the old people, and was a terror to the country-side. Several children's stories contained particulars about the cockatrice.

The serpent, or snake,* was regarded by the Druids as a symbol of the renovation of mankind, which was one of the great doctrines set forth by their religious mysteries. It is known that the snake casts its skin annually, and returns to a kind of second youth. Fine specimens of this reptile were kept by the Druids close under the altar of Augury, and from their motions important divinations and legal decisions were made.

Below the breastplate of judgment the Druids wore, suspended by a chain, the Glain Neidr, or snake-stone. It is sometimes called the adder's stone or adder's egg.

The Glain Neidr, or Maen Magi, of Wales was supposed to possess many virtues. Its origin as a stone of mystery was attributed to the following cause : In the spring, and especially on May Eve, a large number of snakes were accustomed to meet in many secluded parts of the Principality. The creatures apparently formed a congress, which generally ended in snake warfare. After a fierce battle, in which the snakes writhed and hissed fearfully, the spot where the assembly took place was covered with froth. In the midst of this would be found the Maen Magi, or Glain Neidr, or snake-stone. This stone resembles a perfectly round and highly polished pebble. Sometimes the colour is of a pale terra-cotta tint, sometimes light green, and often of a soft azure hue. I have before me as I write, a Maen Magi of a soft pink shade blended with lilac. The tints resemble those of the opal. It is over two hundred years old, and feels extremely cold to the touch, especially if placed against the eyes, lips, or temples. This bead, like others of its kind, was formerly supposed to be of

* Davies, "Mythology," pp. 210-216 ; Meyrick, "Costumes," p. 28.

use in the cure of many diseases. It was especially good for all affections of the eye. The owner of the bead states that for inflammation of the eyes, ulceration of the eyelids, and for sties, it is a never-failing cure if held or rubbed upon the affected part.

Several persons in the Principality said they were eye-witnesses of the great snake congress in the spring. One of them states that it is the time when the snakes select a new king, and the old colony rises up in arms against the younger generation. The newly chosen monarch and his party are victorious. Some of my informants have seen in the midst of the snake froth the Maen Magi. Others have not been fortunate enough to find the mysterious pebble. There were snake congresses on Midsummer Eve or Day. [*C. D. and Family Collection.*]

The snake-stone had not only healing powers, but the possession of it was supposed to render the owner victorious over his enemies, and capable of foreseeing future events. Under certain conditions, it enabled people to discover hidden treasure, and to make themselves invisible. People believed that serpents' eggs were in some mysterious way highly medicinal, and that a quantity of them, made into a kind of decoction, was effectual in cases caused by the stings of serpents, bees, hornets, and wasps, and the bite of any mad animal or infuriated beast. But, while it was effectual in the cure of one person, it would act as a strong poison, fatal in its results, to another.

It was also said that if a man were stung by a snake, and could very soon afterwards catch it, or another serpent, and cut the body open lengthwise, that he would find a long roll of white fat, which, applied to the wound, was a certain cure.

According to an old tradition, whenever a snake is found under or near a hazel-tree on which the mistletoe grows, the creature has a precious stone on its head.

The ash-tree is said " to have a spite against snakes."

In the heads of toads and adders stones of varied power were said to be engendered, and they were always associated with witchcraft and magic.

In stories told by aged people, men and women, it was said that the person who could muster up courage to eat the flesh of the white snake would soon be able to understand the language of " beasts, birds, reptiles, and fish."

Superstitions with reference to reptiles and other venomous creatures were formerly general.

One of the oldest was the belief that when a dragon or a winged serpent was discovered in the act of conveying treasure, food, or a babe to its den, the creature would drop them all if the name of Christ were repeated several times. Another old superstition was that all lizards were formerly women.

It was said in Wales that a snake-skin plaited into a whip and used by a waggoner, or a carrier of any kind, would enable his horses to draw the heaviest load.

A stone of the snake or adder placed in the bottom of a goblet of wine, or any kind of spirit or alcoholic liquor, prevented intoxication. The heart of a snake or adder, or a frog, encased in a locket and worn around the neck, will insure luck in any speculative games or business. If snakes, toads, frogs, or adders enter a house in May, they bring sickness or misfortune. Snakes, toads, frogs, and lizards seem to have played important parts in magic. Witches were supposed to have the bridles for their midnight rides made of snake-skin.

If on your way to market you see a snake, a toad, or a frog crossing your path, you will not have luck in buying or selling. If the first frog you see in spring leaps in water, and not on land, you will have more loss than gain during that year.

Toads, frogs, and adders were called the " flocks of the witches." If an adder is seen in a house, somebody will die within a year.

Transformation into a serpent or snake occurs in a few of the folk-stories. Illustrations of these will be found under that heading. In many localities an unusually bright-looking snake of any kind, which appeared mysteriously and vanished suddenly, was regarded about eighty years ago as the representative of a sensual or divorced woman. [*Family Collection.*]

The blind-worm, or slow-worm, which is about twelve to

eighteen inches long, is an object of terror to Welsh children ;
for the old women say that if this worm were not blind, it
would be a fearful enemy to mankind.

To kill the blind-worm was to bring calamity to the slayer.
To step over it was to put the person in " the power of the
devil." If you crushed this worm you would crush your luck.
To avert its evil power salt was thrown at it. If it came into
the house, it was " a sign of death." If it crawled under the
cradle, the baby would die. If it went into the stable, the horses
would be ill.

Among the lesser snake stories many are to be found in
every part of Wales. In quiet and leafy neighbourhoods snakes
have been known to go to children and infants when alone, and
sip milk with them out of their basins or mugs, and a friendship
has been formed between them.

An old Glamorgan farmer mentioned a snake becoming very
attached to his own child, who, as she grew up, petted and
fondled the reptile. When the little girl was six years old an
uncle, fearing the snake might injure his niece, killed it.
Gradually the child pined away and died.

Several South Wales stories describe a great number of
snakes filling a farmyard and barn, and one amongst them was
the king, distinguished from the others by a glittering golden
crest or crown on its head. The farm-boys and maids were
so accustomed to these snakes that they would fondle
them.

An ancient farm-house in the Vale of Taff was frequented by
a king snake and its courtiers. While these serpents remained
in their old haunt all went well, and prosperity continued.
But when the farmer died, his eldest son immediately killed the
king snake, upon which the others took their departure. With
them went the health, happiness, and prosperity of the family
for ever.

A Vale of Glamorgan story runs thus : To a farmer's
daughter near Penmark a large snake used to come at milking-
time. The girl noticed that it wore a crown on its head. Every
morning and evening the girl gave the snake some warm new
milk. One day the snake vanished, but it left a ring of gold
on the spot where it used to come night and morning. It was

whispered that the girl substituted this ring for her marriage circlet on her wedding-day, and by that means she became very rich. In future years she was ill, and when near death she made her daughter promise to wear her ring. The daughter, either carelessly or wilfully, allowed her mother's ring to remain on her finger, and it was buried with the body. From that moment the daughter's luck waned, and to the time of her death she attributed her adversity to having buried the snake-ring. [O. S.]

In some parts of the Principality there was formerly a tradition that every farm-house had two snakes, a male and a female. They never appeared until just before the death of the master or mistress of the house; then the snakes died.

A small fiery viper, so called because it was very venomous, used to be found in Wales, where, according to tradition, only two of these were alive at the same time. For soon after their birth the young vipers would eat up their parents.

The healing power of snakes appears to have been remarkable. With reference to this many folk-stories are told in North and South Wales.

One from the beautiful Vale of Clwyd, in the North, and one from the fertile Vale of Glamorgan, in the South, will be sufficient as examples of healing serpents.

A few miles from Ruthin, on the banks of the Clwyd, a farmer's son suffered badly from a skin affection resembling erysipelas. The irritation and pain frequently led him to seek seclusion by the river-side. There one day he took a short nap in the dinner-hour. While his companion, one of the farm-hands, enjoyed his noontide meal, he saw a snake coming from the hedge to the sleeper. The workman, instead of rousing his young master, watched the snake's movements. Presently the reptile glided close to the sleeper's face, and appeared to be examining the skin. Then the creature glided slowly back to the hedge, and ate some herbs and grasses. It returned, and gently as possible emitted its saliva over the young man's face. This disturbed the sleeper, but the workman, having heard something about the healing power of snakes, begged his master

to remain quite quiet. " For," he said, " I am rubbing an
ointment on your face." By-and-by the snake went away.
The workman did not say a word about the reptile, but in the
course of a week the painful skin affection vanished, and never
again reappeared. When completely cured, the young farmer
asked the workman the name of the ointment that had wrought
such a cure. Then the man described what he had seen, to the
astonishment of everybody. The herbs and leaves eaten by
the snake were never discovered. [J. R.]

From the neighbourhood of St. Nicholas, in the Vale of
Glamorgan, comes the following story :

Scurvy had broken out in the houses of one or two farmers,
and, as usual, the families were for a time prevented having any
personal contact with other people. Among the sufferers was
a girl aged about eight. It was known that every day she
carried her bowl of bread-and-milk, or flummery-and-milk, into
the orchard, and there, sitting down under a favourite apple-
tree, ate it, at the same time feeding two or three snakes
who came regularly for their portions. The child, like other
members of the family, suffered with scurvy. One day the
father of the child chanced to be in the orchard when the mid-
day meal was served. He watched the snakes gliding from the
long and deep grasses to the child, who, as usual, fed her friends.
Then suddenly one of the snakes lifted its head, and appeared
to be examining the child's face. Presently the reptile glided
away, and soon returned with some leaves in its mouth. These
were deposited by the snake beside its companions, and soon
the reptiles were bruising the leaves in their mouths. Then
each in turn applied the bruised leaves with their saliva to the
child's face and arms. While the snake went for the leaves the
little girl, as usual, laid the empty bowl beside her, and stretched
herself at full length on the grass. The snakes applied their
salve while their patient remained in a reclining posture.
Later in the day the child was asked if the snakes had ever
before " licked her like that." She answered : " Only twice.
This is the third time."

The snakes did not make another application of leaves and
saliva, but three days later the scurvy disappeared " as if by
magic." The farmer told the doctor who was attending his

family of this singular occurrence, and both men searched for
the leaves, but could not find them. Although the farmer was
certain he knew the leaves, not any of them proved successful
in the other cases of scurvy.

The following story about a black snake was told in the
first half of the nineteenth century. It must have been a very
old story, because the narrator always located it on the nearest
mountain to his home, and this particularly black reptile
appeared to have no fixed abode. In Carmarthenshire it was
located among the Van Mountains ; in Pembrokeshire it was
found in the Preceley Range ; while in Glamorgan its home was
the Great Garth, the Llantrisant, or Aberdare Ranges. The
story ran thus : A great black snake was seen coiled in the sunshine. Its head and tail did not exactly meet, but left a small
opening. In the middle of the coil there was a large heap of
gold and silver and copper coins. A working man once saw
all this treasure, and he resolved to have some for himself.
There was nothing to be done but to just pass through the
opening between the black snake's head and tail, and step in.
At first the man was afraid, but, mustering up courage, he
stepped in. He saw that the snake was asleep, and there would
be no harm in having some of the coins for himself ; so he
began to fill his pockets with gold, silver, and copper. When
his pockets were full, he took off his coat, laid it down, and
began filling it with more treasure. Greediness made him
forget the snake, but a fearful roaring frightened him. He
immediately left his coat where it was, and fled. Looking back,
he saw the black snake and the treasure sinking into the
mountain, and the noise ceased. [A. B. and C. D., told also
in Mabsants.]

Castell Gwys, near Haverfordwest, is now known as Wiston.
Centuries ago there were several claimants to this estate. In
the days of old a serpent lived in a hole on Wiston Bank, not
far from the castle. This serpent possessed innumerable eyes,
and it was impossible for anybody to gaze at the creature
without the latter seeing him.

It was agreed by the kindred of the family that the person
who could gaze on the reptile " without the same serpent or
cockatrice seeing him " should be the lawful heir of the estate.

Accordingly, several of the claimants tried every imaginable way to accomplish this object, but without success. One of them formed a plan, but kept the secret to himself until the time came when the others had given up the attempt. Then he took a barrel up to the top of the hill, secured himself in it, and allowed it to roll down the bank past the exact spot where the serpent placed itself. As the man passed the spot where the serpent was stationed he peeped through the bunghole, and said : " Ha, ha ! bold cockatrice, I can see you, but you cannot see me !" In this way that claimant became owner of the Wiston estates. Castell Gwys was formerly the seat of the Wogan family. [O. S.]

Roch Castle, about six miles to the north-west of Haverford-west, marks the spot beyond which the Normans had no need of fortresses. The ruins are approached by a steep path, and the tower occupies the summit of a huge mass of trap rock which rises abruptly from the level plain. It is said that the feudal Lord of Roch built this solitary tower in a very peculiar place because he had been warned by a witch, or in a vision, that his death would be caused by the sting of a serpent or adder. If he passed a certain year in safety, he need not after-wards fear. When the tower was built, the timorous Lord of Roch lived in the top story of his stronghold. The year passed, and he was within a few days of his emancipation from thral-dom. His friends prepared for rejoicings outside, while he quietly but thankfully waited his release. It was cold and wintry weather, and the wind from St. Bride's Bay set the prisoner's teeth chattering. The nights were so bitterly cold that a kind friend sent up a few faggots of wood, so that the Lord of Roch might make a fire therewith, which he did " right gladly." The fire was quickly kindled, and the solitary man warmed his numbed hands. By-and-by he fell asleep, and from the embers on the hearth a treacherous adder crept up and stung the Lord of Roch. When his friends came the next morning he was dead. [J. R. and O. S.]

CHAPTER XIV

CORPSE-CANDLES AND PHANTOM FUNERALS

THE origin of the corpse-candle is supposed to date back to the fifth century. St. David, the patron of Wales, earnestly prayed that the people he loved, and among whom he toiled, should have some kind of warning to prepare them for death. In a vision he was told that through his intercession the Welsh would never again find themselves unprepared; for always before such an event the people in the land of Dewi Sant would be forewarned by the dim light of mysterious tapers when and where death might be expected.[*] St. David apparently prayed particularly for South Wales, because it is said that corpse-candles are seen more vividly and frequently there than in North Wales.

The Canwyll Corph, or corpse-candle, was seen passing along the route to be taken by a funeral, or hovering around the spot where an accident would happen, or fluttering along the edge of the waves where a wreck would be. When two lights were seen, two funerals would take place. A tall light foretokened the death of a man, a lesser one for a woman, and a small one for a child. The colours of the lights varied. Before a man's death a red glowing light was seen; a pale blue light indicated a woman's death; and a faint, pale yellow light appeared before a child's death.[†]

Innumerable stories of corpse-candles are to be found in all parts of Wales, but the South provides the greatest number. As nearly all of these tales bear a striking similarity, with only the difference of location, the following will serve to represent the whole:

[*] Rhys, " Celtic Folk-lore," p. 275.
[†] " Jones of Tranch," p. 30.

178

In passing Golden Grove from Llandilo to Carmarthen, several people in the eighteenth century saw three corpse-candles gliding down the river at various times three weeks in succession. The persons compared their experiences, and wondered what the omen meant. Was it for the villagers, or was it for the noble family who lived at Golden Grove ? At length the solution came. Three members of the nobleman's family died simultaneously in different parts of the country.*

At Disgwilfa, about twelve miles from Carmarthen, a mysterious light was seen glimmering in the corner of a field, where the branches of a tall sycamore-tree made a deep shadow. For quite a year, winter and summer alike, this light appeared, and was seen by several persons, who commented upon the strange occurrence. The light glimmered in the corner, about two or three feet from the gate leading into the field, and was always seen between " dusk and dawn." At last the mysterious light disappeared, and the very next day a gentleman much respected in the district " came to his end " by a fall from his horse. He was hunting, and, while taking the gate, fell over his horse's head, and was killed on the very spot where the glimmering light or corpse-candle had been seen. [A. B.]

Colliers in various parts of Wales even in the present day believe in corpse-candles, and amongst the aged of that class the story about St. David and his omen was formerly prevalent. Before one of the great explosions at Llanbradach people declared corpse - candles without number were seen hovering around the mouth of the pit. At Glyncorrwg, near Bridgend, Glamorgan, " hundreds " were seen before an explosion. At the mouth of the Ogmore River two lights were seen hovering for many weeks along the sands. Later on two brothers, who attempted to cross at low tide, were drowned.

Many people attempt to account for the phenomena by saying that the corpse-candle is the product of noxious gases, and the vapour of swampy places, where the mysterious lights are known as jack-o'-lantern, or will-o'-the-wisp. A distinct difference is made between the latter and the corpse-candle, which is often seen in the house, and sometimes in the room,

* William Howell, " Cambrian Superstitions," pp. 60, 61.

of a person about to die, or in the dwelling of somebody related to the individual.

A correspondent stated that in his own experience the following circumstance happened : In the year 1880 his brother, a native of Carmarthenshire and captain of a vessel, was away at sea. When at home, he occupied a small room only suitable for one person. One evening, about six o'clock, a dim light was seen in that room by a cousin from a neighbouring farm. The young man asked : " Is Jack come home ?" " No," was the reply. " Then who is in the room ?" he asked, and the answer was that " nobody had been there with a candle." The circumstance passed unnoticed, until another member of the family, and an inmate of the house, saw a dim glimmer, " like a rushlight or taper," through the window. Later still the mother one night, going into the room to pull down the blind, turned to go to the door, and over the bed saw a dim hovering light. She went downstairs in considerable agitation, and exclaimed to the members of her family the hope that nothing had befallen Jack. The mail was eagerly waited for, and in the meantime neighbours saw the dim light in Jack's room. A few weeks later news reached the family that the captain died at Singapore of fever about the time the corpse-candle appeared in his room. [*Mr. Price, U.S.A.*]

A well-known family in Glamorgan always see a corpse-candle in the house before the death of a relative. It generally appears in the library or the hall, where it is customary to deposit the coffin in preparation for the funeral ceremony.

Among the peasantry it is common to hear stories about corpse-candles being seen hovering over a spot where soon a burial will take place. An old man said that he remembered one autumn particularly when strange stories were told of numerous corpse-candles being seen hovering along the roads leading to various burying-places in Bridgend, Glamorgan. He was quite a little boy at the time, but old enough to know that mysterious candles were seen, and many of them. He heard his father telling an elder brother that not less than " six candles, two abreast," had come out from a neighbour's house and gone towards the east. In the winter of that year the small-pox scourge carried off numbers of the inhabitants, and six deaths took place in the neighbour's house in rapid succession.

Spectral or phantom dogs were seen before deaths, and these had quite a separate existence from the spirit-hounds of Arawn, Prince of the Underworld, though, as the old people used to say, they " all served the same master."*

There are innumerable stories of an uncanny dog appearing before a death, and in nearly all instances the creature is described as silent and immovable. It makes its first appearance immediately before or just after a person is taken ill, and vanishes when death takes place. Its coming and going are alike mysterious. In colour sometimes it is white, black, mottled, or grey. Its eyes look red around the lids, as though it had been weeping. If driven away, it returns.

These stray and strange dogs were ominous of death.

" For more than three weeks before my master died," said an old and faithful retainer of a Welsh gentleman, " a small white and curly-coated dog planted itself on the steps leading to the front entrance, and would not go of its own accord. When driven severely away it returned. It was a lifeless, sad-looking animal, that never once lifted its eyelids, which were almost hidden by shaggy hair. It never made a sound, not even when beaten away. Every night I drove it out through the front gates, but every morning there it was again. And then I knew it meant death for the master. When the master died the dog went, and never returned."

A lady living in one of the crowded towns of South Wales was followed every evening she went out by a white dog resembling a Scotch terrier. As a rule, it met her at the corner of the street where she lived, and trotted by her side to the door of her house. Sometimes she coaxed it indoors, but it would not go with her. In the morning it waited on the doorstep for the lady's walk out. This happened for several weeks, and the lady's friends " did not like it." They said it was an uncanny dog. The lady was taken ill, and the servants drove the dog unceremoniously away ; but it returned, and remained at its post. The dog's friend died, and the animal was never again seen.

* " Jones of Tranch," p. 38.

A man living some miles out of the town of Brecon had led a life of dissipation, and was notoriously bad in many ways. When he was ill, a small black terrier took its post inside the gates leading to the house. Other dogs avoided the strange animal, which was left severely alone. The dogs of the house—great, strong, and sturdy creatures—sniffed at the strange animal, and in fear and trembling crawled terrorized away. Their owner died, and the strange black dog crept upstairs, concealed itself under the bed, and in the morning was found seated stoically on a chair beside the dead. It was driven downstairs, but returned to its post. On the day of the funeral the servants tried to catch it, but the mysterious creature skilfully evaded their clutches. On the morning of the funeral it was nowhere to be seen, but when the coffin was being lowered into the grave the dog reappeared, and seated itself at the head of the vault. There it remained for an hour, and vanished. Everybody said it was " the devil's dog waiting for the soul of the evil man." The animal was described as " coal black, with very red eyes." [O. S.]

A similar story was told of a wicked woman, who was always very unkind to animals, and certainly had never petted any dog to induce its attention. In this case the animal was a huge black mastiff, with glaring eyes and red eyelids.

In the memory of a few aged people the death-horse survives. Sometimes the phantom animal was white, with eyes that emitted cold blue sparks " like forked lightning." Sometimes it was " coal black," with eyes " like balls of fire." The death-horse came to bear the soul away, and its coming was quiet and stealthy, but its departure was accompanied by the " wind that blew over the feet of the corpses."

To see the white horse on a new-moon night was a " sure sign of death " in the family of the person who saw it. Sometimes it meant death to the beholder.

A few years ago an English visitor in a rural district of Glamorgan asked, and received permission, to see the interior of an ancient manor-house. It was embowered in ivy, climbing roses, and other flowers. After spending an hour in the house, the visitor left, and while proceeding down the drive, he saw a white horse cantering towards him. It was a beautiful animal, with a splendid white mane and long flowing tail. The stranger stood aside, and the horse passed, going straight up to the grand entrance of the mansion. The visitor thought no more of the horse until dinner-time in a small country inn in the neighbourhood. There he happened to remark to the landlord what a fine white horse he had seen in the manor-house drive, expressing at the same time his opinion that it was an Arab. He explained that it was riderless. The landlord asked if any groom or man was with it, and the stranger said it was alone. For a moment or two the host looked grave, and then in a whisper said : " If you please, sir, do not mention this in the village, because it is a token of death in the manor-house family." The visitor remained a fortnight in the neighbourhood, and before leaving he heard that one of the sons of the manor-house had just died in India.

In a field called the Whitton Mawr, on the Duffryn estate, which formerly belonged to the Bruce-Price family, but is now in possession of Mr. John Cory, one of the wealthy philanthropists of Cardiff, a white horse of considerable magnitude used to be seen in the first half of the nineteenth century. It was pure white, and generally was seen grazing quietly as if chained, or gambolling about and snorting. Aged people said its appearance was an omen of death in the family who formerly owned the estate. The then possessors of the property were descended from Admiral Button, who was an Arctic explorer in the reign of Queen Elizabeth. So fond was Admiral Button of his white horse, named Cartouche, that in his will he ordered the animal to be kept for the rest of his days a pensioner in the Whitton Mawr. People said that the horse died the day after his master's death. Ever afterwards the wraith of Cartouche presignified a death in the Button family and their descendants. [O. S.]

An ancient family in North Wales always regarded a white horse as an omen of death. Whenever a pure snow-white horse in the actual flesh passes through some of the villages in West Glamorgan, Carmarthen, and Pembrokeshire, people say there will be a death in the parish.

The same story was formerly common in several of the counties of Wales and the Marches.

In some of the villages in South Wales a coal-black horse was formerly to be seen standing near the " burying-lane " waiting "for orders." When these were given, the animal went slowly and stealthily away, and placed itself in the road-way opposite the house from which it was to " bear the soul away." When this horse, with eyes "like balls of fire," snorted, tossed its mane, and was seen galloping away to its destination, people said a sudden death was imminent. If it went slowly, the illness would be lingering. When it can-tered, the illness would be fluctuating. But, in any case, whether the illness be slight or serious, the coal-black horse meant death. [*Family Collection.*]

Corpse-birds were supposed to appear before a death, and in the rural parts of Wales people do not readily give up this superstition. This bird has been described as having few feathers, and those resembled the downy undergrowth of other birds' wings. It came in the early morning, and remained on the branch of a tree near the house of the sick person until death took place. Its note was a melancholy chirp, that con-tinued with few interruptions all through the day. People always and quickly recognized the note of the corpse-bird, and the " sound and sight of it," says a villager, " makes one shiver."

In some parts of the country the corpse-bird is described as being without feathers and without wings. It is supposed to be continually crying in Welsh, " Come ! come !"

A Breconshire family always heard this mysterious bird before a death in the family. It had a doleful chirrup, and was quite unlike any other bird. In size and shape it resembled a robin, but its feathers were of a dull ashen grey, and bedraggled, while its eyes were " like balls of fire," and remarkably restless. It always appeared " in an old apple-tree " quite close to the house, and sometimes remained for weeks almost motionless. When death took place it disappeared.

The " Deryn Corph," or corpse-bird, was familiar to several people living in the neighbourhood of Caerphilly and Rhymney, Glamorgan, in the middle of the nineteenth century as having a smooth fur-like coat and small fin-like flappers that enabled it to hop from bough to bough. It could not fly, and came and disappeared mysteriously in the night. It was about the size of a starling, and in colour dark, almost black, with a grey breast. Its chirrup had a curious metallic sound, and sometimes it had a strange cooing accent.

In Glamorgan and Carmarthen people said it was more frequently heard than seen, and its note could not be mistaken for that of any other bird.

Closely associated with corpse-candles and other omens of death are the phantom funerals, records of which are to be found in every county of Wales.

The following account was supplied by a native of Denbighshire. He said : " Many years ago my uncle lived in a mining village a few miles distant from Ruabon. In the twilight of a bitterly cold day in December he was hurrying homeward, when, not far from the parish church, his progress was obstructed by what appeared to be in the growing twilight a funeral procession. He could distinctly see the bier, the coffin on it, the mourners, and others following. In order to let the procession pass my uncle stood aside, and then he saw the well-known faces of a doctor and a tradesman who lived in Ruabon. The people were singing, but he could not distinguish the words, although he was familiar with the tune. But presently he observed that the funeral passed the church instead of going into it. Impelled by curiosity, he followed the funeral, which vanished when it reached a house not far from the church. Much impressed by what he saw, he hastened home and told his wife of the vision he had witnessed. About six weeks later my uncle happened to be in Ruabon in the twilight, and a funeral procession passed the spot where he had seen the phantom mourners. Curiously, the real funeral passed the church, and halted at the house he had seen in his vision. In the procession the doctor and tradesman were seen as before. The body was that of a person who had died in the South of England, and was conveyed to the house of the deceased, there to remain until the next day. This explained the remarkable circumstance of a funeral in the late twilight."

The next story comes from Corwen, and was supplied by an eyewitness. He said : " I was coming home late from a neighbouring village, when I suddenly heard wailing sounds a short distance in advance. I paused and listened, and suddenly found myself borne backward in a funeral procession. I distinctly saw the coffin, and recognized one or two persons in the crowd beside me. With the procession I was borne on to the ancient parish church of St. Julian, and not far from the doorway saw a well-known Dissenting minister approaching and joining us. Then the whole phantom vanished. I was greatly frightened, and on reaching home promptly related my experiences. About fourteen days later a friend of ours died in Corwen. I went to the funeral, and, arriving rather late, was pressed backward in the crowd. Near the old church a well-known Dissenting minister joined the procession, and in it I recognized other people who appeared previously as phantoms."

A farmer living in the Vale of Glamorgan had the weird experience of " seeing his own funeral." He had been to Cowbridge Market, and was returning home just before nightfall, when he saw a procession coming down the lane leading from his own house to the highway. His horse appeared to be witnessing the same scene, for the animal halted at the entrance of the lane to allow the crowd to pass. The farmer gazed spellbound as the mourners approached, because immediately after the coffin came his own wife dressed in the deep mourning of a widow! She was supported by her eldest son. The crowd passed and vanished, and the horse, scared by the scene, rushed up the lane and abruptly halted at the garden gate. Hearing the clatter of the horse's hoofs, and fearing the animal was riderless, the farmer's wife and son hastened out, and were thankful to find the husband safe and unhurt. That night the farmer was unusually moody and silent. He could not help thinking of the strange scene he had witnessed. A few weeks later he was seized with a serious illness, from which his family hoped he would soon recover. " I shall never get up again," he said, and then he related his recent experience. One of the sons who told me this story said everybody present was unspeakably thrilled. Three days later the farmer died.

A man living near Porthcawl, Glamorgan, told me he was returning from Sker one evening late in September, when the moonlight, shining on the sea, revealed the huge shape of a wrecked vessel among the dangerous rocks of that wild coast. Wonderment caused him to halt and watch the scene.

Presently he noticed a group of men bearing a burden from the rocks to the land, and thence onward towards Porthcawl. He followed at a distance, and was astonished to see the burden-bearers halting at his own door. He immediately quickened his steps, but when he reached his house the group of men and their burden vanished. The man told his father what he had seen, but begged him not to mention the circumstance to his mother. A week later a ship was wrecked on the rocks of Sker. Among those who lost their lives was his own brother. He had been away on a two years' voyage, and was wrecked in sight of home. His corpse was borne to Porthcawl in the moonlight.

A well-known country doctor of South Glamorgan did not believe in the supernatural, but he was obliged to acknowledge a certain mysterious experience during a professional round. One evening in the twilight he was driving from Sigginston, viâ Llanmihangel, to Cowbridge. Just before reaching the gates of the carriage-drive leading to Llandough Castle his horse suddenly halted. Looking forward in the uncertain light, the doctor saw a very large crowd of people emerging from the castle gates. He drew his horse and gig away to the left side of the road, and so great was the crush that he was almost obliged to pull up into the ditch. Presently he saw a coffin covered with a very handsome pall, and in the bearers he observed well-known men. The great crowd passed on, while the doctor gazed in mute astonishment, and then fell in line with the many carriages and traps that brought up the rear of the procession. Just before reaching Llanblethian the funeral cortège vanished in the growing darkness. Amazed at what he had witnessed, the doctor drove rapidly into Cowbridge, and later on proceeded home. Five weeks subsequently the doctor was called upon to attend an inmate of Llandough Castle, who was seized with a serious illness, which ended fatally. The funeral was announced for a certain hour, and the doctor intended going early to the castle on that day. But, having to pay a professional visit to a farmer in Sigginston, he was delayed, and only reached the castle gates in time to see the procession emerging. Then he remembered the phantom funeral of five weeks previously. As in the illusion, he had to draw up his horse and gig out of the way of the crowd, and then fell into line with other carriages.   In this way he proceeded to Llanblethian Church.

Roger's Lane, a byway leading from St. Athan to Bethesda ar Fro, in the Vale of Glamorgan, was the reputed scene of many phantom funerals.   Long years ago a man was walking through this lane after dark in the late autumn.   Suddenly and in the distance he heard people singing a funeral hymn.   By-and-by from the opposite direction came the sound of another and quite different hymn.   Presently he saw a crowd of people standing and congregating together.   As he drew nearer, he found himself in the midst of two funerals, one going to St. Athan and the other passing to Bethesda.   There was difficulty in passing, one procession eventually doing so by waiting for the other to go by.   The man felt a sense of oppression and being crushed as he struggled out of the crowds, and hastened his steps in advance of the procession going towards Bethesda.   He went on, but after passing the chapel looked back, and there he saw the funeral entering the graveyard.   Some time passed, and he was called upon to attend a funeral that was obliged to go viâ Roger's Lane to St. Athan.   In the midst of the way a funeral coming from St. Athan met the other, and there was considerable difficulty for both to pass.   The man said all was verified to the letter, even two different funeral hymns being heard, and the sense of oppression and being crushed vividly reproduced.

Several years ago a farmer in the Vale of Glamorgan was out in his fields when the first glimmer of dawn appeared in the east.   He was much surprised when the sound of many people singing a well-known Welsh funeral hymn reached him. Hastening to the stile, he looked down the road, and was astonished to see a funeral procession coming from the church, and halting before a house at the west end of the village.   The farmer recognized the mourners, and immediately afterwards the phantom vanished.   Three months later a neighbour's son died in Cardiff, and in the early morning his body was brought past St. Athan Church, and deposited in the homestead, where it remained until the afternoon.   Then the funeral took place in the parish church.

The old chapel of Bethesda ar Fro, in the Vale of Glamorgan, had the reputation of being frequently the scene of phantom funerals.

An aged dame related the following experience of her own in or near the year 1871 : She had been spending the day with some friends, and had remained longer with them than she intended, so that when she passed Picketston it was well on into the gloaming of the September evening. Drawing near the chapel, she saw in the distance a crowd approaching the place. Dim lights were burning in the chapel, and were visible through the windows. The woman halted, and gazed in wonderment at the strange scene. But presently she mustered up courage enough to walk on, and a moment later found herself in the midst of a very large concourse of people, by whom she was jostled and hustled, as she said, "unmercifully." In her eager desire to be quit of the crowd, she pressed through it ; but at the gates of the chapel she was intercepted by a huge white dog running before a piebald pony, which reared and kicked so much that the crowd had to surge back. Taking advantage of this temporary clearance, the woman ran forward and past the chapel, only to find stones hurled after her. But, glad to escape, she ran breathlessly on to Boverton, where in the first house near the bridge she fainted. Upon recovering she related her uncanny experience, and her friends particularly noted what she said about the white dog and the piebald horse. Three weeks later a funeral took place at Bethesda. The woman and her friends attended it, and, to their astonishment, a great white dog ran among the people, and caused a piebald pony ridden by a farmer to rear. In the commotion the stones newly placed on the road were scattered, and several of them struck the woman, thus verifying in every respect the phantom funeral she had seen so distinctly.

· The neighbourhood of Wick, near Bridgend, Glamorgan, had the reputation years ago of being the scene of many phantom funerals going to and from the churches in the district. Some would be going to Wick Parish Church, and others passed on to the village of St. Bride Minor.

The following is given as having taken place in 1836 : Late one evening the daughter of a farmer living in the village of Gileston, near Barry, South Glamorgan, went out for a walk towards a place called The Leys. On her return she fell fainting into a deep armchair. When she recovered, she told her friends that she found herself in the midst of water and a crowd of people who were conveying a coffin in a boat, which they landed at the back-door of the farm. She said there was not a sound to be heard, but she distinctly saw a great crowd. Her friends went forth to ascertain the cause of her terror. The night was fine, and the moonlight so bright that the smallest object could be distinctly seen. When the friends reached the back-door, neither crowd nor coffin could be seen. The farmer said : " Who ever heard of a funeral at ten o'clock at night ?"

No more was thought of the matter until a remarkably high tide occurred in the Severn Sea. Then the waters ran inland for several miles. It flooded the lands and submerged all the low level plain extending from Aberthaw to The Leys, and thence up Gileston Lane, which was impassable. A person who died in an old house on The Leys was to be buried during the afternoon of the high tide. The usual route to Gileston Church was submerged ; therefore the bearers crossed the water in a boat with the coffin. Having laid the latter down at the back-door of the farm, they remained there with it until boats could bring over the mourners and friends. In this way the vision was verified.

An old man sitting in the parlour of an ancient inn near the sea at Porthcawl, Glamorgan, saw a funeral procession, followed by crowds of people, approaching the house. It was twilight, and the shadowy forms were indistinct and unrecognizable with one exception. That was a man in hunting costume, and he rode a spirited and restive horse. The spectator was greatly astonished to see the crowd coming to the house, when the church of Newton Nottage was quite in the opposite direction. Never a funeral or wedding-party passed or halted at that out-of-the-way inn. The old man related his experiences to the landlord, who, after the manner of those days, about seventy years ago, said : " There will never be a church built beyond this house in my time or anybody else's." A few years passed. The landlord of the inn died suddenly in Neath, and his body was conveyed by road to the inn, where it remained during the night previous to the interment in Newton Nottage Church. As a mark of respect to the landlord, who was a keen follower of the hounds, a neighbouring gentleman in hunting costume went to meet the procession, and accompanied it home. It was particularly noticed that he rode a spirited and restive horse.

In former times pedestrians, especially in the twilight and night, kept as closely as possible to the grassy margins of the roadways, so as not to obstruct the passage of phantom funeral processions. There are old people living at present in various parts of South Wales who can well remember stories about phantom funerals, and who, after a little coaxing, are willing to relate their own personal experiences, provided their names are " not printed," as they say.

The Welsh are endowed with second sight, and testimonies of their gifts in this respect are to be found in all rural districts, but particularly in South Wales.

A native of Carmarthen related the following story : He knew a young man who was supposed to be gifted with second sight, but had no personal evidence of it. One evening in the twilight he was out walking with the young man in the neighbourhood of St. Peter's Church. Just as they approached the church the young man stood aside and bared his head, bowing it with a very reverent gesture. A few moments later the young man put his hat on and resumed walking. The narrator of this story asked him why he halted. " Didn't you see ?" was the reply. " But I forgot ; you couldn't. I saw a funeral procession passing into the church." Then he named some of the persons present. " And," he added, " Mrs. So-and-so was there. She was dressed as a widow. Her husband will die." Six weeks later the actual event took place.

A woman who was a native of Carmarthenshire gave her own personal experiences. One day, while standing at her cottage door, which commanded a view of the railway-station, she saw a tall man with sandy hair coming quickly down the roadway. She heard him asking a child his way to a house. His accent was broad Scotch, and she distinctly heard the child reply, as they often do in Wales : " Over by there, to be sure !" The man entered her cousin's house.

Later in the evening she asked her cousin who the Scotsman was. " There was no Scotsman here," replied the cousin. Three weeks later her cousin was taken ill, and they sent for the doctor. The woman was standing at her own door, and was astonished at seeing a tall man with sandy hair coming rapidly down the station road. She heard him asking a child where her cousin lived, and was told, " Over by there, to be sure !" It was the *locum tenens* of a general practitioner in the district.

A Pembrokeshire lady of Welsh origin was walking in her grounds when she met her own counterpart coming towards her. She was greatly surprised, and, with fixed eyes, saw her own facsimile pass by. When she went home she said : " There is not much time for me in the world." As she was in perfect health, her friends asked why she made that remark. She told them of her strange experience, but they advised her not to think any more about it. Three days later she died suddenly.

The apparition of a living person was called Lledrith. It was always regarded as an omen or forerunner of death. Some persons acknowledge the possession of the Lledrith, which means " illusion." An old Glamorgan family who once owned large estates, but afterwards were much reduced, had many stories to tell of the Lledrith. One was remarkable. The head of the family was comfortably seated in a chair on the lawn, enjoying the summer breeze. His wife was indoors reading. The old man saw a man striding quickly along the drive towards the front-door. He wore a suit of brown holland, and on his head was a sombrero. " It is Jack, my son from Mexico !" exclaimed the old man, who remained seated because he could not move without assistance. Presently a lady dressed in deep mourning passed along. It was his eldest daughter, only recently widowed. A few minutes later a girl of ten ran along. She wore a white dress and scarlet sash. Her golden hair fell in waves to her waist. It was one of his granddaughters. When his wife came to him, he related his experiences. She had seen them too ! The next mail from Mexico brought the news that his son died suddenly two days after the Lledrith appeared. His widowed daughter died three months later, and his granddaughter was drowned nearly four months afterwards. The Lledrith, or illusion, did not come as an omen that death had taken place, but was about to happen.

At the same time, this illusion was not confined to apparitions of those about to die. There are many instances of this, but a few will serve for illustration. A well-known townsman of Cardiff in the sixties was seen by two eyewitnesses walking along Crockherbtown, now called Queen Street, towards his house in Windsor Place, which he quickly entered. Those who saw him followed, for they had business to do, and wished to seize the opportunity for an interview. They knocked at the door, and made known their desire. The servant said her master was not in. The men looked amazed, for they saw him entering. They asked to see her mistress, and the latter corroborated her servant's statement. The men at once turned away, and retraced their steps along Crockherbtown. Judge their surprise when they saw their friend rapidly overtaking and passing on before them. Still ahead of them, he turned from Duke Street into High Street, and vanished. Determined to have the interview, the friends went to the business place of Mr. K——. They were ushered into his private office, and found him calmly looking over his accounts. " Well, there is no mistake about it," said one of the men ; " you have played us a fine trick."

Mr. K—— looked up, amused, and asked for an explanation. His friends related their experience. He declared he had entered his office at nine in the morning, and had not been over the doorstep since, in proof of which he called a witness. Convinced of this evidence, one of the eyewitnesses said in Welsh to the other : " It was the Lledrith." Mr. K—— lived many years afterwards, and used to enjoy telling the story of what he called " the Welsh Lledrith," or " unaccountable happening." [*Family Collection.*]

A young man near Talgarth, in Breconshire, said he once chased his wife for a mile and a half up hill and down dale, until he panted for breath, and was forced to halt, when she vanished. Thinking all this was done for a frolic, he went home, to find his wife quietly seated by the window, knitting. " How did

13

you get back ?" he asked. " Get back ?" reiterated his wife. " Why, I've never been anywhere !" " Tut, tut ! Gwen," said her husband. " You looked as roguish as could be beckoning me from the cherry-tree and out into the road. Then you ran, and I followed a mile and a half, until I could follow no more. I was forced to sit down." " Then you must have followed a Lledrith looking like me, for I have not been outside the doors since you went to the barn after tea." This again was an " unaccountable " experience.

CHAPTER XV

GREY LADIES.

A FEW miles above Cardiff, on the eastern side of the river, there is a thermal spring called Taff's Well. Taff is a corruption of Daf, or David, the patron saint of Wales. This well was much frequented by people suffering from rheumatism. A lady robed in grey frequently visited this well, and many people testified to having seen her in the twilight wandering along the banks of the river near the spring, or going on to the ferry under the Garth Mountain. Stories about this mysterious lady were handed down from father to son. The last was to the effect that about seventy or eighty years ago the woman in grey beckoned to a man who had just been getting some of the water. He put his pitcher down and asked what he could do for her. She asked him to hold her tight by both hands until she requested him to release her. The man did as he was bidden. He began to think it a long time before she bade him cease his grip, when a " stabbing pain " caught him in his side, and with a sharp cry he loosened his hold. The woman exclaimed : " Alas ! I shall remain in bondage for another hundred years, and then I must get a woman with steady hands and better than yours to hold me." She vanished, and was never seen again.

In connection with this well there was a custom prevalent so late as about seventy years ago. Young people of the parish used to assemble near Taff's Well on the eighth Sunday after Easter to dip their hands in the water, and scatter the drops over each other. Immediately afterwards they repaired to the nearest green space, and spent the remainder of the day in dancing and merry-making.

A grey lady frequented the neighbourhood of Llanishen, near Cardiff. She was often seen, especially by drovers, who appeared to fascinate her, for she would follow them for a mile or so, and return to St. Dene's Well, where people said she was held in bondage for having done many evil deeds. There was no story about her release.

A woman robed in grey formerly used to frequent a spot on Moel Arthur, overlooking the Vale of Clwyd, in North Wales. Under a rock near which the grey lady was chiefly seen, treasure was concealed in an iron chest with a ring handle. People said that the place of concealment was illuminated by a super-natural light. Occasionally in the evening, or soon after dawn, men dug for this treasure ; but their efforts were rewarded with fearful noises, and they were driven away by thunder, lightning, and rainstorms. One man found the grey lady beckoning to him as he ascended with pickaxe and shovel. He went to her, and she gave him some peas in a pod, and whispered, " Go home." He did so, and the peas turned to gold in his pocket.

In the city of Cardiff a grey lady used to be seen walking along Crockherbtown, now called Queen Street. Her grey robes were partly concealed by a mantle of the same colour, with a hood over her head. Some old houses then stood between the large house on the corner not far from Cory Hall and the Feeder. She generally began her walk there, and proceeded along Crockherbtown, through Duke Street, towards Duke Robert's Tower, and thence to the bridge over the River Taff. There she would stand and signal for a time, and then vanish. Sometimes she signalled to somebody unseen across the river, or, turning her back to the river, she waved her arms in the direction of the castle where Robert of Normandy was imprisoned.

In the eighteenth and early part of the nineteenth centuries a lady robed in grey used to be seen wandering about a spot called Maes Gwenllian among the heights of Mynydd-y-Garreg, near Kidwelly. She had a long trailing robe and a girdle, and her head was concealed by a hood. Once a man met her face to face, and afterwards declared she was headless, while the hood was only a make-up. An old Carmarthenshire man ventured

to address her one moonlight night. Using the name of the
Deity and Jesus Christ, he begged her to tell him what she
wanted. "Alas!" she answered, " I cannot rest until I find
my head. Help me to search for it." For an hour or more
the old man wandered around the spot, but nothing could be
found. Three nights in succession he kept tryst with the grey
lady, and at last he found a stone not unlike a skull. This he
handed to his companion, who concealed it under her robe, and
hastened away from Mynydd-y-Garreg. The grey lady was
never seen again. This folk-story was connected with the tragic
fate of Gwenllian, the beautiful wife of Gruffydd-ap-Rhys-ap-
Tudor, Prince of South Wales in the twelfth century. The
brave Princess and her young sons during her husband's absence
led the Welsh against the Normans, under Maurice de Londres,
who advanced to attack Kidwelly Castle. She was captured
and beheaded on the spot that still bears her name. [A. B.]

WHITE LADIES.

Wales, in common with England, has innumerable white
ladies, and every county of the Principality has several of these
apparitions.

A very pretty and pathetic story about a white lady is told
in the Vale of Glamorgan, where, near the village of St. Athan,
is the site of ancient West Norchète Castle, long ago corrupted to West Orchard.

In a field* near this place the apparition of a slim and graceful
lady, whose white silken robes trailed in the dewy grass, was seen
in the early mornings. She never appeared in the night, but
always soon after dawn during the summer months. Her story
is pitifully romantic.

Long centuries ago a daughter of one of the powerful
Norman De Clares, Lords of Glamorgan, became the bride of Sir
Jasper Berkerolles. When this worthy knight returned home
from the Second Crusade, he accused his wife of infidelity with
Sir Gilbert D'Umphraville, of East Norchète Castle. Lady
Berkerolles vainly protested her innocence, but enemies worked

* Iolo Manuscripts, p. 400.

against her, and her husband condemned her to a terrible doom. In the field not far from the castle Sir Jasper had a hole dug, and up to her neck in this grave the beautiful lady was doomed to a slow death by starvation. Not a crumb was to be given her, and not one drop of water was to moisten her parched lips. She was to linger in misery through this living death. Her sister in pity begged that she might go and see the sufferer at least once a day. To this Sir Jasper agreed, provided that food and beverage were not conveyed to her. At dawn every day the faithful sister carried out her mission. In order that moisture should reach the lips of Lady Berkerolles, the sister wore long silken robes, and allowed them to trail in the dewy grass. Up and down close to Lady Berkerolles the silken folds trailed, and from them the innocent wife received or sucked sufficient moisture to sustain her for ten days.

But sisterly devotion could not save life, and Lady Berkerolles died of exhaustion. Later on Sir Jasper proved his wife's innocence, and went raving mad.

So late as 1863 women who went sheep-milking in the early morning declared they often saw a beautiful lady dressed in white going " round and round " a certain spot in the field, but they " could not make out why."

Aged people in former years always had something to say about the starvation of a Countess and the faithful " Ladi Wen " (white lady).

Probably Lady Berkerolles, as the daughter of the De Clares, who were Earls and Lords of Glamorgan, was known as " the Countess " in her own right, having borne that title before her marriage. The Countess, in Welsh " Iarlles," is the name attached to a lane, a stile, and a hillock or bank called a " Twmpath," all in the vicinity of the tragedy.

In one old story she was described as guarding treasure hidden under the hillock or bank above mentioned, but that every time she attempted to guide anybody to the post a white dog rushed towards her. This dog had red eyes. [C. D.]

Between Ewenny and Bridgend, Glamorgan, there are places named White Lady's Meadow and White Lady's Lane. In former times the white lady was said to appear, and point towards Ewenny. People said she knew where treasure was hidden, but could never go to find it. She was sometimes seen wringing her hands, as if in great trouble. A man once ventured to address her, and she seemed pleased. He asked what he could do to help her, and she answered that if he would hold her tightly by both hands until she told him to stop, her troubles would leave her. The man did as he was bidden, but the loud barking of a dog caused him to look round and release her hands. With a scream she cried, " I shall be bound for another seven years !" and vanished. A later story attributes the white lady to a crime that had been committed in a demolished house in the meadow.

At a place called Rhiwsaeson, near Llantrisant, Glamorgan, a woman in white used occasionally to appear. A farm labourer returning home one evening met her. She approached him, saying : " Your wife has given birth to a babe. Go and bring the boy to me at once, that I may be saved." The man was surprised to find the event had come about. He feared to do this, and the parson advised him to have the infant christened before taking him out, fearing he might die before his return. When he, carrying the babe, reached the spot where the white woman waited his coming, he found her crying bitterly and wringing her hands, for one of the conditions of her soul's redemption was the kiss of a new-born and unbaptized child.

A shepherd, minding his master's sheep on the Llantrisant Mountain, sat to rest in a sheltered nook where a huge rock covered with heather shielded him from the fierce sunshine at noontide. He looked a few paces away, and saw a white-robed girl scattering a few roses. The shepherd waited until she was gone out of sight, and then went from his nook to gather the flowers. He looked at them, and said : " Oh, what beautiful flowers !" He replaced them where they had been scattered. Suddenly the maiden reappeared, looked at him kindly, and smiled sadly, but never uttered a word. That night he took the flowers home, and placed them in water. In the morning he found three gold coins where the flowers had been.

Many years ago at Castell-y-Mynach, or the Monk's Castle, near Cardiff, a white lady used to appear occasionally among the ruins of the ancient monastic buildings. A man who was working in the garden saw the white lady. Her dress was as white as the driven snow, and her long black hair streamed over her shoulders. She beckoned to the man with fingers covered with rings that sparkled in the sunlight. In the left hand she held a bunch of forget-me-nots. The man, terrified, ran into the house, and called his master and mistress to " come and see the white lady." They went, but saw nothing. " There she is," said the man, whereupon the white lady vanished. They said she guarded the monk's treasure.

A ploughman was busy ploughing a very large field near Caer Bannau, the site of a celebrated Roman station, about three miles away from Brecon. In the course of his work from day to day he noticed a maiden robed in white, smoothing her hair in the sunshine, and beckoning the man to her. At first he took no notice of her, but as she repeated the signal he mustered up courage to respond. The maiden told him she was a King's daughter who had sunk with a landslip into the ground. She could only be saved by a man who, without halting or looking round, would carry her to the nearest church-yard, and throw her down with all his might. The ploughman promptly picked her up, and ran with her to the nearest church. He was about to fling her off his shoulders when something tweaked his ears so violently that he looked round, and let his burden fall. The maiden flew into the air, lamenting that she must suffer more severely now, and wait another hundred years for a man with a more steady hand. [*A. B.*]

In the same neighbourhood, but a little nearer Brecon, a woman clothed in white used to be seen. A farmer, curious to see her, went to her haunt, and found her scattering seeds. He was about to run away, when she begged him to return, and, addressing him kindly, she gave him a handful of leek seeds. Thanking her, he put the seeds in his pocket, but threw most of them away. On his return home several grains of gold had stuck in his pocket. He never saw her again.

Ogmore Castle, near Bridgend, Glamorgan, had a white lady who was supposed to guard treasure which was kept under the flooring of the tower. A man accosted her once, and she took him to the spot, where she asked him to lift a large flooring-stone. This he did, and in a hole under the stone he found an old crock full of golden guineas. " Take one half," said the white lady, " and leave the remainder for me." He did as he was bidden, and replaced the stone. One evening he thought he might as well have the other portion, and accordingly lifted the stone, and filled his pockets with the gold pieces. Just as he was leaving the castle the white lady appeared, and accused him of theft. He denied having taken the gold, but she made him take off his coat, and in doing so the money rattled out. The white lady then set upon him, and, to his dismay, he found she had claws instead of fingers, and with these she nearly tore him to pieces. He shouted, and tried in vain to get out of her grasp, but this he was not able to do until she had badly used him. He went home in a dilapidated condition, and was accused of having been mixed up in a drunken brawl, which he stoutly denied. Soon afterwards he was taken ill, and gradually became worse. Nobody knew what his illness was, and in the course of time he wasted away. Before he died he confessed to his adventure, and people called his complaint " the white lady's revenge."

A young man who was fond of frequenting the banks of the River Towy, not far from Carmarthen town, observed on several occasions two parties of white-robed ladies in boats crossing the river. He noticed that they went very swiftly, and vanished almost mysteriously. After seeing them more than once, he concealed himself behind some bushes, and waited there until these white ladies came again. The next time they went very quickly to the margin of the river, and when the boats were in mid-stream the bright moonlight revealed the fact that the ladies sailed in cockle-shells, and when they reached the other side they vanished, and black cats appeared. These were the white witches of Carmarthen, who could transform themselves into cats.

On a farm in South Glamorgan, which was supposed to be under a ban, between eleven and twelve noon a woman robed in white used to be seen. She begged the workmen, in passing, to lay hold of her, catch her tightly by the hand, and never utter a word. The men went on in fear and trembling. One day a man mustered up courage to do as she wished. While he held her, a pack of hounds surrounded him, leaped up his sides, and were ready to tear him to pieces. Terror forced from

him the exclamations, " Christ, save me ! God, protect me !"
The moment the woman was loose from his grasp, she sobbed
and moaned, saying : " I am lost for ever !"   She never appeared again.   [O. S.]

BLACK LADIES.

There are stories of a few black ladies in Wales.

A woman robed in black, with a long black floating veil,
frequented the banks of the River Teifi, in Cardiganshire.
She was always pointing to a bend in the river, and could sometimes be heard wailing and hurrying in search of something.

Not far from St. Athan is Boverton, supposed to be the
Bovium of the Romans.   Carlyle, who visited a member of the
Redwood family at Orchard House in this place, mentions it in
his letters.   The Castle of Boverton was a British stronghold,
afterwards occupied by the Romans and Normans.   In the
reign of Richard I. it was the property of the Earl of Gloucester,
whose daughter Hadwisa became the wife of Prince John.
When, about ten years later, John divorced Hadwisa of
Gloucester, so that he could marry Isabella of Angoulême, his
wife, who has been described as amiable and affectionate,
retired to the seclusion of Boverton Castle.   According to local
tradition, King John once fled from his barons, and was sheltered in Boverton Castle by the gentle woman he had wronged.

Early in the nineteenth century men were employed to dis-
mantle part of this castle.   One dark hazy day they saw a tall,
shadowy female figure, dressed in deep widow's mourning of
antique design.*   Her face was scarcely visible, but her long
dark hair fell in neatly braided tresses down to her waist.   She
wandered from room to room in a slow, disconsolate manner,
and occasionally her sobs and sighs broke the silence.   At first
the workmen were greatly frightened, but as during the progress
of the work they frequently saw this apparition little heed was
taken of it.   One of the men mentioned the circumstance to a
very aged person in the district, and was told : " Oh, she is
Wissie, the King's widow.   I've often seen her."   May not this
dark lady have been Hadwisa of Gloucester ?

* " Vale of Glamorgan," p. 336.

When the dismantling of the old castle was completed the
dark apparition vanished, but for long years afterwards people
declared the black lady haunted Boverton Castle.

A lady robed in black frequented the old sea-lock in the time
when Cardiff was a small and insignificant place. She appeared
to be searching for something which she could not find. In the
twilight she would go down to the sea-lock and return again,
wringing her hands as she went. Mariners and others were
quite aware of her visits, but felt afraid to address her. Sometimes she would stretch imploring hands towards people, and
then go rapidly to the sea-level. At last one evening a skipper
ventured to speak, asking what he could do for her. She asked
him to take her out in a boat to the mouth of the River Ely.
If he would he should be handsomely rewarded. Eager for
gain, the skipper granted her request, and rowed to the mouth
of the River Ely. Never had he ferried such a heavy cargo
before. Every moment he feared that the weight of the black-
robed lady would sink his boat. He was about to express his
fears, when the lady said : " Land me quickly, and draw up the
boat." He did so. The lady beckoned him to follow, and she
led him into the woods far from the river. There she pointed
to a stone, which the skipper lifted at her direction. In a crock
under the stone there were gold coins. " I have found them
at last. They are yours." Then she vanished. Many times
the skipper went for the treasure, and by means of it grew rich.
People wondered how he made his money, but his secret was not
revealed until just before he died. [*Family Collection.*]

Near Penylan Well, Cardiff, a woman dressed in sombre
garments used to be seen. She frequented the spot in the
twilight, and often could be heard wailing or moaning. There
was an old story prevalent in the first part of the nineteenth
century that a Cardiff man once accosted her with " What
dost thou seek ?" She told him she sought freedom, and that
if he held her firmly by the waist and remained silent, her desire
would be granted. He did as he was bidden, but a sharp pain
cramped his arm and loosened his hold upon her. She fled,
crying : " Two hundred years more before I shall be free !" If
people drank of the water in this well, and then dropped a pin
therein, they would get the wishes of the current year granted.

Pwllhelig Pool, in the Vale of Glamorgan, was frequented by a lady robed in black, with a long veil and trailing garments. She was heard murmuring to herself, and sometimes moaning. In the eighteenth century people said that a house once stood on the spot now occupied by the pool. It was under a ban, and for the evil deeds of the owner the house went down in a gap or landslip, which afterwards, owing to the bursting of a spring, was filled with water. The lady was supposed to be the wife of the evil owner, and she was always hoping to find her lost money and jewels. Early in the nineteenth century a man undertook to speak to her. She did not answer, but only smiled sadly and wrung her hands, then vanished.

GREEN LADIES.

In contrast to the white lady and the black lady, there were several green ladies in Glamorgan.

One of them appeared beside the eye-well in Marcross, near St. Donat's. She watched people carefully as they deposited rags on the thorn-bushes around the well.

Caerphilly Castle, some miles to the north-east of Cardiff, had a green lady with " monstrous goggle-eyes " that " glared like great red moons " at people. She has been described as a small person with an " enormously large head," and wore green robes and a " long green veil floating over her shoulders." Sometimes she was alone, but occasionally she was accompanied by apparitions of the mailed and fierce De Clares, who might be seen flitting among the broken and gloomy ramparts of Caerphilly Castle. [C. D.]

Half-way up the Garth Mountain, near Cardiff, a woman robed in green used to appear. She beckoned to men who passed, but they did not heed her. Two men at last ventured to listen to what she said, which was that she guarded hoards of gold, and could not move, but she wished to be released. They should have the treasure if they set her free. If they did not release her then, there would not be a man born for the next hundred years who could set her free. The men whispered to each other, wondering if her tale were true. One of the men, looking down at her feet, said : " True enough. Her slippers are covered with gold-dust." The woman suddenly vanished, but for a long time her sobs and wailings were heard.

Craig-y-Llyn, opposite Glyn Neath, in the Vale of Neath, had a green lady in the seventeenth century. Every seven years she came and sat on one of the rocks, making chains and neck-laces of wild berries. The rowan or mountain-ash was her favourite tree, and she could be seen wandering about gathering an apronful of the bright red berries, which she conveyed to her favourite rock. Once when a man wished to follow her, but stood irresolute, she beckoned to him and smiled. He went towards her, and she gave him a handful of red rowan-berries. He thanked her, and put them in his pocket. Then there came a crash, and the lady disappeared. She wore a green robe and green jewels. The berries changed to gold coins.

On the banks of the River Teifi, in Cardiganshire, a maiden robed in green wandered when the May flowers were in bloom. Her dark hair was plaited in long switches, and bound with bands of gold. She wore a golden girdle, from which was sus-pended a bunch of golden keys. One day two farmers saw her going down to the stream, washing her face and hands, and returning to a spot near a mound. Another day they saw her filling a tub with water from the river, and carrying it to her mound. The tub had broad hoops of gold around it. The men had not the courage to speak to her. It was said there was treasure hidden in the mound, and she had to guard it. [*Family Collection.*]

CHAPTER XVI

WITCHES : THEIR RENDEZVOUS AND REVELS

CEREMONIES connected with the " black art " were formerly common in Wales, where witches and wizards appear to have been fairly fortunate in evading the law.

From the flotsam and jetsam of Welsh witch-lore the following details have been collected. Very aged people refuse information on this subject, but occasionally an old man or woman is willing to relate the stories of their youthful days as " a great secret," and " not to be told to anybody."

Vividly to my mind comes the memory of autumn days spent in farm-houses, where I gleaned all kinds of folk-lore from old farmers who sat in ancient armchairs, and from the aged dames who knitted stockings in the fireside corners of the settles.

The housewives were invariably typical Welshwomen, who " made ends meet " in curious ways. When I asked for " old stories " the candles were " douted "—that is, blown out— and the only light allowed was the fire-glow made by a huge log placed on the burning coals. Reverently, almost with apologies, the old women would answer questions, or relate their grandfather's or grandmother's experiences. The old men were bolder, and would plunge into the subject with considerable energy.

In this way I collected many particulars about witches, wizards, charms, and spells, and added them to those given me by my father, who had obtained stories from his father and grandfather, and other relatives.

Beginning with witches and wizards, the power of " bewitching " anybody appears to have been acquired in various uncanny ways in North and South Wales alike.

The wizard and witch were known by their hooked noses, pointed chins, hanging under-lip, wry teeth, chapped finger-tips, and lump of flesh under the jaw or on some part of the neck.

They all had a knowledge of medicines and poisons.   By the use of certain mixtures they quickened their power.   In Wales it is commonly said that if you look steadily into the eyes of a witch you will see yourself " upside down," and these women have two pupils in their eyes.   When they die their souls pass out of their bodies in the shape of a " great big moth."   Their eyebrows meet over their noses.

Some of the methods were as follows :

1. The members or novices were marked by the prick of a needle while they renounced their Maker.

2. They were compelled to kiss a toad.

3. They must abjure God and promise to obey the commands of the devil.

4. They were obliged to make a pretence of eating the bread of the Holy Sacrament, and place the piece in their pockets. Then, on leaving the church, they would meet a dog, to which they threw the bread.   In this form they would sell their souls to the devil.

5. They were taught to look upside down.

6. A mark was printed on the body of the witch or wizard, and in that part they had no feeling ever afterwards.

7. Their shoulders and feet were anointed with an uncanny salve, by which means they were able to make a broomstick do duty for a horse.

8. They must drink out of a cow's hoof or a horse's head.

An incantation used by witches and repeated in Welsh was translated as follows :

> " In the devil's name
> We pour water among this meal [earth].
> For long doing and ill heal
> We put it into the fire,
> That it may be burnt as we desire.
> It shall be burnt with our will,
> As any bubble upon a kill [kiln]."

One of the witch rhymes or runes ran thus :

" One, two, three, four,
The devil is at the door.
Make him welcome from floor to roof,
Drink to him in a horse's hoof.
Bring the cat and toad and bran ;
Come to the feast. all ye who can.
One, two, three, four,
The devil is here, so no more !"

[Family Collection.]

The favourite haunts of Welsh witches were desolate places far from the busy centres of toil and traffic.

In Anglesea they held their revels near the Druidical stones and beside the Roman watch-tower on Pen Caer Cybi, Holy Island. They were known to frequent the rocky islet of Ynys Gadarn when making compacts with the devil. Lake Coron, near Aberffraw, was another tryst.

In Carnarvonshire, Mynydd Mawr was celebrated as a haunt of the witches, who held high revel among the ruins of the British fortification that crowns the highest point of the summit. Penmaen Mawr, the Gliders, Snowdon, and many of the passes and ravines among the mountains, had the reputation of being frequented by witches.

In Denbighshire the Hiraethog Mountains, the Clwydian Range, the Berwyn Mountains, Lake Alwen, and other places, were patronized by them.

Moel-y-Parc, in Flintshire ; Cader Idris and the shores of Bala Lake, in Merionethshire ; Plinlimmon, the Breiddin Hills, the Long Mountains, and the Kerry Hills, in Montgomeryshire, were reputed places of rendezvous for witches.

South Wales was perhaps even more renowned than the North for these haunts of witches. The Breconshire Beacons ; the Preceley Mountains ; Radnor Forest ; the Black Mountains ; Craig-y-Llyn, near Glyn Neath ; the Pencaer Hills ; the shores of Pembrokeshire, Carmarthen, and Glamorgan ; and the mountains dividing Wales from Monmouthshire, have curious and weird stories connected with them.

All the witches who held their revels in these localities followed their vocation in much the same way.

They were said to anoint their bodies with uncanny salve, and to wear a girdle of snake-skin, and by these and other means they were enabled to bestride a churn-staff, a broom-handle, a distaff, ladle, shovel, pitchfork, or even the branch of a certain twig, and, muttering a spell, could take flight wherever they wished.

An old story about a witch living near the Ogmore River, in Glamorgan, describes a man listening to the muttering of a woman, and instantly giving her chase, with the result that in the " twinkling of an eye " he found himself on the top of the Garth Mountain, near Whitchurch.

An old Welsh agricultural story was to the effect that the site of a dance or a revel of the witches could be traced in the early morning by a perfectly round track showing the print of cows' and goats' feet. Young witches in their novitiate had to nurture and " tend toads." Whoever chanced to see a witches' dance had only to breathe the name of Christ, and all the wicked women would vanish.

Pembrokeshire witches were accustomed to go to sea in egg-shells, because their foremothers came from Flanders by the same means, and settled in West Wales. The Flemings were credited with having imported a " new breed of witches," who were a terror to the South-West and West of Wales.

Witches were attributed with much power and mischief. For this reason it was wise to please, and dangerous to offend, them. The following superstitions regarding Welsh witches have been collected from various parts of Wales :

If a witch walks to the churn and says, " Here's a fine bit of butter coming," the cream will froth and not produce butter.

A woman should never spin or knit in or near a field, for the witches will tangle the yarn.

If a cow is " bewitched," put the milk into a crock over the fire and whip it with switches, or stir it with a clean and sharp sickle. The pain makes the witch appear.

Never throw the combings of your hair into the roadway. If you do you will get into the power of witchcraft.

On Nos Cyn Calan gauaf—that is, Hallowe'en—while conse-crated bells are ringing, witches are hindered from hurting anybody.

If you throw any kind of knife with a cross burnt into the

14

handle out into a storm of wind, you will soon discover the witch, or witches, who raised the tempest. This may account for the appearance of so many sickle, spade, fork, and billhook handles with crosses burnt into them. The agricultural districts of Wales contain many specimens, and the present generation cannot tell why this custom is still kept up

When witches prevent butter coming, put a knife under the churn. If a woman borrows soap and thanks you for it, she is a witch. She that makes butter on a Monday or Saturday is a " witch for sure and certain." In South Glamorgan women, upon being greeted with " Good-morning !" always responded in the same words ; then if a witch met them, they could not be hurt. A witch can never harm a cow that has white feet and a white stripe down its back.

If a thing is bewitched, burn it, and immediately afterwards the witch will come to borrow something of you. If you give what she asks, she will go free ; if you refuse it, she will burn, and a mark will be on her body the next day.

When the kettle is bewitched and will not boil, put under it sticks of three kinds of wood. If you talk about witches on a Wednesday or a Friday, they will brew mischief for you. Eggshells should be broken up small or thrown into the fire, or the Pembrokeshire witches will hurt the people who ate the eggs and the hens that laid them. Pembrokeshire witches hurt the cattle by skimming the dew off the pastures. If you tie pieces of red ribbon or red rags around the tails of the cows the first time they are driven out to pasture, they cannot be bewitched.

A witch in the neighbourhood of Swansea made all the animals in a farmyard very ill. They were all put into an enclosure, and a barrier of hazel wand defied further molestation.

White dimity window-curtains drawn across the window at night prevent witches peeping in. Let the witch have the wall or best side of the path. A limestone pebble with natural hole in it was suspended by a cord to the door to prevent witches' influence. This superstition was only known where limestone was to be found. The pebble often took the place of the horseshoe, or was used with it. Eat, if only a crumb, before you go out in the morning, or you will be bewitched. A hare's foot carried in the pocket defies witches.

Wear your body linen inside out if you would avoid the evil work of witches. When you meet a witch, turn your thumbs inward and close the fingers firmly upon them.

When several people talking together suddenly became silent, they said " A witch is passing." Another expression was," Silence in the pig-market !—a witch goes by."

The baleful influences of the evil eye were at work, the people said, " in every town and village." A woman or man with two pupils to the eye, or a " wall-eye," or with eyes of two colours, or a " squinting eye," or with any defect of that organ, was supposed to be able to fascinate and bewitch people. If any person felt conscious of possessing the evil eye, he or she was told to gaze intently upon a lifeless object, and thus prevent its baneful power. It was formerly said that if a person with the evil eye was the first to enter a shop or market in the morning, the sales would be slow and unsatisfactory for the day. Any person possessing eyes with a spiteful or angry expression had a " touch of the evil eye in them." Amulets of all kinds were worn as a protection against the evil eye.

In the witch stories connected with Wales salt is mentioned as a safeguard against every kind of sorcery. If you had bread and salt in your pocket, you would be safe against witchcraft.

People formerly said : " If you put a few leaves of ground ivy in your hat or coat, and go to church on the Nos Calan gauaf, you will soon see who are witches and wizards in the congregation."

In Glamorgan, about fifty years ago, tailors were always associated with witchcraft. The ancestors of people living there asserted that tailors possessed the power to " bewitch " anybody if they wished. For this reason tailors always looked " lean and miserable."

A twig of mountain-ash was carried in the left-hand pocket of a man, or in the left side of a woman's bodice, to keep apparitions and witches away.

The penal degradation of a man into a beast, as taught in the old doctrine of transmigration, was probably responsible for the belief that the hare and the witch were synonymous. In all the old stories about witches, from one end of Wales to the other, the hare appears. It attended the uncanny revels of the witches' Sabbath, and when the weird sisters took flight upon being disturbed, they were supposed to ascend to the sky on broomsticks, to navigate the sea in eggshells, and to travel the earth in the shape of hares. It is quite common to hear working men in the country calling hares that cannot be caught "the old witch." When a hare is very difficult to skin, the women say: "This one was a bad old witch"; or when a hare is slow in being cooked, they say : "This old witch has many sins to answer for."

A century ago, and even later, many people in Wales refused to eat hare even when given as a present, fearing they would be eating a witch. The peasantry in remote places will now refuse to eat hare, and when you ask them why, they say : "We don't know; but grandfather, and great-grandfather, and old, old [meaning great-great] grandfather, would never eat a hare himself, nor let anybody of the family eat of it."

Yet they will eat rabbits.

Hare-lipped people are supposed to have descended from persons bewitched in the past, or from ancestors who were very evil witches. The hare-lip was formerly called "the mark of the witch."

Fifty years ago it was generally believed that witches and wizards could assume the shape of a hare or a fox. A hare of twenty years was supposed to become a witch, and a witch of eighty turns into a hare again.

In all parts of Wales similar stories of a mysterious hare that baffled the best hounds were told. Many localities had the reputation of providing a good day's sport, but no capture. Huntsmen declared that these hares would continually baffle the hounds.

Some stories describe farmers going forth to kill the objectionable hare, with the result that the animal could not be slain right off; but the men were able to track her course by the drops of blood which fell from her wounded body.   In this way they traced the hare into the house of the witch, who had thrown herself on the bed, and, transformed into her woman shape, was groaning with agony.

Another witch who assumed the hare shape was discovered by means of a maimed ankle, which the huntsmen said she received by falling down a quarry when the hounds were after her.

In a lonely part of South Glamorgan a certain hare baffled the hounds for many years.   The animal's head was described as being quite grey with age, and it was stated that she had lost all her teeth.   She was seen frequently early in the morning running among the cows in the meadows, and the farmers knew she was a witch because the yield of milk was always less when the hare was about.   After years of chasing, both by hounds and huntsmen, the hare was slain.   Because the people thought the hare was a woman transformed into animal shape, they gave the body a " decent burial "; and it was asserted that from the moment the hare was killed the witch disappeared, and was never again seen in the district.

A butcher living near the sea at Cadoxton-juxta-Barry, in South Glamorgan, was reported to be the son of a witch. Whenever he wished to buy stock of the neighbouring farmers the latter were obliged to sell to him, or the animals would surely die..

An old woman, probably the mother of the butcher, could turn herself into a hare at will.   When in this state the hounds could not catch her.   One day three gentlemen took three grey-hounds, and, seeing the hare which they thought was a witch, they hunted the animal through the fields and into the house. By some means the hare's foot was caught in the doorway, and the animal suddenly vanished.   Next day the witch was very lame, and people said she had a hare's foot for life.

Stories of three-legged hares come from Mid-Wales and Pembrokeshire.

Transformation of witches into the shape of a cat appears in the North and South of Wales.

A Merionethshire farmer on his wedding morning threw a stone at a cat, and before nightfall he was indisposed.   He lived only three months after his marriage, because, as the people said, he had struck a witch in the form of a cat.

A Cardiganshire story describes a cat's left paw being cut off by a tailor, who cruelly used his shears for the purpose. The next morning his wife appeared without her left hand.

Transformation into the shape of a wild goose was known in some parts of Wales.

Not far from Porthcawl, in Glamorgan, an old woman who had the reputation of being a witch was supposed to take flight occasionally in the form of a grey goose. She disturbed the operations of sportsmen, who declared that they had a bad day whenever the grey goose appeared. This grey goose frequented the solitary sand-dunes between Porthcawl and Margam.

In North Glamorgan witches sometimes took the form of a fox. The animal baffled the hounds, and led huntsmen into dangerous places. Neither mask nor brush would the huntsmen have when the witch led them.

The mischief of witches is well known, but a few instances of their work may be interesting, as having been obtained from aged people who were eyewitnesses of the deeds.

A farmer's wife in the Vale of Glamorgan was putting cream in the churn ready for butter-making when a local witch looked in. The housewife immediately ordered her away. The witch " cast her eye " upon the churn, and went silently out. From that moment the butter was exceedingly " slow in coming." At last the good woman saw that it was impossible to make butter. Presently she remembered that in the lane leading to the woods not far from her house the hated witches' butter grew. This is a fungus growing on decayed wood. To thrust a pin or skewer into this fungus was supposed to be an excellent remedy for undoing the mischief of witches. But the goodwife of this story heated a poker to a white heat, and with it destroyed the witches' butter, thereby breaking the spell. As the butter melted groans and the sound of flapping wings could be heard. The farmer's wife then returned to the churn, and the butter soon came. [*Family Collection.*]

A notorious witch living in 1859 took a pair of boots to a local shoemaker for repairs She wished to get them done as quickly as possible. The shoemaker said he would not be able to complete them in the time named. The witch went out muttering revenge. Ten minutes later the shoemaker tried to move from his bench, but failed. " It was just as if somebody had glued him to it," said my informant, who saw the man in his uncomfortable predicament. Before the shoemaker could move the people had to send for the witch. She refused to come, but after keeping the man in durance from 10 a.m. to 10 p.m. she released him. [*Family Collection.*]

There were formerly many clever but eccentric men in Wales, who had the reputation of being wizards and familiar with some kind of legerdemain. A few of these, some connected with the North and others with the South of the Principality, will serve to illustrate all. These men healed sicknesses of body and mind. They foretold people's deaths, cured diseases by means of an unknown and mysterious art, and were skilful surgeons. A few of these men never attained more than mediocrity in this respect, while others were reputed conjurers.

The most remarkable man of the South was the renowned Dr. Harris of Cwrt-y-Cadno. He lived in the Vale of Towy, Carmarthenshire. He was popularly known as the " Dyn Hysbys," which, literally translated, means the " manifest or evident person or man "—in other words, a man capable of manifestations. Several stories were told about him. About forty-five or fifty years ago a man of Pontardulais lost ten pounds, which was taken from his house by some person or persons unknown. Every effort to recover the money failed, and at last the poor man who had lost all his hard earnings went in despair to Dr. Harris. The Dyn Hysbys, after a few questions, said that the money would be found in a heap of rags, concealed in a cupboard, beside the kitchen fire, while the thief was his own relative. The man returned home and immediately found the money.

Dr. Harris appears to have been skilful in thought-reading and crystal-gazing. A well-authenticated instance was the following occurrence : Two men living in a rural district went to Swansea to sell corn. On the way home the men in the waggon fell asleep. In the waggon were empty sacks, while in the pocket of one of the sleepers was the money obtained by the sale of the corn. The men awoke to find both the money and the sacks gone. After a fruitless search, they went to consult Dr. Harris. The latter then led the men into a room and placed a round mirror before them. He told them to look at it, and instead of seeing their own reflection, they saw the roadway, their own figures in sleeping attitude, and a neighbour, who was far above suspicion, taking possession of the empty sacks and money !

On some occasions Dr. Harris persisted in marking the thief, so that the person could be known immediately. For this reason many people objected, fearing the mark on the culprit would be permanent, and prove that they had consulted the Dyn Hysbys. An illustration of this happened to a man of Glamorgan. A farmer living not far from Neath sold some cattle in the local fair, and went home with the purchase-money, amounting to about one hundred pounds. In the fair and after it the old man indulged freely in ardent spirits, and soon after reaching home went to bed. The next morning he could not find the money. After searching the house and making inquiries in Neath without success, the farmer, three days later, consulted Dr. Harris of Cwrt-y-Cadno. The doctor told him that he would cause the thief to keep his bed for twelve months as a punishment ; but he would find his bag containing the hundred pounds hanging from a nail behind his own stable door. The farmer returned, and immediately found his lost bag. A few days later a neighbouring farmer was seized with illness, which became so serious that he was confined to his bed for twelve months. The farmer had suspicions, but said nothing, because the money had been restored. Three years afterwards the thief had a fatal illness, and just before his death confessed that after stealing the money he had no rest for two nights, because the Dyn Hysbys came to him in his sleep, awakened him, and urged him to return the stolen money to its rightful owner. Relatives of the persons connected with the foregoing narratives are still living.

If there was anything greatly disliked by Dr. Harris of Cwrt-y-Cadno it was meanness and cheatery. Not far from Carmarthen town a man of considerable means lived, but he was of a very selfish disposition, and almost begrudged the money for food. He once asked two friends, with the Dyn Hysbys, to accompany him into his garden. The party went, and were soon admiring the profusion and quality of the fruit, especially of the apples, pears, and plums. All their admiration passed unnoticed by their owner, who did not offer so much as a pear to his visitors. The Dyn Hysbys challenged him to give them at least one pear each to prove their quality. " They are not fit for picking," said the old man. " Nonsense," said the Dyn Hysbys. " Those up there against the wall will soon drop." " They are as hard as iron," said his host. " Try them," said the Dyn Hysbys, placing a ladder against the wall, pretending he would himself ascend and prove the truth of his assertion. " No, no," said his host ; " I'll go myself." He ascended the ladder, tried the pears, and exclaimed : " I told you so. They are as hard as iron." Then he prepared to descend the ladder. He could not, for his feet refused to reach the next rung, and his hands were glued to the top one. At first he thought it was nervousness, and he began to shake the ladder, but he could not move an inch. Presently he began to fume and fret, but at length he started swearing, to the amusement of his visitors, who laughed immoderately. Then he called the Dyn Hysbys all the bad names in the Welsh vocabulary. There are not many, it is true, but they are remarkably forceful. There he remained for a few hours until his voice was worn out by the repetition of various epithets, which grew milder, and at last became pathetically imploring. Uttering a few words, the Dyn Hysbys released him, saying : " That's how all should serve thee for thy selfishness !" The old man never forgot his tormentor, but in fear he always sent a hamper of the best selected fruit to Dr. Harris every year afterwards.

Another story of this wonderful man was to the effect that when he was visiting a relative in Swansea, his hostess asked him to order and pay for a joint of meat. When the sum was named, he exclaimed at hearing the cost, which he regarded as excessive. The butcher went to the end of the shop to place the meat in the basket, and while he did so the Dyn Hysbys wrote a spell on a piece of paper, and concealed it in a crack of the desk, after which he went to his relative's house. The Dyn Hysbys had not long left the butcher's shop when the man's

wife heard a curious noise. It was of somebody dancing,
stepping, and singing in the shop. Thinking a drunken man
might have entered, she went in, and, to her horror, saw her
husband capering boisterously and singing. This is what he
sang :

> " Eight and six for meat !
> What a wicked cheat !"

She called upon him to be quiet, but it was of no avail, for in a
moment she gave a hop towards her husband, and, joining her
hands with his, began dancing and singing as wildly as he.
The servant came in, and she was seized with the same trouble,
and after her followed the errand-boy and the butcher's two
children. Six individuals were now dancing and singing :

> " Eight and six for meat !
> What a wicked cheat !"

By-and-by the noise surprised passers-by, and the neighbours, many of whom entered to see what the uproar was about.
Everybody laughed right heartily at such a ludicrous scene.
At last somebody asked if the Dyn Hysbys had been there, and
the butcher nodded his head, whereupon the clever man was
sent for. He came, removed the paper from the desk, and the
dancing and singing ceased. " That will teach you not to over-
charge honest people again." [*A. B. and Family Collection.*]

Another Dr. Harris, popularly known as Abe Biddle, and
equally clever as the Dyn Hysbys, his namesake of Cwrt-y-
Cadno, in Carmarthenshire, lived at Werndew, in Pembrokeshire. He was a specialist in certain diseases, and well known
beyond his native county. In the early part of the nineteenth
century the name of Dr. Harris, Werndew, was a household
word all around Fishguard, Goodwick, and the coastline for
his medical skill. His name, Abe Biddle, the magician and
master of all occult subjects, was at once a source of service
in cases of theft and a terror to the wrong-doer, and certainly
a cause of fear to naughty children who refused to obey their
parents.

There are many stories told of him, and particularly of his
discovery of theft, which, if true, would have been a boon to
modern society when valuable jewels mysteriously disappear.

Abe Biddle was once called upon to pay a visit to an English lady of rank who was staying at the seat of a wealthy Pembrokeshire family. The doctor is described as having been tall, slender, and somewhat lanky, with large, deep-set eyes, long and shaggy white hair, and a dreamy or preoccupied manner; but when roused he was fiery and commanding. His voice was well modulated, and his manner particularly courteous. As a doctor and an occultist he was much respected. When Abe was introduced to the English Countess, she was agreeably surprised to find, as she afterwards said, " such a perfect gentleman and remarkable magician." She described the jewels she had lost, and declared they were quite safe in her travelling-bag when she left a certain mansion early in the dawn of the previous day. Abe Biddle opened his very professional-looking bag, and therefrom drew forth a good-sized mirror, which he put to stand on a table. He asked the Countess to look well into the mirror, and tell him what she saw. Turning a chair, he requested the lady to be seated. When she had " composed herself," Abe asked what she saw. She replied : " I see nothing but a mist like steam from a boiler." " Look again," said Abe. She looked, and said : " I see a mist, vapour, clouds . . . they are rolling away. And now I see a woman in a dress of white brocade." " Do you know her ?" asked Abe. " Her back is turned to me," answered the Countess. The doctor told her to pause and close her eyes for a few minutes. The Countess did so, and looked again. She saw the figure slowly turning round, and presently her face was plainly visible. To her surprise, she saw some of her jewels in her hands, others upon her neck and in her hair. The Countess recognized in the lady a personal friend of her hostess, from whom she had recently taken leave. Abe Biddle was asked to make investigations, which he did with considerable tact. The result was the restoration of the jewels to their rightful owner. The lady who had appropriated the gems was a sleep-walker and kleptomaniac.

Abe Biddle was a very clever illusionist, and could alarm and surprise people.

On one occasion some clergymen who had been attending important services in the district assembled in the vicarage for supper. This would be about the end of the eighteenth century, when it was the custom of visitors, male and female, to tell any quaint old tale that came within their knowledge. Conversation turned upon the white art, or astrology ; the black art, or magic and necromancy; and conjuration, or illusion. Some of the friends present, knowing Abe Biddle's repute, wished he would enter into the discussion, but he remained silent. By-and-by he quitted the room, and returned with three small rings, which he placed on the floor. He hurriedly left the room, taking care to quietly lock the door. Immediately everybody's eyes were fixed on the rings. In the midst of each of these a fly suddenly appeared, and began buzzing. These flies grew and developed into hornets. The visitors wondered what was going to happen, when the hornets increased and multiplied, until the room was filled with them. The terror-stricken people cried out, and Abe Biddle opened the door, through which the hornets disappeared, and the clerics were convinced of the magician's power.

One of the well-known men of mystery in the North was Robin Ddu Ddewin, or Black Robin the Wizard, a native of Baradwys, Anglesea. It was said he could do many uncanny deeds.*

On one occasion he went to a farmer to beg a small quantity of wool. His request was refused. On his way home he entered a field belonging to the farmer, and was heard counting the cattle and horses, which numbered six in all. Before midnight the animals were dead.

He could be kind as well as malicious. A poor old woman lived in a solitary cottage. She was half-witted and despised by her neighbours. One day Robin found her crying because the people had refused her the privilege of "leasing," or gleaning, and the boys pelted her with lumps of earth or turf. "They shall rue for it," said Black Robin. Two days later the farmers who had refused to allow the old woman to glean, and the boys who pelted her with earth and turf, were taken ill. Fever held them in bondage, and two out of the number died. Then the people said that "Black Robin had been at work."

* William Davies (Gwilym Glan Ogwy).

One day Black Robin met a farmer carrying hay. The wizard begged a " fork-load " of it for his merlyn, or mountain pony. The farmer sharply refused, and proceeded downhill slowly with his waggon and horses. He had not gone far before the horses went down on their knees, and the load of hay fell over into the road. Every effort to get the horses on their feet failed, and, in despair, the farmer implored Robin to " undo the spell." For a time Robin refused, but when he thought the farmer had been sufficiently punished, he yielded. The horses were soon on their feet again, and the farmer gave Robin as much hay as he required.

Huw Llwyd, who lived in the reign of James I., was renowned as a wizard astrologer and magician. He was a native of Merionethshire, and at a place called Cymorthyn, near Festiniog, on the River Cynfael, where there are some beautiful cascades, stands a rock known as Huw Llwyd's pulpit. From that rocky rostrum, beside a deep, dark pool, the magician was accustomed to deliver his nocturnal addresses and incantations. When Huw Llwyd was in the zenith of his power, Edmund Pryse, Archdeacon of Merioneth, proved himself a rival master of the black and white arts. It is recorded in Welsh lore that these " two of a trade " failed to agree, and quarrels arose between the " masters."

The following story is told about Maentwrog Fair day.

In an ancient hostelry, while music and dancing were the order of the evening, Huw Llwyd merrily passed the time with his convivial companions.

It chanced that Archdeacon Pryse passed, and, seeing him Huw put his head through the lattice, and invited the church dignitary to come in and share the fun. The Archdeacon, who always sternly denounced convivial assemblies, very indignantly refused the invitation. At the same time he was not above exercising his occult powers. In a few minutes he caused two large horns to grow one on each side of Huw Llwyd's head, so that the latter could not be withdrawn from the window. In this position Huw had to remain for many hours, until the Archdeacon was pleased to release his rival in legerdemain. Huw was not slow in revenge. He knew that the Archdeacon would be obliged to pass the old water-mill on his way to his

house, Ty-du. Huw secreted himself in the mill, and it is
gravely asserted that he commissioned two demons to seize
the Archdeacon as he passed by. These demons dragged the
Archdeacon under the large trough which conveyed water to
turn the big wheel, while another let the water on. In this
way the Archdeacon was drenched to the skin, and sent home
in a pitiable condition.

Another story describes Huw Llwyd at midnight near the
deep, dark pool beside his pulpit at Cwmorthyn, summon-
ing numbers of fiends to his presence, and commanding them
to go forth on his missions. His nocturnal incantations were
weird and sometimes terrible, and if anybody offended him,
the revenge was often severe. A farmer who lived not many
miles from Festiniog once disturbed Huw in his incantations,
and it is stated that this greatly offended the wizard, who
pronounced a curse upon the farm and all that was " on or
in it." For a whole year disaster attended all operations
upon the farm. The harvests were failures, the cattle pined
away, the flocks were disturbed by foxes, the fruitage was
scarce, and illness affected the farmer's household. At last
the offender was obliged to go and beg Huw Llwyd's forgive-
ness, which he obtained, and all things came right again.

Huw Llwyd was a poet and soldier in the army of James I.,
and he is said to have held an important commission, and to
have served on the Continent. He was also a poet of considerable renown. In an encounter between Archdeacon Pryse
near Festiniog, Huw quickly prostrated the church dignitary,
but both became friends again. Both could foretell future
events, and their counsel was much sought after by the inhabitants of the northern parts of the Principality. But while
the Archdeacon pronounced the magical incantations, and
practised the black art in his study, Huw Llwyd uttered
his in the spot where his pulpit is still to be seen. Huw
Llwyd died in 1620, and Archdeacon Edmund Pryse of
Merioneth wrote an elegy upon his celebrated rival's death.

A few days before Huw Llwyd died he called his daughter
to his side, and begged her to throw all his books of magic and
black art into the Llyn Pont, Rhyddu, " the lake by the bridge
of the black ford." The daughter much desired to preserve

the books, which were of considerable value, and contained her father's notes upon astronomical lore and the medicinal virtues of certain herbs.   They included astrological calculations " second to none in the world," says the old story. Thrice the daughter went forth with the books of astrology known as the " white art " and magic, or the " black art," and thrice concealed them.   But Huw Llwyd declared he " could not die in peace " until the books were thrown into the lake. Once more the daughter went forth, and this time threw the books into the Llyn.   Just as the volumes reached the surface of the water a mysterious hand was seen to be uplifted from the depths of the Llyn.   It carefully grasped the books, and drew them into the black depths of the water.   Then Huw Llwyd died in peace.*   His grandson was Morgan Llwyd, the great Puritan preacher of Gwynedd, who was buried at Wrexham in July, 1659.   It is said that Morgan Llwyd inherited his grandfather's gift of being able to foretell important events with the greatest possible accuracy.   Huw Llwyd wrote an epitaph upon himself.   It appeared in *The Greal*, a Welsh magazine published in London, 1805.

* Rev. Elias Owen, " Welsh Folk-lore," pp. 252, 253.

'CHAPTER XVII

CHARMS, PENTACLES, AND SPELLS

CHARMS for healing and other purposes and spells of various kinds were popular in Wales so late as thirty years ago, and even in the present day there are several survivals of the old-time beliefs.

Doctors of the old school who failed, or had no patience to cure or find out the complaints from which their patients suffered, invariably recommended the persons to a noted " healer," by which they meant charmer. Some of these men— and women, too—had almost miracle-working powers, and they were much sought after by people of all classes

The power to heal by charms or other mysterious or secret agency was inherited. The gift passed from father to son, or mother to daughter, and was said never to leave the family. Then, again, the healing charm had to be gratuitously done, or the virtue would leave the charmer. Money was never taken for a work, but the person who had received temporary relief or cure was expected to send a gift in kind. In some instances a money gift was accepted, but never a fee. The secrets of the art were seldom divulged, but from time to time the methods of the healer have been discovered.

As a rule, the healer who used charms was the seventh son or seventh daughter in a direct line without alteration of sex. They could heal all kinds of hurts with a stroke of the hand. They could cure wens at the throat and disperse tumours. They had charm remedies for cancer, consumption, and a variety of diseases, but kept them very secretly. Headache was cured in the following way : The charmer, or doctor, filled one bowl with cold water and one with melted tallow. The patient's head was held in the water for a few

224

seconds, while the tallow was poured into the water through a carding comb. This process was repeated thrice, then the water was poured on the nearest elder-tree and the cold tallow was thrown into the fire. Immediately afterwards, the headache was cured.

For convulsions in children or adults the cure was wrought by concealing a horseshoe under their pillows.

If a child was sick, its godfather was called to carry it three times up and down the room. This was a " certain cure."

For children who were late in learning to walk it was customary to make them creep under a blackberry bramble.

For ague the sufferer was to go silently, without crossing water, to a hollow willow-tree. He was to breathe into the hole three times, then stop the aperture as quickly as possible, and go home without looking round or speaking a word. The ague would be immediately cured. The same affliction was cured if the sufferer stuck an elder branch in the ground and bade the ague depart.

A posthumous child, by putting its hands on a tumour, could charm it away.

If a child born with a tooth or teeth in its mouth passed its saliva over the bite or scratch made by any animal, the sore would be thus charmed away.

For hiccough the sufferer was advised to drink out of a mug or jug over the handle.

For nettle stings a few leaves of the field dock are taken, spat upon, and rubbed into the affected part, while the person says : " In dock, out nettle."

Sprained arms and legs were cured by the following charm : A long length of black yarn was made into a kind of thick cord or rope. Nine knots were made at equal distances on this and bound around the injured limb. The person binding had to say :

> "Bone to bone, skin to skin ;
> Satan go out, Christ come in."

The same spell words were used for dislocations.

Earth lifted with the right hand from under the right foot of a child was supposed to heal sores.

A curious spell for healing purposes was translated from a kind of imperfect Welsh in a village near Bridgend, Glamorgan.

15

The translator could not tell for what it was used, but he remembered the rhyme, which was sometimes said in Welsh, and often in English—thus :

> " God the Father down did ride,
> Quick and fast the fork He tried.
> He lifted worms that were out of sight—
> One was black, the other was white ;
> One was mottled, one was red ;
> Soon the worms were killed and dead.
> Heal, O Lord, as soon as said !"
>
> [*Family Collection.*]

Gout was charmed by the patient being put into a bed or bag filled with barley, and over him an old sheepskin would be thrown, and the " sweating " caused thereby was efficacious.

Erysipelas was charmed by means of sparks struck from stone or steel against the face — a very painful and highly dangerous cure, and probably seldom attempted

Earache was charmed in a woman by means of a man's breeches wrapped round her head. A man, for the same malady, wrapped around his head a woman's flannel petticoat or stocking.

To charm boils, " squeeze them with crossed knives " !

A charm for hæmorrhage of any kind was worked thus : The person who exercised the charm dipped his or her finger in blood, and made the sign of the cross upon the patient's forehead. The charmer then recited nine times the following words from Ezekiel : " And when I passed by thee and saw thee polluted in thine own blood, I said unto thee when thou wast in thy blood, Live ; yea, I said unto thee, when thou wast in thy blood, Live."

Apoplexy was charmed by a sharpened hatchet placed on the threshold of the sufferer.

Whooping-cough was charmed in this way : A small lock of hair was cut from the back of the head of the person suffering from the cough. It was then placed sandwich fashion between two pieces of bread and butter. This was given to a dog, and then the animal was driven out of the house. The whooping-cough would then leave the sufferer.

Epilepsy was overcome by a curious charm. When a grave was reopened, people stripped a piece of metal from an old coffin. It was cut in circular shape, a hole was bored in it, and this amulet was worn suspended from a ribbon around the neck.   The metal should drop as low as the heart.

The following charm was recited as a cure for burns and scalds : " Three little angels came from East and West. Each one tried the fire and ice to test.   In frost, out fire !   In the name of the Father, the Son, and the Holy Ghost."   While repeating this the reciter described a circle with the index-finger of the right hand.   Three circles were made from right to left, going " wildershins," or contrary to the sun's motion. Nine circles in all were made, and then the reciter would blow three times on the affected part.   [*Family Collection.*]

For toothache several charms were used.   In Carmarthen-shire and West Wales generally the charm ran thus :

" Jesus was passing by one day, and saw Peter sitting under a sycamore-tree, grievously tormented with the toothache. And Jesus said : ' What aileth thee, Peter ?'   And Peter answered and said : ' Lord, I am grievously tormented with the toothache.'   And Jesus said : ' Arise, follow Me ; thou shalt be tormented by the toothache no more.'   And imme-diately the toothache left him."

This was written on a piece of notepaper, made into a square and sealed.   The name of the sufferer was written across the back of the paper, which was not to be opened.

Another charm for the same ailment ran as follows :

> " Peter sat on a marble stone.
> Jesus came to him all alone.
> ' What's up, Peter ?'
> ' The toothache, my Lord.'

" ' Rise up, Peter, and be cured of this pain, and all who carry these few lines for My sake.' "   [*A. B. and C. D.*]

These words were written on a piece of paper, folded neatly, and kept on the person in a safe place, and so long as it was worn, the toothache did not trouble the patient.

A collier from one of the valleys of South Wales, only recently, declared that his fellow-workmen passed this charm on from one to the other, and with almost immediate relief. In the present day the charm is written on a piece of paper, enclosed in an envelope, and sealed.

For jaundice the sufferer was advised to get by stealth the

grease-pot of a carrier or any wheelwright. If he looked for ten minutes into it, the malady would pass away.

The old charm for jaundice was to put a gold coin at the bottom of a pewter mug, fill it with clear mead, and ask the patient to look into it without drinking any. This was to be done while repeating the Lord's Prayer nine times over without a mistake.

For a peculiar and complicated kind of liver complaint the following formula was carried out. Three visits had to be paid to the healer, and one must be on Sunday. The healer would on the first occasion fill a teacup with oatmeal, then cover it with a linen cloth, and tie it up as a pudding would be tied, so that the meal would not escape. The healer then applied the cup to the right and left sides, the stomach, the back, and between the shoulders. This he did nine times, walking round the patient, but the cup was not applied between the shoulders on the second occasion. During each application of the cup a portion of Scripture was repeated *sotto voce* by the healer. It was from St. Matthew (xv. 22-26). The healer began with the words : " And behold a woman," ending with, " cast it to dogs." This portion of Scripture was slowly recited nine times. After the ninth application of the cup the cloth was removed from the oatmeal. If the disease was slight, there would be a large crack in the oatmeal. If the case was very bad, part of the oatmeal would have disappeared. In extreme cases all the meal would disappear. After the third time of charming the patient recovered. This charm was considered unfailing in working a cure.

A bone-setting charm ran as follows :

> " Lord, set it right again, right !
> Joint to joint and joint to joint !
> Marrow to marrow, bone to bone,
> So that this man can stand alone.
> Blood shall arise with skin to skin.
> Lord, set him right without and within !"
> [*C. D. and Family Collection.*]

For severe pain in the head or colic the charmer grasped the affected part, pressed it tightly, and exclaimed : " In the name of God, of Jesus Christ, and the Mother of Christ I seize thee, I squeeze thee. Go thou to rest in the chest where the

Lord God placed thee." This was repeated nine times in succession.

For the smallpox the charm words were : " In the name of the Lord I command thee to depart out of his skin, out of his bones, his blood, his veins, his joints, and all his limbs. Go thou to the Red Sea, and join Pharaoh and all his hosts."
[C. D.]

When epidemics assailed the people, the charmer would repeat the following incantation :

" God the Lord went over the land ;
Ninety sicknesses came from the sand.
Said the Lord to the ninety sick :
' Whither go ye ?   Answer Me quick.'
Then said the ninety of the sand :
' To take men's health we walk the land.
To hurt their limbs and fester their skin,
To shake them well without and within.'
Then spake the Lord : ' To the elder-bush go
That grows where the healing waters flow ;
See that ye do this thing just now,
And pull the bush down bough for bough.
Name the diseases ye bring from the sand.
Leave God the Lord to walk the land.' "
[Family Collection.]

Carmarthenshire and Pembrokeshire were renowned for the healer who could charm away diseases.   Glamorgan had several who exercised their arts in the nineteenth century.   Some of the healers who did not resort to charms for the cure of complaints had marvellous magnetic power, and they often cured people by merely passing their hands over the affected part. The late celebrated Dr. Price of Llantrisant, Glamorgan, had marvellous magnetic powers, and was known to cure people by a touch of the hand and by the strong power of his will.

An old lady near Swansea had the same power, and she exercised it with much success.

The late Dr. Harris of Cwrt-y-Cadno worked many cures by magnetic influence and will-power, and there are still, as people call them, " men in the West," who are renowned as bone-setters, healers, and makers of remedies which are secrets to them and their heirs for ever.

In South Glamorgan and West Pembrokeshire a curious remedy was used for the removal of warts.   A living snail with a black shell was rubbed on each wart while the person repeated the following rhyme :

> " Wart, wart, on the snail's shell black,
> Go away soon, and never come back."

The snail was then put on the branch of a tree or bramble, and fixed thereon by means of as many prickly thorns as there were warts.   When the snail has rotted the warts disappear.

For the cure of warts there were several charms.   One was to nail a brown snail to the doorpost with a wooden hammer. As the snail dries up the wart fades away.   Another remedy was to fix your eyes in the waxing moon and say three times, " May the moon increase, and may my suffering cease."

Many of the healing wells cured warts.   The method of obtaining a cure was to stick a pin in each wart, and then throw the pins into the well.   The warts soon vanished.   In some places a man undertook, for a small consideration, to " carry the warts into another country."   A blacksmith in Cardiff used to count people's warts, mark their number on his hat, and carry them away over Rumney Bridge into Monmouthshire, a place less than a mile from his smithy.

A Porthcawl blacksmith had a great reputation for removing warts.   He merely examined the warts, passed his hand over them, and told the person not to look at his hands until the next morning.   By that time the warts had vanished.

In several parts of Wales a toad was impaled on a stick, and the warts were rubbed on the creature.   As the toad died, the warts disappeared.   Elderberry leaves, plucked at midnight and burnt, will drive warts away.

An old woman said : " Steal a piece of fat bacon, bury it in the garden, and the warts will soon go."

A charm for driving rats away bore the following inscription :

> "R . A . T . S.
> A . R . S . T.
> T . S . R . A
> S . T . A . R"

This was placed in the mouth of the king of the rats, although how that creature was caught is not explained.   The letters read every way the same.   [*Family Collection.*]

A remedy against drinking habits was composed of the lungs

of a hog, which had to be roasted. If a man ate these after fasting all night, he would not be drunk the next day, no matter how much he drank. The broken bones of a sheep's skull carried in the pocket was a charm against disease.

The Arch-Druid wore upon his girdle the Crystal of Augury, encased in gold. It was part of the Druidical regalia.* " As this crystal sparkled or grew dim, the plaintiff or defendant, the prosecutor or prisoner, shook in his shoes."†

In later times mounted or unmounted crystal balls were used as charms against the evil eye. These balls were sometimes polished and unset, or set in gold, silver, or metal. They varied in size and shape. An old Welshman told me he remembered crystal balls being used for curing sickness and disease in man and beast. Water was poured over one of these stones, and afterwards given to the cattle and sheep to drink. Sometimes the stone was placed in a bowl of water, and the latter was afterwards distributed among people who suffered from any mental or physical malady. People came long distances to the owners of these crystal balls—for water for their flocks and herds, or for maladies that attacked their relatives and friends. If the stone was lent to anybody, the person going to fetch it must not speak nor sit, nor enter anybody's house, nor be found outside his own house after sunset. An incantation or prayer was uttered before the stone was dipped in the water. The following translation of the incantation in Welsh was given me :

> " O thou stone of Might and Right,
> Let me dip thee in the water—
> In the water of pure spring or of wave,
> In the name of St. David,
> In the name of the twelve Apostles,
> In the name of the Holy Trinity,
> And of Michael and all the angels,
> In the name of Christ and Mary His mother !
> Blessings on the clear shining stone !
> Blessings on the clear pure water !
> A healing of all bodily ills
> On man and beast alike !" [*A. B.*]

A stone of this description belonged to a family in South Glamorgan. It is now supposed to be in America, whereto the owner emigrated about 1845.

* Meyrick, " Costumes," p. 28.   † " Welsh Sketches," p. 21.

Some of these crystal balls appear to have been closely connected with the fate of a family. While the crystal remained whole, the owner would be lucky; but from the moment a flaw appeared in it or it was broken, the fortunes of the family would begin to decline. Before a death in the owner's family the crystal became damp and dim.

Various kinds of stones besides the crystals were held in great esteem for their curative powers. A dark red stone, probably the bloodstone, was used in the seventeenth century for murrain in cattle, and hydrophobia in man and animal. This stone was preserved carefully in a family until 1850, but soon afterwards was lost. A Welshman allowed me to look at a curious blue stone, which resembled an uncut sapphire. The owner told me that it belonged to his great-great-grandfather, who once befriended a witch. The witch, who had been much persecuted, was placed in the stocks, and also threatened with death, in the first half of the eighteenth century. While in the stocks she died suddenly. Just before her death she spat the blue stone out of her mouth to the man who had befriended her, as a charm to procure long life and prosperity. The owner of this stone told me he well remembered a collection of charm-stones and kindred objects being taken to a lime-kiln, where, by order of the Dissenting minister and the parson, they were burnt with the limestone. In this way many objects of antiquarian value were destroyed. The lore, which is now regarded as of unusual interest, was at that time suppressed as unholy superstition, but secretly it was cherished by the old people. Occasionally these charm-stones were applied to the seat of disease. Red jasper was much valued. To insure its efficacy the stone, when used, was never to be touched by the first finger of the right hand. Adder-stones and snail-heads were among the charm-workers. At one time amber heads were much used. An aged Welshwoman told me that in her grandmother's days all the girls and women who could buy them wore a string of amber beads around their necks, to protect them from the evil eye, blindness, and the power of witches. [*Family Collection.*]

In an old house-book, dated late in the eighteenth century,

particulars are given of amulets worn to prevent all kinds of
infectious complaints.

One was composed of the roots of plantain, colchicum, and
flowers of lavender. The roots were dried and reduced to
powder, which was placed in a small silken bag, and worn suspended around the neck. This amulet was considered very
efficacious in protecting the wearer against cholera and malignant fevers.

Another amulet consisted of vervain root, dried, powdered,
and worn in a sachet around the neck. This was supposed
to " cure all diseases," especially those of the head.

These amulets were equally efficacious in defeating the designs
of evil spirits and witchcraft as in protecting against sickness
and infection.

A favourite amulet in many parts of Wales in the days of
old was the beginning of the Gospel of St. John inscribed on
parchment, enclosed in a bag, and worn suspended by a ribbon
around the neck.

An amulet used for defeating evil spirits even more than
sickness and infection ran as follows : "Rotas, Opera, Tenet,
Arepo, Sator." This was seen inscribed on a small stone in
the year 1850 in Glamorgan, but the person who copied the
inscription was not allowed by the owner to keep this ancient
relic. What became of it subsequently is not known. It
was probably found among Roman remains, or with Roman
coins, and used by a Romanized Welsh person, for a British
torque was found near it

The following was copied from an old Welsh MS. in 1848.
It was composed of a combination of numbers, thus :

$$\begin{array}{rrrr} ``28, & 35, & 2, & 7=72. \\ 6, & 3, & 32, & 31=72. \\ 34, & 29, & 8, & 1=72. \\ 4, & 5, & 30, & 33=72." \end{array}$$

This, making a total of seventy-two, whichever way added
up, was written in the squares of a square figure, with your
enemy's name under it. The parchment was then neatly
folded, placed in a bag, and worn against the breast. It would
render your enemy powerless against you.

The talisman differed from the charm and amulet in having

power to defeat or summon the aid of supernatural beings or influences.   In Welsh lore a celebrated talisman is mentioned. It was no less than " The stone of the ring of Luned, which liberated Owen, the son of Urien, from between the portcullis and the wall.   Whoever concealed that stone, the stone or bezel would conceal him."*

The Welsh women believe, in common with other nations, that, should anything happen to their wedding-ring, such as the loss or breakage of it, separation or death would ensue.

The modern French word so much in use at present, *la mascatte*, is described in up-to-date dictionaries as " a luck piece, fetish, or talisman, whose presence is supposed to be a cause of good fortune."

A very mystic sign of talismanic power was the pentacle. It consisted of five straight lines joined and intersected to form a five-pointed star.   In the middle ages it was held in great veneration.   They were often cut into the bark of trees to charm away or banish ghosts, witches, and evil spirits that haunted the neighbourhood.   Sometimes they were painted on barn-doors, the inside doors of houses, and often on cradles. The art of making them descended from father to son, until people could not tell why they made these signs, which were seen so late as 1850 in some places.   Trees felled at St. Donat's, Tresillian, Beaupré, Cwmciddy, and Porthkerry in the first half of the nineteenth century had pentacles cut into the bark. All these places are in South Glamorgan.   They were found on the doors of old houses in many parts of Wales.   [*Family Collection.*]

Cradles bore this mystic sign, either carved or painted on them.   An old oak cradle that had been in the possession of a family more than a hundred years had a pentacle cut into it. The owner valued it highly, for it had come into her possession at the birth of her first child, in the year 1801.   This old woman was born in 1783, and died in 1879, leaving the cradle to her great-grandson.   In 1878 the cradle was jealously guarded by the good old dame of the Vale of Glamorgan ; but when her descendant, a Rhondda collier, obtained possession of it, he valued it so little and considered it so old-fashioned that he cut it up for firewood.

* " The Mabinogion," p. 54 *notes*.

It is doubtful whether many, if any, of those quaint old cradles carved with the pentacle remain in Wales.

These mystic signs were generally carved, scratched, or painted on wood or stone. They were to be found in many curious places so late as 1858, when stones inscribed in this way were broken up for road repairing in Glamorgan. An old gatepost at Tresillian, in the Vale of Glamorgan, bore these mystic signs when the last of the Mal Santau were held there. Soon afterwards it was taken down, and the house restored for a gentleman's residence.

Love spells included many kinds, and were in use until quite recent dates. In remote places they are tried in the present day—more for the fun of doing so than for peering into the future.

To find out the Christian name of husband or wife, it was directed that an apple must be peeled in one unbroken strip from beginning to end. This peel should be placed behind the front-door. The first person who enters the house of the opposite sex to the one who peeled the apple will have the same Christian name as the future husband or wife.

To know whether your husband or wife will be tall or short, go to the place where you store wood or sticks, and with your back to it, pull out a piece on Christmas night. If it happens to be long, the future wife or husband will be tall, or *vice versa*.

On Christmas Eve at midnight take a brush and sweep the floor backwards. If the girl hears a whip, she will marry a man connected with horses. If the sound of music comes, he will be fond of dancing and pleasure.

Girls in some of the farm-houses take each an onion, and name it after a bachelor of their acquaintance. The onions are then put away in a loft. The man whose onion first " begins to grow," or bud, will soon declare his love. If the onions fail to bud, it is a proof that the men will not marry.

When spinning of yarn and flax was general in Welsh homesteads, the girls stretched the first piece of yarn or thread they spun on Christmas Eve or the day of the Twelfth Night outside the door of the house. The first man who passed over it would bear the same Christian name as the future husband.

It was customary for girls to perform the following spell :

Place a knife in the corner of the leek-bed, on a dark night and in absolute secrecy, after ten o'clock. Walk backwards around the bed, and be careful not to stumble or look back. If you are to be married, the apparition of the future husband will come and lift the knife from the leek-bed. If two apparitions appear, the girl will be married twice.

Another spell was accomplished thus : A key and a gold ring were placed in a Bible or Prayer-Book. The volume was then bound securely with a garter, and placed under the pillow of a spinster or bachelor. The sleeper would dream of his or her future wife or husband.

To find the name of your future husband or wife, a door-key was placed in Ruth, chap. i., v. 16. The Bible was then tied so that the book could be lifted by the end of the key. The Bible was next suspended by the two index-fingers, and the above verse repeated. The person kept in her mind any name she wished, hoping it was that of her future partner. If she had fixed on the right name, the Bible would turn round during the recital of the verse ; if not, the book would not move.

To prove whether any two young people would be man and wife, take two small wisps of straw or pieces of stick, name them after the persons, then set them on the surface of the water in a pan ; if they float close together, there will be a marriage. If one floats away from the other, they will not be married. The fault will rest upon the one that first floats away. If it is wished to know which of two married people shall die first, the same operation is performed, but the twig or straw that is the first to go under water will die first.

It was customary for girls to go to the nearest cross-road, and, having brought some hemp-seed with them, to scatter it to the wind. Meanwhile the following couplet was repeated nine times :

" Hemp-seed I sow, hemp-seed I sow,
Hoping my true love will come here to mow."

The girls then secreted themselves, and waited to see what men passed along the cross-roads. From among these the future lover was to come.

Another spell was worked by means of the cleanly scraped

blade-bone of a lamb. While scraping the meat off the bone, the following rhyme was repeated :

> " With this knife this bone I meant to pick ;
> With this knife my lover's heart I mean to prick,
> Wishing him neither rest nor sleep
> Until he comes to me to speak."

Dragon's blood in its powdered state was sprinkled on the fire at midnight to insure the presence of the future husband or wife.

If a girl who has lost her sweetheart throws dragon's blood and quicksilver on the fire at noon or midnight, she will regain his affection. If a husband or wife who has lost the partner's affection does the same thing, happiness will be regained.

An old woman told me that she threw dragon's blood on the fire at noon and midnight, and, turning around from the hearth, she saw in the doorway the figure of a man, who afterwards became her husband.

If a girl wanted to see her future husband, there was another way of procuring her wish. On Midsummer Eve she laid supper on the table for nine persons. She invited seven guests, each one of whom sat at table. Each had to sit with eyes fixed on the plate, and not a word must be spoken, or the spell would fail in its purpose. The house doors were left open as widely as possible. At midnight an apparition would come and sit in the vacant seat next to the prospective wife. Or a funeral procession would be heard passing through the house, and the corpse would sit next to the girl who was to die before the end of the year. The seven friends remained seated, and the girl who invited them always occupied the eighth chair. The ninth seat was left vacant for the apparition. In ten cases out of twelve, said my informant, terror prevented the visitors remaining to see the apparition or the corpse. [*O. S.*]

Even in the present day the girls in rural districts place an apple-seed in the palm of the left hand and cover it with the right, meanwhile shaking both hands up and down, and repeating the following verse :

> " Kernel, kernel of the apple-tree,
> Tell me where my true love be.
> East, west, north, or south ?
> Pretty kernel, tell the truth."

At the conclusion they examine the kernel, and whichever way the pointed end is found, from that direction the true love will come.

To find out the occupation of their future husbands, the girls take what they call " wishing grass," and, touching alternately each sharp blade, they say :

> " Tinker, tailor,
> Soldier, sailor,
> Apothecary, ploughboy, thief !' "

Or this :

> " Tinker, tailor,
> Soldier, sailor,
> Gentleman, tradesman,
> Farmer, rogue, or thief !"

Old people in the first half of the nineteenth century mentioned a love-drink. It consisted chiefly of metheglin, mead, rhubarb, cowslip, primrose, or elderberry wine. But there was something else in it which they would not name, although they knew what it was very well. This beverage was put into a drinking-horn, and quaffed off by man or maiden, as the case may be. The old folks said that by means of this beverage the man secured the love of the girl, or the maiden that of the sweetheart. This drink was very pleasant, and people said the person who drank it would forget father, mother, heaven, earth, sun, and moon. A rich man in Glamorgan discovered the secret, and used it to obtain the love of a beautiful village maiden, who ever after followed him everywhere. An eyewitness said : " It was pitiful to see her following him. She would run through pools, over hedges, up hill and down dale, only to catch sight of him. At last he got tired of her, and wished to undo the spell, but could not ; and eventually, worn out with mental anguish, the poor girl died." [*Family Collection.*]

It appears that sometimes with the love-drink cakes were offered.

When a maiden saw her lover becoming indifferent towards her, she used to take small pieces of dough of nine bakings or batches in succession, and, after making a small cake, which was duly baked, she gave it to him to eat. By this means his former affection was supposed to return. Wives did the same with husbands whose affections grew cool or passed away. [*O. S.*]

In the eighteenth and first half of the nineteenth centuries people believed that some places and individuals were under a ban or curse; therefore certain farm-houses were avoided. People refused to rent them, because the curse prevented the crops growing, flocks and herds thriving, and poultry fattening. All dealings with persons supposed to be haunted were very carefully managed. Even in later times it was quite general to speak of people whose affairs go wrong as " That man seems to be under a curse," or " A curse seems to be hanging over him." It was the opinion in Wales that a curse, once uttered, lasted seven years, and may at any time descend upon the person aimed at. In some parts the curse was supposed to last until the third, fourth, or seventh generation. An old man in the year 1858 remembered a form of curse that was once in use in South Wales, and probably in the North as well. It ran, as nearly as possible, thus :

" I curse thee ! I curse thee ! I curse thee standing, walking, riding, driving, running ; awake and asleep ; at morning, noon, and night ; both eating and drinking, going out and coming in. I curse all that is made and done by thee, all that is touched by thee. May thy crops and fruit be cankered, thy flocks and herds diseased ; thy daughters be ailing, and thy sons be maimed ! May thou die thrice accursed, and may thy descendants for seven generations reap the harvest of this my curse ! Then shall thy house be the home of the raven and the bat, the snake and the viper !" This was uttered in Welsh, and the old man named several families and old houses in various parts of Wales where the curse had been verified to the letter. [*Family Collection.*]

· Here and there in the Principality the ruins of old mansions and farmsteads are pointed out as having been " under a curse." Although some instances have been mentioned as probably the work of priestcraft, the greater number are attributed to malicious people, witchcraft, and " righteous indignation for a grievous wrong suffered."

An expression that frequently falls from the lips of the

Welsh people is " Bless you !" in the vernacular.   It is not used in an irreverent way, but rather as an appeal to God on somebody's behalf, and the exclamation, " Bless me well !" has the same meaning. If a person slips in walking, or if anything goes wrong, he says " Bless me well !" If his neighbour has a fall or is in trouble, they say " Bless you !" " Bless him !" or " Bless them !" In the days of old the people went out and, with much ceremony, blessed the corn-fields. A blessing uttered in the morning protected people from the influence of the evil eye. It was customary for the fishermen of Wales to turn their boats sunwards, which was equivalent to asking a blessing on them. Some of the old people in the past turned their faces sunward, thus suiting the action to the words—" Bless you !"

CHAPTER XVIII

DAYS AND MONTHS

IN Wales they say Monday is a bad day for beginning any new undertaking. On that day you should "lend nothing, give nothing, pay for all you buy, and fasten no legging on the left leg first." [O. S.]

Work begun on Monday will never be a week old. A Monday marriage is a "bad beginning." If a stranger looks through a house or room door without coming in on a Monday, the husband and wife, or the inmates, will quarrel.

Tuesday was a very fortunate day, and for this reason, doubtless, it is a stock-market day in many parts of Wales. It was considered an excellent day for making journeys and getting married. At the same time, "devils appeared" on Tuesday. It was lucky to meet a stranger on Tuesday.

Wednesday was one of the "witch days." A woman who churned butter on Wednesday had "dealings with a witch." Pigs driven to pasture on Wednesday would go astray. The boy who went first to school on Wednesday would be a dunce. It is unlucky to be married, to begin a new undertaking, to open business, or go to a situation on Wednesday. If people talked of witches on Wednesday, they would punish them. The most curious of the lore concerning Wednesday was the belief that if a woman consented to be churched on that day, her child would "come to the gallows"! Finger- and toenails were trimmed on Wednesday for luck.

Thursday was unlucky for removing from one locality or one house to another, for people said birds never carried anything to their nests on that day. Thursday was a good day for a christening. It was unlucky to spin or hew wood on

Thursday evening.   Men who trimmed their own beards on Thursday were lucky.

Friday was a " witch day," and generally unlucky.   Eggs put under a hen on Friday would be addled ; or if chicks crept out, the fowl would eat them up.   If women neglected to brush and comb their hair on Friday, vermin would breed in it.

New undertakings on a Friday were unfortunate.   If a man cut his hair on Friday, it would grow quickly.   To remove from one house to another on a Friday foretokened many obstacles in the new abode.   It was lucky to churn on Friday. Fruit-trees pruned on Friday will not bear blossoms for three years.   If you put on clean underwear on Friday, you will not have gripes.   To pare the finger- and toenails on Friday is good for luck and the toothache.   The Welsh used to say that Adam and Eve were expelled from Eden on Friday.   It was considered unlucky to bathe children in the sea or a river on Friday.   A wet Friday, a wet Sunday ; a fair Friday, a fair Sunday.   Friday is better than no day.   If you wash garments on Friday, you will iron on Sunday.   The Welsh said that the fairies controlled and disturbed the waters of springs, rivers, lakes, and the sea on Friday.

Saturday was regarded as a lucky market-day for poultry, butter, cheese, and meat.   It was unlucky to do any laundry-work on Saturday, or to do any kind of labour after sunset on that day.   In the days of old they said if a woman had not cleared her distaff by Saturday night, the threads would never bleach white.   If a dressmaker could not finish the buttonholes of the dress she was working on before midnight on Saturday, she would long have to wait payment.   A Saturday's moon is regarded as being seven years too soon.   The woman who spun or wove on Saturday night would walk after she was dead.

In many parts of the Principality the Ystafell, or household goods and chattels, were always conveyed to the bride and bridegroom's new home on a Saturday for luck.   A Welshman of the past would not begin a new undertaking on a Satur-day, if he could possibly avoid it.   He firmly believed that if he married on Saturday, either he or his bride would not live the year out, or there would not be any children of the marriage.

Sunday was regarded as particularly fortunate.   At one time marriages were celebrated on Sunday for luck. Farmers said that if a person carried in his pocket a harrow tooth found on a Sunday, he would be able to see witches with tubs on their heads in church. The first three Sundays after a child's birth the babe should be " dressed up fine," so that it might grow up with a " good figure." Its clothes would always " sit well " on it. A wound made with a knife or any instrument sharpened on Sunday would be slow to heal.

Whoever sews any bed-linen or clothing on Sunday, if taken ill, she cannot die until it is unpicked. The man was doomed to the moon for gathering sticks on Sunday. Sticks picked on Sunday for lighting fire will not burn. Cabbages planted on Sunday will never thrive. Early in the nineteenth century it was considered lucky to dance after church service on Sunday evening. Card-playing on Sunday was regarded as very unfortunate to the players, for the devil helped to shuffle the cards.

St. Dwynwen's Day, January 25, was formerly celebrated with many festivities, the trying of love-spells, and the giving of love-tokens. This saint was the patron of lovers, friendship, and all ties of affection. The story of Dwynwen was at one time familiar in Wales. Maelon Dafodrill, a Welsh Prince, fell in love with Dwynwen, one of the beautiful daughters of Brychan Brycheiniog. But the stern parent had already arranged a marriage between his daughter and another Prince. Maelon's proposal was rejected. This angered Maelon Dafodrill so much that he at once left his lady-love, and in great bitterness of soul, to spite her father, he cruelly aspersed her. Dwynwen was so distressed that she retired to a lonely woodland, and there prayed long and fervently that God would cure her of love. Then she fell fast asleep. In her sleep an angel administered a delicious potion to her, which quite fulfilled her desires. But in a dream Dwynwen observed that the same liquid, administered to Maelon Dafodrill, caused him to be turned into ice—a statue of ice. The angel then asked her to express three wishes. She did so. The first was that Maelon should be unfrozen, which, after all, proved she still had place in her heart for the old love. The second was that by means of her supplications all true lovers should either obtain the object

16—2

of their affections or be cured of love. Thirdly, that they should never wish to be married. The three wishes were granted, and Dwynwen devoted herself to a religious life. Faithful lovers who invoked her either obtained the object of their affections or were cured of love. Dwynwen's symbol was the crescent moon; her magical girdle had the same attributes as the Cestus of Venus, and she carried a bow of destiny. During her last visit to earth she left her bow on the yellow sands of her southern shrine, wherefrom it was seized and turned into stone by the Hag of the Night, who fixed it about ten feet below the roof of Tresillian Cave, Glamorgan, where it is still to be seen. It is customary in the present day for people to visit this cave to try their luck under the bow of destiny. The trial consists of flinging a pebble over the natural arch of stone. If successful the first time, the person will be married within the current year. Each failure represents one year of life. In South Wales, on the shores of the Severn Sea, the festival of Dwynwen was held in April, when, it is asserted, she last visited the earth, and left in her footprints the blossoms of spring. In North Wales her festival was held in January, at her shrine, the church of Llandw-wynwen, in Mona (Anglesea). [*Family Collection, the David Jones Manuscripts.*]

On Candlemas Day in several places it was customary many years ago for people to light two candles, and place them on a table or high bench. Then each member of the family would in turn sit down on a chair between the candles. They then took a drink out of a horn goblet or beaker, and afterwards threw the vessel backwards over his head. If it fell in an upright position, the person who threw it would live to reach a very old age; if it fell bottom upwards, the person would die early in life. [*Family Collection.*]

If the sun shines on the altar on Candlemas Day, there will. be an abundant harvest in the ensuing year. It was considered unlucky if a single crow hovered or circled over a house on the eve or day of Candlemas.

St. Valentine's Day was a favourite date for festivities. In the old Mabsant times dancing was the greatest feature of the festivities. It was customary to make true lovers' knots, and distribute them like favours. These were sent anonymously, and great was the amusement, and sometimes the consternation, of the youths and maidens when these favours appeared on the bodice or coat of anybody present at the revels. Dreams of St. Valentine's Eve were supposed to be fateful. A child born on Valentine's Day would have many lovers. The farmers said a calf born on St. Valentine's Day was of no use for breeding purposes. If hens were set to hatch on Valentine's Day, all the eggs would be rotten.

St. David's Day, the national festival of Wales, was kept up in rural parishes with much festivity in the past. The Mabsant revels and orgies were prevalent, and the wearing of the leek was popular. People believed that if they went to the churchyard at midnight they would see corpse-candles on the graves of families who were to expect a death during the year. They threw a shoe over their heads on this day, and if the toes pointed out of doors, they would either quit their present abode or die within a year If they walked around the leek-bed three times and in silence at midnight on St. David's Eve, they would see their future husband or wife, as the case might be.

St. Patrick's Day was celebrated with revels. Strict people sixty years ago much objected to the proximity of March 1 and 17, because it gave good excuse for holding the Mabsant. Smugglers, wreckers, and dealers in contraband goods· held high revelry in the seaboard parishes of Glamorgan on this day. A native of South Glamorgan gave me valuable information on this subject. He said he well remembered the people when he was a boy singing the praises of St. David and St. Patrick in the same song, but he had forgotten the exact words and the melody. There was something in the song about a boy being carried away by the Irish, and becoming one of them. This boy was lost to his native Morganwg (Glamorgan) for ever. The song expressed great detestation of the Irish for having carried the boy away, and afterwards claiming him as their very own, when he was " pure Welsh." [C. D.]

Palm Sunday, called in Welsh Sul-y-Bledau, was celebrated in several ways in Wales. In South Wales a curious custom prevailed. The image of a donkey was made of wood. On this a stuffed effigy was placed, and these were glued fast to a platform, which was set upon wheels.   The donkey and the effigy were decorated with flowers and bunches of evergreens. When brought to the church door by the procession, each member carried a sprig of evergreen, seasonable flowers, or herbs, box-wood predominating.   The people were met by the clergyman, who blessed the procession and the evergreens and flowers.   The sprigs were carefully preserved for the year as a charm to keep away evil spirits and witches, and a protection against mishaps.   [A. B. and C. D.]

This old custom has long since become obsolete.

In some parts of Wales Palm Sunday is called " Mothering Sunday," and all the graves in churchyards, cemeteries, and burial-places are decorated with flowers.   But in rural places Easter Day is celebrated in this way, particularly in South Wales.

Palm Sunday was formerly considered an unlucky day for a birth, because people born then were more in the power of elves, fairies, and witches than on any other day.

If you walk around the boundaries of your land or garden on Palm Sunday, you will keep thieves away.

In many parts of Wales on the Monday before Shrove Tuesday it was customary for the children to call at the neighbours' houses, and sing the following lines in Welsh.   Translated, they run thus :

> " Lent crock, give us a pancake,
>   A fritter, or bread and cheese ;
>   A few fine eggs, or a dish of flour,
>   Or anything else you please.

> " I see by the latch
>   There is something to catch,
>   And I see by the string
>   There's a good dame within.

> " Lent crock, throw and throw ;
>   Give me my dole, and I'll go."

Shrove Tuesday was favourable for all new enterprises.   If pancakes were not made and tossed on this day, there would be little prosperity during the ensuing year.   If you drank butter-milk on Shrove Tuesday, you would never have freckles or sunburn.   If you buried a piece of pancake, you would have luck during the next twelve months.

Ash Wednesday was formerly a day of gloom, and at one time silence was enforced upon young people on that day in remote parts of Wales. Witches were supposed to " groan " on this day.

Maunday Thursday was important for doing good deeds. It was customary for schoolboys to put up a target of wood or stone, and pelt it with pebbles on this day. If anybody performed unnecessary work on this day, he would be in danger of being stricken by thunder and lightning.

Good Friday is regarded as a very bad day for any new work. On this day it is unlucky to meddle with earth, to plough, sow, or to do any kind of gardening. If you use a sewing-needle on this day, lightning will destroy you or your premises.

If you endure thirst on Good Friday, whatever beverage you drink during the year will not hurt you.

Bread made on Good Friday quickly turns sour. Some of this bread was given by sailors' wives to their husbands in the days of old, because it was supposed to protect them against shipwreck and disaster at sea.

Easter festivals in Wales were not particularly striking, but superstitions connected with the season were curious and interesting. The Baltân fires were lighted in some parts of the Principality, and the festivities attached to them resembled those of the May and Midsummer celebrations.

Among the lower classes in many parts of North and South Wales a ceremony called " lifting " took place. It consisted of lifting a person three times, in a chair or on a stool, from the ground. On Easter Monday the men lifted the women, and on Easter Tuesday the women lifted the men. But the ceremony must cease at noon on each day. The lifted person was expected to give, if only a few coppers, to all who exalted him for luck.

In Glamorgan the last man to be married in the parish before Easter Sunday was on that day immediately after morning service accompanied by a number of people to the highest hill in the neighbourhood. Each man carried a branch of gorse. When they reached the hill, the newly-married man ascended a hillock or heap of stones and delivered an address.

In conclusion, he ordered that all men under sixty years of age were to be up and dressed before six o'clock, all men under forty were to be presentable before four o'clock, and all under twenty were not to go to bed at all, but to be ready in the streets or market-place on Easter Monday morning. If they neglected this command, the offenders were to be put in the stocks in turn for a certain number of hours. At dawn on Easter Monday the stocks were placed in a prominent position in the main street. Near it was a cart ready to convey the sluggard to the scene of his punishment. The house of a lazy, bed-loving bachelor was generally the first to be attacked. Then woe betide the lazy man who slept while his wakeful friends called him ! To force an entry, the villagers either burst in the door or entered the house by means of a window. Two or three of the men roused the culprit, commanded him to get dressed as soon as possible, and come downstairs. Then they lifted him over the threshold, placed him in the cart, and drove him to the stocks. There they made fast his feet. The latest-married man, who acted as master of the revels, lectured the culprit on the sin of idleness, and reminded him of the sluggard and his fate. Taking the right hand of the victim, the lecturer administered several strokes of a gorse-branch. Between each stroke he was asked a number of questions. If he evaded them or told an untruth, the stroke was harder and the reprimand severe. With his hand looking rather the worse for scratches, the man was released amid cheers. He in turn joined his tormentors in pursuit of another victim. If a girl was caught peeping at these proceedings, her shoe was snatched from her foot, and she could not reclaim it without giving a kiss or two as ransom. If a married woman or elderly dame visited the scene, she was obliged to pay a contribution under sixpence towards the roistering. All the fun was over by eight o'clock on Easter Monday morning. [*Family Collection.*]

This custom ceased in Carnarvonshire and North Wales generally about the year 1825, it is said, but it was known in Glamorgan so late as in 1840.

On Easter Day the sun was supposed to dance as it arose in honour of the Resurrection of Christ. Young people were advised to " rise early to see the sun dancing." Traces of this belief have come under my own notice in several parts of South Wales. Children in their play on Easter Eve said : " If you'll only get up early enough, you shall see the sun dancing." On being asked for more information, the children said : " The sun always dances on Easter morning, and if you will get up early enough, you will see it."

In the days of old, and even now in rural districts, it was regarded as absolutely necessary, in order to insure " good luck for the whole year," to wear something new, if only a small bow of ribbon.

A cold Easter, a warm Whitsun.

Children born or baptized on Easter Sunday were supposed to be very fortunate.

It was considered a very evil omen for Wales when Easter Day fell on March 25, or Lady Day.

Ascension Day is regarded as unlucky by miners and colliers in North and South Wales alike.

The *South Wales Daily News* of June, 1878, recorded a superstition of the quarrymen of Penrhyn, where thousands of workers refused to do anything on Ascension Day. The paper stated that " this refusal did not arise out of any reverential feeling, but from an old and widespread superstition, which has lingered in that district for years, that if work is continued on Ascension Day an accident will surely follow. A few years ago the agents persuaded the men to break through the superstition, and there were accidents each year—a not unlikely occurrence, seeing the extent of the works carried on, and the dangerous nature of the occupation of the men. This year, however, the men one and all refused to work."

In many parts of Wales it is considered unlucky to dig the earth or to plant or sow anything on Ascension Day.

Whitsuntide was regarded in Wales as a more secular festival than that of Easter. The morris dancers were all alert at Whitsuntide, as at Christmas. Sometimes at this season the dancers were accompanied by a man dressed in green, and completely covered with ivy, leaves of trees, and flowers. When the whole party assembled in an open space, the leading person in the village was allowed three chances to guess the name of the man or youth concealed under the green. If the guesses were wrong, the person who guessed had to pay a forfeit in beer.

On Whit Monday morning the farm-boys and others went out very early, and with noise, merriment, and song awakened the lazy people in the village. At every sluggard's door they placed a bunch of nettles, which were generally tied to the latch.

In the latter part of the eighteenth century, about a fortnight before Whitsuntide the boys of the farms and villages were accustomed to go into the woodlands, and in a very secluded spot tell each other their sweethearts' names. The girls used to do the same. One person in each party kept the roll-call, and when the Whit Monday dancing began the recorder paired the young people. Those who refused to be paired had to pay a fine of some kind. As a rule, the girls had to give beer, and the boys were expected to give a nosegay or neck ribbon.

At that period a boy dressed in a girl's dress, and adorned with flowers and foliage, was led from house to house on Whit Monday morning. He was surrounded by other boys, who kept singing merry ballads until gifts were bestowed upon them. A girl gaily dressed and wreathed and garlanded with flowers also went from house to house, accompanied by other girls, who sang and sometimes danced until they received presents. [*A. B., C. D., and Family Collection.*]

On Whit Monday people were expected to be up between three and four o'clock in the morning. Any breach of this duty brought upon the offending individual the penalty of the stocks.

Whitsuntide was thought the best season for making a bargain. During the week it was the custom to throw pins into certain wells for luck.

On the eve of Corpus Christi it was customary in some parishes for people who had any kind of ailment to kneel before the altar of the parish church, and fervently pray for their own and their friends' recovery. This was regarded as the health-restoring time, when prayers for that purpose could not fail to be effectual. It is said that a Welsh squire living among the mountains in the north of Glamorgan determined to put down the superstitious assembling of the " sick, lame, and lazy " in his parish church on the eve of Corpus Christi. He had the doors of the church locked, and ordered the people away. Lamenting sorely at the abolition of an ancient usage, the villagers returned to their homes, and the squire heartily enjoyed his triumph in the old Hall of his forefathers. His pleasure was short-lived, for at midnight, to his surprise, the church bells began ringing merry wedding-peals, mingled with funeral knells. He sent his men down to the church to pre-vent the people ringing the bells, but when his messengers reached the belfry they found it empty ! The moment they reached the Hall the bells began ringing again. Once more the messengers returned to the church, only to find the belfry empty and the bells silent. But as soon as they entered the Hall the bells were ringing merrily or tolling dolefully. From that night forth the squire allowed the villagers to enter the church when they liked on the eve of Corpus Christi. [C. D.]

A similar story used to be told about a church in South Glamorgan.

Midsummer Day was formerly associated with curious customs prevalent in many parts of Wales. One of these was an old tenure which consisted of paying suit of court and a red rose.

Waterton Farm, near Coity, Bridgend, Glamorgan, was held by paying the lord of the manor suit of courts and a quarter of a pound of pepper, which the said lord was to fetch away on or about Midsummer Day in a wain drawn by eight milk-white oxen.

St. John's, or Midsummer Day, was an important festival. St. John's wort, gathered at noon on that day, was considered good for several complaints. The old saying went that if anybody dug the devil's bit at midnight on the eve of St. John, the roots were then good for driving the devil and witches away. In the days of old, if the cuckoo was heard " singing" after St. John's Day, dearth might be expected in the winter. If you lop a tree on St. John's Day, it will wither. People said that if man and beast leaped over St. John's (Midsummer) fire, they would be free from fever and all illnesses for a year. A curious way of forecasting the length of life, even so late as the middle of the nineteenth century, was as follows : Take as many St. John's worts as there are people in the house. Clean these free from dust and fly, and hang them on the rafters of a room. Each wort was named after an individual. Those whose plants wither first will die first. To forecast marriage, spinsters used to make a wreath or garland of nine different kinds of flowers. Walking backward, they endeavoured to throw the garland on a tree. The number of times it falls to the ground indicates the years they will remain unmarried.

If it rains on St. John's Day, nuts will spoil and wicked women will thrive. There was formerly an old superstition in Wales that between June 22, or the eve of St. John, and June 26 a disastrous thunderstorm must be expected. It was lucky to be born on St. John's Eve or Day.

St. Peter's Day was selected by farm-wives for making nests for their hens, and by doing so on this day they would insure a plentiful supply of eggs. On St. Peter's Night unmarried women were accustomed to tie a small key on each wrist, and when in bed their hands were folded in prayer, while the sixteenth and seventeenth verses of the first chapter of Ruth were repeated nine times. The keys were to remain on the wrists all night, and in a dream the future husband would appear. At his appearance the keys would fall off. If the keys remained where they were tied, the girl would not be married or have an offer that year.

St. Swithin's Day is considered a lucky birthday for a boy, but unlucky for a girl. If it rains on St. Swithin's Day, people expect the same kind of weather for forty days in succession ; if fair on that day, sunshine comes for a like period.

Lammas Day was not much regarded in Wales, but on the seacoasts it is said that if on this day geese and ducks run about carrying straws in their beaks, there will be destructive storms in the late summer, and the autumn will be very boisterous.

St. Michael's Day was celebrated in Wales in former times. A Michaelmas goose was always on the tables of those who could afford it. Even now in many parts of Wales the Michaelmas goose makes its appearance. It is a general custom for the Welsh housewife to make and bake a very large loaf-cake made of currant dough well risen with barm. It is called the Michaelmas cake. Pieces of this were distributed to every member of the family, the domestics, and any strangers who might call at the house. This is done for luck. At the present time the Michaelmas goose and the Michaelmas cake make their appearance in the houses of well-to-do Welsh people. According to the age of the moon on Michaelmas Day, the number of the floods after it will be decided. Wheat sown during Michaelmas week turns to cockle. Many acorns at Michaelmas, much snow at Christmas. Michaelmas Day was formerly regarded with suspicion in Wales. It was credited with uncanny power. There was an old superstition that on this night the Cistfaens, or warriors' graves, in all parts of the Principality were illuminated by spectral lights, and it was very unlucky to walk near those places on Michaelmas Eve or Night ; for on those two occasions the ghosts of ancient warmen were engaged in deadly fray around their lonely resting-places. [C. D. and Family Collection.]

Nos Cyn Calan Gauaf, All Saints' Day, or All Hallow's Eve, was a time of much festivity in the Principality. In the days of old it was attended by many superstitious rites and ceremonies. A huge log was thrown on the fire for purposes of heat and light. As a rule, the only illumination of the great farmhouse kitchen was that of the ruddy fire-glow. All sorts of tricks were performed, and charms were tried. The younger folk amused themselves by catching apples with their teeth from a tub of water, or suspended from a cord tied to the rafters. This cord was strung with apples, and had a farthing dip at the end. The greatest fun arose when somebody took a bite of candle and missed the apple. In the case of the tub and the cord, those who entered into the game had their hands tied behind their backs. Nut-burning or grains of wheat substituted for nuts, and all kinds of games, were the order of the evening. When the people were tired, they congregated around the old hearth, and became attentive and sometimes scared listeners while the aged grandfather or grandmother related fairy-tales and ghost-stories in the fire-glow. Meanwhile, in secret and silence, uncanny tricks were attempted. Hallowe'en festivities are still kept up in Wales.

It was firmly believed in former times that on All Hallow's Eve the spirit of a departed person was to be seen at midnight on every cross-road and on every stile.

This was the weirdest of all the Teir Nos Ysbrydion, or three spirit nights, when the " wind blowing over the feet of the corpses " bore sighs to the houses of those who were to die during the ensuing year.

If at midnight any persons had the courage to run three times around the parish church and then peep through the keyhole of the door, they would see the apparitions of those who were soon to die.

If crows caw round the house in the afternoon of Hallow-e'en, there will be a corpse of an inmate or the dead body of an animal belonging to the inhabitant soon.

If people on this night go to cross-roads and listen to what the wind has to say, they can thereby learn all the most important things that concern them during the next year.

If you sit in the church porch at midnight on Hallowe'en, or all through the night, you will see a procession of all the people who are to die in the parish during the year, and they will appear dressed in their best garments.

In some parts of Wales the girls used to go at midnight and strip the leaves from a branch of the sage-bush. The apparitions of their future husbands were supposed to pass at the time.

The yarn-test was another means of obtaining peeps into the future. Two girls would agree to make a little ladder of yarn without breaking any portion from the ball. The ladder was then thrown through the window. Then one of the girls would begin winding the yarn back, meanwhile repeating a rhyme in Welsh. This was done three times, and during the process the watcher would see the apparition of the future husband ascending the yarn ladder.

Divination with reference to matrimony was carried out by means of bowls or basins. Three bowls were placed on a table. One contained clean water, one dirty water, and one was empty. The girls of the household, and sometimes the boys too, entered into this with much spirit. They were blindfolded and led to the table, then asked to dip their hands in a bowl.

If they chanced to dip into the dirty water, they would be widows or widowers ; if into the clean water, they would marry spinsters or bachelors ; if into the empty bowl, they would live unmarried.

On this night people would cast stones or pebbles into the fire, and sometimes walnuts or hazel-nuts. When these were shot out by the heat, or if the nuts burst, the younger folk ran aside, fearing the " goblin black-tailed sow " would come and drive them into the fire.

People said if a girl went backward and placed a knife among the leeks on this night, and concealed herself near at hand, she would have the pleasure of seeing her future husband taking the blade up and throwing it into the middle of the garden.

Until the first half of the nineteenth century the poor peasantry of many parts of Wales went about begging bread on All Souls' Day, November 2. The bread bestowed upon them was called Bara Ran, or dole-bread. This custom was a survival of the Middle Ages, when the poor begged bread for the souls of their departed relatives and friends.

In almost every parish there was a holy well, and on All Souls' Day old women generally washed their eyes in the waters, so that their eyesight might retain its strength.

St. Martin's Day decided the weather that might be expected during the ensuing winter. If the geese on this day stood on ice, there would be mire at Christmas. There was formerly a superstition that if meteoric stones fell on this day, some trouble would happen in Wales. The hooting of owls on the evening of this day was regarded as a very bad omen for the district or village where it was heard.

St. Andrew's Day was selected for working several love-spells. Spinsters who much wished to know who their future husbands were to be were advised to go without nightdresses into bed, and invoke the saint. They would then see their sweethearts in their sleep. If the maidens took notice from which quarter of the compass the dogs barked on St. Andrew's night, they would know wherefrom to expect their future husband. If the sound of barking came from the north, the man would come from that quarter. A curious test was by means

of a pewter tankard of beer.   If the froth of the freshly-drawn
beer ran over, they might expect a year of moisture ; if the froth
stood heaped on top, they were certain of more dry weather
than wet all through the year.   It was customary for girls to
melt lead on St. Andrew's Night, and pour it through a key
that had a cross in its wards into water that was drawn between
eleven and twelve. The lead would reveal the shape of the
future husband's tools, implements, or instruments.   This was
also done on Hallowe'en and other " spirit nights."

It is still customary for the wives and mothers of the labour-
ing classes to go from house to house before Christmas, to
receive their annual dole of money and other good things.
They chiefly visit the houses of well-to-do farmers, who are ready
with their annual gifts.   The aristocracy and country gentry
bestow these gifts according to a prepared list, but some of the
farmers are ready to receive the annual applicants.

On New Year's Day the children used to go round the
district, wishing their neighbours " A happy New Year," and
soliciting gifts.   They carried an apple or an orange on a
skewer or stick.   The fruit was decorated with gold and
silver tinsel, and the girls and boys wore paper flowers in their
hats and caps.   This custom has become obsolete in many
parts of Wales.

In old Welsh superstitions it is said that if you feed your hens
on New Year's Day with any available fruits chopped well and
mixed together, you will make them lay whether they will or not.

A sudden noise heard in a house on New Year's night fore-
tells the death of an inmate.

If the log on the New Year's fire does not burn brightly,
and if it will not burn out, but smoulder, there will be disaster,
sickness, or death in the family.

If on New Year's Day you wash a dish-towel and throw it
to dry on a near hedge, and then rub your horses with it,
they will surely grow fat.

The dreams of New Year's Night are generally fatal, or
come true.

Among the women of Wales it was customary, when the
first batch of bread was made after New Year's Day, to make
as many small round cakes as there were inmates of the house.

Each cake was given a name, and a hole was made in it with the thumb. If any hole became baked up, it was a sure sign that the person to whom the cake was assigned would die within the year.

Those who desire to get their wishes realized during the year should be the first to go to the well for a pitcher of water immediately after sunrise on New Year's Day.

It is regarded as fortunate to begin any new undertaking on New Year's Day.

It was considered unlucky for anybody to see a girl first on New Year's Day, while in some localities it is lucky for a man to see a woman first and a woman to see a man.

Holy Rood Day was set apart for a festival. In Glamorgan large parties of men and boys went out nutting, and brought the results of their labours to ancient hostelries famed for keeping up the Mabsant. The nuts were equally distributed among the assembled visitors, and games were played, with fines and forfeits discharged with nuts. This day was celebrated in a variety of ways in centuries gone, and the festival was kept up until the old Mabsantau became obsolete.

So late as the years 1840 to 1850 the day dedicated to the patron saint of the locality was celebrated by feasting, preceded by religious services and processions, and succeeded by dancing and merriment. These celebrations were called the " Mabsant " or " Gwyl Mabsant," which ultimately degenerated into noisy meetings and convivial excess.

Old people in Wales still remember the Mabsant, and talk about it with considerable fervour and amusement. Very often practical jokes provided much mirth, and in days when there were no railways and penny postage they were a source of great delight to young and old alike. One narrative will serve to illustrate the Mabsant, which was conducted all through Wales in much the same way.

Young people saved money in readiness for the Mabsant. and on the morning of the day to be celebrated each one did his best to appear well dressed and in holiday style. In one locality the patron saint's day was February 7, but for some reason the festival was held in the nutting season. The afternoon was spent in games of various kinds, and when the

17

twilight came, the people assembled in the long room of the village inn, where very often the sexton's fiddle and the parson's flute provided music for the dancers.   In those days musicians went from Mabsant to Mabsant regularly every year, and were in great repute for their skill.   My father and many others remembered an old Glamorgan harpist who for sixty years had made the same circuit.   He began his itinerary at the age of twenty-three, and continued it until he was over eighty-three.   The dancing in the Mabsant was excellent.   Wales was renowned for good dancers in those days.   Originally the Mabsant was a pleasant gathering of old and young, when mirth and melody were at their best, and the dancing would have done justice to any mansion.   Subsequently the Mabsant became the rendezvous of objectionable people, who held orgies of the worst kind.   Then it died and passed out of memory.

When a poor family wished to raise a little money for some useful purpose, or to make good a heavy loss, the founder of the object made a large brewing of metheglin (mead) or small beer.   A notice was then sent out to the effect that a Cwrw Bach was to be held in the house on a certain date.   Then young and old attended the meeting, and bought the beverage or treated their friends.   In the early times the company drank but little of the metheglin or beer, and conveyed a good quantity home, or paid for much, and thus helped the family. Legal restrictions were not severely enforced, and a few occasions sufficed to raise an ample sum of money.   But in time the Cwrw Bach, like the Mabsant, degenerated, and eventually passed into disuse.   While the Mabsant became completely stamped out, the restrictions of the Sunday Closing Act in Wales secretly revived the Cwrw Bach and its attendant Shebeenings, which are suppressed, but not wholly obliterated, in the present day.

Gwyl-y-Cwltrin, Cooltrin Court, was a custom in many parts of Wales, and intended as an exposure of quarrelsome husbands and wives.   Frequently these trials had a salutary effect, especially upon offenders, and served as a warning to young couples.   My father well recollected one of the last of the Cooltrin Courts, and could name the leading characters in it ;

but as their descendants are still living, I forbear doing so.
The court was conducted with all the mock ceremonial of a
real court of justice. Sometimes the Cooltrin Court was held
in the parish in which the offence was committed, but occasionally it was held in a neighbouring parish. The object
of the court was to expose and hold up to public ridicule
husbands and wives who had quarrelled and come to blows,
or actually fought, during the year. But the court was never
held unless the wife had punished or assaulted her husband,
and persisted in the molestation, and actually drawn blood
from her spouse. The last Cooltrin Court my father witnessed
was that held because a nagging woman had belaboured her
husband with various instruments, including a flat-iron and
a poker. The poker had been the means of drawing blood
from the man's head, hence the trial of Gwenni. Her husband,
Dewi—by no means a saint—had complained to the neighbours, who took little notice of the domestic troubles until
Gwenni overstepped the bounds and shed the blood of Dewi.
The arrangements for the trial of Gwenni were conducted thus :
a judge was appointed, and a jury of parishioners. Sometimes the jury was called from another parish. The judge
had the power to select counsel for the prosecution and defence,
and these men had the reputation of being the best talkers
in the district. In the trial of which I speak, as in all other
Cooltrins, the judge, counsel, and officers of the court formed
a procession near the Town Hall. A waggon, drawn by four
horses, formed the centrepiece of the procession. In the
waggon two men sat face to face in fighting attitude. One
was disguised as a woman, representing poor Gwenni, and the
other impersonated Dewi. The procession paraded the town,
and halted by the house where the quarrelsome husband and
wife lived. Then they proceeded to the steps of the Town
Hall, and, with a fanfare of tin pots, kettles, pans, and a
trumpet, the judge entered the hall. After the assembling of
the court, the case for the prosecution was heard, and the
counsel for the defence replied. The counsel on both sides
were quick-witted men, who provoked much mirth. It was
a perfect burlesque. The judge summed up, and the jury
retired to consider the verdict. In this case it was to the

effect " that Gwenni shall forbear to use the poker against Dewi and keep the peace for twelve months. For any breach of faith, the penalty was the ducking-stool." Dewi was also enjoined not to be " aggravating or in any way provoking to Gwenni." After the Cooltrin trial, the judge, counsel, jury, and officers of the court assembled at the Old Swan Inn, opposite the Town Hall steps, and there drank to the " good health and happiness of Dewi and Gwenni."

A green winter makes a full churchyard ; a cold winter a warm summer ; too much sunshine in winter, a rainy summer.

A mild and sunny January promises a cold spring and an uncertain summer.

If February blows the wild goose off her nest, poultry will be scarce that year. A fine February, a cold November.

In Wales there is an old rhyme similar to the English couplet. It runs thus :

> " March will test, April will try ;
> May will prove whether you'll live or die."

This is especially applied to consumptives and people who are subject to pulmonary complaints.

There is also the Welsh equivalent for the proverb, " If March comes in like a lion, it will go out like a lamb," and *vice versa*. They say :

> " March winds and April showers
> Bring forth May flowers."

April floods carry away frogs and their brood. A windy April is good for hay and corn. If there are many weeds in April the meadow-lands and cornfields will flourish. Thunder in April foretokens a fruitful and joyful year. If you are made a fool in April, you will be a fool or get befooled all through the year. The older Welsh people used to say that Cain was born on April 1. An April cat is a good mouser. A rainy April, a burning June. In April the cuckoo primes her bill. Barley sown in the first week of April turns to hedge mustard.

Fogs and mists in May promise heat in June. Rain in May promises much hay. A swarm of bees in May is worth " eight oxen-loads " of hay. A very showery May will bring a very full harvest. A cold May makes full barns and empty church-yards. A very cold May promises a summer of very little

sickness.   May was considered a good month for all contracts
excepting that of marriage.   The May bug was the devil's
servant.   Promises made in May are seldom kept.   In May
the cuckoo sings all day.   Cats born in May are supposed to
bring snakes into the house.

Crosses were formerly marked in chalk or lime on every
door on May Day Eve, to keep the witches away.

The person who on May Day goes to church with ground
ivy under or on his hat, or on any part of his wearing apparel,
or in his belt or buttonhole, will soon find out who are witches in
the congregation.

If consecrated bells are rung on May Eve, the " witches
who dance with the devil on the cross-roads at midnight will
not be able to hurt anybody."

The witches held some of their revels and excursions on
the first night in May.

If early in June the stones or paving around a house or
the pantry flooring " gives," and is quite damp with moisture,
you may expect a very warm summer.   Warm mists in June
foretoken great heat.   A cold June brings an uncertain summer.
June 25 was one of the important days of the year in Wales.
It was one of the Baltân days, and a time of great festivity.
Many of the customs in connection with it have become obsolete.   When in this month the hay-crop is light, the Welsh
farmers say : " There is no need to rake it very clean ; we shan't
want it all."   If the crop is heavy, they say : " Rake every
bit : you'll want it all and more before next May is in."   In
June the cuckoo changes her tune.   June 22, Llantwit Fair
Day, decides the weather for the autumn.

July fogs are supposed to bring the blight in their folds.
When the sea makes a great noise in July storms are coming.
This is considered a month for " no good anchorage."   If
an aged person is taken ill in July, he or she will " surely die."
The children say that the " devil's messenger," the dragon-fly,
comes " to spy in July," therefore they must be careful in
their actions.   July is considered an uncertain month for
weddings.   Marry in July, you'll live to sigh.   In July the
cuckoo " prepares to fly."   If there is rain on July 1, it will
be a rainy month.   If it rains on St. Swithin's Day it will rain

for forty days.   A shower of rain in July, when the corn begins to fill, is worth two oxen.   The dog-days are unlucky for new undertakings.

August is regarded as a royal and exalted month.   It is very favourable for weddings and journeys.   There is an old saying in some parts of Wales that a child born in August will " rise in the world."   Of the cuckoo in August they say " fly she must."   In the early part of the nineteenth century old people used to say that the destruction of Sodom took place in August.   Fogs in August promise a severe winter, with frost and snow.   Heavy dew in August promises heat. If St. Bartholomew's Day is fine, a prosperous autumn may be expected.   According to a Glamorgan saying, there is a complete change in the weather on August 26, St. Mary Hill Fair Day, when it generally rains.

September was the " reaping month," and a very fortunate time for marriage.   September gales were attributed to witches, and were often called " the witches' frolics."   This month, on or about the fourteenth, it was customary to go " a-nutting," and bring the nuts to the Mabsant, where they were distributed.   If three cold days came in the middle of September, the frosts would not begin in October.   " Mid-September dry would make a cellar full of Cwrw Da [good ale], but a ' mitty copse ' foretokened a ' mottled harvest.' "

From an eyewitness the succeeding account of an old Welsh harvest custom was received :

He said : " On every large farm in many parts of Wales, especially in the South, a harvest celebration known as ' Y Gaseg Fedi ' (the harvest mare) was popular.   There are many people who are at present able to give accurate descriptions of what was done before and after the harvest supper, and it is certain that ' Y Gaseg Fedi ' was the most important of all the customs.   When the harvest-fields were reaped, a handful of corn was left uncut by the reapers.   This was bound or plaited, and left standing in a prominent place on the field.   When the corn had been carried, and sometimes while the shocks still remained standing in the field, a mark was placed within a certain distance from the uncut portion of the corn.   Here the reapers stood, with spectators behind them. At a given signal the leading reaper, followed by all his fellow-workmen in turn, aimed their sickles at the ' Gaseg Fedi,' or sheaf of standing corn. Often more or less danger happened when an inexperienced hand aimed badly, with the result that the sickle would spring back among the onlookers. By-and-by the coveted shock of corn would fall, cut down by a well-aimed sickle. Then followed struggles for its possession. This often entailed a free fight, after which the captor carried it in triumph and with difficulty to the harvest dinner-table.

" But before reaching the farm-house he had to encounter a throng of merry maidens, who stood ready to throw small bowls of water over the corn and its bearer. Quick-footed and capable of dodging the girls, the bearer was supposed to carry his trophy high and dry into the hall of the house. He was then the hero of the evening. Lazy farmers came in for a share of ridicule when the harvest dinner was finished. For then the roisterers went forth to plant the ' Gaseg Fedi ' in the field of uncut corn. Sometimes the farmer took the joke pleasantly, and heartily joined in the laugh when the ' Gaseg Fedi ' was placed in his field. Still, I have known instances in which the farmers resented the intrusion, and with their men opposed the intruders, and a free fight ensued ; but, as a rule, this harvest custom was conducted in a merry mood by the neighbours. The last celebration of this kind took place in our neighbourhood in 1863 or 1864."

In some parts of Wales this custom was called " Y Wrach." In Pembrokeshire it was called " Neck " ; in North Wales it was known as " Ysgub-y-Gloch," or bell sheaf.

When the orchards were stripped of their fruit, it was formerly, and still is, customary in many parts to leave three, seven, or nine apples hanging on each tree, so that the next crop may be a heavy one. In many large and old orchards apples, pears, plums, and other fruit-trees are to be seen every autumn bearing their tributary numbers.

October is regarded as a month of mystery. The last night of this month, the Eve of All Saints, called in Welsh " Nos Cyn Calan gauaf," the first night of winter, is one of the " three spirit nights " when quaint old customs are prevalent.

It is still kept up in the Principality. On this night spells and love-charms were formerly worked.

November was considered as not lucky for weddings. Witches were supposed to have great power in this month. Their November Sabbaths were scenes of the wildest orgies, so the old people said. Children were told not to remain out after dark in November, for the witches would catch them. If there was sufficient ice in November to hold a duck, the winter would be a muddy one.

If there is ice in December, clover can be cut at Easter. A warm December, a warm Easter; but a green December promises snow at Easter. A windy Christmas Day promises trees heavily laden with fruit. If there is much rain for twelve days after Christmas, the next year will be wet. The people in South Wales say:

> " If it rains on Christmas Day,
> It will rain from May to May ;"

and:

> " If the sun shines on Christmas Day,
> There will be frost and snow in May."

Sunshine in December foretokens peace and plenty during the next year. A stormy December is a sign of sickness in the spring. Some people foretell the weather in the following way: On December 25 or 26 twelve onions are named after the twelve months of the year. A pinch of salt is put on each. If the salt has melted by Epiphany, the corresponding month will be wet ; if the salt remains, the month will be dry.

CHAPTER XIX

BIRTHS, WEDDINGS, AND FUNERALS

THERE is a Welsh proverb to the effect that a good workman is known in his cradle. If a child in the cradle does not look up at you, it will be deceitful. A child with two crowns to its head will be lucky in money matters. If seven girls are born in succession, the youngest will be a witch or gifted with second sight. If seven boys are born in succession, the youngest will have the power to heal by the passing of his hands over the affected parts. He will also be lucky in planting and sowing, for " everything will grow after him."

Children born with cauls around their heads will be very fortunate, and they will never be drowned. The caul is bought by master mariners for their ships. So long as it is on board the vessel will not be shipwrecked. Fastened securely to the figure-head of the ship, it is a protection against lightning and disasters by fire or meteoric showers. A child born on a Sunday will be fortunate. If born three hours after sunrise on that day, the child will be able to converse with spirits. Babes born on the last two days of the week are said to marry late in life. When a child suffers from hiccough, he is said to be thriving. If two children who cannot talk kiss each other, one will surely die within the year. The first time a child is carried out, one of its garments should be put on with the wrong side uppermost for luck. If a newly-born infant cries, three keys should be placed in the bottom of the cradle. If an infant learns to say " Dada " first, the next child will be a boy; if it says " Mam " first, the next child will be a girl.

In the past it was customary for the nurse to place a Prayer-Book or a hymn-book in the bed until a babe was baptized. A fire was always kept burning in the room where the infant was born. This was done to keep the devil away, and prevent the fairies from changing the child. The Welsh would never have a child baptized after a funeral, for they said it would thus be prevented from following the dead to the grave during its infancy or early years. They disliked christening a babe on the anniversary of its brother's or sister's birth.

If a babe holds its head up during the christening ceremony, it will live to be very old ; if it allows its head to turn aside or sink back on the arm of the person who holds it, you may expect its early death.

Christenings never take place on Fridays in Wales. The old people say : " The child that is christened on Friday will grow up to be a rogue."

Whatever a baby first clutches will indicate its future occupation.

While a knife, a ball of yarn, and a key remain in an infant's cradle, it will not be under the influence of sorcery.

A woman who is about to become a mother is not allowed to salt a pig or touch any part of the killed meat, or make butter, or do any kind of dairy work. This is of general occurrence in the present day, for the touch of the woman is regarded as pernicious.

She must not walk or step over a grave. If she does so, her child will die. If she dips her fingers in dirty water, her child will have coarse hands. If she ties a cord around her waist, her child will be unlucky. If she turns the washing-tubs upside down as soon as she has finished with them, her child will be tidy and orderly. If she passes through any kind of tangle, her child will have a life of confusion. If she meddles much with flowers, her child will not have a keen sense of smell. If she has a great longing for fish, her child will be born too soon, or will soon die. " She must not spin," said people in the eighteenth century ; " for if she does, flax or hemp will be made into a rope that will hang her child." If, instead of eating at a table, she goes to the cupboard and " picks at food," her child will be a glutton.

If she dusts her furniture with her apron, her children will be very disorderly.

It is lucky for mother and child if a spinster passes in and out of the room at the time of the birth.

Children should not be weaned at the time when birds migrate to or from Britain. If they are weaned at that period, they become restless and very changeable. If weaned when the trees are in blossom, they will have prematurely grey hair.

Old Welsh nurses would not allow rattles to be given to the children, because they made the latter " late in talking " or " very slow of speech." If you bathe babies in rain-water, they will talk early and be good conversationalists.

If you rock an empty cradle, you will take the infant's rest away.

The first time a baby's nails need paring the mother bites them off. If she cuts them, the child will be a thief.

If you blow the baby's first food to cool it, the child will never be scalded in the mouth.

A horseshoe placed under the pillow of a child subject to convulsions would cure the malady. Children beloved by the fairies died young. When babies smiled or laughed in their sleep, the Welsh nurses in the long ago said the fairies were kissing them. If a child in the cradle would not look at you, it would be a witch. It was customary to place a small bag of salt in the cradle until the babe was baptized, to protect the babe from witches.

To insure good luck for a newly-born babe, a pair of tongs or a knife was placed in the cradle the day before the christening. A piece of braid made of the child's mother's hair was used for the same purpose.

The Welsh peasantry believe that children born when the moon is new will be very eloquent. Those born at the last quarter will have excellent reasoning powers. Girls born while the moon is waxing will be precocious.

People formerly said if you wanted your children to attain a long age, you should see that the godparents come from three different parishes. If you stride over a child who is crawling on the floor, you will stop its growth. Newly-born babes should not be laid on their left sides first, for they will be awkward in shape and clumsy in movement. If a babe is weaned, and afterwards suckled again, it will become a profane swearer when grown up. If you measure a child for garments in the first six months of its life, it will often want clothes. When a child dies, they say it visits the person who was fondest of it. If a new-born babe is wrapped in fur, its hair will be curly.

A child who has not yet talked should never be held up to a mirror, for this encourages vanity.

A child with small ears will never grow to be rich, while a babe with very large ears will live to be selfish and a great talker. A near-sighted baby will be a saving man. Red birth-marks around the neck of a child are called the "hangman's sign," and he will come to the gallows. If the baby's eyes are beady, he will be untruthful. The old women say: "Watch well when the child has finished cutting its first teeth, for if there is a parting between the two front teeth to admit the passing of a sixpenny-piece, that individual will have riches and prosperity all through life." The child who enters the world in an abnormal manner will be gifted with courage, and be able to conquer his enemies. A very precocious child dies early.

It was formerly the custom in Wales to make a large rich cheese for luck, in readiness for the expected birth of the first child. This was made in secret, and not a man was allowed to know of it, especially the husband. When the gossips congregated at the birth, and the husband invited the women to take refreshment, they stolidly refused; but the moment his back was turned out came the cheese and beer! Part of the cheese was eaten, and the remainder was divided among the women, who were expected to take their portions home. All this was done secretly for the sake of good luck and the prosperity of mother and infant.

In many parts of Wales baptisms were sometimes held at the residence of the parents. After the ceremony the christening water was removed, and thrown over the bed of leeks. If the garden did not contain leeks, the water was thrown over cabbages or any green-topped vegetables. This was done to insure wisdom and prosperity to the infant, and to prevent any illness or unlucky circumstance happening to the babe or the family. Font water was disposed of in the same way. If some of the christening water was thrown high up against the belfry wall, the child would attain an exalted position. Children that cried at their christening would never live to a great age. If the babe's arms were left free at the christening, the child would be expert and industrious. If a sponsor looked around during the christening ceremony, the child would be able to see ghosts. Sponsors at a christening should not wear dirty or soiled linen, or witches would have power over the babe. If the godparents refused any dish at the christening feast, the babe would dislike that food all through life. If the sponsors whispered during a christening, the babe would walk and talk during its sleep.

A christening immediately after a funeral is of ill omen to the babe and its relatives, for the child or a member of the household will soon " follow the dead." If the christening takes place immediately after a wedding, the child will be rich and happy. Children who die unbaptized are said to be for ever hovering between earth and heaven. In the days of old the nurses said these children were claimed by the fairies, or were doomed to follow Mallt-y-Nos and Arawn, King of the Underworld.

With reference to the churching and christening ceremonies of the past, the following quaint custom was general : The monthly nurse, carrying the child, accompanied the mother to church. A slice of white bread and butter or bread and cheese was also brought by the nurse. White or wheaten bread was very scarce in the past. The slice was given to the first person met by the christening party on the way to church ; but the person to whom it was given must be of the opposite sex to that of the child which was to be christened. This custom was supposed to insure plenty and prosperity to the child all through life, and to keep it from poverty and want.

When Welsh parents brought their tenth child to be christened, people said they were " holding Hunger at the font."

It was customary for young people to take the breast-bone or " merry-thought " of a chicken or fowl, and conceal the joint, then to offer either end to a friend. It was then cracked, and the person who obtained the larger side of the joint would be married first, while the other would be the first to rock the cradle.

Three lights accidentally burning on the same table fore-token a wedding. If a person stumbles in going upstairs, the one who comes after will soon be married. If a girl steps on the cat's tail, she will not be married in that year. If a girl lets her knife fall, her lover and future husband is coming. If a girl or a wife loses her garter, her lover or husband is unfaithful to her. When thorns or brambles catch or cling to a girl's dress, they say a lover is coming. Boys born on New Year's Day will be unlucky in love affairs and marriage. The unexpected advent of a girl baby on January 1 means prosperity and a wedding in the family within twelve months. Girls born on Christmas Eve will be lucky in marriage.

Saturday is considered a lucky day for a wedding.

The bride and bridegroom are advised not to look round on their way to church. They are to stand as closely as possible together, to prevent witches creeping in between them. If at the altar the bride and bridegroom stand far apart, they will not agree. The person who gets up first from the altar will die first.

If a woman bursts her wedding gloves or shoes, or splits any article of her raiment, she will be beaten by her husband.

Snow on a wedding-day indicates a very happy marriage.

If rain falls on the bridal wreath or bonnet, the married pair will be prosperous.

If there is a grave open in the churchyard during a wedding, it is considered unlucky. If the grave is for a man, the bride will be a widow ; if for a woman, the bridegroom will be a widower ; if for a child, their children will die early. If two weddings take place at the same time, one of the husbands will die, or a separation will take place.

To marry at the time of the waning moon will cause the luck of the bride and bridegroom to wane. It is lucky to marry when the moon is new.

A bride must not keep the pins that fasten her wedding dress, or those used in any part of the toilet. The pins must be thrown over her left shoulder, or into the fire for luck. If the bride preserves a piece of her wedding-cake, she will never know the want of bread.

It is unlucky to be " called " at church at the end of one quarter of the moon, and to be wed at the beginning of the next.

If a woman loses her wedding-ring, or even if it falls off, it is a sure sign that she will lose her husband's affection or there will be a separation.

In the days of old it was customary to ride on horses to the wedding ceremony. On the return journey, when the bride rode on the same horse as the bridegroom, it was considered unlucky for the husband to turn the animal or to rein it in until home was reached. If he did so, the marriage would be childless.

It was considered unlucky for a stone to roll across the path of the newly-married pair. If the bride and bridegroom placed a small silver coin in their right shoe, the marriage would be happy. If the bridal procession chanced to meet a funeral, the wife would soon be a widow. For a bridal party to meet a cartload of dung was considered very unfortunate. If the bridegroom rode a mare to the wedding, his wife would have daughters, but no sons. If the bride slightly stumbled on her way to the altar, her first child would die early. Brides never went through the same gateway to church as that through which corpses were borne. If the chief groomsman gave the bride a small piece of bread and butter to eat before the wedding-cake was cut, her children would have pretty and small mouths.

A Cardiganshire correspondent writes as follows : " In some parts of this county we, until recent years, retained the old practice of marriage by capture. On the wedding-day the bridegroom and his friends proceeded to the bride's house. There they found the doors locked, and resistance was offered to their entry by the bride's friends. Scuffling and horse-play ensued, and when order was restored the spokesmen on each side held a dialogue, generally in verse. The bridegroom was then allowed admission. In the meantime the bride would be disguised, and was eventually found, dressed as an old crone, nursing a

baby boy. The child was a boy for luck, so that the first babe
of the marriage might be a male. After that the bride and
bridegroom went to church. Before the wedding the father
or person who gave away the bride rode off with her, and a wild
chase ensued. When at last the bridegroom overtook the
bride, the latter was delivered into his keeping, and they went
to church, where the ceremony duly took place. The day
after the wedding was devoted to the ' Tiermant ' or ' Tur-
mant,' which resembled the English tournament, only on a
smaller scale."

Welsh weddings,* especially among the peasantry in the
past, were considered incomplete without the customary
bidding. This was a general invitation to all the friends of
the bride and bridegroom to attend the house of one of the
contracting party's parents or a friend's residence. It was
understood that each visitor brought a small sum towards
making up the purse for the young people with which to begin
their finances. These donations were registered, and regarded
as debts to be repaid when the next friend's wedding took
place. In connection with the bidding was the Gwahoddwr,
or Bidder, whose business it was to go from house to house to
proclaim the date of the wedding. The Bidder carried a white
wand decorated with ribbons, while his hat and buttonhole
were decked with flowers. Into each house he went, and,
taking his stand in the centre of the living-room floor, he
struck his wand thereon to enforce silence. Then he announced
the wedding in prose or verse, according to his capabilities.
In addition to the Bidder's address, people who could make
rhymes contributed their share of verse to the proceedings.
Sometimes a written or printed circular was sent out instead
of a Bidder. The following is a copy of one of these circulars :

" *September* 25, 1801.

" As we intend to enter the matrimonial state on October the
25th next, we are encouraged by our friends to make a Bidding
for the occasion at the house of the bride's father, at Penmark.
There the favour of your company is most respectfully invited.
Whatever donation you may be pleased to bestow upon us

* Llewelyn Pritchard's, " Twm Shon Catti," pp. 48-59.

will then be thankfully received, and cheerfully repaid whenever called for on the like occasion.

" Yours obediently,

" J. H.

" G. G."

" The parents, brothers, and sisters of the young bride and of
the bridegroom desire that all gifts of the above nature due to
them be returned to the betrothed pair on the same day,
and will be thankful for all favours granted." [*A. B.*]

This custom is called in Welsh Pwrs-a-Gwregys, or purse and
girdle, and is doubtless of very ancient origin.

A peculiar kind of dance was popular in all parts of Wales,
and it was freely indulged in on the eve of the wedding and
the night of the marriage day. The harpist or fiddler would
play a gay tune, and then invite the young people to dance.
When the couples had been selected, one of the girls would
invite her partner to dance, and he would refuse. The girl
would then appeal to the harpist, and a very amusing dialogue in
verse was heard between them. The harpist would advise the
girl to make a second appeal to her partner. This she would
do with success. The same proceeding was followed by all the
girls in turn, and much mirth was the order of the evening.
Steps and reels, and various dances well known in Wales, were
popular on these occasions. [*Family Collection.*]

It was considered very unlucky for a bride to place her
feet on or near the threshold, and the lady, on her return from
the marriage ceremony, was always carefully lifted over the
threshold and into the house. The brides who were lifted
were generally fortunate, but trouble was in store for the
maiden who preferred walking into the house.

" Chaining " the bride and bridegroom is common to all
country weddings to-day. A rope is held across the road at
various points from the church to the house, and the bridal party
is not allowed to pass unless they pay their footing. It was
formerly customary to pelt the bride and bridegroom with
flowers as soon as they came out of church. .This custom,
which was pretty and harmless, is now superseded by rice and
confetti throwing.

18

Bridal flowers in Wales were the pansy, roses of all colours (excepting yellow), prick-madam, gentle heart, lady's-fingers, lady's-mock, and prickles. In some places the golden blossoms of the gorse or furze, red clover, old-fashioned crimson fuchsia, golden rod, shamrock, and ivy, were popular. Whole straws, in token of partnership, were interspersed with the flowers.

The bride should always buy something as soon as she is married, and before the bridegroom can make a purchase. " Then she'll be master for life !" say the old women. It is customary for brides to buy a pin from their bridesmaids in order to retain their privilege in the mastery of their husbands.

If the youngest of a family was married before the eldest, the seniors had to dance shoeless for penance to the company.

Funerals were formerly associated with many peculiar and melancholy customs, strangely mingled with feasts, convivial meetings, and speech-making.

It was the rule when a person was dying to keep the bedroom door open, so that the soul could easily go out. In some parts of Wales the windows were set open for the same purpose.

In hushed whispers the old people of the Principality used to mention the name of Margan, a spirit supposed to conduct the soul on parting from the body to the place assigned to it in the other world. [C. D. and A. B.]

One of the obsolete customs of Wales with regard to funerals was the Gwylnos, or wake-night—the evening before the body was conveyed to the grave. When the relatives and friends of the deceased person had assembled, the coffin containing the body was lifted on four men's shoulders. These men then proceeded to tramp up and down the room with slow and measured steps. Meanwhile the immediate relatives would hide their faces in their hands and moan incessantly. Groans and sighs sounded dismally, and occasionally a muffled scream or shriek varied the monotony. Hot spiced beer, or hot elderberry wine, was handed round, and it was considered unlucky if anybody refused a sip. The coffin was frequently changed from one set of men to another, and this proceeding was carried out all night. The purpose of this strange custom was to scare away the evil spirits, goblins, and hobgoblins who were supposed to be lurking in dark corners of the house to carry away the soul. These spirits, according to the old folk-lore, would not quit the premises until the body was borne to the grave. [*Family Collection.*]

In the words of an aged Welshman, this custom was intended " to give or bestow upon the corpse the fosterage of friends, who undertook to chastise or punish evil spirits who tried to prevent the soul from passing through the portals of death into the fair and blessed life which it panted for, and would reach in spite of any dark covering that might be placed in its way."

The Gwylnos, or wake-night, of Wales was succeeded in the nineteenth century by other customs which allowed the body reverent rest, but were not free from superstition.

When the coffin had been borne out of the house and laid upon the bier, the nearest of kin in the female line gave over the body a quantity of small white loaves, and sometimes pieces of cheese with money stuck therein, to certain aged people. The loaves were placed in a large pewter dish kept for the express purpose. Then a cup of wine, or metheglin, or small beer, was handed around, and every recipient of a loaf was expected to take a sip. After this everybody knelt down, while the clergyman or minister present repeated the Lord's or any other prayer. It was customary for the bearers to set the bier with the coffin on it three times on the threshold. When the body had left the premises, the gate was bolted. The procession then left the house. At every cross-road between the house and the church the bier was laid down, the people knelt, and the clergyman or minister prayed. The same proceeding was carried out when the procession entered the churchyard. All the way from the house to the church psalms and hymns were sung.

A pewter dish containing salt was sometimes placed near the coffin, and people were expected to take a pinch of it before the funeral procession left the house. The distribution of bread and salt kept the people free from the thrall of sorcery, and the body of the deceased safe from the power of evil spirits and witches. During the funeral the caretaker, who remained in the house, sprinkled salt in the bedroom, then swept it away, and the sweepings were always burnt.

In bygone times it was customary for all people who attended a funeral to place a coin on the coffin or on a table near at hand for the benefit of the bereaved family. These offerings, known as Cymmorthau, were given by those who had ample means to people of limited means or the poorer classes.

A service known as " the month's end "—meaning the last Sunday in the month after a person's death—is held in the church or chapel of which the deceased was a member. To this service the chief mourners, all the relatives, friends, and acquaintances of the deceased come, and a funeral sermon is preached. Sometimes this service is held on the Sunday after the funeral. This latter arrangement is still customary in Wales.

Nearly all the old funeral customs have become obsolete, but in some of the rural parts of Wales " the singing procession " survives, and is one of the most pathetic and solemn accompaniments in connection with the mournful occasion.

At Rhayader, in Radnorshire, an ancient funeral custom was continued until quite recent years. On the occasion of every funeral procession all the mourners carried small pebbles from the house to the church. When the men bearing the body arrived at the turn of the road leading to the church, each mourner threw a pebble to a large heap of stones which had accumulated there by the offerings from previous processions. Each person throwing a pebble said, " Careg-ar-y-ben "—that is, " A pebble on thy head." The old church associated with this curious custom fell in 1722, and a new building was erected in 1888. It is dedicated to St. Clement.

An ancient custom, which prevailed in remote districts so late as the last half of the eighteenth century, was formerly remembered by aged people. When a person died, the relatives sent for a local bard or another individual to perform the following ceremony : Upon this man's arrival, he placed a pinch of salt on the breast of the deceased, and upon the salt a piece of bread. He then recited the Lord's Prayer or the Apostles' Creed over the bread, and then ate the latter. When this was done, he was paid a fee of not less than two shillings and sixpence. Then he went away. In superstitious times this man was regarded with loathing, and as one absolutely lost, because he had, as it were, eaten the sins of the deceased. In remote centuries he was called the "sin-eater." An aged man living in the year 1826 had the reputation of having been in his earlier days a sin-eater. [*Family Collection.*]

This custom was in no way connected, as some people assert, with Druidism. It seems to have been a survival of mediæval times.

In the early part of the nineteenth century people arranged funerals to take place after nightfall, either by moonlight or torchlight, and very often in the twilight. This custom has long become obsolete, but even now the sunset hour is often chosen for funerals.

Previous to the year 1852 it was considered unfeeling to leave a dead body in a room by itself during the interval between death and burial. By day and night the corpse was watched, and candles were kept burning in the death-chamber.

Every village and rural town in Wales formerly had its traditional road by which the dead were carried. Many of these still remain, and are locally called " the burying lane." It was thought that if the funeral procession went along any other road, the soul of the deceased would have no peace. The ancient town of Llantwit Major, Glamorgan, still retains its " burying lane," but it is no longer used by funeral processions. In some places this was called the " death-road," and in earlier ages it was connected with Hades, or the intermediate state between earth and the abode of the blessed. The " death-road " was a remnant of pre-Reformation times, and has long since become obsolete ; but the " burying lane " is still to be found in many parts of Wales.

There was an old belief that this road or " burying lane " must always be kept level, smooth, and in good repair, for Death was supposed to walk up and down it three days before the soul parted from the body, and, if it was in good order, the better it would be for the deceased.

Death was sometimes described as riding a horse up and down this road. When dogs barked and howled in the night, people said, " Death is riding about, and the dogs see him."

If a funeral procession had to pass through arable land,

whether the grain was standing or the soil fallow, people said misfortune would follow the bereaved family.

If people walk quickly in a funeral procession, another will soon follow.

In some of the old village churchyards there were double stiles, known as " coffin-stiles," on which the coffin was rested before conveying it into the churchyard, and where the officiating clergyman always met the funeral procession.   Death was supposed to wait for his horse there, or to pace up and down three nights before the decease of any person.

When some of the " burying lanes " and " coffin-stiles " were diverted from their purposes, and the corpse was borne along another road, or gates were substituted for stiles, there was a general outcry, because the change would prevent the dead resting.

In former times the route of a funeral procession from the house to the church was swept, and sometimes sanded.   For the young and old alike the road was strewed with evergreens and ivy, mingled with sweet-smelling flowers.   White blossoms were used for young spinsters and persons under thirty, while red flowers—chiefly roses—were scattered on the grave-path of people who were distinguished for goodness and benevolence of character.   Sprays of the yew, with sprigs of rosemary, also found places among the foliage.

In those days wreaths, crosses, and other floral emblems were not known, but " posys," or nosegays, were sometimes carried by the mourners, and loose flowers were scattered over the coffin after it was lowered into the grave.   Bowls with sprigs of box were placed near the door of the house when a coffin was carried out, and the mourners and friends were expected to help themselves to this evergreen, and to throw them into the grave.   People said that if the chief mourners threw three clods or a handful of earth on the coffin at the commitment, it " helped the dead."

Flowers were used for the decoration of the death-chamber, and after a body was laid out, the coverlet was adorned with beautiful and seasonable blossoms.

Graves of the humbler classes even in the present day are planted with fragrant flowers.   These are generally gillyflowers, white pinks, polyanthus, mignonette, thyme, hyssop, camomile, rosemary, and balsam.   A flower called " snow on the mountains " is much used for graves.

In olden days a white rose-bush or the " maiden's blush " rose was always planted on the grave of a girl who died in her teens.

The graves and the clearings around them were covered with black earth, and carefully sanded.   Sand and black earth protected the dead against the devil, witches, and body-snatchers. For the same reason the little head- and footstones of the humbler graves were whitewashed.

CHAPTER XX

DEATH : ITS OMENS AND PERSONIFICATIONS

SUPERSTITIONS with reference to death are numerous. When a coffin sounds hollow in nailing it down, there will soon be another death in the house. The dead are laid out, if possible, with their faces to the east, "for fear that the wind from the west, blowing over the feet of the corpses, will bring a catching complaint" into the parish.

It was customary, whenever a death took place, to shake the vinegar and wine for luck.

People who commit a crime which remains undiscovered are doomed to walk in spirit form, with their heads under their arms. Wales has the reputation of having innumerable headless ghosts—an indication of many undiscovered crimes! If a person buries or conceals money or treasure of any kind before his death, he must afterwards walk ceaselessly in search of it, or he will have no peace in the hereafter. If you beat down the undertaker's charges, the dead cannot rest.

Dead children visit in spirit form the people who loved them best. The dead always reappear on the ninth day after death, but only a few are privileged to see them.

A dead person's linen is always washed immediately, "for fear he will not rest in his grave."

Two persons who, wearing mourning, meet for the first time, must never fall in love, or they will "come to quarrels."

If three thumps are heard in the house at night, a death will soon follow.

If a mole burrows under the washhouse or dairy, the mistress of the home will die within the year. If a molehill be found among the cabbages in the garden, the master of the house will die before the year is out.

If the wind blows out a candle on the altar, or lights grow dim in the chancel or around the pulpit, the clergyman or minister will soon die. If the house candle gutters in a long length, it indicates a shroud or a coffin.

When people experience a cold shiver they say, " A donkey is walking over my grave," or, " Death is picking my grave."

If the pall be placed on a coffin wrong side out, there will be another death soon in that family.

To prove whether a sick person will live or die, place a hand-ful of nettles under his pillow. If they keep green, the invalid will recover ; if they turn colour, he will surely die.

When a screech-owl is heard crying near a house, it is an indication of death on the premises. When a barn-owl alights on a house, hoots, and then flies over it, an inmate will die within the year.

A solitary crow or goose flying over a house portends the same sorrow. If any person is ill when this happens, there will be no recovery. A cock crowing at an untimely hour is a death-warning.

If a swarm of bees enters a house or settles on the dead boughs of a tree near the premises, the old people say " death will soon follow." When there is a death in a household the head of the family whispers the news to the bees, and the beehives are turned around before the funeral.

If crickets suddenly desert a house, death will soon enter.

It is said that the house cat can tell whether the soul of the dead person has " gone to heaven or hell." If immediately after death the house cat ascends a tree, the soul is " gone to heaven " ; if it descends, the soul is " gone to hell."

The ticking of the insect called the " death watch " is an omen of the inevitable.

The death of a near relative was prophesied by a white weasel.

If any person saw a white mole, he might expect his own death.

A white crow presaged death or disaster in the house near

which it appeared. A white pigeon was also a harbinger of death. A white dog, a white hare, or black foxes were regarded as messengers of death. A dove or doves circling above the head of anybody were supposed to indicate serious illness or death.

It is unlucky to call the dead by name. If there is sudden thunder in mid-winter, the most important person for twenty miles around will die. If a body is lying dead in a village on a Sunday, there will be a death in the same parish almost immediately.

In many parts of Wales it is asserted that if when you hear the cuckoo for the first time you are standing on grass or any green leaves, you will certainly live to hear the bird next season; but if you are standing on a roadway, or the earth, or even upon stone, you will not live to hear the cuckoo when it comes next.

If after receiving the Sacrament a sick person asks for food, he will die for certain; but if he asks for water or any kind of beverage, he will recover.

If a man dies exactly at the time of new moon, he will take away all the family luck with him. It is not good for a corpse to be reflected in a glass or mirror of any kind, because the dead will not rest. If two people express the same thought at the same moment, one of them will die before the year is out.

A funeral on a Saturday was considered good for the dead person's soul. In Wales they say, " Blessed are the dead that the rain rains on."

If a small silver coin is placed in the mouth of the dead, the latter will not come in spirit form to earth in search of any hidden treasure. If a corpse retains its colour or looks red in the face, one of the relatives will soon follow to the grave.

Any person can pray that his enemy be dead, if he wishes to repeat Psalm cix. every night and morning for a whole year. If he misses one night or morning, he must certainly die himself.

When prayers are said by a sick-bed while complete silence is maintained the patient will die. If anybody coughs or makes the slightest noise, the patient will recover.

If a smell as of fresh-turned earth pervades a house, people say, " There will be a death in the family soon." A wind called the "Gwynt-Traed-y-Meirw," or " wind blowing over the feet of the corpses," is felt by a relative of a person who is about to die, and by that they say, " Death is coming." If a person shivers before a roaring fire or in the heat of summer, the people say, " The spirits are searching for your grave."

If a watch or small clock falls to the floor, there will be a death in the house. When the house clock fails to strike it is an omen of death. If the town or church clock fails to strike, an important inhabitant or the incumbent of the parish will soon die. If two clocks strike exactly at the same moment, a married couple will die in the village. If the town or church clock strikes while the passing bell or a funeral knell is tolling, there will soon be another death in the parish. When the church bells sound dull or not so clear as usual, there will soon be a death in the parish. If a raven or rook perches and caws upon or near a house where a sick person is lying, it foretokens the patient's death. A long, narrow cinder falling from the fire denotes the coming of a shroud or coffin to the house. If a cinder called a coffin flies out of the fire, the person that it alights nearest will die first. If a mouse nibbles any part of a person's clothing, he or she will surely die soon. White beetles in a house are called " death-bringers." If two white lice are found in the hair or on the body of any person, a death in the family may be expected. If you allow your tears to fall on the dead, they will have no rest.

If a strange dog howls near the house, it is an omen of a death in the family. In some Welsh households it is considered an omen of death or misfortune for the house-dog to get up in the night and howl. The trouble may not actually fall upon the inmates, but upon their relatives or family connections.

It is considered very unlucky to pluck a flower that is growing on a grave. Persons doing so will experience death or disaster in their own families before a year has passed.

Mysterious marks, generally very dark, or " black and blue," that appear on a person's body, especially the arms, and cannot be accounted for, are called " the death pinch." After their appearance people said there would soon be a death in the family.

A sudden and startling noise heard on New Year's Night foretokens a death in the family.

A person cannot die easily if there are pigeon's feathers in the bed.

In Glamorgan and several other parts of Wales the yarrow is called " the death flower." People will not allow it to be brought into their houses, for it is said that if it is taken in, one, two, or three funerals will soon come out of the same house, or will happen in the same family.

The omens of death included the Cyhiraeth and the Tolaeth.

The Cyhiraeth was a doleful cry proceeding from the home of a sick person, and traversing the way leading to the place of interment. Sometimes it assumed a sad, wailing sound, heard at a distance. Occasionally it sounded like a smothered shriek, or a rushing noise resembling the whirring of birds' wings, or a flight of starlings. When heard on the seashore it foretokened wrecks. If the moaning passed up and down among the houses in a hamlet or village, it indicated epidemics.

The Tolaeth was only apparent to one sense at a time. When heard it could not be seen, and it could not be heard if anybody saw it in any form.

As a rule, the Tolaeth is described as rapping, or knocks, or heavy thuds. Sometimes it sounded like the shuffling or tramping of many feet, or the noise of people bearing a heavy burden.

The following experiences describe the Tolaeth in North and South Wales.

A tailor living in Carnarvonshire said he always knew when a customer was going to die by the sounds he heard. One day he was repairing the breeches of a huntsman, and presently he heard a mysterious rapping or tapping on his work-table. If he set the breeches aside for a few moments whilst threading a needle or cutting a piece of cloth, the sounds ceased; but when he took up the work again, the rapping or tapping was resumed. In this way he was able to foretell deaths in the parish.

A fisherman living on the shores of St. Bride's Bay said that for three successive nights in 1903 he was disturbed by the sounds downstairs of shuffling feet, doors opening, chairs being moved, and a grunting sound like that of men laying down a heavy burden or load of something. The man was much troubled in mind about these noises, and mentioned the subject to his wife, who admitted having heard the same sounds. Both agreed that they were nothing less than the Tolaeth. The noises were only heard in the kitchen. A week later their only son was drowned, and his body was brought home on a ladder. The mysterious sounds were exactly reproduced. The shuffling of feet, moving of chairs, and grunting sounds of the men setting down the ladder with its burden—all were heard as in the solitary watches of the night.

A man who was accustomed to letter breastplates for village carpenters and undertakers kept a stock of material for this purpose in a corner cupboard at the top of the stairs leading from the kitchen to his bedroom. He always knew when a death was going to happen in the district, because of the rappings, knocks, and rustling of trimmings in the corner cupboard.

Even in the present day carpenters in the rural districts of Wales assert that they are often forewarned of a death by mysterious rappings and knockings among the timbers in the workshop.

A curious story was told me by a Glamorgan carpenter. Early in 1904 an aged and much-respected man frequented the workshop. He had not long returned from America, where he had made a small fortune. Seeing a piece of timber in the end of the shop, the old man struck it with his stick. " That is the stuff for my coffin," said the old man. " There's plenty more like it," remarked the carpenter. " No, no," added the old man, who pointed out a peculiarity in the timber. A little controversy arose between the two men about the quality of the different timber on the premises. Before the old man left, he said, " That is to be the timber for me." The carpenter thought no more about the conversation, until one night, while working late, he quickly took up a piece of timber and laid it on his table. Suddenly he was disturbed by rappings and knocks. Thinking somebody sought admission, he several times called, " Come in," but without response. Again and again he set to work measuring the pieces of timber he had taken up, and each time he touched it the rappings and tappings continued. He was called away, and did not return to his work until early the next morning, when he moved the piece of timber, and placed it against the wall. But no sooner had he done so than the noises were resumed, and in vexation he threw the timber into the yard ; but the apprentice replaced the piece among others of the same kind and quality. The carpenter then remembered that the piece of timber was the very one that the old man from America had bespoken for his coffin. Thereupon, believing the omen meant something, he set the timber carefully aside. A week later the old man died, and the bespoken timber was used for his coffin.

Mysterious coffin-making has been heard in many villages. An old woman in South Glamorgan said she knew when an important death was likely to happen in her locality ; for she said, " There is always a noise of coffin-making in the dead of the night in my grandson's workshop." This had been the experience of four generations of the same family.

In a village a few miles west of Cardiff, a farmer had the following experience : He lived in a farm-house the e t windows of which overlooked a carpenter's shop and small timber-yard. Just before midnight on a Sunday night, looking out of his window, he was startled by seeing a dim light burning in the shop. His thoughts immediately turned to thieves, who were apparently making free with his neighbour's goods. Dressing himself in haste, he quietly left the house and entered the narrow lane leading to the yard. When there, he distinctly heard the sounds of coffin-making. First thoughts prompted him to return indoors, as he was by this time under the impression that the carpenter had received a hurried order for a coffin. Second thoughts urged him forward, and, quietly crossing the yard, he approached the workshop, where the dim light was still burning. Through the open doorway he distinctly saw the big and burly form of a labourer who was well known to be a notorious poacher.

Returning as quickly as possible, the farmer went down to the village, and sought the aid of the policeman, who was just starting on his night beat.   Both men went up the lane to the yard, but by this time the light had vanished, and no trace of the poacher could be seen.   The door of the shop was tried. It was locked.   Early next morning the farmer told the carpenter what he had seen, and both entered the workshop with the policeman.   A careful examination showed that everything was in order.   Apparently nothing had been touched, and there was absolutely no evidence that anyone had been in the building.   But the farmer persisted in asserting he had seen the light and the poacher.   The story was the topic of conversation in the village, and presently it reached the poacher's ears.   He declared he was in Cardiff on that very night.   A few weeks later the poacher was accidentally shot in a field beyond the farm.   His body was conveyed to the workshop, and laid therein, pending the inquest.

Folk-stories concerning the personification of Death are to be found in Wales.

Evan Bach—" Little Evan "—of Porthcawl, Glamorgan, desired to live to a very great age.   When Death came to look for him at sixty, he thought it was " foolishly soon." Evan was very pleasant to Death, and invited him to be seated at the fireside corner of the settle.   " I have no time," said the visitor, " and there are several calls to make in this neighbourhood."   " Half an hour isn't much to miss in a night," remarked Evan.   " I am in a hurry, and you must come with me," said Death.   " Isn't it a bit soon ?" asked Evan. " Only sixty, an' able to do a good many things 'fore I'm eighty."   " That may be," said Death, rattling his bones ominously ; " but I have set my mind on having a man of your age to-night, or, at latest, to-morrow.   People of sixty are getting too sure of themselves."   " Well," said Evan, " there's Billy James down in Newton.   He's jest gone sixty.   Iss, indeed ; an' now I do come to think of it, Billy 'll be glad to go.   He's had rheumaticks since he was forty.   There's one to be a warnin', if you like."   Death looked gravely into Evan Bach's eyes, and said : " I want a healthy man, of whom it shall be said, ' Died by the visitation of God.' "   " Well,

well, to be shure," said Evan ; " an' I can tell you of one sound in wind and limb—just the thing for you. Iss, indeed ! An' that's Dewi Mawr [Big David] of Pyle. He can walk forty miles without feeling tired. Come, now, isn't that likely to suit ? You be uncommon hard to please." This with the rubbing of hands and a smile. " There's plenty riper then me down this way," continued Evan. " There's Ned of Merthyr Mawr, an' Jack o' Cornelly, an' old Uncle Dick o' Newton, an' all of 'em over eighty." " Too old for me. just now," said Death. " Well, now," said Evan, " supposin' I wass to give you all my savin's—a big lump, too, only you'll keep it a secret, I know "—with a wink at Death—" jest on three thousand pound." " Money is of no use to me," said Death ; " but for once I will break my rule, if you are prepared to make a bargain with me." Evan was elated. " Dear anwyl [beloved], I will do anything you do like. Iss, indeed." Death lowered his voice, and said solemnly : " My terms are these : You must work more on the land than you have been doing since your savings reached three thousand pounds." " I will work agen every day but Sunday," said Evan. " You must support your old aunt, who has only parish pay." " Agreed. Iss, indeed !" exclaimed Evan. " You must give a new fishing-boat to your nephew who is soon to be .married," said Death. " To be shure. Iss, indeed !" exclaimed Evan. " And you must be more generous than you have been during the past few years," continued Death. " Anything you do tell me to do, I will do it. Iss, indeed," answered Evan. " Finally," said Death, " you must give more to the poor-box and the collections in the parish church. If you fail in these things, I shall come for you." " But if I do all these things, and never fail, I shall live for ever," said Evan. " Nay," replied Death ; " but you shall live over a hundred years—that is, forty or so years from your sixtieth year." " Dear anwyl," said Evan, " I'd be satisfied with comin' at ninety-nine. Iss, indeed !" Death went his way, and Evan kept his part of the bargain. Modrỳb (Aunt) Molly was in his house ; his nephew had the new boat ; he was wonderfully generous, and he gave handsomely to the collections and the poor-box in church. For many years all went well, but when he approached his ninetieth year he began to feel miserly. Modryb Molly was long dead ; his nephew was well off. Evan became selfish, and he gave less to the collection in church and the poor-box. When he was ninety-three all his good work ceased. A little later Death came for him. Evan pleaded for the other six years of life, but it was too late ; the bargain had failed. This story, called " Evan Bach," was popular in Glamorgan in the early part of the nineteenth century, and formed part of the répertoire of wandering minstrels. [*Family Collection.*]

A folk-story of the same period was well known in the first half of the nineteenth century. At Millincourt, about four miles from Neath, lived Modryb Nan, who on several occasions had been carried off by main force over mountains and streams, through woods and glens, and returned again, but never would let people know what her experiences had been. Rumours were current that a few times in her life she had been visited by a stranger—a grim figure in a long grey cloak and a curious slouching grey hat. He had been seen, but his face was never visible, for the reason that people always observed him going to Modryb Nan's house, and never coming from it. They also heard something like the clanking of keys or fetters, as the stranger moved along. Modryb Nan's nephew came home from sea, and hoped while he remained ashore to solve the mystery of the stranger, if the latter paid a visit to his aunt. One night in December his wish was gratified. He slept upstairs, and as there were wide cracks and small holes in the flooring, anybody could play the spy therefrom. In the dead of the night Jack, who was snoring, heard a knock at the cottage door. Modryb Nan, who slept on the ground floor, did not immediately hear the knock, which was repeated thrice. Then she got up, and called out, " Who's there ?" Somebody answered, " You know who." Modryb Nan unbolted the door, and Jack from the flooring saw the grey-cloaked stranger entering, while his aunt sat down on the settle. " I am come for you," said the stranger." " Sit a bit," replied Nan ; " I'm not quite ready. It's a cold night." And she shivered. Some talking went on, and presently the stranger threw his cloak off, revealing no more nor less than a complete skeleton. Jack shook with fear, and eagerly watched

19

the couple. " This is the third time of asking," said the
stranger, " and to-night I come to claim my bride." Modryb
Nan moved uneasily on the settle. Then there was more
whispering between the pair, and presently the skeleton seized
the old woman and compelled her to dance with it. Wildly
they whirled, until Modryb Nan was giddy, and begged permission to rest. While she did so the skeleton resumed its
cloak and hat, and prepared for departure. It threw the door
wide open, snatched Modryb Nan under its arm, and when
Jack went to his window to look out into the dim moonlight,
he saw a grey horse waiting, upon which there was a bundle.
The skeleton, placing Nan in front, mounted the horse, and
rode away like lightning. The people said Death had come
for Modryb Nan, who was never again seen. [O. S. and C. D.]

Dewi of Cwmdyfran, near Carmarthen, cheated Death
twice, according to an old folk-story. He entered into a compact with the devil by which the latter should have his soul if
he saved him from Death until he reached his hundredth
birthday. This the devil promised to do without fail. So he
gave Dewi instructions that when Death approached or
knocked at the door for admission, he was to have ready a
sack filled with old rags. This was to be tied around the neck
with one of Dewi's cravats, and on the mouth of the sack an
old hat was to be placed. Dewi was to go into the cupboard
near the bed, and snore loudly. When Death came and
knocked Dewi snored and snored. After three knocks, Death
called upon Dewi to answer, but there was no response. " He
sleeps soundly," said Death, and Dewi heard him. Growing
impatient, Death forced the window, seized the rag figure,
and fled, leaving Dewi to laugh heartily. The next time
Death came Dewi again cheated him in the same way. When
Death paid his third visit Dewi was ninety. It was his birthday, and the old man had celebrated it with his friends in a
convivial manner. Upon reaching home, Dewi went to bed,
and when Death knocked at the door he was fast asleep and
snoring. He did not hear his visitor, and therefore could not
put the rag effigy in the bed. Death entered by the window,
and seized Dewi, who, awakened by a rough shaking, tried to
wrestle with his visitor. In vain he struggled and lamented

his lapse. He failed this time to cheat Death. When his neighbours came in the morning they remembered his story about how he had cheated Death twice, and meant to be " up-sides " with him the third time. " After all," said the neighbours, " he had lived long enough, and 'twas better to die than live to a hundred, and then give his soul to the devil !" This old tale was sometimes called " The Lucky Escape of Dewi Cwmdyfran." [*A.B. and C. D.*]

Similar stories were formerly told in many parts of the Principality, and some of them had morals attached, or were related in a manner to inspire awe in people who boasted of the longevity of themselves or relatives. When men passed over eighty-six, they invariably said they were " good for another twenty years." Very often their assertions were true.

CHAPTER XXI

TRANSFORMATIONS AND TRANSMIGRATION

TRANSFORMATIONS from human shapes to those of animals, birds, and sometimes flowers, are illustrated by many old stories connected with the folk-lore of Wales.

In "The Mabinogion" account of Math, the son of Mathonwy, the story of Blodenwedd is beautifully told. It has already been stated that this lovely lady was changed into an owl by Gwydion. Before her transformation into a bird, she was the wife* of Llew Llaw Gyffes, "the lion with the steady hand," and her romantic origin illustrates the wonderful magic powers of Gwydion.

Arianrod, the mother of Llew, declared that her son should never have a wife "of the race that now inhabits the earth." Whereupon Gwydion said : "A wife he shall have, notwithstanding." The magician then went to Math, the son of Mathonwy, and complained of Arianrod's malice. Math promptly decided to seek by charms and illusions "to form a wife for him out of flowers." Then, it is said, the two magicians, Math and Gwydion, took "the blossoms of the oak, and the blossoms of the broom, and the blossoms of the meadow-sweet, and produced from them a maiden, the fairest and most graceful that man ever saw. And they baptized her, and gave her the name of Blodenwedd."

Llew Llaw Gyffes was delighted with the bride, known as "Flower Aspect," and they lived happily together until the latter fell in love with the Lord of Penllyn. Then the beautiful wife plotted like Delilah, and found means to kill her rightful lord, who, though pierced with a poisoned dart, was

* "The Mabinogion," p. 426.

transformed into an eagle. He was discovered by Gwydion, and ultimately restored to human form. With Gwydion and others, Llew returned to his rightful possessions and the palace of Mur-y-Castell. When Blodenwedd heard that her husband was returning, she fled to the mountain. Through fear, the guilty Princess and her maidens kept looking backward,* and "unawares fell into the lake." All the lovely maidens were drowned, excepting Blodenwedd herself, and she was overtaken by Gwydion. In the words of the Mabinogi, he said to her : " I will not slay thee, but I will do unto thee worse than that, for I will turn thee into a bird ; and because of the shame thou hast done unto Llew Llaw Gyffes, thou shalt never show thy face in the light of day henceforth, and that through fear of all the other birds. For it shall be their nature to attack thee, and to chase thee from wheresoever they may find thee. And thou shalt not lose thy name, but shalt always be called Blodenwedd."

The Llyn-y-Morwynion, or Lake of the Maidens, where the unfortunate ladies were drowned, is not far from the Cynfael, or Festiniog River.

According to local folk-lore, the mist that arises from the Cynfael is the spirit or wraith of a traitress, possibly the beautiful but faithless Princess of Gwynedd.

In the same Mabinogi, Gwydion, by means of magic, transformed Gilvaethwy first into a deer, then into a hog, afterwards into a wolf, and lastly back again into human form.

Gwrgi Garwlwyd, whose name is mentioned with Medrod and Aeddan in the triads, was called in English the " rough brown dog-man." He was a cannibal, and for his atrocities as an eater of human flesh he was killed by Difedell, a Welsh Prince, whose murderous attack on the dog-man is celebrated in the triads as justifiable homicide.

In the Mabinogi of Manawyddan, the son of Llyr,† the wife of Llwyd, the son of Kilcoed, was turned into a mouse, and at his death King Arthur was transformed into the shape of a raven, for which reason the peasantry of Wales, Cornwall, and Brittany will not kill that bird.

The power of assuming animal shape is illustrated by many

* " The Mabinogion," p. 431.   † Ibid., p. 409.

old Welsh stories, in which men are changed into a wolf or hog, a raven, an eagle, or a hawk ; while the women become swans, wild geese, serpents, cats, mice, or birds.

These metamorphoses were either voluntary or compulsory. Invariably the important personage or wizard assumed the shape that best suited his purposes, or he doomed a man to wear it in vengeance or punishment. The lesser people had their shapes changed with or without the aid of any wizard or witch.

From these ancient myths probably arose the belief in later ages that certain people could be transformed by magical aid into various shapes, or were directly descended from animals.

With reference to the former, the following stories have been well authenticated, though, for obvious reasons, the names of the families cannot be divulged.

In the last half of the eighteenth century the tale was extant that the son of a rich landowner in North Wales exercised peculiar and evil influences over his own eldest brother and heir to the estate. When the father died the heir mysteriously disappeared, and the second son succeeded to the inheritance. Wherever the new squire went, he was accompanied by a white crow with black wings. In the course of a few years, just before going to London, the Squire was persuaded by his friends to leave the crow at home. He did so, and, after remaining in London for a few weeks, he started on his homeward journey, but halted at Shrewsbury. While there he visited a friend. One night, while at dinner, the door was blown open by a gust of wind, and the white crow flew in, and perched itself upon the Squire's shoulder. The company expressed surprise, but the Squire assured them that the bird was his most faithful friend. During dinner the crow kept to its perch, but as the party entered the drawing-room a pet dog chased the bird, and a quarrel ensued. One of the visitors, in attempting to strike the dog, accidentally struck the bird. The crow, croaking piteously, wheeled around twice, and then fell dead. The Squire, who had lingered behind talking to his host, pressed forward, and, seeing the dead white crow, cried : " Alas ! you have killed one who was to me like a brother !" Then, turning to his host, he begged leave to proceed home at once ; " for," said he, " I have but three weeks more to live." The host and his guests regarded the Squire's remarks as peculiar, and credited him with being superstitious. Three weeks later the Squire died, as he prophesied, and it was rumoured that, according to the terms of a spell by which the brother disappeared and was transformed into a crow, the owner of the latter could only survive the bird three weeks. The third brother succeeded to the estates, and to this day, before a death in the family, a white crow with black wings appears in or near the house. [*Family Collection.*]

A small farm in Breconshire was occupied by a tenant whose ancestors had the reputation of being remarkably ugly and very eccentric. The man himself had exceedingly pointed and hairy ears, and his seven children inherited this peculiarity. Three or four generations of the same family had occupied the farm, and the father of the fourth succession left it owing to a windfall. The neighbours rejoiced at this departure, for everybody secretly feared " the wolves," as they were called. It was rumoured that the family traced its origin to a race of people, half men and half wolves, which formerly inhabited the forests of Wales. After the family left the farm, people said the shadow of the wolf-man haunted the place. In the course of time, it is said, the farm fell under a ban. Flocks and herds died ; the hay-crops were meagre ; the corn would not ripen, and yield of fruit ceased. It was generally believed that this place had been cursed because the wolf-man and his family had received notice to quit. Tenant after tenant left the unlucky house, and before the first half of the nineteenth century it became a complete ruin. [*A. B.*]

The story of a wolf-woman comes from Mid-Wales. A young man met a very pretty but impulsive girl on the borders of Radnorshire. He loved her very much, but had to " put up " with her violent temper. By-and-by adversity came, and the man could not any longer bring sufficient food into the house to feed himself, his wife, and child. The wife declared she would have enough to eat, even if she begged, borrowed, or stole it. True to her words, she obtained a constant supply of meat, and after the first few weeks the husband became fearful lest she had stolen it. He told her of his trouble, and she promised to reveal her secret, provided he did not call her by name during the revelation. Then she led him away to a lonely spot, where a few lambs had strayed from the fold. Quietly the woman went towards one of the lambs, and afterwards uttered a few words. Instantly she was changed into a wolf, and when in that form, she seized a lamb and ran off into the woods with it. Later on she came home, as usual, laden with meat. But one day, when doing this, a farmer, with his dogs, chased the wolf, and the husband in terror exclaimed : " Come home, Gwenllian—come home !'' The wolf vanished, and on the field, in its stead, lay his wife, bereft of every shred of clothing. From that moment everybody called her the " wolf-woman." After the revelation of the secret the wife was never again able to get meat without paying for it. [J. R.]

In old Welsh stories the wolf-people's eyebrows are described as meeting in a point near the bridge of the nose.

An old story, prevalent in many parts of Wales, was to the effect that in former times witches were capable of transforming men into werewolves. The men thus treated became wolves for three, seven, or nine days, or as many years. The peasantry said that werewolves only thirsted for the blood of young children and maidens, and in order to satisfy their thirst, they carried their victims away to the woods. There they sucked the blood until death ensued ; then the werewolf left the body in disgust.

Wenvoe and Cadoxton-juxta-Barry, Glamorgan, were credited with having werewolves. A man born early in the nineteenth century remembered hearing his father talking about the Witch of Wenvoe having a spite against a young man who once proposed marriage to her niece, then jilted her. The man lived in Wenvoe near the Bear's Wood, and the girl resided at Cadoxton, some little distance away. A year or so afterwards the man jilted his sweetheart and married another girl. The Witch of Wenvoe twisted her girdle and laid it on the threshold of the bride's house. The married couple stepped over it into the house, and, to the surprise of everybody, the bridegroom was turned into a werewolf. He rushed away to the Bear's Wood, and the bride was left disconsolate. Every night the werewolf ran howling around the witch's house, to the terror of everybody in the village. He frequented Cadoxton, and his pitiful cries nearly distracted his former sweetheart. So shocked was his poor bride that she pined away and died in less than a year. Then the Witch of Wenvoe, wishing to have the man for her niece, threw a charmed lamb-skin over the werewolf, and he resumed his human shape. Later on he married the witch's niece, but treated her so badly that the aunt once more bewitched him, and soon afterwards died. After her death no charm could restore him to human shape, and as a werewolf he remained to the day of his death, about nine years later. The narrator of this story said the people called him the " wild man of the woods," and when he was accidentally shot there was much rejoicing.

There used to be an old story told in Mabsant days of an innkeeper's wife at Candleston, Newton, or Cornelly, all near Porthcawl, who, for her cheating propensities, was transformed by a wizard into a wild goose for more than a year. In this shape she flitted along the dreary tracts of sand stretching away towards Aberavon and Margam. One day the wild goose quarrelled with other geese, and in a sharp encounter, the enchanted woman lost a piece of ribbon that was tied to her wing, and by which she was known from the other birds. The loss of the ribbon broke the spell, and the innkeeper's wife was able to reassume her human shape.

Swan-women in Welsh lore are closely connected with the fairies, and many stories are told of these. But there are several instances in which the swan shape has been given as a punishment for neglect of duty.

The most notable of these is the story of Grace, or, as she is called in Wales, Grassi.

At Glasfryn in Lleyn, Carnarvonshire, there is a small lake, which, according to tradition, owes its origin to the following circumstances : In former ages a well was on the spot, and it was called " Grace's Well."* A maiden named Grassi was the keeper of this well, over which there was a door. When

* Rev. Elias Owen, " Welsh Folk-lore," p. 256 ; Rhys, " Celtic Folk-lore," pp. 367-372, 394, 401.

people wanted water, Grassi opened the door, and carefully shut it immediately sufficient water had been taken. One day the maiden forgot to shut the well. Owing to this, the waters overflowed and formed a lake. For her neglect of this important duty she was instantly changed into a swan. In this form she is said to have haunted the lake for more than three hundred years, and always about 2 a.m. she was heard crying plaintively. The lonely lake is now frequented by swans. Grassi never resumed her human shape, but it is said her wraith, robed in a soft white silk gown, walks around Glasfryn House, and haunts Cae'r Ladi, or the Lady's Field. The former tenants of Glasfryn could not keep servants in the house, because it had the reputation of being haunted by Grassi, who kept the ancient well.

Old Morgan, an ogre, is said to be dwelling at the bottom of this lake, and when the children are naughty in the district they are told that " Morgan will swallow them."

On the wild coast of Gower, and with reference to Whitmore Bay, Barry Island, in Glamorgan, the following stories used to be told : In connection with the former it was said that a young farmer, while busy working in a field near the sea, saw a beautiful swan alighting among the rocks. There she laid aside her feathers and wings, turned herself into a lovely maiden, bathed in the waters, and after a time put on her swan shape and flew away. This he saw repeated on several occasions ; so one day he lay in wait for the swan, and as soon as she was in the water he seized her bird garments. The beautiful maiden came from her sea-bath, knelt before the young man, and begged him to restore her swan wings. But he would not. He loved her so much that they were soon married, and for three years the swan maiden was a faithful but plaintive-voiced wife. Her husband carefully preserved the swan's wings and feathers, and generally kept them under lock and key. But one day he chanced to leave the old oaken chest open, and from it his wife took the swan wings and feathers, and flew away. Her husband reached home, to see his beautiful swan-wife with outstretched wings slowly flying into the sunset, and as she went, her voice could be heard plaintively crying farewell. The man so bitterly lamented his loss that he pined away and died within a few months of his wife's departure.

The story of Whitmore Bay was well known in the early part of the nineteenth century. A young man from Rhoose went to visit a friend at Cadoxton-juxta-Barry. At that time it was only possible to reach Barry Island when the tide was out. For the purpose of shooting wild-fowl the young men crossed to the island, and soon reached the broad and sandy expanse of Whitmore Bay. There they lingered, and forgot the time until sunset, when the rising tide had surrounded the island, and made their return for some time impossible. To while away the period between the flow and the ebb, the young men went to the Friar's Point. There among the rocks they saw two swans. Thinking they would be fine birds to capture, the young men went nearer, and when they fixed their gaze upon the birds, it was to see them changed into very lovely maidens, who forthwith began to plunge up and down in the sea. Then gently the men went among the rocks, and gathered the two sets of swan wings and feathers, so that the maidens were obliged to beg and pray for them when they came out of the water. But the men refused, and the swan-maidens were forced to promise to become the wives of their captors. Ultimately the wife of the Cadoxton man was accidentally killed by being run over by a waggon, and when the people went to pick her up she quitted her human form, and flew away in the shape of a swan. The man of Rhoose, after seven years of happy married life, threw the swan-wings, with other rubbish, out into the farmyard. His wife went to examine the collection, and, finding the old plumage, put it on. A few minutes later the husband saw his wife slowly flying away in the shape of a swan. The children of these marriages were said to be somewhat conspicuous by reason of their swan-shaped necks. [*Family Collection.*]

A young man in Radnorshire had the reputation of being very cruel to cats. On his wedding-day he saw a cat crossing his path, and immediately he threw a stone at it. From that moment his health failed, and occasionally he went away to recuperate his strength. During his absences people said he was transformed into a cat, and ran wild about the woods.

After his death it was gravely stated that in cat shape he wandered in lonely parts of the district, and was a terror to naughty children.

An old superstition in the South of the Principality places all sandy-haired people and those with dull red hair among the races descended from foxes.

About a century ago there were several dens of foxes well known to people on the seaboard of the Vale of Glamorgan. Because these could never be caught, killed, or trapped, the country folk attributed to them superhuman attributes. It was gravely asserted that these animals were very old, and twice a year—at midsummer and midwinter—they were able to change themselves into human shape, and prowl about the lonely villages and hamlets. Whenever a vagrant with sandy hair appeared, the housewife promptly gave him something good to eat, and sent him away with a blessing. Then the " old fox " would not harm the children. The fox men and women were said to be quiet and playful if pleased and fed, but dangerous when angry and famished.

In the eighteenth century a fox that frequented the woods near Porthkerry, South Glamorgan, was known as " Catti Cwmciddy," the " c " being pronounced as " k." This meant Catherine of Cwmciddy. Everybody knew this fox, by reason of a grey patch across its shoulders, and people at a distance said that twice a year Catti might be seen in her human shape if anybody cared to roam through the woods of Porthkerry between sunset and sunrise during the three longest and three shortest days in the year.

Llancarfan Woods, in the same part of Glamorgan, had more than one semi-human fox, so the old people said ; and Tresillian Cave, on the shore between Llantwit Major and St. Donat's, was the reputed haunt of similar foxes. These latter, according to tradition, were, when in human shape, notorious wreckers, who hid their ill-gotten gain in Tresillian Cave, which had a subterranean passage leading to St. Donat's Castle. Old folk-tales describe the spot as " Reynard's Cave," afterwards changed to " Reynold's Cave "; and people said the wreckers and smugglers who frequented the place had obtained from Kate the Witch a charm which transformed them into foxes when the emissaries of the law came in pursuit.   Kate the Witch lived in a farm called " Flanders," an old, half Flemish, half Celtic homestead in the neighbourhood.

To assume the shape of a snake, witches prepared charms and amulets for themselves and others, and sometimes a ban was placed upon enemies, by means of which they involuntarily became snakes for a time.

Two stories about snake-people—one from the North and one from the South of Wales—will illustrate this old superstition.

A young farmer in Anglesea went on a visit to South Wales, and there, not far from Swansea, met a very handsome girl. Her eyes appear to have attracted everybody, especially the young man from the North.   They were described as " sometimes blue, sometimes grey, and sometimes like emeralds," and they " glittered and sparkled like diamonds."

In due course the Swansea maiden was wooed and won by the Anglesea man.   On the eve of the wedding the bride-elect told her husband to be that twice a year she would be obliged to leave him for fourteen days each time.   He was not to question her as to where she was going, or to whom.   The husband agreed.   For the first few years the periodical disappearances of his wife did not trouble him in the least.   He was perfectly satisfied with his wife's outgoing and incoming. But by-and-by the spirit of curiosity was roused in him by his own mother, who had been trying to solve the mystery of her daughter-in-law's repeated absences.   Advised by his mother, he disguised himself, and followed his wife to a lonely part of the woodlands surrounding their home.   Hidden by a huge rock, he saw his wife removing the girdle from her waist, after which she threw it into the deep grass beside a dark pool. A moment later his wife had vanished, and where she stood a large and handsome snake went gliding through the grass. The man chased it, but the snake swiftly passed into a large hole near the pool.   The husband went home, and for fourteen days eagerly waited his wife's return.   When she came, he questioned her closely about her absence, but she refused information, and only blushed in silence when he asked her what she did with her girdle in the woods. Just before the time for the next absence approached he secreted his wife's girdle, and for several days the woman's departure was deferred. To his astonishment, his wife was seized with a sudden illness. Then the man, hoping to get rid of a baneful charm, threw the girdle into the fire. His wife's agony was very severe, and when the girdle was consumed the woman died. For this reason the people in that part of Anglesea called her the " Snake-woman of the South." [A. B.]

The next story is more gruesome in its details.

A shoemaker in the Vale of Taff married a widow for her money, and in the course of time was not too kind to her. Soon the rumour was current that the shoemaker and his wife had serious quarrels, and words turned to blows. The neighbours remarked it as strange that the shoemaker's wife constantly appeared in their midst without even a bruise or the trace of a blow upon her person. Yet cries in the night were heard, and deep groans, and much commotion. One night a prying person found ways and means of witnessing the twain quarrelling. The spy secreted himself in a loft over the kitchen, and through the cracks in the flooring he beheld much, but said nothing. It was at last declared that the spy was " paid by the shoemaker for keeping the family secret." Ultimately the spy and the shoemaker had a dispute over a boundary wall, and then the truth was revealed. The spy said that when angry words cropped up between the husband and wife, the latter assumed, from the shoulders upward, the shape of a snake, and deliberately and maliciously sucked her partner's blood, and pierced him with her venomous fangs. Hence the cries and groans in the night. Never a mark was left on the man's body, but in time the poor fellow became emaciated, and was ailing for months, after which he died. At his death the doctor expressed his opinion that he died from the " poison and stings of a venomous serpent." This settled the matter to the credit of the spy. But both the spy and the doctor were found in a helpless condition in the churchyard at sunrise one morning. When roused from what might have been a fatal slumber, they said the shoemaker's widow invited them to taste her metheglin, and drink to the memory of her dear

departed second husband. They did so, and, in revenge for
the tales that had been circulated, the woman sprang upon
them, and stung them severely. After fighting against her
for some time, they were exhausted, and crawled to the churchyard, where they would have died, if a neighbour had not roused
them from the torpor which had bewildered them.   The shoemaker's widow vanished from their midst, and was never again
seen ; but for many years afterwards a snake that was frequently visible in the neighbourhood, and could not by any
means be killed, was called in Welsh " the old snake-woman."
[*Family Collection.*]

Toad-men and frog-women are found in Welsh lore, and
of these the following instances are well authenticated :

An old grange in Glamorgan had the reputation of being
haunted by a well-known M.F.H., who strode forth at midnight, mounted his favourite horse, and led the hounds to the
meet.   People heard the cry of the huntsmen and the yelping
of the hounds, and shrank in terror at the sounds.

In later years the lodge of the grange was occupied by a
labourer and his wife, who had but one child, a boy born in
another neighbourhood. When the family came to the
lodge the child was about three years of age, but was never
seen walking. By-and-by the truth came out that the child
was malformed, and could only move after the fashion of a
toad.   In the course of time he was called the " toad-boy."

The child developed into youth, but was good for nothing,
said the people.   Still, he appears to have been fairly intelli-
gent, though sharp in speech and often spiteful.   His parents
were kind and patient, and bore their sorrow with great forti-
tude.

One day the master's pet dog flew at the lad and bit his leg,
inflicting a painful, but not a dangerous, wound.   The lad
took the attack to heart so much that he gradually pined away
and died.

A few days before his death he cried, " I'll pay them back,"
meaning the master of the grange and his wife, who owned the
dog.

The youth was buried in a neighbouring churchyard, and in
less than a year the parents left the place.   It was rumoured

that they never had any peace in the lodge after the boy died. Other people came to the lodge, who declared that the carriage drive was haunted by a shape of mystery resembling a toad, and the house was troubled by the same evil creature. At last, after repeated tenants, the lodge was deserted, and to this day the people in the district declare that the place is haunted by the toad-man ! [O. S.]

A frog-woman was known to frequent the road between Llandaff and Cardiff. Country people said she was only to be seen on moonlight nights. It was rumoured that she belonged to a " high family," but had been sent " out of the way " to live with the wife of an agricultural labourer near Llandaff, who was paid for keeping her. This woman had the movements of a frog, and her croak was unmistakable. Eventually she fell into the River Taff, and for many years afterwards people believed that about midnight on moonlight nights the frog-woman could be heard croaking and screaming for help to get out of the dark waters. [O. S.]

Transformation from human to bird or animal shape is accompanied by stories of the transmigration of the soul.

It is stated that when M. Henri Martin, the French author, visited South Wales, he found the peasantry still believed in the transmigration of souls.* Traces of this belief existed between fifty and sixty years ago in the remote parts of the Principality, where some of the people asserted that the spirit of a wizard or witch descended from body to body for three, seven, or nine generations.

The history of Taliesin is the oldest Welsh story of the transmigration of the soul. In this story Gwyddno Garanhir is described as asking Taliesin what he was, whether man or spirit, whereupon Taliesin answered :

" First I have been formed a comely person.
In the Court of Ceridwen I have done penance.
Though little I was seen, placidly received,
I was great on the floor of the place to where I was led.
I have been a prized defence, the sweet muse the cause,
And by law without speech I have been liberated.
By a smiling black hag, when irritated
Dreadful her claim when pursued.
I have fled with vigour, I have fled as a frog,

* Rhys, " Celtic Folk-lore," Preface.

I have fled in the semblance of a crow scarcely finding rest ;
I have fled vehemently, I have fled as a chain ;
I have fled as a roe into an entangled thicket ;
I have fled as a wolf cub ;
I have fled as a wolf in a wilderness ;
I have fled as a thrush of portending language ;
I have fled as a fox, used to concurrent bounds of quirks ;
I have fled as a martin, which did not avail ;
I have fled as a squirrel, that vainly hides ;
I have fled as a stag's antler of ruddy course ;
I have fled as iron in a glowing fire ;
I have fled as a spear-head of woe to such as has a wish for it ;
I have fled as a fierce bull bitterly fighting ;
I have fled as a bristly bear seen in a ravine ;
I have fled as a white grain of pure wheat,
On the skirt of a hempen sheet entangled,
That seemed the size of a mare's foal,
That is filling like a ship on the waters ;
Into a dark leathern bag I was thrown,
And on a boundless sea I was sent adrift,
Which was to me an omen of being tenderly nursed,
And the Lord God then set me at liberty.''*

There was an old Welsh belief that new-born babes who died immediately after their birth became a new kind of flower on the land.

Very old women were peculiar with regard to children until they reached the age of six, because their souls might be taken away by their first owners. A person born in the early part of the nineteenth century asserted that when his sister died at the age of five, his grandmother said : " I knew she would not live long. She had the soul of my grandmother. I could see it in her. And the old woman could not stay long in one place !"

An aged woman said that her grandmother referred to one of her children as " old Modryb Gwen come back to life again." She had also heard old people connected with farms referring to horses and dogs as having almost human characteristics. " He was a good man once," they would say of a horse or a dog ; or, in the case of a female animal, it would be : " She

* Taliesin was the laureate of the Christian bards or poets of the sixth century. Translations of his poems appear in Thomas Stephen's " Literature of the Kymry," in Professor William Skene's " Four Ancient Books of Wales," and one of his most brilliant compositions was contained in the manuscript collection of William Morris of Gare-gybi, who lived in 1758. There are also poems and particulars of this poet by Dr. Owen Pughe in the *Cambrian Quarterly*, the Iolo Manuscripts, Jones's " Welsh Bards," and the " Myfyrian Archæology."

was a woman of spirit and mettle," perhaps adding, " more's the pity, poor thing !"

When a child was too precocious or wise for its age, people in Wales would say : " He has been in the world before." When a child looked prematurely old they said : " This is his third chance in the world." They did not know their ancestors believed in that literally. These expressions are still in use.

If any person suffered from hæmorrhage, or lost blood owing to a severe cut, or had bleeding of the nose, a great dread seized his neighbours, who believed that if the blood could not be quickly stanched, he would lose his soul. The latter was supposed to pass with the flowing of blood. Aged people in the eighteenth and early part of the nineteenth centuries believed that the seat of the soul was in the blood.

Trances and catalepsy were known in Wales in the eighteenth century, and in some parts so late as the first quarter of the nineteenth century. It was then gravely asserted that the soul had left the body, and would not return until the sleeper awoke. It was customary in such cases to ask the sleeper where he or she had been in the interval. On one occasion a Carmarthenshire girl living in Glamorgan was asked to relate her experiences through a slumber of fourteen days, during which time she neither spoke nor took food, and was only sustained by the moisture of a feather dipped in cream and applied to her lips. She stated that she found herself flying through the air at great speed, and soon reached a very high mountain with a door in the side of it. There she was met by a crowd of people all beautifully dressed. The strangers led her into a hall, where, at a banquet, Kings and Queens, with crowns on their heads, were seated. From the hall she was conducted through beautiful rooms into lovely gardens, where flowers and fruits grew in profusion and the sunshine was glorious. From this her friends judged she had been in heaven during her long sleep. [A. B. and Family Collection.]

A man rescued from drowning at Breaksea Point, on the coast of Glamorgan, firmly believed that while efforts were being made to restore animation, his soul left his body. This happened in his twenty-fifth year, an age when experiences seldom fail to leave indelible traces upon the memory. To the last years of his life he retained a vivid recollection of his sensations. He felt conscious that, a few minutes after being completely submerged, his soul or spirit felt an unusual sense of freedom. He seemed to be gazing down on his helpless body, to be watching its rescue, and the subsequent efforts for restoring animation. He recognized both the rescuers and those who readily helped in the work of restoration. Then he felt conscious that his soul re-entered his body, and a keen sense of imprisonment succeeded the previous sensation of delightful freedom. In proof of his perfect knowledge of all that took place while his soul was absent from his body, he mentioned having seen two sailors fighting near a wrecked ship among the rocks. They were fighting for a keg of spirits, probably rum. It was a moonlight evening, and he saw them distinctly. Those engaged in restoring animation to his body declared nothing of the kind happened. But a few days later the two sailors admitted they had fought over a keg of rum. To the last hour of his life the man who had been rescued from drowning declared that the memory of his experiences would remain fresh until his soul could finally quit his body. [*Family Collection.*]

It was formerly a common belief that every soul after leaving the body hovered between earth and the moon. Vestiges of this, by force of habit, were prevalent in the first half of the nineteenth century; for it was customary among husbands and wives in a joking way to threaten that, if their partner married again too soon, they would torment the person by hovering over him or her between the earth and the moon.

Aged people used to say that white moths were the souls of the dead, who in this form were allowed to take farewell of the earth. When any kind of moth fluttered around a candle, people said somebody was dying, and the soul was passing.

When a ship foundered or was wrecked, the watchers said the souls of the victims ascended to heaven in the shape of doves.

The first-born daughters of an ancient Welsh race were turned into doves if they died unmarried, while the married ones became owls. The death of each female member of the family was presaged by the appearance of these birds or " by their bite " or pecking.

20—2

Shooting stars were supposed to be the souls of dying Druids and bards. When a shooting star was seen, people said, " Another Druid or bard is dead."

The custom of burning or breaking empty eggshells is said to have arisen from the belief that souls were supposed to sail over the River of Death in them, and unless they were smashed, witches would get in and disturb the soul in its passage.

In all the old stories of King Arthur his soul was supposed to be conveyed away by ship. A swan-ship conveying corpses was an old Celtic belief, and generally it was without sail or rudder.

The ancient Celtic bards believed that, in order to reach the underworld, souls were obliged to sail over the Pool of Dread and dead bones, across the Vale of Death into the sea, on whose shore there stands the open mouth of hell's abyss.*

Procopius the Byzantine recorded a story with reference to the passing of souls from Gaul to Britain. He stated that on the coast of the Continent, and under the Frankish sovereignty, there were fishermen and farmers exempt from taxation, whose duty it was to ferry the souls of the dead to Britain. They undertook this duty in turn. Those to whom this duty fell went to bed at dusk. At midnight they heard loud knocking at their doors, and muffled voices calling them. Immediately the men got up, went to the shore, and there saw empty boats—not their own, but strange ones. These they boarded, and at once seized the oars. When the boat was under way they saw that it was " laden choke-full," with its gunwales scarcely an inch above the water. Yet they did not see anybody. Upon arriving at " Brittia," the boat was quickly unloaded, and became almost dangerously light. Neither during the voyage nor on landing did they see any-body, but they heard a voice loudly asking each invisible pas-senger his name and country. Women gave their husbands' names, rank, and position.

In old Druidical lore the clouds were composed of the souls of men who had recently quitted earth, and their influence either inspired courage or struck terror into armies and people. These souls were capable of terrifying mortals with

* Davies, " Mythology," p. 231.

howlings, cries, apparitions, and luminous phantoms. Their agency was seen in dreams and nightmares. They vainly endeavoured to soar above the atmosphere, but an irresistible force impeded their flight into the purer spheres. There they waited until a new body was formed. This they entered with impatience, and animated it. Not having attained the higher purity which could unite them to the sun, they were compelled to wander in the forms of various birds, animals, and fishes, or, as they said, " creatures that peopled the air, earth, and seas."

Millions of higher souls occupied vast ice-plains in the moon. There they lost all perception but that of simple existence. They forgot the kind of life in which they lived. On bridges, or more correctly " tubes," or tunnels caused by eclipses, they returned to earth, where, revived by a particle of light from the sun, they began a new life career.

The sun consisted of an assemblage of pure souls " floating in an ocean of bliss." This glorious orb contained the souls of good, brave, and wise people, who were friends and defenders of mankind. These souls, when thrice purified in the sun, ascended to a succession of still higher spheres. From there they could not again descend to those stars which occupied a less pure atmosphere.

Souls sullied by earthly impurities were refined by repeated changes and probations until the last stain of evil was worn away, and they were ultimately ripened for immortal bliss in a higher sphere.

This was a purely Druidical belief.

The Druids divided existence into three circles : (1) The Circle of Space, which God alone could pervade ; (2) the Circle of Courses, pervaded by material creation or state of humanity ; (3) the Circle of Happiness, which would be ultimately obtained by mankind.

In the Circle of Courses man, with other works of Nature, began in the Great Deep or lower state of existence. This contained a mixture of good and evil, of which the soul of man could make his choice, or balance his propensities. This condition was called the Point of Liberty. Thence the man's soul went through the Gate of Mortality to the Circle of

Happiness, where there would be neither want, adversity, sorrow, nor death. If he permitted evil affections and passions to govern him, he would sink down from the Circle of Happiness. In that case Death would return him to the Circle of Courses, where he would suffer punishment in proportion to his sins. Here the soul was to do penance in the form of a beast or reptile, or in several of them successively. From this degradation it again arose and reassumed human form. Repeated corrections and probations would ultimately subdue all evil propensities. The Point of Liberty would at length be attained, and the " Divine particle " would be introduced by Death to infinite happiness.

It was stated that the " Clych yr Abred," the mystery of the " Abred," or the " Circle of the Courses," was the corner-stone of British Druidism.*

* Davies, " Mythology," p. 220 ; Owen W. Richards, " Cambro-British Biography," p. 32 ; Smith, " Religion of Ancient Britain," p. 37 ; *Cambro-Briton*, vol. i., p. 251 ; " Voyage dans le Finisterre," 1794, 1796.

CHAPTER XXII

COLOUR-LORE AND OLD-TIME REMEDIES

OLD-TIME remedies associated with folk-lore are peculiar and curious. In some instances remedies that were formerly laughed at as " old women's superstitions " are, by means of modern science and its advancement, turned to use again. I refer particularly to colours used for the cure, or at least the alleviation, of certain human maladies.

Red is regarded in Wales as a colour of many virtues, and from the far past even until so late as twenty years ago red flannel was considered to be excellent for rheumatism. A piece of red flannel or any kind of woollen stuff worn around the throat, especially with a layer of thinly cut bacon placed between two folds of the fabric, was considered to be a sovereign remedy for all kinds of sore throat.

In 1859 a doctor of the old school ordered a patient suffering from scarlet fever to be dressed in red night and day clothing. Red curtains were suspended from the window-pole, and the old-fashioned four-posted bedstead was draped with red material.

Smallpox patients were also enveloped in red, and red blinds or curtains were drawn across the windows. At the first approach of scarlet fever or smallpox, the person was subjected to red treatment.

There was an old superstition that if scarlet fever or small-pox were epidemic, red flannel worn around the neck, or next to the skin on any part of the body, warded away the disease. Even in the present day the peasantry of Wales cling very closely to the old superstition about a bit of red flannel as a preventive against fever, smallpox, and rheumatism.

At the same time, the people believed that if a person gazed very long at scarlet or bright red, he would be driven to kill somebody, especially his nearest and dearest relatives. Red placed before the eyes of a person beginning to be light-headed would send him mad, but in later stages of delirium the colour would cure him.

Purple and shades of " puce," as they called it, had a tendency to drive men mad, and I heard an old woman saying that if " you look too long on laylock [lilac], you'll get crazy."

In South Glamorgan between fifty and eighty years ago blue was regarded as a " flighty colour," and had a tendency to make women have a longing to be " show-girls and play-actors." It was also " very bad for the nerves to look too long on blue."

Yellow was considered very bad for the " sterricks " (hysteria), and country folk said that if you gazed too long upon a " yellow rag," you would become " silly and moon-struck." The plague was often called the yellow sickness, or the yellow complaint. At the same time, a person suffering from jaundice was advised to wear a yellow ribbon or woollen rag around his throat. But in some parts of Wales it was asserted that yellow worn on any part of the body would induce or " conjure " the jaundice.

If a yellow-hammer could be caught and held before the face of a person afflicted by jaundice, a cure might be expected. A piece of amber or a topaz put in a drinking goblet or cup, and the latter filled with mead, was a cure for jaundice. The skin of a lizard or viper placed under the pillow served the same purpose.

The cure of hydrophobia in mankind and animals appears to have exercised the minds of the Welsh very much. Many of the remedies are now forgotten, and before referring to the testimony of one who made up a hydrophobia decoction for man and beast under the direction of her father, mention may here be made of the antidotes well remembered.

On the sea-coast of Wales, north, west, and south, a patient suffering from the bite of a mad dog was taken out to sea in a boat. Before starting, he was securely bound by the hands and feet, and when out at a distance from the shore two men plunged him in the water three times. Each time the man or woman, as the case might be, was asked if he or she had had enough. But just as he opened his mouth to reply, he was dipped again. This dipping was repeated nine times, with a pause between each three dips, to enable the patient to have an opportunity for " breathing." The shock or temporary fright caused by repeated dips into the sea and the quantity of water swallowed worked the " cure," so the people said.

Another remedy consisted in a visit to the wonderful stone at Mynyddmelyn.* A bit of this stone reduced to a fine powder and mixed with milk was given to the sufferer, and the cure " never failed." Friends of the person bitten made a pilgrimage to the stone for the purpose of obtaining a small portion of it, or else the patient was conveyed to the stone, where, with bound hands and feet, he was forced to lick it. The stone of Mynyddislwyn, Monmouthshire, was also regarded as curative and almost sacred.

Among other remedies well remembered was the buck's-horn plantain. This formerly grew in abundance among the sand tracts of The Leys in South Glamorgan and the sand-dunes of Newton, near Porthcawl. In those sandy and barren places the leaves of this plantain spread star-shaped upon the ground. They are narrow, long, notched, and divided so as to resemble a buck's-horn. The root is long and slender. The root and leaves were made into a decoction, sweetened with honey, and administered to the patient.

Scarlet pimpernel was also used as a sovereign remedy, not only for the bites of mad dogs and other venomous animals, but for the stings of vipers, adders, and snakes.

An old woman in the Vale of Glamorgan told me that this remedy was prepared in the following way : The herb was dried and reduced to a powder, just as the housewife prepares mint for winter use. The leaves and root were also made into an infusion. A teaspoonful of the latter, or about twenty grains of the former, were put into a cup, with fifteen drops of spirit of hartshorn, and a dose was administered every six hours. The patient had to continue using this for fifteen days. Rags steeped in the decoction were applied to the wound, and whenever practicable, the underlinen or flannel

* William Howell, " Cambrian Superstitions," pp. 23, 25.

worn next to the body was soaked in the same liquid.   White poppy and scarlet pimpernel were sometimes used at the same time, or in alternation.

A North Welshman said the remedy often used in the Snowdon region was a kind of moss found on wild heaths, dry pastures, and in woodlands.   He said it spreads on the ground, and is a leather-like substance.   To the botanist this lichen is known as ash-coloured liverwort, or *lichen caninus*.   This lichen was dried and reduced to a powder.   When used as a remedy for hydrophobia, two parts of the powder were mixed with one of pepper, which should be the black variety.   This was commonly used in Wales.

Milkwort was used for slight bites of dogs, cats, and venomous animals, or for the sting of a snake, viper, or any reptile.

Elecampane was much used for the same purpose.   A correspondent recently wrote to me thus : " There lived about sixty years ago an old woman in a cottage, one of a row that stood on the site now occupied by the present new Nolton St. Mary's Church, in Church Street, Bridgend (Glamorgan), who cultivated elecampane in her garden.   She was noted for curing hydrophobia in cattle, and farmers in the surrounding district came to her for the remedy.   She made a decoction of it mixed with milk and a quantity of fowls' feathers.   The other ingredients were kept as a profound secret, which she took to the grave and never divulged.   Elecampane was generally known and very plentiful in the Vale of Glamorgan a century ago."*

Angelica, vervain, and rue were used with other remedies.

The person to whom reference has already been made who prepared a hydrophobia decoction under the direction of her father gave me some interesting particulars, but would not name the herbs.   From her description I gleaned there was something mysterious or even magical in the gathering and preparing of the herbs.   Shaking her head gravely, she said that some of the things done in preparing the decoction would be laughed at by the present generation.   Six or seven herbs were used, and they were brewed into a kind of beer.   One kind of brew was for man and one for beast.   This beer would

* William Davies (Gwilym Glan Ogwy).

keep for years. The afflicted person was to bathe in the sea, then walk home and take a dose of the mixture. It was to be taken when the moon was either new or full, or at both periods. This beer was in great request all through South Wales, and people even came from North Wales to obtain it. It was generally known and used in Wales so late as 1870. The maker of it says she could prepare it now, if necessary, but she will not divulge the names of the herbs. The receipt for making this beer is in her possession, and it has descended from father or mother to son or daughter for more than two hundred years. This beer would cure any scratch as well as bite of animal.

At Disgwilfa,* about twelve miles from Carmarthen, a white stone, " the size of a giant's head," was found. It was scraped by a knife, and the powder swallowed for hydrophobia. For curiosity a healthy man took some of this powder, and experienced a sensation as if the blood boiled in his veins. People said the stone had fallen from the sky.

Dog's madness was attributed to a worm seated under the tongue, and this could be cut out if seen to in time. The same worm caused distemper in cats, and could be cut away. An ailment of horses was called the " blow-worm," and this affected sheep and other animals, in all cases causing a kind of frenzy or temporary madness. An old story used to be told that a Welshman, having caught the devil, asked him what was a cure for this worm. The devil said when all the cattle or any other animals were dead but one, that one must be carried around the field or pen three times, and then no more would die but the last one ! [C. D.]

Syrup of elderberries with water of wormwood was a remedy for colic, and so also were boiled leeks. A poultice of blueberries was supposed to be a cure for sore throat. The mouth affection known as the thrush in infants was cured by allowing the child to suck the raw " mouse bit " of beef. Violets and their leaves stewed and eaten as a preserve with honey or sugar was regarded as good for cancer. Dandelion-leaves and flowers, sometimes with the addition of the roots, was considered good for liver affections. Rue-tea was the remedy for fits. Rosemary tea or beer, sweetened with honey,

* William Howell, " Cambrian Superstitions," p. 102.

cured hoarseness, loss of voice, and coughs. Sage tea or beer served the same purpose. The dew shaken from camomile-flowers was used as a cure for consumption.

May-dew was collected and used as a lotion for improving the complexion. For the same purpose elder-flowers, alone or with parsley, were boiled and strained, and the water used as a face-lotion. The old people said that the dew collected from pure white June roses would bring beauty to a new-born girl, if sprinkled on her face every morning before sunrise.

Sty on the eyelid was cured, they said, by means of a new bride's or grandmother's wedding-ring rubbed across it nine times. This was done in turns of three, each divided by a pause. To look at a person with a sty on the eyelid was to catch it yourself.

It was generally believed that shingles could be cured by the application of cat's blood to the affected part. The blood could be obtained from the ear or tail of the animal. Other remedies were lard or the slime of a snail rubbed into the shingles. A charmed girdle was sometimes worn around the waist. If the shingles gradually crept around a person's waist, and at last actually surrounded it, forming a complete girdle, it was regarded as a fatal sign, and the sufferer must die.

To cure a tongue-tied child, people took two loaves that had stuck together in the baking, and broke them loose over the sufferer's head.

For cramp, a ring made from the handle of a decayed coffin was to be worn on the finger all night. Armlets and ankle-rings of the same metal were worn for cramp in the arms or legs.

For toothache people were told to take a sharp twig of willow and therewith pick their decayed teeth until they bled. After that the twig was to be thrown into a running stream. This was a perfect cure. It was customary to peel the bark of the elder-tree upward, and make a decoction with it, which was administered three times a day for toothache. The same remedy was used for ague and all shivering fits.

For feverish chills the patient was recommended to walk over the boundaries of nine fields in one day, and he would be rid of it. It was also thought that for the same ailment the patient should go in silence, and without crossing water, to a hollow willow-tree. He must breathe through it three times, and go home without looking round or speaking. This last remedy was recommended for ague.

If a person ate the first three sloe-blossoms he saw, he would not have heartburn all through the year. A hare's foot kept in his pocket was equally effectual. He who would be free from all pains and aches through the year must be careful not to step barefooted on the floor on Easter Day.

For erysipelas, burns, and inflammations of the eyes, the remedy was to strike a fire by means of stone or iron in " front of the person " afflicted ; or the sufferer was recommended to stand before a forge fire and allow the sparks to fall freely upon him ! To stir or blow a fire before the patient, so that the glow overspread his face, was a remedy for the same ailment.

The marl of certain wells and springs at Llancarfan, South Glamorgan, was made into a paste and applied to the parts affected with erysipelas. Water running through cliffs near St. Donat's Castle, Glamorgan, was a well-known remedy for erysipelas in the end of the seventeenth and early part of the eighteenth centuries.

An old custom with regard to consumption died out in the middle of the nineteenth century. Old women who were skilful in making herb-tea, ointments, and decoctions of all kinds, professed to tell for certain when a person was consumptive. This was by measuring the body. They took a string and measured the patient from head to feet, then from tip to tip of the outspread arms. If the person's length was less than his breadth, he was consumptive ; if the width from shoulder to shoulder was narrower than from the throat to the waist, there was little hope of cure. The proper measure was made of yarn. Snail-broth was an old-time remedy for consumption, and the malady would be alleviated, if not cured, if the patient stood every morning for one hour after sunset in a stable among horses.

Gout was often attributed to the malicious work of witches. There were several kinds of this complaint, but all could be cured by flint-broth, snail-soup, or limestone-tea ! Each of these remedies was boiled for half an hour, strained, and drunk by the sufferer, who was invariably told he must have faith in them !

An old Welshman told me that his grandfather said the people in his youth mentioned several different kinds of gout. They were designated as flying, running, staying, trembling, morning, evening, growing, wasting, swelling, splitting, blowing, riding, deaf, dumb, and blind gout. The flying gout shifted from one part of the body to another. The running gout kept to one part, and ran up and down that particular place. The staying gout affected one part, and continually remained there. The trembling gout gave quiverings in various parts. The wasting form of this malady caused great emaciation. The splitting variety caused the finger and toe nails to break. The blowing gout caused bladders and scales to form and break on the fingers and feet. The riding gout was worse at night, and caused nightmares. The deaf, dumb, and blind gout affected the hearing, speech, and eyesight. For the flying gout the patient was completely swathed in clean hay or flax, and afterwards wrapped in a sheepskin. A sweating medicine was administered.

For rheumatism people formerly kept a piece of raw potato or a small lump of sulphur in their pockets. The tooth of a weasel was recommended for the same purpose. The various forms of rheumatism were treated in the same way as gout, and similar charms were used for both maladies.

Apoplexy was always called the " stroke of God " or the " touch of God's hand." The old people said the first stroke would " bring, the second would try, the third was the touch to make you die "! A hatchet laid on the threshold sometimes prevented the third stroke.

Epilepsy or falling sickness was pronounced incurable, and patients were encouraged to " bide their time in peace." Charms were used to relieve the fits. Epileptics were supposed to have double vision, and sometimes everything before them was trebled. If children ate chervil, they would become epileptic, and see everything double or blurred.

In some parts of South Wales dropsy was referred to as a moon-sickness. It was a water-calf or moon-calf, and always destroyed people's hearts.

Ringworm was the work of a witch, and was cured by means of seaweed poultices and powdered cuttlefish sprinkled on the sore place. This, with stone, gravel, affections of the spleen, and gripes, were singled out for exorcism of a special kind. The same method was followed in cases of tumour, fistula, whitlow, cancer, " king's evil," or scrofula, and boils of all kinds.

The old people used to say that if you desired to die you should eat cabbages in August. A dry, hoarse cough was formerly called the " churchyard cough," and the " trumpet of death." A cold head and warm feet insure long life. If you feed a cold, you will have to starve a fever. In some places the people say, " Feed a cold, and starve a fever." Light dinner, little supper. Sound sleep, long life. Plenty bread, but little beer. Salmon and sermon in Lent. Tongue-tied children should eat a beggar's bread. An egg, and to bed. After dinner rest awhile ; after supper walk a mile. In many parts of Wales the people say :

> " Early to bed and early to rise
> Makes a man healthy, wealthy, and wise."

If a draught comes through the keyhole, make your will at once.

The wick of a candle that had been burning in a dying man's room was supposed to be a certain cure for goitre. It was rubbed on the affected part.

A piece of oak, or the blood of birds or foxes, passed lightly over the body in perfect silence before sunrise on St. John's Day would heal open sores and wounds of all descriptions.

A stone from a virgin's grave was formerly tied to any person who had been bitten by an adder.

Mouse-pie was to be eaten by children who stammered, and by people who suffered from bladder affections.

In some parts of Wales snails are facetiously called " wall-fish," and one of these rubbed on any inflamed part of the body effected a cure.

Brimstone and treacle, and salts and senna, are still the common remedies used in Wales for purifying the blood in spring.

Creeping through gaps in trees, the earth, or stone was a remedy for many complaints in the early part of the nineteenth century. The young pollard ash-trees and oaks were cleft asunder and held open by wedges, so that any patient, from the infant to the adult, could be pushed or drawn through the aperture. A naturally hollow tree was still more valuable. When the operation was over the part of the body affected was rubbed, stroked, and bound. This was an invaluable remedy for rupture.

For animals a hole was bored in the oak or ash, and a living field-mouse was placed in the hollow. It was then customary to plug the hole, and to rub the affected part of the animal with the leaves of the tree, of which a poultice was made for application to the sore.

Children troubled with rickets were put to crawl or creep under blackberry brambles three times a week, and the same remedy was used for infants slow to walk. Sometimes a natural archway was made of raspberry-canes or blackberry brambles, so that both ends were in the earth, and the child was taught to crawl through it three Fridays in succession.

Children suffering from whooping-cough were formerly drawn three times through a hawthorn hedge.

A trout's head put into a child's mouth answered the same purpose, and in some parts a dead spider or the tooth of a weasel, sewn up in a tiny silk bag, was considered effectual. It had to be suspended around the sufferer's neck.

One of the most popular remedies was to take the sufferers daily to the edge of the tide at low-water mark, and allow them to walk up and down before the flowing sea.

To bury in the earth was another curious method of curing any physical affection. A piece of fat bacon enclosed in a few ash-leaves, and secretly buried in the earth, was supposed to cure warts. The same remedy relieved toothache and sore throat. For fever, people stole three small pieces of bread from a neighbour's house. Two empty walnut or hazel-nut shells were then filled with crumbs moistened by saliva. The shells were closed and tied with some yarn. They were then secretly buried in earth close to a churchyard wall. It was customary to repeat an old rhyme while doing this, the only line remembered now being, "Fever, fever, go to the wall." Another remedy for the fever was to catch a moth, kill it, roll it in bacon, and bury it in the earth. For gout take a nail from a dead man's boot, and bury it a foot deep in earth under an ash or oak. To bury an old tooth in the churchyard will relieve the owner of toothache. Headache would be cured if a small piece of fat bacon were buried in earth under lavender or in an ant-hill.

Stroking and rubbing were remedies for many ailments. The patient's body was commonly stroked with the hand or sleeve, or the back of a knife. Very often a thread was tied around the affected part, or the medicine or healing herbs were tied on by it. In the first half of the nineteenth century there were men and women known as marvellous rubbers, whose profession it was to rub patients. Their efforts bore similar results to those obtained by the massage of the present day. These people are still called "rubbers."

The rubber was, and is still, to be found in many remote parts of Wales, where also people called "bone-setters" live. It is strange to hear of people still going to the rubber and the bone-setter, in whom they have great faith, when surgeons and hospitals are available near at hand. The herbalist is another with potent influence among the peasantry and the colliery population of North and South Wales.

"Y frech wen," or the smallpox, was always treated in the following way in Wales : The patient known to be suffering from this complaint was placed in bed and kept as warm as possible, in order that he should have a "good healthy crop." To induce as much heat as possible, he was enveloped in blankets, and had to drink gruel with strong rum in it, or beer made as hot as possible, with sugar and ginger in it, or egg-flip. The latter was made with beer, beaten eggs, sugar, and a small quantity of gin. These were heated, and served smoking hot. The patient drank until he perspired freely, and was afterwards kept comfortably warm during the course of the complaint. When the modern system of reducing the temperature was introduced, the old people were shocked, and declared that the smallpox would "turn in" and be fatal. A Welsh doctor of the old school so late as 1870 treated the smallpox in the old-fashioned way, with the result that his patients had not a mark ; while those of a neighbouring surgeon, who favoured the new treatment, had several deaths among those under his care. Whereupon the old doctor boasted his triumph!

In the days of old, charms were used for the cure of small-pox, and also for measles. Patients of both maladies were recommended to wear yellow or red night-clothing while ill, and during the early stages of convalescence.

Personifying disease appears to have been general in Wales in the far past, and down through later centuries it can be vaguely traced.

The sixth-century plague was described as a woman so hideous to behold that to look upon her would be death. When a pestilence known as the " Fad Felin " raged in the district between Duffryn Clwyd and Conway, Maelgwyn shut himself up in Llan Rhos Church, to avoid seeing the creature ; but, incautiously looking through the window, she crossed his sight, and he died. In this way the prophecy came true which was uttered by Taliesin :* " A strange creature will come from the marsh at Rhianedd to punish the crimes of Maelgwyn Gwynedd. Its hair, its teeth, and its eyes are yellow, and this will destroy Maelgwyn Gwynedd."

It was customary, so late as the eighteenth and early part of the nineteenth centuries, to say, when a sultry mist and a blight passed over the country, that there soon would be " sickness and suffering in the parish." More especially was this said when the mist took the shape of a grey-blue cloud or fog that moved rapidly. It was called the " fever blight," and people said it was always seen before epidemics of various kinds of fever. In the days when smallpox (frech wen) was a dreaded disease, people said an epidemic of it was always preceded by a sultry, yellow, and poisonous mist, that had a depressing effect. A heavy, dull, and dark-looking mist, moving slowly along when all sounds were deadened and the foliage was seared thereby, was " a sign before cholera."

Certain flying moths that become very troublesome in some years were called " fever moths," and were supposed to carry disease in their wings. When these moths infested a house, people said somebody would die of fever therein.

* Welsh poet, fifth century.

Some kinds of butterflies were called " fever flies," and it was asserted that they carried germs of fever under their wings. A number of these seen flying together were carefully watched, and when they entered a house, it was a foretoken of malignant fever and death.

Bluebottle flies were called " fever flies " or " death flies," and were supposed to bring fever or death to the person upon whose body they alighted. When a persistent bluebottle could not be got rid of from a bedroom, people said the occupant of the apartment would either have the fever or die within the year.

There was a " fever bird " resembling an owl, but without legs, or else with very short ones, and large, red-looking eyes. When this strange bird looked in at a window, or perched itself on a window-sill, somebody in that house would die of fever or " burning illness " within a year and a day. It was a fever-bringer.

Animal disorders were foretokened.

In some parts of Wales people used to say that when a strange ring-spotted calf mysteriously appeared among the herds, and cried mournfully, the kine and oxen would be stricken with disease. It killed by its cry, and was the bringer of disease of various kinds.

When a mottled sheep, unidentified by the farmer, was seen and heard bleating near the flocks, he called it the bringer of death to the fold. A stray horse of two colours neighing near the stable foretokened or brought disease or death to the horses.

In the poultry-yard a stray and strange chanticleer brought sickness or death to the fowls or scarcity at sitting-time. This omen was fatal alike to turkeys, geese, ducks, and fowls.

CHAPTER XXIII

THE LEASING

IN the days of old, when the harvest sheaves had been borne away, the " leasers," as gleaners are commonly called in Wales, were allowed into the cornfields to gather stray ears of wheat that remained in the stubble. Generous farmers took care that the " leasing " should yield a plentiful supply for the women and children of the parish, so that all might have enough bread and to spare.

Wales takes the place of the kindly farmer. There are ample supplies for those who care to search, and this book contains only a handful of wheat-ears from a very small " leasing."

People say it is fortunate to find a horseshoe, or part of one, or a limestone pebble with a hole through it, on the sea-beach or elsewhere. It is lucky to find three whole grains in a baked loaf. If you find a needle on the floor with the head towards you, pleasure will come unasked. Beg some small silver coins, get them made into a finger-ring, and so long as you wear it you will be fortunate. If you cut a loaf quite evenly, you will be successful and rich. To find a silver sixpence with a hole in it is lucky. When you first wear a new dress, put a coin in the pocket for prosperity. When crickets sing under the hearth, it is regarded as a token of pleasure and plenty. If a stocking or any other article of wearing apparel is worn with the wrong side out all day without your knowing it, you will have a present of money. Stockings hung crossways at the foot of the bed, with a pin stuck in them, will procure luck and prevent nightmare troubling you. Always keep a crooked sixpence in your pocket for luck. If you see a wandering fox in the morning, you will have a good day. A flight of birds to the right of you is a good omen. The four-leaved clover brings luck and love. A candle that burns roses, or red wick-heads, indicates prosperity and a letter. If a woman on New Year's Morning sees a man first, she will have prosperity all through the ensuing year. It is fortunate for a dark-haired person to be the first to cross your threshold on New Year's Day. It is lucky to find a crow's feather stuck in the ground before your feet.

It is in the Principality, as well as in England, considered good to find a horseshoe, and when found it is invariably nailed to the door of the house or the barn. A rusty horseshoe is always kept for luck.

Hazel-nuts are regarded as emblems of good fortune. In some old farm-houses in South Wales hazel-nuts are always kept in the house until they are brown with age. When quite rotten, they are burnt in the fire, to insure prosperity.

Ringing in the right ear is lucky.

If the right eye quivers or twitches, you may take it for a good omen.

If the left eye quivers or itches, you will have cause for laughter.

Itching of the soles of your feet is a token that you will have good news, or an invitation to a dance. If your feet itch, you will soon tread on strange ground.

If you throw an old shoe after a bride, she will have good fortune.

Throw a shoe over your head, and whichever way the toe points will be the most fortunate direction for you to take.

When the hand itches, the Welsh say, " Rub it against wood, it will come to good." When people are saying how successful, fortunate, or lucky they have been, they immediately touch wood. These actions are probably descended from a reverential source. " Touch the wood of the cross, and remember, and be humble," was an old saying ; therefore in Wales they touch or rub wood when the hands itch. If your right hand itches, you will receive money ; if your left itches, you will spend it.

Swallows' nests and crickets bring blessings to the house. If you cry before breakfast, you will laugh before supper, and *vice versa*. There was an old saying that if you slept with your feet near the window, you would have consumption, but if with your head to the window, you would never have that complaint. They say " Three chances for a Welshman," and if he is successful the third time, he will be very fortunate afterwards. If on the morning of Christmas Day, May Day, or Twelfth Day the embers of the previous night are still glowing, you will have a year of great prosperity and success. You will easily win favours if you dig up a root of cinquefoil on the eve of May and wear it in your coat. It is very fortunate if swallows build under your eaves. To find money in unexpected places is fortunate, and you will remain successful so long as you conceal it, and do not let anybody know you have found it.

To sneeze while you are putting on your shoes is a good sign.

There is an old story in Wales that if a man sneezes in the morning, he should lie down again for three hours, or his wife will be master for the ensuing week.

Sneezing between noon and midnight was considered a good omen, but it was very unlucky between midnight and noon. If a person sneezed while getting up in the morning, he would soon go back to bed with pain.

If you sneeze thrice in succession, they say you will be kissed, cursed, or shake hands with a fool.

People in Wales formerly would instantly use every endeavour to suppress sneezing, for there was an old story prevalent in some counties that a man was once killed by a single sneeze.

When people sneeze, it is customary to utter the exclamation, " Bendigedig !" which means blessed.

They say that if you make any remark or express any desire, and sneeze immediately, it will be confirmed and come true.

The Welsh say if you sneeze on Christmas night, your cattle will die. To sneeze to the right is lucky, to the left unfortunate ; right in front of you, good news is coming.

He who sneezes when a narrative is being told proves its truth. In some parts they say that if you sneeze once you will have a kiss, twice a wish, thrice a letter, four times a disappointment.

Foretokens of sorrow appear to be more numerous than those of joy.

It is bad to meet an old woman early in the morning, or to pass between two old women in the forenoon.

If a man sees a woman first on Christmas morning, he will have sorrow.

It is very unfortunate if, when you first go out in the morning, you meet a clergyman or a minister of any denomination.

If when going to market you meet a person carrying water, you will be unlucky in buying and selling that day.

To meet a beggar, a blind man, a lame man, or a person with a squint the first thing in the morning was unfortunate.

A crowing hen is prophetic of evil.

> " A whistling woman and a crowing hen
> Are only fit for the devil and his den."

If a hare crosses your path in the morning, expect misfortune.

On setting out early in the morning you will have misfortune if swine or weasels cross your path.

To open an umbrella in the house is unlucky. If a person lets one fall and picks it up himself, he may expect a disappointment. He should ask somebody else to pick it up for him.

If you gather pansies, you will have a disappointment.

Heather—the emblem of good luck in Scotland—is regarded in Wales as a token of misfortune or death if brought into the house.

Old women, known as " crones," and clergymen, formerly called " parsons," appeared in the folk-lore of Wales as subjects for scorn. In the eighteenth century they said if " an old crone meets you in the morning, you will have affairs going wrong all day." If a man chances to walk between " two old crones," he has no luck that day. Never forget to greet an old crone in the morning, or you will be unfortunate. Old and very aged women, known as " crones," were much despised because people said they brought misfortune. Generally they were dirty, untidy gossips.

With reference to the clergyman, he was supposed to be meddlesome, always prying into people's affairs, and, in the far past, neglect of his duties caused him to come under derision. It was an old saying that if a person met the parson the first thing in the morning, something bad would happen during the day. If the parson walked out early, bad weather was coming. When people talking became suddenly silent, they said, " The parson is passing ; no luck to-day." The huntsmen in the eighteenth and early part of the nineteenth centuries thought it so unlucky to meet a parson that they turned home again with the hounds. If the parson was in the hunt, " well and good," but it was " bad to meet him." He that wore the parson's left-off shoes or clothes would be unlucky. [*C.D., J.R.*]

It is considered unlucky to keep peacock's feathers in the house.

If you break the looking-glass, there will be misfortune for seven years. To break anything made of glass is a token of death or misfortune. If one piece of crockery is broken, three will go. It was bad to meet anybody on the stairs. To go out of the house early in the morning having forgotten anything, and return for it, is an omen of evil. It is very unfortunate to find money on the highroad. Never put on any garment trimmed with crape, unless you are in mourning, for it foretokens sorrow. So, also, if a spinster puts on widow's weeds, she will never marry ; and if a married woman " tries on the weeds," she will soon be a widow.

Two blackbirds sitting together on a window-sill or doorstep indicate death to one of the inmates of the house. Creaking rafters and squeaking tables foretoken disaster or death. If a fire crackles or salt is spilt, you may expect quarrels. If a goose lays one soft and one hard egg, or two eggs in a day, it means misfortune to the owner. A deserted rookery means misfortune and probably death in the mansion. A white cock brings bad luck. A spider running towards you in the morning is a token of misfortune. If a candle spits, or a log from the fire falls to the hearth, it is a bad sign.

When several locomotives let off steam at the same time, the railway men say it is a token of rain.

If your left ear rings or looks red, it is a token that somebody is slandering you or misfortune is approaching. If your right ear rings or looks red, somebody is praising you.

If your fingers become yellow or dead-white—in other words, benumbed—without a cause, there will soon be a death in your family.

If in going out your skirt catches in the doorway, it is a token of misadventure or misfortune. If you ·stumble on the threshold, you are liable to have a fall during the day. If you turn back after crossing the threshold the first time in the morning, you may expect worries all day

You should never tread upon the sweepings on the floor. Strangers should always sit down the moment they enter the room, or the children will not rest. If men watch women putting new feathers into the tick, they will be uneasy all ·night. To get out of bed the wrong side is to have things go contrary all day. At market, do not let the first customer go ; sell under value rather than lose him. If the crows make much noise by the house, you will have unexpected guests. If you spill salt, do not scrape it up, or you will be unlucky. If you help anybody with salt, you will help him with sorrow. Those who tread their heels inwards will be rich ; if outwards, they will be poor. If the new moon peeps into your purse, you will be short of money all through the month. It is customary for people in the markets in Wales either to spit on the first money they take in the morning, or to throw the coin on the ground and tread on it. If this is not done, they believe they will be unfortunate all day. It is unlucky to find money in the morning, unless it is on a board. In settling a bargain, it is customary to hand back a shilling to the seller. If this is not done, the transaction will prove unsatisfactory. If the three-legged stool falls and lies upside down, you will be worried that day. It is unfortunate to permit strangers into the farm-yard at milking-time.

English names were regarded as very unlucky for fishermen in Wales. The names Davis, Davies, Thomas, and John were unlucky for sailors and fishermen. Jones, Yorath, Howe, Lloyd, and Leyshon were fortunate. In and around Cardigan town it was considered unlucky for a person named Thomas to be the first to enter the house on New Year's Day. At Llanybyther, on the same day, John and Jenkin foretokened misfortune, while David and Evan were fortunate. In some parts of South Wales, if a man named David with red hair came first on that day, it was unlucky ; but if a person named Jones with dark hair came, all would be right. In South

Cardiganshire, if a person named Thomas with red hair came, he brought misfortune.

In former times, if anybody called the Llantrisant people "The Black Army," they would be ready to fight. This arose from the fact that a great number of Llantrisant people and others in the district went out to fight with the Black Prince. Instead of being honoured by the Welsh, they were bitterly reproached for joining the "Sassenach" (the English).

People living in Pentyrch, near Llantrisant, were called "the peacemakers of Pentyrch." In the days of old, when feuds were many and fighting was common for the slightest pretext, the men of Pentyrch were celebrated for their efforts in "coming between" opponents and settling differences.

The "Boys of Llantwit" had the reputation of being notorious fighters. A story used to be told that in the far past an inhabitant of their town was slain in Brecon. To have what was known in those days as the "revengement of blood," the men of Llantwit went to Brecon, and wrought so much havoc with their fists alone, that those who shielded the murderer were "fayne," to let them go, fearing dire calamity.

The "Men of Dinas Mawddy" in the North were renowned for their strength and brigandage. They were bandits, and their name struck terror in the hearts of the people. But in times of emergency they were powerful and patriotic.

Among other curious nicknames in Wales were the "Whelps" of Carmarthen; the "Pigs" of Pembrokeshire; "Sneering" Llanarth; "Long" Llanrwst; the "Mules" of Flint; the "Snakes" of Aberdare; the "One-A-wantings" and the "Vipers" of Llantwit; the "Thieves of Merioneth"; the "Pigs of Mon"; and the "Calves of Lleyn."

An old Welsh couplet describes a Queen journeying through North Wales, and receiving gifts at certain places. Anglesea gave her a beautiful pig; Lleyn presented a calf; and Merioneth people stole both from the Queen.

The Anglesea people were called "the Pigs of Mon," the Welsh name for that island. The inhabitants of Cowbridge, in the Vale of Glamorgan, were described as "Call Again To-morrow." As all know, Welshmen are called "Taffy" —a corruption of Dafydd, or David.

The origin of " The Cuckoos of Risca " is attributed to the following cause, the story of which was transcribed from an old eighteenth-century house-book : " On a time the men of Risca were wishful to have perpetual good luck and fine weather all the year round. As these could not be expected without the aid of the cuckoo, the men decided upon a safe and sure plan. In the midst of the town they built a high hedge, quite round in shape, and green with leaf. Then they got a cuckoo, and put her into it, saying : ' Dear bird of good omen, sing here always, and you shall lack neither meat nor drink nor comfort, all through the year, and for years to come.' When the cuckoo perceived the high hedge shutting her in, she quickly flew out, crying, ' Cuckoo, cuckoo !' Thereupon the people said, ' A vengeance upon her !' The wise men who had encompassed the bird shook their heads, and cried out : ' Alas ! A-lack-a-day ! If we had built the hedge higher, she would have stayed.' "

Llangynwyd, near Bridgend, Glamorgan, was formerly derisively known as " The Old Parish." This title is said to have originated in the following way : Centuries ago a young man of that parish died. It appears that a new apprentice of the village carpenter was very boastful of his scholarship. His master had always used Roman numerals. The youth, eager to give evidence of his talent, searched the alphabet and numbers generally used for a pauper's coffin. He had some difficulty in satisfying his requirements. Presently he found the correct initials, but not the number twenty-eight, representing the man's age. Equal, as he thought, to the occasion, the apprentice promptly nailed four sevens on the coffin, and rendered the age 7777 ! The inscription was not noticed until the coffin had been lowered into the grave ; then the clergyman's attention was arrested by the four sevens. He then asked the carpenter where the deceased was born, and the answer was, " In this parish, sir." " And where has he been keeping himself all these ages ?" added the clergyman. " In this parish, sir," was the reply. " It is indeed a remarkably old parish," concluded the clergyman.

On the shore near Conway a mermaid was stranded during a storm. She begged the fishermen to put her back in the sea, but they refused. Then she entreated them to put at least her tail in the water; still they refused, and the poor mermaid died of exhaustion. Just before her death she uttered a curse against the people of Conway, and said they would always be poor. The old story goes that ever since the mermaid's death Conway has been under the curse; and if a stranger brings a sovereign to the town, the inhabitants have to send across the water to Llansantfraid for change.*

Sir Gawaine's rock and fountain in Pembrokeshire were protected by supernatural power. In the dark and deep hollow of the tall and beetling cliffs on this part of the coast there is a vertical cleft, where the hero of Arthurian romance was hidden from his enemies by enchantment. It is said that the rock opened to let him in, then closed upon him; and when the foes were gone it opened again, and still remains open, with the impression of Gawaine's body visible. The name Gawaine was corrupted to Gofen, then to Gowan, by which it is now known. The cleft in the rock grows larger for a tall man, and decreases in size for a small person; and if anybody wishes in this hollow before turning round to come out, his desire will be gratified. Then, again, the steps leading to the tiny chapel of St. Gowan never can be counted by a mere mortal; but whatever hopes may be in a person's mind when going up and down these steps, if they are breathed lightly in the wind, they will be fulfilled. Below the steps are magic stones, which ring like bells when touched. In a little arch over the roof of the church St. Gowan's bell hung for many centuries, and often sounded without the touch of human hand. It is said that sometimes the mysterious sound of a bell is heard ascending from the lonely and romantic ravine, and it is always regarded as an omen of death in the neighbourhood, or disaster at sea. The Huntsman's Leap, close by, indicates the spot where they say a reckless man who had sold his soul to the devil was told by the latter that the only way to save it was to ride across the chasm. It is said the devil did not think this possible, but the rider persuaded St. Gowan to bless the horse, and the feat was accomplished in one marvellous leap.

Bosheston Mere, or Meer, in the same neighbourhood, was

* Rhys, "Celtic Folk-lore," pp. 30, 199.

frequented by apparitions and mysterious wailings, moans, and
cries. A scrap of folk-song is attached to this spot. It runs thus:

" There is nothing to hope and nothing to fear
When the wind sounds low on Bosheston Meer ;
There is much to fear and little to hope
When unseen hands pull St. Gowan's rope ;
And the magic stones, as the wise know well,
Promise sorrow and death like St. Gowan's bell."

On the coast of Glamorgan, in the town of Llantwit Major,
the omen bell of St. Illtutus used to be heard before a death
in the parish. Sometimes, it is said, the sound would be heard
over the house of the person who was to die, or whose relative
would die within a few months. Like St. Gawaine, St. Illtyd
was a knight of King Arthur's Court, but afterwards became
preceptor of the fifth-century college bearing his name at
Llanilltyd Fawr, now known as Llantwit Major.

St. Teilo, at one time Bishop of Llandaff, took a journey to
Jerusalem, and on his return brought a wonderful bell. Un-
touched by man, it struck the hours regularly. People were
in awe of it, and when it struck mysteriously at midnight they
said some bad deed had been done during the day. It detected
crimes, and when the suspected man or woman was brought
before it, if he or she were innocent, the tone of the bell was
gentle ; when the genuine offender appeared, the tones were
harsh and severe, almost to abruptness. It also worked wonderful cures. In the course of time it was polluted by profane
hands, and its miraculous virtue was lost. In the eighteenth
century people said the bell was heard tolling before the death
of anybody in the parishes of Llandilo and Llandaff.

A very old folk-story is connected with a farm, still called the
Wolf House, Lisworney, near Cowbridge, Glamorgan. The
story dates back to the time when wolves were plentiful, and
probably long before measures were taken for the extirpation
of those animals in South Wales. The ground now known as
the Pinklands was covered with dense woodlands, part of those
stretching around Penllyne Castle. On the outskirts of Lisworney village there was a farmstead. The farm-wife had
several children. One day, while her husband was away, the
wife went into the garden, but before going she closed the
door, for her baby was in the cradle. When she returned, to

her horror, the cradle was empty. Instantly she suspected a wolf of having been there. She at once rushed to the Pink-lands, and there, in a clearing of the woods, she found her babe, asleep and uninjured. In an instant she snatched up her babe and ran breathlessly home. Scarcely had she reached the house when a wolf was at her heels, and she had only time to bolt and bar the door before the animal was howling fero-ciously around the house. This memorial of a mother's bravery at the present day retains the name of the Wolf House. [*The David Jones MSS.*]

Penllyne, near Cowbridge, in the Vale of Glamorgan, had a miraculous cow owned by a very benevolent lady, who be-stowed the milk of the animal on the poor only. The yield of milk was enormous, and at whatever time of the day she was milked the supply never failed. This animal lived to be very venerable and was regarded as almost sacred. From this story arose the proverb " It's like the Penllyne cow," when supplies appeared to be inexhaustible, or when people were unusually generous in the district.

The site of the place called Castell Teirtud is in Breconshire, near Builth. It is mentioned in the " Liber Landavensis." Connected with this spot there are two stories.* One is that a giant named Teirtu lived there, and he was the maker of a wonderful harp. In the Welsh nursery-tale a dwarf named Dewryn Fychan desired to possess this harp. He visited the Castle in the night, and when Teirtu was fast alseep, stole the harp. All went well for a time, but when the dwarf was out-side the giant's premises, the harp began to play without the touch of any visible hand. The music was very harmonious, and it immediately awakened the giant, who went in pursuit of the dwarf and recovered the harp.

The other was to the effect that near Castell Teirtud the form of a " big man " was sometimes seen wandering about with a triple harp in his hand, and in the eighteenth century the country-folk said that where the fortress once stood strange sounds were to be heard, as if coming up from the ground. 'When these sounds were heard in the summer, they foretokened a wedding in the district ; but if heard in the spring or autumn,

* " The Mabinogion," p. 287 ; Jones, " Welsh Bards," vol. i., p. 44.

a funeral might be expected. Heard in the winter, they indicated storms and severe weather, accompanied by sickness and death. [*Family Collection.*]

A story often told by the firesides of South Wales is connected with the ruined towers of an ancient mansion on the summit of Pencarreg, by the road leading from Lampeter to Llandovery. Formerly the place was shunned at night, and people declared cries, groans, and moans were heard coming from the towers, and a strange wailing went wandering down to a certain spot beside the River Teifi. Several generations ago Squire Vaughan was the owner of the mansion called Maesyfelin. He had one daughter and three sons. These latter proved so reckless that he struck their names out of his will, and left all he possessed to his only daughter. Very soon the Squire and his wife died, and Helen, the heiress, came into possession of the estates. The brothers rejoiced in the fact that she was very delicate, and not likely to live long. They were pleased to see how gradually she became weak and pale and sad when she met her brothers' frowns, or witnessed their recklessness and revelry. But in a year's time she was stronger and more spirited. This puzzled them, and they attributed it to a probable lover. Setting a spy on her track, the Vaughans discovered that she was betrothed to young Prichard, the son of the Vicar of Llandovery. All through the country-side this young man was known as the " Flower of Llandovery." His father was the celebrated Rhys Prichard, vicar of the parish, and the author of the poems entitled the " Canwyll y Cymry," or the " Welshman's Candle." Helen and Prichard met by stealth. He would signal from Pencarreg, and she waved a handkerchief from Maesyfelin. One day the brothers waved a signal, and went down to the riverside, where they concealed themselves among the bushes. Young Prichard hastened down, and not finding Helen at their usual trysting-place, hastened to the Hall. He was pursued by the brothers, but, outstripping them, entered the house, to meet the astonished girl, who swooned with fright. The brothers seized young Prichard, carried him to an outhouse, and, after strangling him, placed his body in a sack. This they conveyed to the River Teifi, where, weighted by stones, it was thrown in. The mystery of the murder remained undiscovered for some time, Helen being the only witness. She became insane, and was looked after by the Vicar of Llandovery, but she died soon after the tragedy. Later on the body of young Prichard was found by a fisherman, who chanced to see spurs in the water. These spurs had broken through the sack that contained the body. The brothers soon became more reckless than ever, and one was killed by the other two. The third son killed the second, and there was at last only one of the Vaughans remaining. This one went raving mad, and poisoned himself with a concoction of hemlock. The mansion became a ruin dreaded by all. This is the story of the Maid of Maesyfelin and the Flower of Llandovery.*

Rhys Prichard, the father of the " Flower of Llandovery," was a sturdy Royalist vicar and poet, who has been called the " Hudibras " of Wales. One of the saddest poems was that on the cruel murder of his son. But he is best known by his collection of poems entitled " Canwyll y Cymry," or " Welshman's Candle," which is still familiar in Wales. This book was first published in 1646, consisting of Parts I. and II. A third part was issued in 1670. The second edition, with the addition of Part IV., was published in 1672. In all, fifteen editions have been issued, the best being that printed by the Llandovery Press in 1841. In 1771 an English poetical translation was published by the Vicar of Llawhaden.

An old man was walking along the road leading from Canton to Leckwith many years ago, when he was joined by a strange-looking companion, who either dogged his footsteps or kept beside him persistently. Fast or slow, the stranger was not to be shaken off. The old man saw imploring glances in the sunken eyes, but not a word was uttered. " At last," said the old man, " I called nine names, but it did no good. He only kept looking at me, and then I got into a rage, and cursed him, but he didn't say nothing. At last I says, ' In the name of God, what do you want ?' Then tears ran down his face, and he said very slowly : ' I couldn't speak until you asked me in the name of God. I am dead, but I cannot rest till my head is buried. I was a boatman down the Ely River, and my head is

* Llewelyn Pritchard's " Twm Shon Catti," p. 143.

on the bank, and the devils do play with it continually, using it as a football. If you will come with me and get it from them, and bury it, I shall rest.' Then the old man agreed to go down the river-side in search of the skull. It was late, and the night was dark. Guided by the poor spirit, the man went to a bend of the River Ely, just above the present Taff Vale Railway bridge. There, by a bluish light, he saw a group of people, as he first thought, playing ball, instead of which they were little devils kicking football like hooray with the poor man's head. The old man said, ' I was feared at first, but then I knew what to do. I thought I would go to them praying (for I had often engaged in the prayer-meetings at Bethel). So I did, and as I came near to them, they all flew away, and I took the poor man's head and buried it in a soft place, digging a hole with my knife ; and the ghost, he stood all the while looking at me, until I finished the job, and then he did go away like a puff of smoke."*

Stories of the Wandering Jew have been heard and chronicled in Pembrokeshire and Glamorgan, and both were connected with county families, whose names, for obvious reasons, were suppressed. The following story was obtained direct from a Glamorgan farmer. He said his grandfather had three sons and two daughters. Of the latter, one was married and the other was single. The unmarried girl was very handsome and spirited. One day a strange man came to the farm, and asked if they could accommodate him with apartments. He wanted to be in the heart of the country, to have quiet for studies. As he offered generous terms, they let him two rooms for an indefinite period. It was late in the autumn, and after the stranger had been there two months the farmer and his family felt quite at home with him. Soon the stranger made friends everywhere in the neighbourhood. The Vicar, the Squire, and the doctor invited him to their houses, for he was not only a man of intellectual attainments, but " good company " in conversation. Spring came, and the stranger still remained. " Towards the summer," said my informant,

* T. H. Thomas, R.C.A., " Old Folks' Tales." This is published privately, and there are copies in the Cardiff Free Libraries. It is also to be found in the Transactions of the Cardiff Naturalists' Society, vol. xxxvi., 1903, p. 52 *et seq.* Cardiff, 1904.

" Mr. W—— went away for a few days, and came back again.
While he was away my Aunt Winifred was not the same girl
—at least, so the neighbours said. She seemed spiritless.
Rumour was abroad that Mr. W—— had been paying atten-
tions to the Squire's daughter. At the same time, my uncles
knew that he had been equally attentive to their sister. This
displeased them, and when Mr. W—— came home they were
determined to speak to him about it, ' lodger or no lodger,'
they said, and he paid them handsomely. So they told him
it was not honourable to pay court to two girls at the same
time. Mr. W—— expressed surprise and sorrow, which my
uncles knew was genuine, for he spoke so kindly and sadly.
' It is my fate,' he said, ' to win love ; it is my doom never to
marry.' Very soon after that he went away. The Squire's
daughter and my Aunt Winifred soon came to know that they
had been in love with the same man, and became fast friends.
Mr. W—— was remarkably handsome. In two years' time
my Aunt Winifred died, having gradually pined away from
the moment Mr. W—— left. Twenty years afterwards, when
the roses were blooming over Aunt Winifred's grave, the
Squire's daughter, who married a neighbouring baronet in less
than two years after her early love-affair, went with my father
to the churchyard. They stood together at the graveside of one
who died too early. ' He was a mysterious man,' said Lady
L——. ' He was,' said my father. ' The Squire declared he
was the Wandering Jew,' remarked the lady ; and they left the
grave. A moment later they were face to face with the very
man, who passed on quickly to my aunt's grave. Lady L——
touched my father's arm. ' There he is,' she said ; and as the
stranger stood bareheaded, they both whispered, ' There is a
mystery about him.' He was never seen again, and both Lady
L—— and my father always declared the mysterious stranger
to be the Wandering Jew.''

The other story was told by a Carmarthenshire Squire.
When his father was a youth he met a remarkably clever
stranger, who appeared to have studied all that was possible
in the world. Languages, art, science, music, and a host of
other things, were at his fingers' ends. He had travelled
all over the world, and was a most interesting companion.

For six months they travelled together, and then parted. Before parting the stranger told his companion that they would meet and be together on three separate occasions of their lives. " After our third meeting and parting," said the stranger, " you will die, but I shall continue to wander until the day of doom." The young man in due course became Squire, was married, and had children. When he was about fifty the stranger reappeared again in Carmarthenshire, and was as interesting as ever. The Squire invited him to his seat, and when alone, laughingly reminded the stranger of his prophecy. " It will be verified to the letter," said his guest. Later on the visitor took his leave. The Squire lived until he was eighty-six, and then revealed his story to his son. The latter thought it was an old man's fancy, and humoured it but little. A year later the stranger reappeared, and visited the old Squire, who was delighted to see his former friend. Two days he stayed, and when taking leave of the Squire he said : " Good-bye, my dear old friend. You will never see me again." The next night the Squire died, murmuring, as he peacefully passed away : " The Wandering Jew ! Poor man ! He is the Wandering Jew !"

In old stories told by the firesides fifty years ago the Red Goblins, or, as some called them, the Red Robbers, took a prominent place. It is not known whether these men derived the appellation " red " from the colour of their leader's hair or from the hue of their caps and cloaks. Some people said they were descended from a race which mated with goblins and hobgoblins. Others declared they were given that name for their goblin-like tricks. These men were notorious freebooters, famed for their cunning and bravery, and often for their generosity. It was their custom to kidnap adults and children, and restore them on payment of a ransom. Their headquarters were in the fastnesses of the Moelgillian Hills between the Garw and Llynfi Valleys, to the north of Bridgend, in Glamorgan. Among those hills there is a large cave, in which, tradition asserts, the chieftain of these brigands lived, while his men dispersed themselves in lesser caverns and hollows near at hand. The Giant's Cave was occupied by the chief of the Red Goblins, whose name was a terror to people in the neighbourhood and elsewhere. These men sometimes made raids into other parts, and on a few occasions visited the Vale of Glamorgan. Two stories told in Mabsant celebrations were well remembered by old inhabitants. One was to the effect that the Red Goblins traversed the Vale, and near Cowbridge intercepted the Carmarthenshire drovers on the way to London with cattle. The robbers surrounded the herdsmen and their companions, bound them hands and feet, and drove the cattle to their own strongholds. This story was told in Welsh, with fantastic accompaniments, shouts, and mimic display.

The second story was about a young lady captured by these men. One version described her as being a very rich English heiress visiting the Carne family. The other stated she was a daughter of the Carnes. The Red Goblins seized her when she was riding, accompanied by a groom. After binding her man-servant to a tree, they carried her off to the mountains, and there kept her until ransom was demanded and paid. Many pathetic incidents were woven into this story, and it was asserted that they moved people to tears. It was quite understood that the Red Goblins included in their number several reckless young men of good families. Aged grand-dames and old nurses in the first half of the nineteenth century quieted noisy children by saying : " Hush, or the Red Goblins will come and take you !" The palmy days of these robbers were probably during the seventeenth or eighteenth century, and among the stories of the Vale of Glamorgan, allusions were made to the mad pranks and merry tricks of the Red Goblins [*Family Collection.*]

INDEX

AUTHORITIES CONSULTED

In writing this book, the following authorities were consulted :

I. Printed Sources.

Davies' "Mythology and Rites of the British Druids," and "Celtic Researches," 1804 and 1809.

"The Mabinogion." This work was translated by the late Lady Charlotte Guest from the Welsh "Llyfyr Coch o' Hergest," or the "Red Book of Hergest," in the library of Jesus College, Oxford.

Iolo Morganwg. The Iolo MSS. form the celebrated collection of the late Edward Williams, under his bardic name. He died in 1826.

The Cambro-Briton, The Cambrian Quarterly, and *The Greal.* These are periodicals of the early nineteenth century.

Edmund Jones of Tranch: "A Relation of Apparitions of Spirits in the Principality of Wales, etc."; published "at Trevecka," 1780. A copy of this is in the Cardiff Free Library.

William Howells, Carmarthen: "Cambrian Superstitions." This book belongs to the early nineteenth century. A copy was lent to me by the author's granddaughter, Mrs. Evans. A volume, dated 1831, is in the Cardiff Free Library.

Professor Sir John Rhŷs, M.A., F.S.A., Jesus College, Oxford: "Celtic Folk-lore."

The Rev. Elias Owen, M.A., F.S.A.: "Welsh Folk-lore."

Hoare's "Giraldus Cambrensis."

Froissart.

"Welsh Archæology," vol. ii.

Pennant's "Tours in Wales."

Geoffrey of Monmouth.

Owen, in Richard's "Cambro-British Biography."

Smith's "Religion of Ancient Britain."

Rees's "South Wales."

Meyrick's "Costumes of Ancient Britons."

"Welsh Sketches," 1850.

Llewelyn Pritchard's "Twm Shon Catti."

Thomas Hughes, F.S.A.: "Handbook to Chester."

"Voyage dans le *Finisterre,*" 1794 and 1796.

Charles Redwood: "The Vale of Glamorgan." This work was published anonymously in 1839. For some years the authorship remained undiscovered. The collection was subsequently attributed to the late Mr. Charles Redwood, of London, Cowbridge and Boverton, Glamorgan. Thomas Carlyle visited him when preparing the memoirs of Captain John Sterling, the "Thunderer" of *The Times,* who lived at Llanblethian, near Cowbridge.

The David Jones MSS. This collection was bequeathed by the late Mr David Jones, formerly of Llanblethian, Glamorgan, and afterwards of Wallington, Surrey, to Mr. Iltyd B. Nicholl, J.P., F.S.A., of the Ham, Llantwit Major. The MSS. were lent by the latter to Mr. T. C. Evans, author of " The History of Llangynwy," for his " Welsh Tit-bits " column in the *South Wales Weekly News*, where it appears under the bardic name of " Cadrawd."

Mr. T. H. Thomas, R.C.A.—" Arlunydd Penygarn," herald bard of the Welsh National Gorsedd : " Old Folks' Tales."

To Mr. Iltyd B. Nicholl I am indebted for the use of many books in preparing this work, while from volumes in the public libraries of the British Museum, the city of Cardiff, and elsewhere, I have derived much information.

The Welsh collection in the Reference Department of the Cardiff Free Library is invaluable to students of Celtic literature.

II. ORAL STATEMENTS AND MSS.

For various reasons—chiefly religious—the names of persons who either remembered the stories or allowed access to private documents have not been mentioned, but I reserved to myself the privilege of naming the localities from which my material has been drawn. Oral statements and MSS. are accompanied by initials, of which the following is a list :

A. B.—These initials cover the names of clergymen, Dissenting ministers, and others whose itinerary profession or trade gave them opportunities of hearing folk-stories in North and South Wales.

C. D.—These initials indicate an old inhabitant who related stories well known in the first half of the nineteenth century. His surviving relatives have religious reasons for desiring anonymity.

O. S.—Old servants—some retainers of ancient families, and others personally employed.

J. R.—This old man requested anonymity in the personal interests of his family.

Mrs. E—— requested anonymity for private reasons explained.

Mr. William Davies, whose bardic name is Gwylim Glan Ogwy, is an indefatigable collector of all kinds of lore about Wales.

Family Collection and MSS. This indicates my late father's collection.

THE END

Elliot Stock, 62, Paternoster Row, London.